UNDERSTANDING

AS *level*

COMPUTING

AQA

Ray Bradley

Published in 2004 by:
Nelson Thornes Ltd
Delta Place
27 Bath Road
CHELTENHAM
GL53 7TH
United Kingdom

04 05 06 07 08 / 10 9 8 7 6 5 4 3 2 1

A catalogue record for this book is available from the British Library

ISBN 0 7487 7703 2

Page make-up by Mathematical Composition Setters Ltd

Printed and bound in Great Britain by Scotprint

Acknowledgements

We are grateful to the following awarding body for permission to reproduce
questions from their past examinations:
Assessment and Qualifications Alliance (AQA)
All answers provided for examination questions are the sole responsibility of the
author.

Contents

How to make the best use of this AS level book

Introduction and resources

Although this book is written specifically for the AQA Computing Subject Specification, it should prove extremely useful for Computing and Computer Science related examinations for other boards, and similar examinations held at this level. This is the first of two books in this series. The second book, Understanding A2 level Computing for AQA follows on with the second-year work, and completes the material needed for the full 'A' level Computing course. A useful set of Examination Hints and Tips is included, together with key words that often need to be understood in the context of an AQA examination. There is a separate Glossary of AS and A2 level Computing Terms for AQA, also available from Nelson Thornes.

Numerous margin entries offer helpful advice in the form of 'hints and tips'. Both the AS and A2 books are in full colour, and the **'bold purple entries'** flag terms that have corresponding entries in the comprehensive 100-page glossary mentioned above. This glossary is special, because it is written specifically with AS and A2 computing students in mind. It is not burdened with unnecessary terms, or with over-complicated definitions. It thus makes definitions much easier to learn, and provides a comprehensive snapshot of the material which needs to be covered. Each glossary entry has a colour which flags it as belonging to the AS or the A2 course, and it is therefore ideally mapped to both the AS level and A2 level Computing for AQA books.

Electronic resources

In addition to the above three books, there are two sets of interactive electronic resources, one for AS level Computing and one for A2 level Computing. There is also a revise computing website (www.revisecomputing.com) which offers additional help and information, including careers advice for students thinking of pursuing a career in Computer Science or a related subject.

Modular Structure

This book is arranged in a modular fashion, which corresponds to the three AQA modules, as follows.

- Module 1 – *Computer Systems, Programming and Network Concepts*
- Module 2 – *Principles of Hardware, Software and Applications*
- Module 3 – *Practical Systems Development – The Practical Exercise*

The material is split up into easy to digest chapters, many of which can be studied independently of each other. At the beginning of each chapter you are told which key concepts are going to be covered, and whether the material you are reading depends on material in other chapters. The end-of-chapter exercises will check that you have understood the work just covered, and there are comprehensive answers to each of these exercises at the end of this book. Two further chapters on examination questions for modules 1 and 2 complete the range of material available for the theoretical modules.

Project Work

AQA module 3 consists of a board-set exercise known in advance of the examination. A real AQA project exercise has been undertaken in great detail in the module 3 section of this book. It fully covers the analysis, design, implementation, testing, maintenance and evaluation phases of the project, including a fully worked sample write up. A module 3

A 100 page glossary of AS level and A2 level Computing Terms for AQA is available in addition to this AS book.

There is also an A2 level book, interactive electronic resources and a revision web site.

A real AQA AS computing project has been analysed, developed and tested in this book. It is also accompanied by a module 3 examination paper which has fully worked solutions.

This is used to give invaluable project advice for AS students.

examination based on this case study is also provided, and many of the questions are taken from a real module 3 AQA examination. The answers to this practical module 3 are covered in great detail; including the important annotation techniques needed to ensure high marks in this particular component of the AQA AS level Computing course.

Keep up to date

The subject specification, mark schemes and Examiner's reports for AQA AS computing are all available from www.aqa.org

It is not possible for any book to keep you right up to date, and you must, therefore, read computer magazines, newspapers, watch the news and look at specialist programs which cover computer-related material. This will help considerably with the moral, ethical, social, cultural and other issues about which you are expected to be able to comment in a knowledgeable fashion.

Set up an effective revision schedule

Before you take your AS examinations it's essential to be organised. *Start weeks before the examinations are due*. AQA Computing is usually taken in June, so March/April is a good time to start thinking about building up your revision schedule.

Download a copy of the current AQA Computing specification from the internet. *Don't forget to download the correct one for the year in which your examination will take place*. They will probably have next year's on-line too, and some things may change. You can search for the current Computing specification on the AQA internet site which is at www.aqa.org.uk.

You will need Adobe Acrobat Reader, a free program available on the web, (from www.adobe.com) to read the pdf (page description format) files containing information for AQA AS level computing.

After you have downloaded the pdf file, print it out, and then work through Module 1 by using a highlighter pen. Highlight any topics which you do not understand, then use this book or get your teacher to go through them. You will find that the glossary for this course (mentioned at the beginning of this chapter) is particularly useful for revision purposes. You could make use of the glossary to test your friends and classmates. Do the same with Module 2, and also with the theoretical components of Module 3, which are covered in Chapter 19. *You may be asked questions on these topics in addition to the practical work submitted for the Module 3 examination.*

Find a revision pattern which works for you

Work out suitable time slots which are best suited to *your* revision routine. Some students get up at the 'crack of dawn', and others prefer to work 'late into the night'. Make sure that the work you are doing is productive. If you get stuck for long periods of time or find yourself doing nothing, then stop and do something completely different. There is no substitute for writing things down, usually by highlighting key points. Simply looking at a book is no good for most students. Make notes in your own words, then categorise the material into manageable sections.

Do as many past papers as possible

At the time of writing AS computing has been undertaken for a number of years. Don't forget that there are AQA AS Computing examinations in both January and June. Make sure that you get all the papers that are available, but do this early, because they often take several weeks or more to arrive. In addition to the actual papers you will need access to the mark schemes, which are also available on the web. This will save your teachers/lectures a lot of time, and *you will be able to see what the examiners are looking for*. Finally, get access to the Report on the Examination. This is where the Principal Examiners write down where many of the candidates go wrong or loose marks each year. *You can learn an enormous amount from reading this material, and by learning from the mistakes that students have made in the past.*

Make use of the past examination questions in this book, but most importantly of all, save one or two papers that you can do *under timed examination conditions*. It is only by doing this that you will really know what you are capable of.

Examination hints and tips for AQA AS level computing

Examination technique

Good grades in examinations are usually the result of good examination technique. *A good knowledge of the theory may not be enough to get you a top grade unless you know the rules.*

Examination jargon

It is important to know what the examiners expect, and the list of key words produced by AQA is essential reading. These key terms, referring to the key words used in AQA examinations are as follows.

Name (What is the name of?) usually requires a technical term or its equivalent. Answers to this type of question normally involve no more than one or two words.

List A number of features or points, each often no more than a single word, with no further elaboration of detail required.

Define (What is meant by?) 'Define' requires a statement giving the meaning of a particular term. 'What is meant by ... ?' is used more frequently as it emphasises that a formal definition as such is not required.

Outline A brief summary of the main points is required. The best guide to the amount of detail required lies in the mark allocations; approximately one to one and a half minutes should be allowed per mark. This generally works out at around two or three lines in a standard answer booklet for each mark.

Describe Means no more than it says, that is, 'Give a description of ... ' So, 'Describe one feature of a graphical user interface (GUI) which is likely to be helpful to a non-technically minded user' requires a description of a feature such as a pictorial icon in terms of making the selection and execution of a program easier. 'Describe one relationship that can be inferred form the data requirements' means supplying its name and degree.

Explain This creates major difficulties for many candidates. A reason or interpretation must be given, not a description. The term 'Describe' answers the questions 'What' and the term 'Explain' answers the question 'Why?'

Suggest 'Suggest' is used when it is not possible to give the answer directly from the facts that form part of the subject material detailed in the specification. The answer should be based on the general understanding rather than on recall of learnt material. It also indicates that there may be a number of correct alternatives.

Give evidence for (Using examples from ...) Answers to questions involving these phrases must follow the instructions. Marks are always awarded for appropriate references to the information provided. General answers, however, comprehensive, will not gain maximum credit.

Calculate This term is used where the only requirement is a numerical answer expressed in the appropriate units.

The definitions shown on this page have been produced by AQA examiners.

Understand these terms and you can maximise your chance of getting a good grade in the examination.

State 'State' falls short of 'Describing' and amounts to no more than making bullet points. For example, 'State one advantage of writing a program as a collection of modules' the answer might be, 'Teams of programmers are able to work on producing individual modules at the same time'.

Computing content

Some computing questions are difficult to answer for the following reasons.

- Innovations happen so quickly that old criteria may no longer apply
- The number of ways of doing things is so vast that it is difficult to mark some of the material.

The AQA and other boards have their work cut out to make sure that all questions are still relevant. Not many subjects have to check for possible new responses so close to producing the mark schemes for the examinations.

Answer you questions wisely and stick to the specification

Don't try to be too clever when you answer questions, and go for the obvious answers if you have a choice. Consider, for example, the following question:

Hard disks and floppy disks are both secondary storage media; state three differences between these two devices.

Three 'correct' answers could be as follows.

- A floppy disk has a read/write protect tab.
- A floppy disk does not rotate very quickly, a hard disk does.
- A hard disk is sealed; a floppy disk is open to the elements.

Better answers, containing more obvious differences, would be as follows.

- A hard disk is able to store a huge amount of data compared to a floppy disk.
- Data may be read much more quickly from a hard disk.
- A hard disk is usually fixed; a floppy disk is usually portable.

All bulleted points above are 'correct', but the ones below would probably be in the mark scheme, along with others like a 'hard disk is more reliable than a floppy disk'.

Students at 'A' level, especially those who know a great deal about computers think that the required answers are so 'obvious', there must be a catch! Some of the simpler questions at AS level are obvious, and it's important to realise that the technical intricacies of the hardware are not usually required, but the functionality of the hardware is.

Check what you need to know from the AQA AS level computing subject specification. It seems unfair, but 'right answers' often gain no marks because they are not in the specification, and hence not in the mark scheme. Sensible suggestions are usually in the mark scheme, so make sure that your answers are sensible in the context of what you are meant to know.

Remember, carefully following the guidance given here could gain you a grade or even two.

There are many ways that different concepts can be explained in Computing.

Using the AS level and A2 level glossary will give you a feel for the depth that is required for the AQA Computing specification. (See the 'How to make the best use of this AS level book' section.

1 Data, information and coding

In this section you will learn about:

- Character codes like ASCII and Unicode
- Data, information, bits, bytes, words and multipliers
- Basic binary and conversion between decimal and binary
- Octal, BCD and hexadecimal
- Simple floating point numbers, binary fractions
- Negative binary numbers, two's complement, sign and magnitude explicit sign

Data, information and binary encoding

Data is the raw material on which the computer operates. When structure has been applied to the data it becomes **information**. Throughout your course you will be applying increasingly sophisticated structures to data, so that the data may be processed in efficient ways.

Computers use **binary digits** or **bits**. These binary digits ('0's and'1's) build up codes inside computers. A group of eight binary digits is called a **byte**, a unit of storage in a computer system. 1 **Kbyte** (**Kilobyte**) is actually 1024 bytes of data, and 1 **Mbyte** (**Megabyte**) is 1024 × 1024 or 1 048 576 bytes. A **word** is a group of bits, usually 16, 32, 64 or 128 bits, although other word lengths may also be used. Some multipliers are shown in Table 1.1. Larger multiples, *when used to describe memory size*, are not used in the same way as in other branches of science. This is because **pure binary** multiples are used in computer science.

Table 1.1 Some common multipliers used in computing

Name	Letter	Derivation	Words	Exact number
pico	p	1×10^{-12}	trillionth	0.000 000 000 001
nano	n	1×10^{-9}	billionth	0.000 000 001
micro	μ	1×10^{-6}	millionth	0.000 001
milli	m	1×10^{-3}	thousandth	0.001
				(Memory size only)
Kilo	K	1×10^{3}	Thousand	1024
Mega	M	1×10^{6}	Million	1 048 576
Giga	G	1×10^{9}	Billion	1 073 741 824
Tera	T	1×10^{12}	Trillion	1 099 511 627 776

Several more multipliers exist, both for larger and smaller numbers. However, the ones shown in Table 1.1 are sufficicent for the purposes of AS level.

When using larger multiples for anything other than memory size, don't use binary multiples, because the normal rules will apply.

For example, a 5 GHz processor, would operate at 5 000 000 000 Hz, or a 56 Kbit/sec modem would literally mean 56 000 bits/sec.

Various methods of **encoding** exist. Codes like **ASCII** (the American Standard Code for Information Interchange) allow computers to transfer text information, because everybody has agreed on this standard. A few **ASCII** codes are shown in Table 1.2.

Table 1.2 A small selection of ASCII codes

	(Binary column headings or decimal place values)							
Character	128	64	32	16	8	4	2	1
A	0	1	0	0	0	0	0	1
B	0	1	0	0	0	0	1	0
%	0	0	1	0	0	1	0	1
é	1	0	0	0	0	0	1	0

Using one **byte**, codes 00000000 to 11111111 are used, giving **256 combinations**. This is enough for most Western languages, but others, like the Arabic and Chinese require extra codes. The more versatile **Unicode**, based on a 16-bit character representation (2 bytes) is now popular. 16 bits means **65 536 characters** are available.

Basic binary

The **binary system** (or **base two**) uses 'column headings' or 'decimal place value headings', as shown in Table 1.2. The next column heading to the left may easily be generated by multiplying the previous column heading by two. Looking at the first row reveals that the letter 'A' has a decimal value of '65', because it is made up of 1 lot of 64 (the 1 under the 64 column) and 1 unit (the 1 in the 1 column).

Example

Using the small extract from the ASCII table shown above, what is the decimal value for the character 'é'?

Solution

Place a suitable bit pattern underneath the column headings as shown in Table 1.3

Table 1.3 Table for working out the decimal value of the ASCII code for é.

	A small selection of ASCII code (Binary column headings)							
Character	128	64	32	16	8	4	2	1
é	1	0	0	0	0	0	1	0

You may find that some of the extended ASCII characters like é have different codes on different systems.

By observation we see that we have **1 lot of 128** and **1 lot of 2**, which, when added together, gives us a decimal value for the ASCII code for 'é' of '**130**'.

Conversion between binary and decimal

Convert from **binary** to **decimal** by adding the values of the column headings containing a binary '1'. Conversely, if we are told that the decimal value for the ASCII code representing the '%' sign is '37', we can work backwards from this decimal number to find the binary pattern having the same value. Do this by writing down the largest column heading we can take away from the decimal number – in this case 32.

Take one lot of 32 away from the original number 37, and we are left with 5. This means that there are no lots of 16, no lots of 8, 1 lot of 4, no lots of 2 and 1 unit, as shown in Table 1.2. Not forgetting to put the two leading zeros back in to make a **byte**, the original bit pattern for the '%' sign, which has a decimal code of '37' is therefore 00100101.

If **ASCII** is used to code a decimal number like 237, then the ASCII code for 2 is followed by the code for 7, which is then followed by the code for 3. You should note that this pattern is different from the **pure binary** representation for 237, which would be found by using the methods outlined in the previous paragraph.

Example

(a) **Find the 8-bit pure binary number patterns for the following decimal numbers:**

   (i) 61   **(ii) 100**   **(iii) 273**

(b) **What is the ASCII code for 237?**

Solution

Part (a) is solved using the binary column headings in Table 1.4.

Table 1.4 The solution to part (a)

	Binary column headings (decimal values)							
Decimal	**128**	**64**	**32**	**16**	**8**	**4**	**2**	**1**
61	0	0	1	1	1	1	0	1
100	0	1	1	0	0	1	0	0
237	1	1	1	0	1	1	0	1

(b) By looking up a table of ASCII codes you will find that the ASCII code for '2' is 'decimal 50', the **ASCII** code for '3' is '51' and the **ASCII** code for '7' is '55'. Therefore, the **ASCII** code (*using decimal values*) for '237' is '505155'. Note that this is very different from the **pure binary** code for '237', which is '11101101', as shown in Table 1.4.

Simple binary arithmetic

Binary digits may be added together, assuming that the correct digits are lined up underneath each other. When doing addition in **base ten** (**decimal**) we carry one to the next column when ten is reached (*i.e. 13 would be 1 lot of 10 with 3 left over*). In the binary system, the same ideas are used, but we carry 1 when we reach 2 (*i.e. 3 would be 1 lot of 2 and 1 left over*). These ideas are demonstrated in the next example, where the small subscripts (a 2 in this case) are used to denote a pure binary number. (For example, 101_2 should not be confused with '101' or 'one hundred and one' in decimal.) Sometimes these suffixes are omitted if the base in which we are working is obvious.

Make sure that you can use your calculator to work out numbers in binary or hex. Make sure that you can also convert between different number bases using your calculator. It's far easier than working it out by hand.

Examples

(a) Work out $10010_2 + 1011_2$. (Note that the subscript denotes a number in base two (binary).)

(b) Work out $101_2 - 11_2$.

Solutions

(a) When the number 2 is reached, we carry a 1 to the next column, as is the case in the second column from the right in this sum.

1	0	0	1	0	
	1	0	1	1	+
1	1	1	0	1	
			1		← This is the carry

(b) When we attempt to take '1' from '0' in the second column we can't. Therefore, we borrow a '1' from the previous column. In decimal this would mean borrowing 1 lot of 10, but in binary it means borrowing 1 lot of 2, as shown by the purple numbers at the top of this sum.

When we borrow a '1' we really borrow 1 lot of 2, as shown here in red:

	0	2	
	1̶	0̶	1
	0	1	1	−
	0	1	0	

Hexadecimal

Long binary strings are tedious to deal with and mistakes are common. **Hexadecimal** (base sixteen) is often used instead. **Hex** (short for hexadecimal) uses the numbers {0, 1, 2, 3, 4, 5, 6, 7, 8, 9, A, B, C, D, E, F}. 'A' represents '10', 'B' represents '11' and so on up to 'F' which represents '15'. When adding hex numbers, we carry lots of 16. When using octal numbers, we carry lots of 8.

Example

Add $35B2_{16}$ and $247C_{16}$.

Solution

3	5	B	2	
2	4	7	C	+
5	A	2	E	
	1			← This is the carry

'2 + C' is the same as '2 + 12' which is '14' (i.e. E). 'B + 7' is the same as '11 + 7' which is '18' (i.e. 1 lot of 16 (the carry) and 2 left over). '5 + 4 + 1' is the same as '10' which is 'A'.

Conversion between hex and binary

To convert a binary number into an octal number, group the binary digits into lots of 3, starting at the right-hand side. Then write down the value of each group in octal, and that's the answer.

To convert a **binary** number into a **hex** number, group the binary digits into lots of 4, starting at the right-hand side, then write down the value of each group in hex.

Example

Convert $10\ 1100\ 1100\ 1111\ 1010_2$ into hex.

Solution

10	1100	1100	1111	1010
2	C	C	F	A

Therefore, $10\ 1100\ 1100\ 1111\ 1010_2$ is $2CCFA_{16}$.

Binary coded decimal

An alternative to binary is **binary coded decimal** or **BCD**. This is *not* a number base like **binary** or **hex**, but a system of coding groups of 4 binary digits to represent decimals.

Example

What is the BCD equivalent of 345_{10}?

Solution

3	4	5
0011	0100	0101

Write down the groups of 4 binary digits under each decimal digit. Therefore, 0011 0100 0101 is the **BCD** representation of 345 in decimal.

Fractional binary numbers

A **binary fraction**, like a conventional fraction, contains two parts. The **integer** part appears before the binary point and the **fractional** part appears after the **binary point**. The idea is shown in Table 1.5, where three simple examples are given.

Table 1.5 Three examples to demonstrate the idea of binary fractions

A fractional binary number consists of two parts								
	Integer part				Fractional part			
Decimal number	4	2	1	Binary point	$\frac{1}{2}$	$\frac{1}{4}$	$\frac{1}{8}$	$\frac{1}{16}$
3.5	0	1	1	●	1	0	0	0
1.25	0	0	1	●	0	1	0	0
4.75	1	0	0	●	1	1	0	0

Therefore $3.5_{10} = 11.1_2$, $1.25_{10} = 1.01_2$ and $4.75_{10} = 100.11_2$.

Most calculators can't handle binary fractions and binary floating point numbers, so you will have to work these out by hand. Nevertheless, you can use your calculators to help with parts of the problem, like adding up the integer part and then adding up the fractional part.

Floating point binary numbers

Numbers may be written in scientific notation, for example: $2.3 \times 10^3 = 2300$. In computing, we use a similar system in binary. For example: $101 \times 2^3 = 101000$. The binary point, implied to be at the end of the number 101, is shifted 3 places right, as indicated by the index. The '101' part of the number is called the **mantissa**, and the 'power of two' (i.e. the number on the top of the two) is called the **exponent**. When combined in this way, the number is called a **floating-point number**, because the binary point floats backwards and forwards, dictated by the value of the exponent. Floating-point numbers are usually contained in a **register** (*an electronic place into which binary digits may be stored*), split into two parts as follows:

Floating point binary number									
Mantissa							Exponent		
0	●	1	1	0	1		0	1	1

To work out the value of the number that is contained in this register, we move the binary point 3 places to the right in the mantissa (as indicated by the exponent). Thus the original mantissa '0.1101' becomes '0110.1' after the binary point has been moved, giving us a decimal value of 5.5.

Example

Floating point binary number									
Mantissa							Exponent		
0	●	1	1	1	0		0	1	0

What is the decimal value of this binary floating point number? In this register the mantissa is a fractional number and the exponent is an integer number.

Solution

See Table 1.5 if you are not sure about binary fractions.

The exponent has a value of two, therefore move the binary point two places right, to get 11.10, or decimal for 3.5.

Negative binary numbers

Negative binary numbers work using a system called **two's complement**. It is like a tape-recorder counter and is demonstrated in Table 1.6.

Table 1.6 Positive and negative binary numbers

Number types	Binary (3 digits)			Decimal equivalent
Negative binary numbers	1	0	0	−4
	1	0	1	−3
	1	1	0	−2
	1	1	1	−1
Zero	0	0	0	0
Positive binary numbers	0	0	1	1
	0	1	0	2
	0	1	1	3

The number of digits used must always be specified, like the **3-digit two's complement representation** shown here. Make a note of the patterns. Positive numbers start off with a '0' and negative numbers start off with a '1'. To find the two's complement of a number use the following rule: *Write down the binary number using the correct number of digits. Starting at the right-hand side, move left until the first '1' is encountered. Write this first digit down, and then continue moving left, inverting the other bits (i.e. changing the 0s to 1s and 1s to 0s).*

Example

How is −6 represented in binary if a 4-bit two's complement representation is used?

Solution

First write down the binary number for +6, making sure that 4 bits are used, as shown in Table 1.7.

Table 1.7 How to find the two's complement representation of a 4-bit number

Instructions	Result			
Write down the binary number for +6	0	1	1	0
Move left, writing down the number until the first '1' is encountered			1	0
Invert the remaining digits	1	0	1	0

The answer is shown at the bottom of the table. Therefore, −6 = 1010 using 4 bits.

Don't forget that you can find out the size of the negative numbers by using the a similar method (*i.e. write down the negative number, then follow the same rules as used above*).

There are alternative ways of representing negative numbers in binary.

Sign and magnitude is sometimes used, where the first bit (the sign bit) is '0' for positive and '1' for negative.

The remainder of the digits are represented using a pure binary number, which is the same for positive and negative numbers.

Self-test questions

1 What is meant by the terms ASCII and Unicode?
2 What is meant by:
   (a) a byte
   (b) a word
   (c) a bit.
3 How many bits are needed to represent the following?
   (a) a byte
   (b) 23_{10}
   (c) A_{16}
4 Change the decimal number 39 into the following:
   (a) binary
   (b) BCD
   (c) hexadecimal.
5 Convert 10000101_2 into decimal.
6 Express 9.125 in binary.
7 Convert 237_8 into
   (a) binary
   (b) decimal.
8 Change $A2B_{16}$ into binary.
9 Explain how to convert between binary and hexadecimal numbers.
10 Why is BCD not a true number base?
11 Work out $1011_2 + 1111_2$.
12 Work out $1100_2 − 110_2$.
13 What is a floating-point number?

14 Work out $2BC_{16} + B4_{16}$.

15 Convert 111111111111111_2 (fifteen ones) into decimal.

16 What is the largest positive integer that can be represented using 16 bits? (No negative numbers are needed.)

17 Making use of 8-bit sign and magnitude notation, what is the representation of the decimal numbers −29 and −56?

18 What are the two's complement representations of −29 and −56 using 8 bits?

19 If a two's complement 8-bit representation is used, what is:
(a) the decimal equivalent of the number 11110000; (b) the maximum positive and maximum negative numbers that can be stored using this system?

20 What is the binary representation for +30 if 8-bit sign and magnitude is used, where the eighth bit represents the sign?

2 Images, sound and analogue data

In this section you will learn about:

- Methods of encoding graphics, sound and other information
- Analogue to digital converters and sound synthesis

Other encoding methods

All information on the computer must eventually be coded into **binary**. Here we look at other methods in addition to coding numbers covered in Chapter 1.

Graphical methods

A pattern of bits may be used to represent image information. A bit controls the **colour** in a monochrome image, as shown in Table 2.1. We could also arrange 3 bits to be used, giving 8 different colours (or shades of grey), as shown in Table 2.2.

Table 2.1 1-bit colour

Colour	Bit pattern
Black	0
White	1

Table 2.2 3-bit colour

Colour	Bit pattern		
	R	G	B
Black	0	0	0
Blue	0	0	1
Green	0	1	0
Cyan	0	1	1
Red	1	0	0
Magenta	1	0	1
Yellow	1	1	0
White	1	1	1

Using 4 bits would give us 2^4, which is 16 different colours or shades of grey. 8 bits would produce 256 colours or shades of grey, and the familiar 24 bits would produce 2^{24} or **16 777 216 colours**. The system used here is the **additive colour system** (red, green, blue) as used inside computer monitors. **Subtractive colours** – cyan, magenta, yellow and key (black) – would be used when driving a printer.

Bit-mapped graphics

Individual bits are used to represent an image on the screen in the form of **pixels**. The position is controlled by **mapping** locations in memory to adjacent parts of the picture, and the colour of each pixel is controlled by groups of binary digits in ways identical to those described in the last section. A **bit-mapped image** is made up of tiny squares called **pixels**. If the image is made larger, then the quality degrades (lots of jagged edges). This is characteristic of **bit-mapped graphics**. If **high resolution** is used, near-photographic quality is achieved (several million pixels).

The additive colour system is used inside monitors, where different coloured lights (red, green and blue) are added together to give the illusion of lots of other colours.

The subtractive colour system (cyan, magenta, yellow and key (black)) is used in printers where light is absorbed into the paper and other light is reflected to present the illusion of lots of other colours. The black (key) is needed to produce pure black, which is difficult to reproduce on a printer by using the other colours.

Example

How much memory would be required for a 300 dpi coloured image, the size of an A5 sheet, if 24-bit colour is used?

Solution

An A5 sheet is approximately 8.25 inches by 5.75 inches. At 300 dpi (dots per inch), we need 8.25 × 300 = 2475 pixels horizontally and 5.75 × 300 = 1725 pixels vertically, which gives us 2475 × 1725 = 4 269 375 pixels altogether.

At 300 dpi, this means there would be 4 269 375 dots on the page to make up the picture. Now each pixel requires 3 bytes (24 bits) to define one of the possible 16 777 216 different colours. We therefore need 4 269 375 × 3 = 12 808 125 bytes. Dividing by 1024 (see Chapter 1) gives us 12 808 125/1024 = 12 507 Kbytes. Dividing by 1024 again gives us 12 507/1024 = **12.2 Mbytes**. Setting up an image with the same number of pixels in Paint Shop Pro, for example, confirms the above calculations, as can be seen from Figure 2.1.

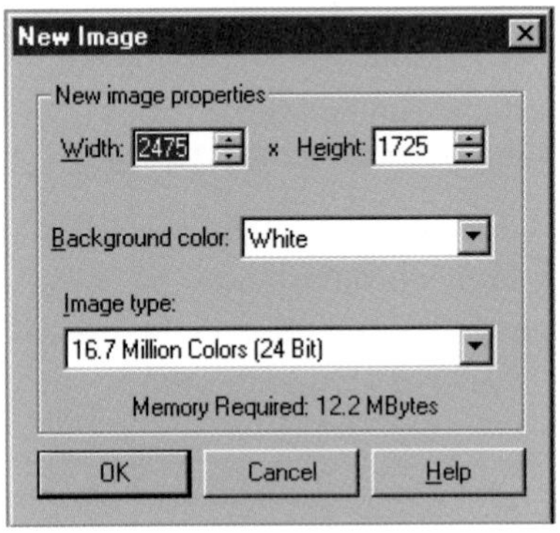

Figure 2.1 Setting up a bitmap

Vector graphics

A good example of a CAD package is the industry standard AutoDesk's AutoCAD. This has a huge number of add ins depending on the industry (e.g. mechanical, civil or aeronautical, for example.)

A good example of an art package is the industry standard Adobe PhotoShop.

Another way to derive a graphic is by using vectors. Mathematical equations determine attributes of the image, made up from straight lines (called **vectors**). These straight-line segments build up into complex **objects** like squares, rectangles and circles. The resultant graphic components are called **objects**. Vector graphics are also known as **object-oriented graphics**. Vectors are used extensively in **CAD packages**, whereas bit-mapped images are usually associated with **art packages**.

Example

Compare and contrast the use of bit-mapped and vector graphics, giving reasons why each is suited to a particular application.

Solution

Bit-mapped graphics are made up from lots of tiny dots called pixels. They are used extensively in art packages like Adobe PhotoShop or Corel Photo Paint. Vector graphics are made up from lines, which build up into objects like circles and squares, etc. They are used extensively in CAD packages like AutoCAD.

Many packages like CorelDraw or Adobe Illustrator, for example, enable us to use both vector and bit-mapped images in the same program. Bit-mapped images tend to be able to do more subtle fancy effects, and vector graphics are much sharper. Bit-mapped images take up a lot of memory. Vector images are less memory hungry and, unlike bit-mapped graphics, can be zoomed in by vast amounts with virtually no loss of image quality.

Other forms of encoding binary data

Sound can be represented by binary data. **MIDI, the Musical Instrument Digital Interface**, has been used for many years, enabling us to transmit binary data in the form of bytes between different electronic musical instruments, or ordinary instruments that have a MIDI interface added. Data in a typical MIDI transmission consists of bytes containing **channel information** (i.e. which of the 20 synthesisers you have connected to your computer pays attention to this data!), a program number like 15, for example, which would tell a standard MIDI keyboard to sound like tubular bells, and a **MIDI value** containing the note information. The channel and program numbers are sent less frequently.

Recording sounds

Most people are aware that sound forms an important part of any multimedia computer system. You can record your own sounds into the computer by using a standard Windows recorder like the one shown in Figure 2.2.

The quality of the recorded sound depends on the amount of binary data used to represent it. Figure 2.3 shows the Windows dialogue box, which determines the quality with which the sound is recorded. For example, we can have CD quality sound, which takes up 172 Kb/sec (172 K bits/sec) of bandwidth.

Figure 2.2 Recording from Windows

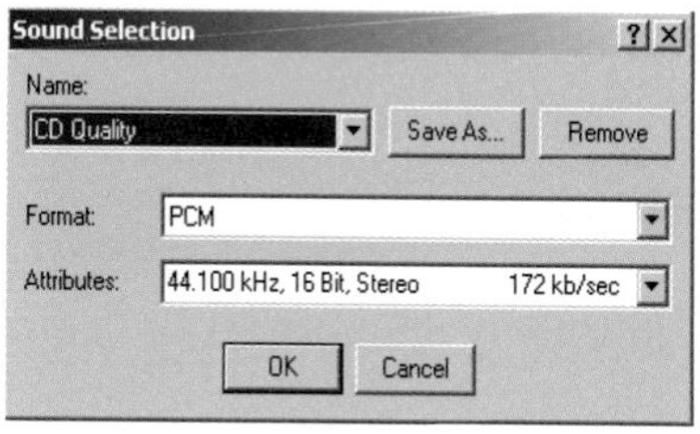

Figure 2.3 Sound quality

It is important to realise that CD quality sound takes up an enormous amount of space. A compression system like MP3 is used, if sound is to be sent over the internet.

Example

Explain exactly why the CD-quality sound in Figure 2.3 takes up 172 Kb for each second of sound recording.

Solution

16-bit stereo means 2 bytes for each sample for each channel. There are 44 100 samples each second (giving CD quality). With 44 100 samples/sec, each sample requires $4 \times 8 = 32$ binary digits (two bytes for each channel for each sample.) Thus $44\ 100 \times 2 \times 2$ gives us 176 400 bits/sec. There are actually 1024 bits in 1K, we get $176\ 400/1024 = 172.27$ Kbits/sec. Therefore, this particular sound recording would take 172 Kb/sec, as shown in Figure 2.3.

A to D converters

An A to D converter (analogue to digital) is an electronic circuit, usually present on most computer sound cards or data logging cards, which transforms an analogue signal, like the one shown in the left side of Figure 2.4, into digital values, like those shown in Figure 2.4.

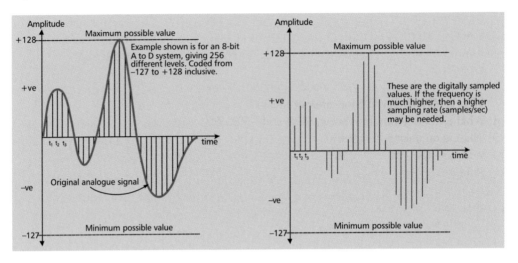

Figure 2.4 Analogue to digital conversion

Example

How many different levels could be sampled with a 16-bit A to D converter?

Solution

1 bit gives just 2 levels: 0 and 1 (2^1).
2 bits give 4 levels: 00, 01, 10 and 11 (2^2).
3 bits would give 8 levels (2^3).

Therefore, 16 bits would give us 2^{16} or 65 536 different possibilities of digital values. If positive and negative values were required, as is the case in Figure 2.4, then we could go from −032 768 to +32 767 including 0, this gives us the 65 536 different possible levels. This is the **two's complement method** (*see Chapter 1*).

Sound synthesis

Making electronic sounds (pure tones) is easy because any sound can be made up from groups of alternating-current signals at different frequencies. This is called **additive synthesis**. It is difficult to make the exact sound required, because more and more complexity is needed if true fidelity is to be accomplished. Other modern techniques used on computer sound cards include **FM synthesis** and **wave table synthesis**.

Self-test questions

1 What is meant by 24-bit graphics?
2 How many colours would be possible if the following graphics systems are used?
    (a) 2-bit
    (b) 8-bit
    (c) 16-bit
3 What's the difference between bit-mapped and vector graphics?
4 How much memory is needed for a 100 dpi 8-bit graphical image 2 by 3 inches?
5 What is MIDI?
6 How does MIDI differ from encoding sound and music?
7 Why is MP3 important for internet music?
8 What's the difference between MP3 and MPEG 3?
9 What is an analogue signal?
10 What is an A to D converter?
11 Sound is a continuously variable or analogue signal. Name three other physical quantities that are analogue in nature.
12 How might sound be encoded into binary?
13 What is the name for a device that converts a digital signal into analogue form?
14 What resolution is available from an 8-bit A to D converter set up to monitor a signal that has minimum amplitude of 0 and maximum amplitude of 5?
15 What is RGB, and how does it differ from CMYK?
16 An A to D converter uses 12 bits. What is the maximum positive and negative amplitude if they are both equally spread in either direction?

3 Microprocessor fundamentals

In this section you will learn about:

- The internal components of a microprocessor
- The bus systems and other components like memory and the clock
- Machine code, parallel processing and mainframes

The internal components of a processor

At the heart of most modern computer systems is a **microprocessor** chip. One or more of these chips, housed on the **motherboard** inside the computer, determines the **hardware** platform on which the machine is run. An understanding of these basic principles leads to a better understanding of how a computer system operates at the most basic level.

There are interactive learning materials available to help you understand more about the microprocessor architecture.

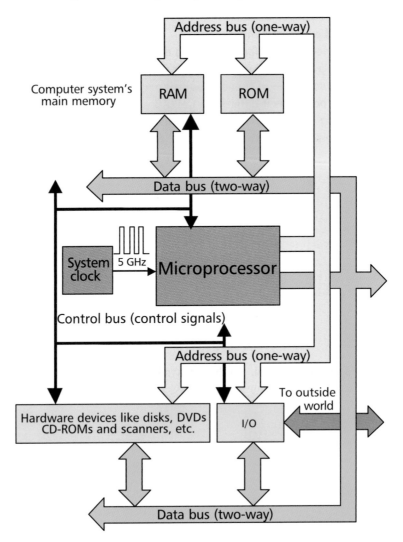

Figure 3.1 How a simple microprocessor is connected to a typical computer system

A simplified system, shown in Figure 3.1, consists of a **microprocessor** chip, which is activated by an electronic circuit called a **clock**. This clock can generate very fast pulses, like the '5000 million tick-tock cycles per second' shown here. This not only controls the speed, but synchronisation of the system too. A **bus** is a parallel group of wires, connecting different parts of the computer system. Binary digits, which form the **data** on which the computer operates, flow along the **address**, **data**, and **control buses**. Some data may go from a DVD disk to the main memory, for example.

The **address bus** is used to address memory and other devices, and the data travels along the **data bus**. Special control signals, like the one telling the memory chip if a 'read' or 'write' operation is taking place, go along the smaller, but equally important, **control bus**.

Main and secondary storage systems

The contents of **main memory** (**RAM** or **Random Access Memory**) are lost when power to the computer is switched off, but the computer needs **instructions** (a **program**) to follow as soon as it's switched on. Therefore a set of program instructions are permanently held in **ROM** (**Read Only Memory**), which never loses its data, even when the power is removed. These instructions, together with settings in the **BIOS** (the **Basic Input Output System**) help the computer to know which hardware devices are available when it **boots up**. During this booting process, the computer will search for the appropriate **operating system**, load it from disk and finally pass control over to it. **Applications** and **user's programs** are usually stored on **secondary storage** devices like magnetic and optical disks (**M/O disks**), and these form an important part of most computer systems.

For more about operating systems see Chapter 16.

Applications and **user's programs** are usually stored on **disk** until they are needed, when they are loaded in the computer's **RAM**. Devices like **hard disks**, **CD-ROMs** and **DVDs**, etc. are connected to the processor by the address, data and control buses too, and are dealt with in ways similar to the main-memory devices mention earlier. In fact any device can be hooked up to the processor in this way, and Figure 3.1 shows a general **I/O** (Input Output) connection to the outside world. This connection might go via a sound card and an A to D converter so that a microphone could be connected, or data lines might go via some electronics to control the lights in your house, for example.

Modern computers have a huge variety of ways of getting data into and out of the system; **USB** (the **Universal Serial Bus**) and **FireWire** to name but two. The USB system is popular for the connection of a large number of devices ranging from **printers** and **keyboards** to **modems**, **PDAs** (**Personal Digital Assistants**) and **mobile phones**.

Example

Based on what you have just read, list three ways in which the speed of execution of a microcomputer system can be improved, explaining why each method is effective.

Solution

- The **speed of the clock** can be increased. This means that more cycles can be carried out each second.

- The **width of the data** bus can be increased. More data can be transferred to and from memory for each clock cycle.

- **More than one processor** could be used, thus giving a parallel-processing capability, in which more than one thing can be carried out at the same time.

3

Real microprocessors are getting more complex with each new addition, and the simplified microprocessor architecture considered so far does not do justice to the latest innovations. Nevertheless, if you look at diagrams showing real microprocessors, you can see important parts of our simplified processor, like the ALU and cache memories and bus systems, for example.

Microprocessor and internal components

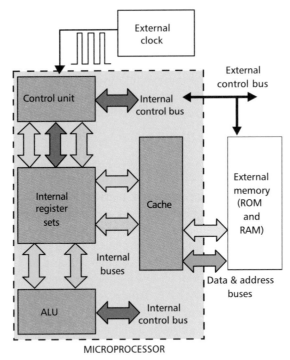

Figure 3.2 A simplified internal structure of a typical microprocessor

Considering the simplified **microprocessor** architecture shown in Figure 3.2, you should be able to quote the roles played by the ALU (the **arithmetic logic unit**), the **control unit**, and **internal memory** (cache). Detailed work regarding registers and assembly-language programming are covered in the A2 modules. (*See the second book in this series.*)

The **ALU** is the part of the processor that carries out arithmetical and logical operations. It is this unit that would accept the binary data on which to perform these operations, and pass back the results ready for the next process. It is quite a task to make sure that all data gets routed correctly, and in our simplified system it is the job of the **control unit** to do this.

Although getting data from the **main memory (RAM)** is very fast indeed, the internal parts of the processor often require data even faster than this. Therefore, some memory inside the processor, usually called **cache**, is used for this purpose. It speeds things up by keeping copies of instructions that are likely to be needed soon. The instruction decoder is also considered to be part of the control unit in our simplified system.

Machine code and the stored program concept

Groups of **binary digits** (*see Chapter 1*) represent the special instructions that form the **program** on which the computer operates. These instructions are called **machine code**, and they usually reside in the computer's **main memory (RAM)**. It is the job of the computer system to **fetch** a machine-code instruction from memory, decide what the instruction is telling it to do (called **decoding**), and finally carry out the required actions (called **execution**). The next instruction is then **fetched** from memory, so that the next part of the program may be carried out. (This is known as the **fetch-decode-execute cycle**.) Under the 'metronome-like pulses' from the **clock**, complex sets of instructions can be carried out serially (i.e. one after the other). The idea of operating in this way is called the **stored program concept**, because groups of instructions (or **programs**) stored in the main memory, are being executed serially. The sort of instructions that can be carried out at this level are quite simple and may be **arithmetic operations** like 'add' or 'subtract', or **logical operations** like 'AND' and 'OR'.

Example

Briefly explain how a microprocessor, running sets of machine code instructions, can appear to exhibit intelligent behaviour like making a correct decision.

Solution

Machine code instructions consist of a variety of different forms, some of which can help make decisions, based on the results of simple arithmetical or logical operations. Therefore, using machine code, you could program the computer to take action after adding a couple of numbers together. It could, for example, carry out one action if the result was too big, or it might carry out a different action if the result was too small. In this way it is possible to make the computer take an appropriate decision and therefore appear to be intelligent.

Machine code and the stored program concept

So far we have looked only at single-processor microcomputer systems. Add an extra processor and you have the ability to literally do more than one thing at the same time. Network files servers, for example, commonly have two, four or even eight processors, so that the enormous workload of dealing with many users simultaneously is shared between them.

The next stages up the hierarchy are **mainframe** and **supercomputers**. Historically these were very large machines, found in university and government research labs. However, recent **mainframes**, and even **supercomputers**, are built up using a larger number of microprocessors. SGI's Cray SV1 can handle hundreds of processors simultaneously! Computers such as these are awesome, and would handle complex military projects, or work out the results for weather forecasts and hurricane prediction, for example. They can handle hundreds of processors because they are designed with scalability in mind. This means that you can add another bank of processors should the need arise.

Example

Why do we need supercomputers like those described above to predict the weather?

Solution

Running a simulation for weather forecasting is an extremely complex business, involving billions of complex interrelated calculations, even for forecasting today's weather. If much slower computers are used, the results of tomorrow's weather might be ready in about a month, assuming that the mass of data could be correlated in time. As computers get more powerful, better prediction methods are being developed.

Self-test questions

1 Explain the functions of the following bus systems inside a microprocessor:
    (a) The data bus
    (b) The address bus
    (c) The control bus
2 What determines the hardware platform for a particular microcomputer?
3 What is the difference between primary and secondary storage?
4 What do the letters ALU stand for and what is the purpose of the ALU?

5 There are usually two types of primary store associated with a microprocessor, **ROM** and **RAM**. What are these and why are both types usually used when a microprocessor is set up as a microcomputer?

6 What is machine code? Why does the machine code for a particular microprocessor not work with any other type?

7 What is cache and why is it used?

8 What is the function of the control unit inside a simplified microprocessor chip?

9 What does the fetch-decode-execute cycle mean?

10 What is the stored program concept?

11 A typical computer system would have a variety of ways of connecting peripheral devices. Suggest four different interface systems which enable us to do this.

12 What is the function of a motherboard inside a microcomputer?

13 List three different types of machine-code instruction.

14 Use the world wide web to find a diagram of the inside of the type of microprocessor in your computer.

4 Fundamental ideas about software

In this section you will learn about:

- The difference between hardware and software
- A brief look at operating systems and some application software
- System software, library and utility programs
- High- and low-level languages and language generations
- A brief introduction to compilers, interpreters and assemblers

Hardware and software

An important distinction is made between **hardware** and **software**. **Hardware** is *equipment* like the microprocessors, memory and disks, and **peripheral** equipment like printers, scanners and bar-code readers. **Software** is the **programs** or **instructions**, like the machine code described later in this chapter. Examples of software are **operating systems** and **application programs**. An often-used but slightly silly definition of hardware is 'anything that you can stub your toe on', but this is actually quite informative and should be remembered!

Different types of software

Software can be split into two major categories – **application software** like word processors and databases, and **systems software** like the Windows 2000 or Linux operating systems.

Application software can be subdivided into **general-purpose applications software** and **special-purpose applications software**. Applications like word processors and spreadsheets belong to general-purpose applications. Microsoft Word is a good example of this. **Special-purpose applications software** covers less general applications like the 'QuArk' game-editing software shown in Figure 4.1, where James Marriot, a pupil at the author's school, is producing a map of the Technology block for the computer game Quake.

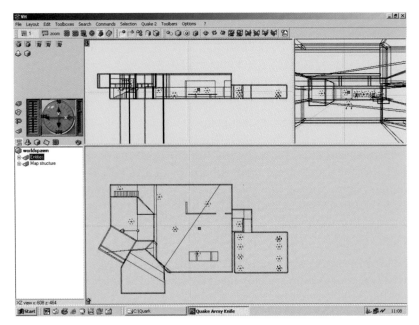

Figure 4.1 QuArk – a good example of a special-purpose application software

Other examples of special purpose applications software would be the 'AutoCAD design software' made by AutoDesk, and the '3D Studio Max' software made by Discreet. The 3D Studio Max software was used to develop Walt Disney's film *Toy Story*.

If software is written or tailored to a unique situation, it is often referred to as **bespoke software**, which simply means 'built to order'. **Bespoke software** is usually created by a professional, either 'in house' or by a third party that specialises in this sort of work. It may be written using a **high-level programming language** (*see later*) or by using the advanced facilities in **application packages** like Microsoft Office. A good example of bespoke software could be **word processors**, **databases** and **spreadsheets** set up specifically for an organisation like a school or college to run their administration systems. Such a system might handle registration, examination entries, class and teacher timetabling and parents' evenings to name just a few of the hundreds of different possibilities. It's up to the school to specify all the things that the bespoke software solution should provide. Some companies now provide special purpose application software for schools to do a similar job, and the CMIS system (covered in detail in Chapter 10) is a good example of this.

Application software is often referred to as an **application package**. Typical of these application packages are office suites like Microsoft Office, which consists of fully blown word processors, spreadsheets, databases, presentation packages and organisation programs, etc. There are also cut-down versions of these application packages, which are known as **integrated packages**. A good example of an integrated package is Microsoft Works, which has simpler versions of a word processor and a spreadsheet. These are ideal for use at home by non-professionals because the software is generally easier to use, and it's easier to transfer data between various parts of the system. An integrated package does not contain all the 'bells and whistles' available in the main suites. However, due to some compatibility problems, it can be annoying if you wish to share work with others. You often have to remember to save the work in a special way to be able to do this.

Introduction to system software

System software is the heart of any computer system. It can be thought of as *software specifically used for the management of the computer system*, rather than application software, which is software for use by the user (i.e. software that enables the user to write documents, draw pictures or surf the net, for example). System software is designed to help out with the efficient running of the computer, and to enable the user to maintain the system. It includes **software** like the **operating system**, **utilities** and **libraries**. (*See later.*)

The **operating system** is the software that polices and controls the computer, and gives the computer its special characteristics, like a **GUI** (**Graphical User Interface**), for example. It enables the user to customise the computer to their exact needs, and, if properly set up, should prevent other people from inadvertently or deliberately messing up the system. The operating system is the single most important piece of software on the computer, without which nothing else (except, the ROM BIOS – explained on the next page) would work. It is a tribute to the modern operating system that computers are now so much easier to use than previously.

Command-based operating systems like 'DOS' are very much harder for novices to use than the **GUI-based operating systems** like Windows. This is because the user interface is less intuitive. As a comparison, Figure 4.2 shows a typical **GUI interface**, and the less intuitive **DOS-based command line interface**.

Visit www.ccmsoftware. com to look at the CMIS special-purpose application for educational administration.

DOS is the name for Microsoft's Disk Operating System. A version of DOS is still available from Windows. You can access it by running the MS-DOS command prompt. Figure 4.2 shows a typical DOS interface. Don't assume that this type of interface is less useful than a GUI; on many occasions it can be much more useful and powerful.

Figure 4.2 Comparison of typical GUI and command-line operating systems

Example

List two advantages and two disadvantages of GUI-based operating systems like Windows compared to command-line operating systems like DOS.

Solution

A GUI, like the Windows-based operating system, is easy to use by a novice; a command-based language like DOS is not. A GUI takes up a lot of computer memory, but a command-based system does not. (Note: command-based systems are still very powerful, and are often the only convenient way of doing tedious administrative tasks, like setting thousands of file permissions on a file server.)

The ROM BIOS

Another important part of the system, called the **ROM BIOS** (Basic Input Output System), is located in a ROM chip housed on the **motherboard** (the main electronic board inside the PC). After this software (often called **firmware** as it is stored on a chip), has done its job, the operating system boots up so that the computer ends up in a useable state. Think of the software inside the ROM BIOS chip as an *interface* between an **operating system**, like Windows, for example, and the **hardware**, like the motherboard, disks and DVDs, etc. Together with the **software drivers**, this software ensures that different pieces of hardware are compatible with different operating systems and motherboards.

The **BIOS** has many special software routines embedded in it. The function of these is to check the hardware, and correctly configure all the settings for the disks and graphics displays, etc. (via the **CMOS RAM** settings). The **bootstrap loader** is then run so that the computer is in a useable state, and then the main **operating system** can be loaded from disk. After all this system software has been loaded, the computer is ready to load any application software.

If some piece of hardware does not work properly, it is a good idea to surf the internet to find the latest software drivers for your particular operating system. You will often find that this cures a problem.

If no drivers are available, you many not be able to use a particular piece of hardware with your operating system.

Example

How is it possible to have operating system software like Windows interface to different types of hardware, and how do we customise this for individual users?

Solution

The ROM BIOS provides an interface for the hardware on which an operating system may sit. Therefore, if you have different types or sizes of disk, different motherboards or different amounts of memory, the software inside the BIOS, together with the hardware drivers, can interface your particular hardware to a standard operating system. Each type of motherboard needs a different BIOS, and each piece of hardware will need a different software driver which is compatible with a particular operating system. The same graphics card, for example, will probably need a different driver to interface it to Windows XP, Windows 2000, Windows Me, Windows 98 and Windows 95. Without these facilities we would need a different version of the operating system for each version of hardware available! Some settings may be customised to your individual requirements by altering data in the CMOS RAM.

The role of the operating system

At AS level you should be able to make a long list of things carried out by the operating system, but need to know little about how it actually implements these systems in practice.

Apart from providing a computer system with 'special characteristics', like a command line or GUI, it is the function of the operating system to manage all resources. For example, the **memory allocation** for each application being run, managing the **security systems** on file servers and workstations, managing the **disk-space allocation** for different users on a network system, accounting for how many colour printouts each user might have made or producing an **audit** about who has done what, where and when.

All other software that runs on the computer depends on the correct functioning of the operating system. If, for example, an errant application uses memory that belongs to another application which is running at the same time, one of the applications could crash, resulting in the familiar 'Page protection fault' error message, which frequent users of PCs have probably encountered at some time or other!

Example

Most professional operating systems have the ability to produce an audit trail. Outline two typical scenarios that might lead to certain activities needing to be audited.

Solution

For the purposes of AS level you need to appreciate the function of the operating system, but need few details about how it goes about these tasks. Operating systems are covered in more detail in the A2 book.

Two scenarios where an audit might be required are as follows:

(a) A program is causing errors. The network manger is not sure if it is a bug in the software or whether the user is doing something silly without realising it. An audit trail is put on the user's activities when this suspected errant program is being run.

(b) The security of a file in a database is being compromised. The network manager has set up an audit to monitor who is accessing the file, and what they are doing to it.

Utility programs

Each day we take for granted many of the mundane things carried out on our computer systems like 'backing up work onto tape', running a 'recovery program' in case we delete something by accident, or 'finding a file on a disk'. A **utility** is therefore *related to aspects of computer management*. Some of these **utilities** may be part of the **operating system**, and third parties may provide others. A good example of a utility program is the program to defragment a disk, shown in Figure 18.3. Other common examples are 'setting file permissions', 'creating directories' (folders), renaming files and folders and making a list of all the files created before a certain date.

Library programs

Other **routines** may reside inside what's called a **library**. In Windows, for example, there is a **Dynamic Link Library**. This library contains files (**DLLs**), stored and ready to be used by any program that can link to them. In this way, **applications** and **users' programs** can share these routines. Other libraries exist too. For example, **programming languages** like C++ have their own library files, usually stored in a special directory. Programmers may call up and use these when needed. Library routines can literally be anything programmers care to dream up, and examples of simple ones could be anything from 'reading a password' via 'handling special interfaces' to 'working out complex mathematical relationships'. When an application or program requires a library routine, it loads it into memory and leaves the executable code and data in memory ready to be used by it or any other application.

Example

What is an operating system? Outline three major functions that are typically performed by the operating system.

Solution

An operating system is the software that controls the computer and, via the BIOS, interfaces it with the hardware. It gives the computer its characteristics like a **GUI** or **command line system**, and helps to make the system much easier to use for non-specialists. Three functions typically performed by the operating system are as follows:

- the allocation of memory to different parts of the system

- allocating CPU time (microprocessor time) to different tasks

- managing the disk space on the hard disks attached to the computer.

Machine code – a first-generation language

The computer works only with **pure binary codes** called **machine code**, which, cleverly encoded, can represent anything from colours on the screen to sounds from the loud-speaker (*see Chapter 2*).

Machine code is the only language a computer 'understands'. All other languages are for the convenience of humans, and all programming instructions, in whatever language they are written, must eventually be translated into machine code before they can be run on the microprocessor controlling the computer.

4

Machine code (low-level language)						Visual basic (high-level language)
58EC:0000	CD	20	00	A0	00 ..	Dim Number, Digits, MyString
58EC:0010	7B	27	B5	0A	7B ..	Number = 53
58EC:0020	05	FF	FF	FF	FF ..	If Number < 10 Then
58EC:0030	CD	21	CB	00	00 ..	Digits = 1
58EC:0040	6E	70	75	74	30 ..	ElseIf Number < 100 Then
Assembly language (low-level language)						Digits = 2
MOV	AX,	5B71				Else
MOV	DS,	AS				Digits = 3
PUSH	AX					End If

Figure 4.3 Some examples of low level and high-level languages

Working only with **binary digits** is a tedious and error-prone task, as can be imagined from the small machine-code extract at the top left of Figure 4.3. In this example, lots of **binary digits** representing the machine code are presented as **pairs of** hexadecimal **digits**. Looking at this particular code is like taking a snapshot inside the computer's memory. **Machine code** is a **first-generation language**, and is the only language a computer 'understands'.

Assembly language – a second-generation language

More progress could be made if the machine-code instructions were easier to interpret by humans. **Assembly language** was the next stage (**second generation language**), and **mnemonics** (aids to the memory), representing machine-code instructions inside the microprocessor, replaced the tedious groups of binary digits. A typical assembly-language program segment is shown at the bottom left of Figure 4.3. **Mnemonics** like 'MOV' and 'PUSH' represent simple operations on registers (electronic places to store numbers) inside the microprocessor. Typical of these might be a hex number '5B71', for example, being 'MOVed' into the AX register. Although not very user friendly, this is much better than the machine code equivalent for the same operation. If you wish to move these numbers using pure machine code, then the hex numbers 'B8715B' would be used!

When using **assembly language** an extra stage has been introduced. The computer must therefore translate the assembly-language mnemonics into the machine code that will actually run on the computer. To do this we use an **assembler** (*see later.*) Both **machine code** and **assembly language** are examples of a **low-level language**.

High-level languages – the third-generation languages

Programming in a **low-level language** required programmers to be experts. It was not an ideal environment for other professionals (non-computer scientists) who wished to program computers to solve specific problems, like those found in mathematics, engineering and commerce. New ways had to be developed if computers were to become easier to use. **High-level languages** were the answer to this, as program instructions were much easier to understand.

A segment from a typical high-level language is shown on the right of Figure 4.3. Note that English-like words have been used, and variable names, like the variables used in mathematics, help clarify this routine, which determines how many digits are in a number < 1000. Key words like 'IF', 'THEN' and 'ELSE' are easier to understand, and are related to human logic, instead of the operations required by a particular machine. This is why it is called a **high-level language**. Imperative (see next section) high-level programming languages belong to **third-generation languages**. All high-level languages contain an imperative programming element.

Imperative high-level languages

Imperative languages typically give **sets of instructions** (called 'imperatives') to the computer. You will also come across other language definitions (or paradigms) such as 'object-oriented languages' or 'declarative languages'. However, an understanding of these other language paradigms requires an understanding of imperative programming too, and this is why imperative languages are considered first at AS level.

*Object oriented programming **and** declarative programming **are** covered in the A2 book.*

Other generations of language

There are two other language generations. Examples of these are the **macro languages** used to program databases, spreadsheets and word processors, which typify **fourth-generation languages**, and high-level languages like **Prolog** which typify **fifth-generation languages**.

Fourth and fifth generation languages are also covered in the A2 book.

Example

List two conditions under which it would be essential to use machine code or assembly language instead of a high-level language? Explain your answers.

Solution

- High-level languages have to be converted into machine code. Therefore, if speed is of the essence, as might be the case in a **real-time operating system**, (*see Chapter 16*) then machine code or assembly language could be the only language that is fast enough. Assembly language needs minimal translation, but machine code needs none.

- Sometimes a high-level language may not have the facilities to do exactly what you want. Therefore, some routine may have to be written in machine code or assembly language to carry out the desired function. Anything that it's possible to think up can be done with machine code, provided, of course, that you can find a suitable solution to the problem (*see* **algorithms** – *Chapter 16*).

Other system software

We need special software to '**translate**' code written in a **high-level language** or **assembly language** into the **machine code** that will run on the computer. You must never lose sight of the fact that *only machine code can run on a computer*, and other languages must eventually be translated into this form. **Interpreters** and **compilers** are '**translators**' (software), which translate **high-level languages** into **machine code**, and an **assembler** is a program that translates **assembly language** into **machine code** (*see next section*).

Assemblers

An **assembler** is a piece of software that translates **assembly language** into **machine code**. It also gives much help to the assembly-language programmer in terms of error detection and organisation. Without an **assembler**, the program writer would have to translate the assembly language instructions into machine code by hand. They would have to work out where to put the program in memory, and calculate any jumps from one part of the program to another. This would be a tedious and error-prone task. There would be no checks performed on the **syntax** (grammar) of the code, and any errors not detected could easily cause the machine to crash. To get over these and many other problems, a program called an **assembler** (see Figure 4.4) is used. This program enables you to type the assembly-language mnemonics, '**assemble**' the code (change it into **machine code**) and save the **source code** (the list of assembly language instructions) and **object code** (the **machine code** that will run on the computer) onto a disk. If you need to change the code at a later date the **editor** that is built into the assembler can be used.

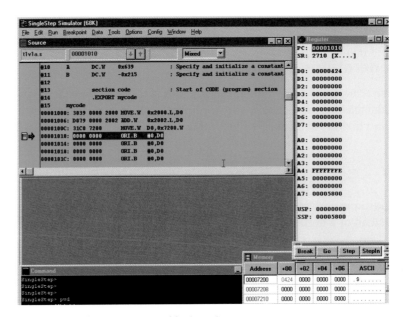

Figure 4.4 A GUI interface showing an assembler in action

Compilers

A **compiler** is a piece of software which converts a **high-level language** into **machine code**. Code is typed into a special editor, and an executable file (one that will run on a computer without the compiler being present) is produced. A compiler changes all the **high-level language code** into **machine code** at the same time. Any errors in the code, would involve recompiling all the code (i.e. you need to load the source code, change it, resave it and then recompile it). This is not a good environment for beginners to learn to program. A compiler enables companies to produce code which is very hard to reverse engineer (i.e. to work out how the original program operates). As with the assembler described in the last section, most compilers provide lots of help. This would include syntax checking, the ability to add comments and produce printouts, etc.

Interpreters

An **interpreter** is a piece of software that converts a **high-level language** into **machine code**. It does this in a much more user-friendly interactive environment compared to a compiler. This means that you are instantly aware of any errors in syntax that you have made, and are able to correct these errors without having to recompile the entire program. Many students would learn to program making use of an interpreter, because most versions of the high-level language **BASIC** are interpreted.

An **interpreter** has most of the advantages of a **compiler**, but is usually a lot slower because only one line of the high-level language is converted into machine code at a time. Moreover, code inside a loop in the language (code to be executed over and over again) will need to be interpreted (translated) over and over again. The biggest advantage is that errors may be identified and corrected very easily, and this is thus a friendlier environment for the novice user. Some high-level languages, like **Visual Basic**, for example, enable you to compile code after you have developed it using the interpreter.

Example

Outline a typical scenario where the following would be most appropriately used:

(a) machine code

(b) assembly language

(c) use of a compiler

(d) use of an interpreter.

Solution

(a) Machine code is rarely used for programming a computer. It is occasionally used for programming some computer-controlled devices.

(b) Assembly language is used if a particular facility needed by a program is not available in a high-level language. It is also used if great speed is required, as might be needed for military equipment.

(c) Programs are compiled if speed of operation is important. Because the final code is compiled into machine code, this is a convenient way of selling your software without giving your customers access to the actual high-level language code you have used to solve the problem.

(d) An interpreter is ideal in a learning and development environment, where instant feedback regarding errors is more important than speed or efficiency.

Self-test questions

1 Explain the difference between hardware and software.
2 List ten different items of hardware and ten different items of software.
3 Give two examples of general-purpose software, bespoke software and systems software.
4 What is the difference between applications software and systems software?
5 What is the ROM BIOS? Outline three different functions performed by this system.
6 List three things that can be accomplished most easily by using a command-line operating system like DOS.
7 List three different things that can be accomplished most easily by using a GUI.
8 What is the difference between a high-level language and a low-level language?
9 Give two examples of a low-level language.
10 What is meant by a first-generation language?
11 What is a third-generation language? Give an example.

You may need to make use of the internet to answer question 20 in the self-test questions.

4

12 What is an imperative language?

13 Java is a high-level programming language. Name four others, and outline a typical use of each.

14 Name three different utility programs on a typical microcomputer.

15 What is the difference between a compiler and an interpreter?

16 An interpreter is more easy to use than a compiler. Explain why this is so.

17 Library programs are often used by a variety of applications. What is a library program and why is it used?

18 List two different things that might be accomplished with a library program.

19 Which of the following is the odd one out?

keyboard, USB port, operating system, motherboard or graphics card

20 Would a compiler or an assembler be used to translate the high-level language Delphi into machine code?

21 Make a list of three useful functions that are carried out by compilers.

Use the Internet to answer Q20 if you are unsure

5 Programming fundamentals 1

In this section you will learn about:

- The basic principles of high-level language programming
- The idea of writing programs using pseudocode
- Key words, identifiers, variables, constants, assignment and arithmetic operations
- Data types, simple functions and inputting data
- 'For to next', 'do while' and 'repeat until' loop structures
- The importance of comments and dry running

High-level language principles

Most **high-level languages** have much in common. Without these common features programmers would need to learn brand new concepts from scratch, and this would be counter productive. Here we concentrate on these common features, using elementary concepts from high-level languages and some Microsoft **Visual Basic** examples.

If you have no access to the Visual Basic programming language, don't worry; *you will not be asked for details of any particular language during AS examinations.* Some schools may use '**Pascal**' or '**Delphi**', and others may use '**C**' or '**C++**'. During examinations (and at other times too) it's acceptable to use **pseudocode**. This is 'made up code' that mirrors common features in most high-level languages. **Key words** like 'FOR TO NEXT', 'REPEAT UNTIL', 'WHILE', 'DIM' and 'PROCEDURE', for example, will be familiar to all who have studied programming. However, *it's essential to write programs using your particular language.* The work is much easier to understand if you write some real code.

The basic ideas

Learning a programming language is like learning a foreign language. The rules and regulations (or '**grammar**') covering the layout and use of words, etc. is called the **syntax**. All high-level languages are made up from sets of **reserved** or **key words**. These words are used in special contexts, and should not be used for any other purpose. Key words are added to **variables** and **constants** and are grouped together to form **statements** (see below). The meaning conveyed by these **statements** is called **semantics**.

Most high-level language programs are made up from **statements**. These are *descriptive phrases that generate one or more machine code instructions.* A high-level language statement will always have to be turned into machine code before it can be run on any computer. This is just one reason why high-level languages are organised in this way. It is fortunate that we can solve many AS level problems with just a few ideas and a limited knowledge of high-level language principles.

Identifiers, constants and variables

Each language has a character set, which usually consists of 'letters of the alphabet' and 'numbers', plus other symbols like 'arithmetical operators' (+, −, etc.) and 'punctuation'. An **identifier** is the general name given to a 'string of characters' that acts as a **label** to represent **data items** or elements of a program. Some examples of **identifiers** now follow.

The work in this chapter is not intended to teach you any particular high-level language. There are plenty of excellent textbooks and manuals written specifically to do this.

This work is related to the common principles associated with any imperative high-level language, and will help you to develop pseudocode solutions to problems posed in AS level examinations.

This work should also provide a good foundation for those who choose to do a programming project during their A2 year.

```
Pi = 3.142    Stock_Level = 300    TestString$ = "revisecomputing.com"
```

Pi (or π) is an example of a **constant** (a value that does not vary). However, Stock_Level could be a constant (indicating a minimum level of stock) or it might represent a **variable**, indicating the actual level of stock. A **variable** is a name given to an **identifier** (not clashing with any other key or reserved word) that is allowed to take on a range of values. Note that an underscore '_' is used instead of a space to represent variable names using multiple words. Most high-level languages don't allow the use of a space inside a variable name. Most also don't allow a variable name to start with a number; therefore, '1ton' would be an invalid variable name. These are examples of errors in the rules of **syntax**, and would be picked up as errors by the **compiler** or **interpreter** during the translation phase.

It makes programs easier to understand if the programmer explicitly states at the beginning of a program whether an **identifier** is a **constant** or a **variable**, and this is usually done by means of a dimension or **Dim statement**. The following statements at the beginning of the program would have solved the problem we had with identifiers mentioned in the last paragraph. In practice, words like 'integer', 'real' and 'boolean' would be used instead of the word 'variable' (see later).

```
Dim Pi, Stock_Level As constant
Dim TestString$ = "ReviseComputing.com" As variable
```

Here the **key words** have been shown using green text, to distinguish them from the identifiers representing constants, variables and other data. This technique is used to good effect in the **editing software** used to compile the high-level language code, because it makes the programs easier to read. When constants and variables are set up this way, usually at the beginning of a program, this process is called **declaration**. You are *declaring* or *defining the types of data* to be used during the execution of the program.

Examples

1 Using the rules outlined above, which of the following are valid variable names?
   (a) `My Bank Balance`   (b) `Route66`
   (c) `76Trombones`   (d) `Fifth_Generation`

2 Write some pseudocode to declare two valid constants and three valid variables.

Solutions

1 Only (b) and (d) are valid variable names. (a) contains illegal spaces and (c) starts off with a number.

2 The following pseudocode declares two constants and three variables:

```
Dim Target, Destination As constant
Dim Radius, Circumference, Area As variable
```

Assignment and simple arithmetical operations

It is a common requirement to work out simple arithmetic. Most high level languages use the arithmetical operators '+', '−', '*' and '/' to represent addition, subtraction, multiplica-

All high-level language code is produced by using suitable editing software. It's possible to use a text editor like 'Microsoft's NotePad' to create the text which is then used as the source code for the compiler.

Most modern languages now come with their own editor built into an integrated program development environment. Microsoft's Visual Basic and Borland's Delphi studios are good examples of this modern approach to writing high-level language code.

tion and division respectively. To work out the perimeter of a rectangle having sides of length a and b, we can make up a statement like the following:

```
perimeter = 2*a + 2*b
```

Here the variable called 'perimeter' is put equal to the value of '2 times a' plus '2 times b'. This is called an **assignment statement** because the value of the variable on the left-hand side is put equal to the result of the operations on the right-hand side.

Students are often confused when they use assignment statements like the following:

```
counter  = counter + 1
```

Don't think of this as a mathematical equation, because it is not. It is an **assignment statement** that means take the current value of the variable 'counter', add 1 to it and place this value in the variable called 'counter'. If counter = 387 before this **assignment statement** is encountered, then after this statement is executed the value of the variable counter would be 388. Because of this confusion, some high-level languages make use of ':=' as the assignment operator instead of the equal sign. However, once you realise what is happening, it's one of the simplest and most useful concepts about programming.

Example

Work out the value of the variable called 'result' for the following pseudocode:

```
DIM a, b As variable
DIM result As variable
a = 2
b = 3
result = 3*a + b
```

Solution

The result would be 3 * 2 + 3 = 6 + 3 = 9. Therefore result = 9. (*Multiplication is worked out before addition – the normal rules of mathematical precedence apply.*)

Data types

Most high-level languages support a rich range of **data types**. These allow you to express the solutions to problems in more elegant ways. Just like the 'constant' and 'variable' declarations considered earlier made the programs easier to understand, using data types like **integer** and **real** makes the program easier to follow too. It also helps the **compiler** or **interpreter** (*see Chapter 4*) to set up the memory inside the computer more efficiently.

We have used simple numeric variables in the last few paragraphs, but languages like Microsoft **Visual Basic**, for example, have integer, long, single, double and currency numeric data types. You will be aware from reading Chapter 1 that binary numbers can be stored in a variety of different ways like '**integer**' and '**two's complement**'. This is why programs specify which numeric data type is required. Currency, for example, stores 4 decimal places after the decimal point, and 15 places before the point. It would be silly to store somebody's age in this way, because an integer would be more appropriate. It's up to the programmer to

Table 5.1 A typical range of numeric data types

C++ numeric data types		
	Range	
Name	**From**	**To**
char	−128	127
int	−32 768	32 767
short	−32 768	32 767
long	−2 147 483 648	2 147 483 647
float	3.4×10^{-38}	3.4×10^{38}
double	1.7×10^{-308}	1.7×10^{308}
long double	3.4×10^{-4932}	1.1×10^{4932}

make sensible use of these data types. The language C++ also supports a rich diversity of numeric data types, and Table 5.1 shows the range available in one version of C++. Note how the ranges of numbers correspond closely with how binary is used to represent numbers. The numeric data type 'char', for example, is an 8-bit two's complement number.

There are many other data types, like **boolean**, **string**, **arrays**, **file**, **records** and **enumerated** to name but a few. Some of these other data types will be covered in the next few chapters.

Other operations and functions

Brackets are used in the normal way, and **exponentiation** (raising a number to a power) often uses the '^' key. Hence $x = 2^2$ would be written as $x = 2\text{\textasciicircum}2$. Many other **mathematical functions** like **square root**, **sin** and **random numbers** exist in most high-level languages. However, not all functions available within a programming language are mathematical. Functions such as **eof** (end-of-file), for example, could be used to determine if the end of a computer data file has been reached.

Examples

Write out the following three formulae, making use of pseudocode, or by using a high-level language of your choice.

$$x = \sqrt{a^2 + b^2} \qquad \text{Area} = \tfrac{1}{2}h(a+b) \qquad r = \frac{\sqrt{s(s-a)(s-b)(s-c)}}{s}$$

Solutions

```
X = SQR(a^2+b^2)   Area = (1/2)*h*(a+b)   r = SQR((s*(s-a)*(s-b)*(s-c))/s)
```

The 'for to next' structure

A common mistake is to forget to put in the * for multiplication. Students are so used to writing abc to mean 'a multiplied by b multiplied by c' that they forget to write a*b*c when using a high level programming language.

So far our programs have a **linear structure**. This means each program statement is executed (carried out) one after the other until the end of the program. Without the use of **loop structures** we would not make very much progress, because carrying out a large number of similar things would need a large amount of code. An important name for looping is iteration. Iteration and looping are essentially the same thing.

Suppose we wish to print out even numbers between 1 and 20 000. A rather inefficient linear structure, consisting of 10 000 lines of code might be as shown on the left! A more efficient loop structure, making use of a **for to next loop** is shown on the right.

Example of a linear structure involving no loops	Example of a 'for to next loop'

Print 2
Print 4
    etc.
    etc.
Print 20000
	For counter = 2 to 20000 step 2
	    Print counter
	Next counter

The **variable** called 'counter' is being used as the number to be printed. The **for to next loop** sets the counter to two, then increments it in steps of two until 20 000 is reached. When counter = 20 002, the loop terminates without printing the value of counter.

Note how *indentation has been used to show the extent of the loop* i.e. the statement/s inside the loop (only one in this case!) are **indented** to show that it is these statement/s that are executed each time we go round the loop.

'Do while' and 'Repeat until' loop structures

Other useful loop structures, available in many high level languages, are **do while loops** and **repeat until loops**. Some examples, similar in nature to the **for to next loop** structure now follow. The variable 'counter' is set up in the first line of each program.

Example of a 'do while loop'	Example of a 'repeat until loop'

Dim counter = 1 As integer
Do while counter < 50
    counter = counter + 1
    Print counter
End while
	Dim counter = 1 As integer
	Repeat
	    counter = counter + 1
	    Print counter
	Until counter >50

On the left the **do while loop** is executed as long as the value of the counter is less than 50. Therefore, the numbers printed for this loop would be 1, 2, 3 ... 48, 49. On the right the **repeat until loop** would print out the numbers 1, 2, 3 ... 48, 49, 50.

The **do while** and the **for to next loops** may be used interchangeably. It is nevertheless important to realise that the **do while loop** *tests the condition before carrying out any of the statements inside the loop*, but the **repeat until loop** *will carry out the statements at least once before testing the condition*. This could be crucial to the logic of your program.

Examples

Making use of suitable pseudocode or a high level language of your choice, write small program segments using *loop structures*, to carry out the following:

(a) **print out the odd numbers from 1 to 99 inclusive**

(b) **print out the first 100 square numbers, (i.e. print 1, 4, 9, 16, etc. up to 10 000)**

(c) **print out the sequence of numbers 200, 190, 180, 170 ... 30, 20, 10, 0**

(d) **print out the sequence of the first 20 Fibonacci numbers 1, 1, 2, 3, 5, 8 ... (The next number in the sequence is obtained by adding the previous two.).**

Solutions

(a) Pseudocode to print out the odd numbers from 1 to 99	(b) Pseudocode to print out the first 100 square numbers
| ```
For counter = 1 to 99 step 2
    Print counter
Next counter
``` | ```
For counter = 1 to 100
    Print counter^2
Next counter
``` |
| (c) Pseudocode to print out numbers 200, 190, 180 ... 10, 0 | (d) Pseudocode to print out first 20 Fibonacci numbers |
| ```
For counter = 200 to 0 step -10
    Print counter
Next counter
``` | ```
Dim a = 1, b = 1 As integer
Dim counter = 2 As integer
Print a
Print b
Repeat
    counter = counter + 1
    c = a + b
    Print c
    a = b
    b = c
Until counter = 20
``` |

Program comments

When programs become complex, it's good to include **comments**. Even a simple program like part (d) in the previous example would benefit from a few comments as follows:

Program to demonstrate the use of comments
| ```
Rem Program to print out the first 20 Fibonacci numbers
Dim a = 1, b = 1 As integer
Dim counter = 2 As integer
Print a 'set up first two numbers
Print b
Repeat
    counter = counter + 1
    c = a + b 'work out next number
    Print c
    a = b 'set up conditions for next time round the loop
    b = c
Until counter = 20
``` |

It is usual to use a 'REM' (Remark) or ' ' to indicate the start of a **comment**. When the compiler encounters a comment it will pay no attention to it because it does not form part of the code. A comment is put at the beginning of the program, indicating what it does. Suitable comments are placed at strategic points throughout the program where it may not be clear what is happening. It is bad practice to have no comments, or too many.
```

Inputting data

A common requirement is for a user to type in data, like a program to convert Fahrenheit temperatures into Celsius. A simple formulae to do this is C = 5(F − 32)/9. The following routine shows how the user is prompted to input data by the use of an **input statement**.

Program to demonstrate user input
Rem Program to convert from Fahrenheit to Celsius.
Input "Please type in a Fahrenheit temperature"; far
cent = 5*(far-32)/9
Print "The centigrade temperature is"; cent

A prompt for the user can usually be appended to an **input statement**. Without this the user would be expected to input data without knowing what they are entering or why.

Dry run

It's important to manually test a program. This is especially true if it does not produce the expected output. Manually working through a program and working out what is happening by noting the variables, etc. is called **dry running**. An example now follows.

Example

Part (d) of the previous set of examples shows some code to work out the first 20 Fibonacci numbers. Dry run this code, showing the values of the variables and the printed output expected for the first ten numbers.

Solution

The code is as follows, and the dry run shows the variables in various states. The black numbers at the beginning show the values before the 'repeat until loop' is entered and the red numbers show what's happening during the execution of the loop.

Code from example (d)	Variables for dry run				
	a	b	c	counter	Printed numbers
Dim a = 1, b = 1, c = 0 As integer	1	1	0	2	1
Dim counter = 2 As integer	1	1	0	2	1
Print a	1	1	2	3	2
Print b	1	2	3	4	3
Repeat	2	3	5	5	5
counter = counter + 1	3	5	8	6	8
c = a + b	5	8	13	7	13
print c	8	13	21	9	21
a = b	13	21	34	10	34
b = c					
Until counter = 20					

Don't forget that you don't need to understand the maths. You are either copying the formulae into an appropriate form, or using these simple series to explain what you need to do in your loops.

Examples like these are ideal for producing the simplest loop structures.

Self-test questions

1 Define the terms 'identifier', 'constant' and 'variable'.
2 Explain what is meant by the term 'pseudocode'.
3 Define the terms 'syntax', 'semantics' and 'statement'.
4 Using a high-level language to which you have access, write down the names and the ranges of the 'numeric data types'.
5 Making use of pseudocode or a high-level language of your choice, write out a statement to work out each of the following mathematical formulae:

$$r = 20x^2 + 10x - 1 \qquad \mathbf{a} = \tfrac{1}{2} + \tfrac{1}{4} + \tfrac{1}{8} \qquad \mathbf{b} = \frac{-6}{k+1} + t \qquad y = \sqrt[3]{a^2 + bc}$$

6 Making use of pseudocode, or a high level language of your choice, write small program segments *using loop structures* to print out the following sequences of numbers:
   (a) *sum* $= 1^2 + 2^2 + 3^2 + 4^2 + ... + 100^2$ (i.e. the sum of the first 100 square numbers)
   (b) *sum* $= 1000 - 10^2 - 9^2 - 8^2 - ... - 22 - 1^1$ (i.e. 1000 – the squares of the numbers from 10 down to 1 inclusive.)
   (c) *sum* $= \sqrt{100} + \sqrt{99} + \sqrt{98} + ... + \sqrt{1}$ (i.e. the sum of the square roots of the first one hundred numbers.)
7 Explain what is meant by a dry run. Dry run the following code and make a note of the final number printed out:

```
Dim a = 1, b = 3 As integer
Dim counter = 10 As integer
Repeat
    Print a + b
    a = a + b
    counter = counter + 2
Until counter = 20
```

8 Explain a fundamental difference between a 'do while' and a 'repeat until' loop structure.
9 What is the relationship between high-level language statements and machine code?

6 Programming fundamentals 2

In this section you will learn about:

- The use of selection structures to make decisions
- Functions and procedures, including parameter passing by reference and by value
- Using sensible variable names and comments to make programs more readable
- A modern visual programming interface
- A small project enabling the development of a well structured program

Selection structure

It's important to jump from one part of a program to another, usually based on some particular decision. A typical **selection** structure needed to do this is an **IF-THEN-ELSE** statement. These are also called **conditional branch statements**, because a condition is tested, and based on the results of the test (usually **true** or **false**), other statements may be executed or not. A **true/false** decision is also known as a **Boolean** decision.

An `IF-THEN-ELSE` structure is shown here. A selection is made, based on the value of the **variable** called result. If result is more than 50 'You have passed' is printed, else 'You have failed' is printed instead. **Statements** may be **nested**, which means that new `IF-THEN-ELSE` statements may appear inside other loops. Elegant code can be written, and selections made on a variety of criteria.

```
If result > 50 Then
    Print "You have passed"
Else
    Print "You have failed"
End if
```

Throughout this chapter you come across the important term structured programming. *It is really a method for ensuring that a program is logically written, which makes it easier for other people to understand.*

You should always try to modularise *your programs, and this important technique is demonstrated throughout this chapter.*

Example

Examination mark	Result
Mark <40%	Fail
40% <= Mark < 60%	Pass
60% <= Mark < 80%	Merit
80% <= Mark <= 100%	Distinction

An examination system uses the categories of marks shown here. By making use of pseudocode, or by using a high-level language, write some code to implement this decision-making problem using a suitable selection structure.

Solution

The solution shown here uses nested **IF-THEN-ELSE** loops. Notice how **indentation** helps to make the code understandable. It clearly shows which pairs of the 'Else' and 'End if' go with a particular 'If Then'. It's easy, for example, to work out that if the exam mark >= 40, then you execute the embedded loops; else you print 'Fail'. Without suitable indentation it's easy to get confused. Indentation is just part of our arsenal of tools to produce good **structured programming** style.

```
If exam_mark >= 40 Then
    If exam_mark >= 60 Then
        If exam_mark >= 80 Then
            Print "Distinction"
        Else
            Print "Merit"
        End if
    Else
        Print "Pass"
    End if
Else
    Print "Fail"
End if
```

Further functions

Most high-level languages have a rich selection of built-in **functions**, plus the ability for programmers to define, name, and call their own. Examples of **intrinsic** (or *built in*) **functions** might be 'sine' and 'cosine', 'square roots' or 'end of file'. There are usually hundreds of built-in functions in a typical high-level language.

Functions may be *called by name*, and **parameters** (values) may be *passed over to them*. The *result is then returned* to the calling routine. As an example, if we wish to find the square root of 9, then we might use the following typical high-level language **statement**:

```
result = Sqr(9)
```

The **function** called **SQR** (square root) is **called**, and the **parameter** 9 is passed over to it. This is done by placing the number 9 inside the brackets. The answer is then **assigned** to the variable called **result**, which would end up in this particular case having a value 3, because 3 is the one of the square roots of 9.

Functions may be **intrinsic** (*built-in*) to the language or they may be user-defined. **User-defined functions** are called by using a name defined by the user. It's important to remember that *a function can only return a single value*. If you want more than one value returned, then **procedures** or **subroutines** should be used instead (*see later*).

Example

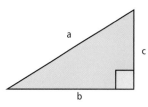

By making use of pseudocode, or by using a high-level language of your choice, write a *user-defined function* that works out the longest side of a right-angled triangle having sides a, b and c as shown. You are to pass the values 'b' and 'c' over to your function.

Use the formula $a = \sqrt{b^2 + c^2}$

Solution

There are two parts to consider in this problem: the *function definition* and the *function call*.

1 Calling the function is shown first. We assign a name 'LongestSide' to our function, and pass parameters (b, c), the two shorter sides of the triangle over to it.

2 We now define our function, and this is shown in the second part. The key words 'function' and 'end function' are typical, and parameters passed over to this function are declared to be real numbers. Inside the function we tell the computer what to do

```
Rem this is the function call
a = LongestSide(b,c)

Rem this is the function definition
Function LongestSide(b,c As real)
    LongestSide = SQR(b^2 + c^2)
End function
```

with 'b' and 'c' to generate the parameter to be passed back to the calling routine. This parameter (the eventual value of a) is placed into this variable by the function when the value is returned.

Procedures

Procedures enable us to modularise programs. This is essential if we are to follow modern **structured programming** techniques. **Procedures** make programs easier to understand, and enable programmers to undertake different parts of larger projects by writing separate modules. Modules may be tested individually, and joined with other modules to form larger systems. As with passing parameters over to a function (covered earlier), passing parameters over to a procedure is important, and this is considered next.

Parameter passing by value and reference

When parameters are to be passed over to a procedure, two methods exist for this, called **passing by value** and **passing by reference**.

This is an example, using Visual Basic, of **passing by value**:

```
Sub My_Procedure(ByVal My_Variable As Integer)
    .
    . Rem Other code goes here
    .
End Sub
```

A **copy** of the variable called 'My_Variable' is **passed over to the procedure** called 'My_Procedure'. As only a copy of the original variable has been used, if this gets altered in the procedure, then **the original variable won't be altered**. Inside the procedure the variable is treated as *local*, which means that any variables with the same name outside of this procedure won't get changed. This is a good idea if different programmers are working on different modules. They can use the same variable names used by others, so long as it's local to their procedure.

It is also possible to **pass by reference**, as shown here:

```
Sub My_Procedure(My_Variable As Integer)
    .
    . Rem Other code goes here
    .
End Sub
```

The word 'ByRef' is not used. This is the default way Visual Basic, for example, passes variables to procedures. The original variable is **referenced**, and is thus irrevocably altered by this procedure. In this case the variable is **global**, as all instances of the use of this

Procedures are considered more fully, with examples, at the end of programming the house picture covered later in this chapter.

variable throughout the program will be altered. You declare **global variables** at the start of a program. This makes it unlikely that you will use the same name again for something entirely different.

A visual programming interface

Before proceeding with a detailed programming example, we take a brief look at a typical interface used for programming in a modern high-level language. The Microsoft Visual Basic 6 interface is shown in Figure 6.1, but it's very similar to interfaces in other project environments like 'Delphi', 'Visual C++' and other visual programming languages.

There are several major parts to a typical software development environment. From Figure 6.1 you can see the active window where the high-level language **code** (like that being developed in this chapter) is typed in. You can see that **key words** are coloured blue, and **variables**, and **assignment statements**, etc. are coloured black.

Although complex to look at, you can build effective programs using just a fraction of the facilities. Professional programmers spend years coming to terms with all the bells and whistles, and Microsoft's newest version, Visual Studio.NET, ensures that there is another steep learning curve to climb.

There are many important principles of structured programming covered here.

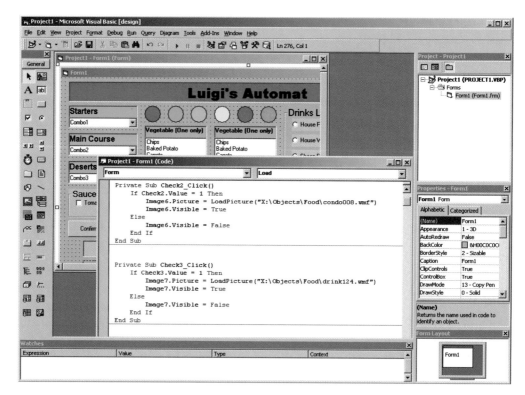

Figure 6.1 Microsoft's integrated programming environment for Visual Basic 6

The window at the back shows the form which will be displayed when the program is run. In this case it shows an automatic 'dinner making machine' created by the author. This program instructs Luigi the robot to make your lunch!

There are a huge variety of tools available for placing controls on the form (these allow the user to interact with the program by clicking the mouse, etc.). A **properties window** shows the properties of the forms (e.g. if a window has a scroll bar on not). A **project window** shows where the forms and projects, etc. are stored, and a **watch window** can help if you are trying to find some bugs in your code. These modern visual development environments enable relatively inexperienced users to construct professional programs very quickly and very easily, and this is why they are mentioned now in an introductory chapter on programming. Without them, writing code in a Windows environment would be very hard.

The house project

You have now learnt enough material to be able to do some fancy things with loops and procedures. Modularising a program making use of procedures is similar to modularising any project, like building a house; so let's build a house! The idea is to write some code in a suitable high-level language to draw a house similar to that shown in Figure 6.2.

Example

By making use of pseudocode, or by using a high-level language of your choice, write a program to draw a house similar to the one shown here. Your code should be efficient by making use of suitable loops and procedures, and use good structured programming techniques and style.

Note: We will use Microsoft's Visual Basic 6 language to illustrate this, but any high-level language could be used as an alternative. *The most important thing is to use the computer and language to which you have access to actually write some code.*

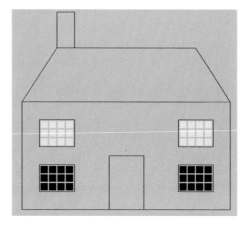

Figure 6.2 This house will be used to demonstrate good structured programming techniques

The house project will take up the remainder of this chapter.

Solution

Making a start

You need to investigate how to create simple graphics in your chosen high level language. The screen resolution we will use in our example is 1024 by 768. This is therefore the maximum co-ordinates that can be used for the house picture.

To draw a line in Visual Basic 6 is very simple, and the following **syntax** is used.

```
Line (x1, y1)-(x2, y2)
```

(x1, y1) is the start co-ordinates, and (x2, y2) are the end co-ordinates of the line to be drawn. Therefore, 'line (0,0) − (200,300)' would draw a line from position (0, 0) to position (200, 300) on our 1024 × 768 grid as shown in Figure 6.3(a). Note that the x numbers go from left to right, but the y numbers go from top to bottom. This is unfortunately not exactly the same as a conventional co-ordinate system.

It's possible to construct the entire house using a long sequence of 'line statements', but this would not be a **structured program**! VB (**Visual Basic**) provides a modification of the line command which draws a box, and the syntax of this is as follows.

```
Line (0,0) − (200,200), ,B
```

After this project you will be better placed to write modern well structured pseudocode in AS level examinations.

Figure 6.3(a)
Result of `line (0,0) - (200,300)`

Figure 6.3(b)
Result of `line (0,0) - (200,200),,B`

Thus the walls, door, windows and window panes can all be drawn more efficiently by using the box method, which uses opposite diagonal co-ordinates as shown above.

Setting the scale mode

VB can make use of a variety of scale modes to draw pictures. To make the system work as suggested we need to work in **pixels**. We also need to embed the code in the form that will display the diagram, and if you don't see any graphics set the 'AutoRedraw' property to 'True'. The code to draw the box shown in Figure 6.3(b) would actually be as follows.

```
Private Sub Form_Load()
        ScaleMode = VbPixels    'Set scale to pixels
        Line (0,0)-(200,200),,B
End Sub
```

We are now ready to draw the house using VB6.

Comments as an aid to good program structure

The importance of **comments** was stressed in the last chapter, and we can now see why. Let's suppose that several errors are made in your code, and your house ends up looking similar to the picture shown in Figure 6.4! The code (with errors) used to construct this house is shown next, but which lines are wrong? It's difficult to tell, even with a simple program like this, but do try! You could spend some considerable time finding out, and then get into a complete mess. Imagine what a mess you would get into if you were writing a complex program!

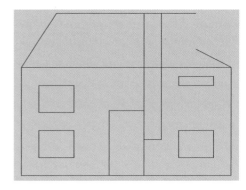

Figure 6.4 Some mistakes have been made!

```
Private Sub Form_Load()
   ScaleMode = vbPixels      'Set graphics units to Pixels
        Line (200, 300)-(800, 600), , B
        Line (300, 150)-(700, 150)
        Line (550, 500)-(600, 150), , B
        Line (450, 420)-(550, 600), , B
        Line (250, 475)-(350, 550), , B
        Line (700, 250)-(800, 300)
        Line (250, 350)-(350, 425), , B
        Line (650, 475)-(750, 550), , B
        Line (200, 300)-(300, 150)
        Line (650, 350)-(750, 325), , B
End Sub
```

A better organised program, with some suitable **comments** and **indentation** is as follows:

```
Private Sub Form_Load()
   ScaleMode = vbPixels
   Rem Walls
        Line (200, 300)-(800, 600), , B
   Rem Roof
        Line (200, 300)-(300, 150)
        Line (700, 150)-(800, 300)
        Line (300, 150)-(700, 150)
   Rem Chimney
        Line (300, 50)-(350, 150), , B
   Rem Door
        Line (450, 420)-(550, 600), , B
   Rem Window1 - Bottom left
        Line (250, 475)-(350, 550), , B
   Rem Window2 - Top left
        Line (250, 350)-(350, 425), , B
   Rem Window3 - Bottom Right
        Line (650, 475)-(750, 550), , B
   Rem Window4 - Top Right
        Line (650, 350)-(750, 425), , B
End Sub
```

It's now far easier to locate the errors, because we can see from Figure 6.4 that something is wrong with the chimney, and window 4 roof. Simply locate the 'Chimney', 'Roof' and 'Window 4' sections, and alter the code accordingly. This program is better **structured**.

If you still find the above frustrating, draw the house on a piece of graph paper and work out the co-ordinates needed. *This is actually the best way to proceed*.

Making good use of loops

We could write some of the previous code more efficiently using **loops**, but until you write the code for the window panes this may not become apparent. I hope that no student would think of writing 48 different statements for producing the window panes!

There is often no substitute for using a pencil and paper to work out simple problems like the co-ordinate systems being used here.

It's amazing how many pupils will struggle for hours on the computer trying to get these numbers right, when five minutes spent with a piece of graph paper and a pencil will usually solve your problem!

If you are unable to identify how the variables inside a loop may work, write down a few lines of code that the loop needs to replace. This method will always establish the appropriate patterns.

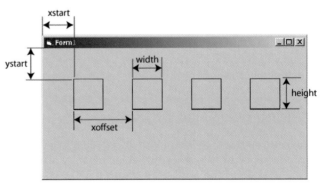

Figure 6.5 Breaking down the problem into simpler structures

As with all **modular** or **structured** problems, we need to break them down into simpler steps. By looking at the house in Figure 6.2, we see that each window consists of 12 separate panes, but each group of 12 panes consists of 3 groups of 4 panes. Finally, each group of 4 panes involves drawing 4 boxes as shown in Figure 6.5.

Our problem now becomes a simpler one of 'how to draw four boxes equally spaced in a row'. To solve this we can write code without the use of a loop, and then identify the number patterns to help us work out the loop. As an example, consider the following four lines of code, which draws four boxes, each of side 50, starting at position 50, 50 from the top left-hand side, and having spaces of 50 between each box.

```
Line (50,50)-(100,100),,B
Line (150,50)-(200,100),,B
Line (250,50)-(300,100),,B
Line (350,50)-(400,100),,B
```

It's now more obvious how the generation of these boxes work, and you should be able to write a suitable **loop structure** based on the following patterns, which are explained in more detail the next paragraph.

```
For x = 1 To 7 Step 2
    Line (50 * x, 50)-((50 * x) + 50, 100), , B
Next x
```

By incrementing x from 1 to 7 in steps of 2, and by using 50 * x, we generate the numbers 50, 150, 250, etc. i.e. (50 * 1 = 50), then (50 * 3 = 150) and (50 * 5 = 250) etc. The second co-ordinate pair can be generated by noting that these are simply 50 more than the first numbers. We could generate the second numbers by adding 50, giving (50 * x) + 50.

Using meaningful variable names

One of the goals of structured programming is to make sure that other people (and you!) can understand and therefore modify code at a much later date. If you can't do this it's very difficult, if not impossible, to maintain the code, and this would render the code useless.

You should be able to understand the above code because you have been taken through the stages of development. However, imagine coming back in six months time, and having only the above three lines of code to look at. It would be difficult, for example, to quickly find out what variable controls how many panes of glass are printed, what variable controls the width of the pane and what variable controls the distance between the panes? A better, more **structured** strategy is needed. Consider Figure 6.6.

Figure 6.6 A general approach using meaningful variable names

We can now re-write the code making use of **meaningful variable names**. Our original code consisted of the following lines, but can now be replaced by more structured code.

```
Line  (50,50)-(100,100),,B
Line  (150,50)-(200,100),,B
Line  (250,50)-(300,100),,B
Line  (350,50)-(400,100),,B
```

The new code, using **meaningful variable names** and **comments** is as follows.

```
xstart = 50 'Set the x position of the top left window pane
ystart = 50 'Set the y position of the top left window pane
xoff = 100  'Set the x offset distance from one pane to the next
w = 50      'Set the width of the window pane
h = 50      'Set the height of the window pane
Line (xstart + 0*xoff, ystart)-(xstart + 0*xoff + w, ystart + h),, B
Line (xstart + 1*xoff, ystart)-(xstart + 1*xoff + w, ystart + h),, B
Line (xstart + 2*xoff, ystart)-(xstart + 2*xoff + w, ystart + h),, B
Line (xstart + 3*xoff, ystart)-(xstart + 3*xoff + w, ystart + h),, B
```

In Visual Basic the words 'Width' and 'Height' clash with key words, therefore 'w' and 'h' have been used instead. The use of the letters 'w' and 'h' are explained with comments.

The above code, put inside a **loop**, could be as follows.

```
xstart = 50 'Set the x position of the top left window pane
ystart = 50 'Set the y position of the top left window pane
xoff = 100  'Set the x offset distance from one pane to the next
w = 50      'Set the width of the window pane
h = 50      'Set the height of the window pane
Xpanes = 4  'Set the number of windows panes in the horizontal direction
For  Xpanes = 0 To  Xpanes -1
   Line (xstart+Xpanes*xoff, ystart)-(xstart+Xpanes*xoff+w, ystart+h),, B
Next Xpanes
```

This may look complex, but suitable comments have been added to aid **readability**. It is now trivial to alter the 'number of panes', the 'width and height of the panes' and the 'offset between the panes' without much thought. Compare this to the code developed earlier, which looks easier, but is, in fact, very hard to use, especially if we need different windows in different places, as is the case with the house shown in Figure 6.4. Strive to make your code readable. This is one of the aims of **structured programming**.

Making good use of procedures

All **parameters** set up in the last block of code can be passed over to a **procedure** called WindowPanes, in which the 'number of panes', the 'width' and 'height of each pane' and the 'distance between them' can be controlled. It's easier to introduce **procedures** now, *before* we complicate the code further by setting up the number of panes vertically. The idea of a procedure is something that can be called up by name, and parameters passed 'over to' and 'back from' the procedure. The following code is in two parts:

1 Setting up the variables and the **procedure call** to 'WindowPanes'

2 The **procedure definition** for 'WindowPanes'.

Modularisation of programs is easily possible when procedures are used. This is one of the most useful sets of tools in our arsenal of structured programming techniques. Always make use of procedures unless your program is trivial.

```
Private Sub Form_Load()
  ScaleMode = vbPixels
  xstart = 50 'Set the x position of the top left window pane
  ystart = 50 'Set the y position of the top left window pane
  xoff = 100  'Set the x offset distance from one pane to the next
  w = 50      'Set the width of the window pane
  h = 50      'Set the height of the window pane
  Xpanes = 4  'Set the number of windows panes in the horizontal
direction

  Call WindowPanes(xstart, ystart, xoff, w, h, Xpanes)
End Sub

Sub WindowPanes(xstart, ystart, xoff, w, h, Xpanes)

  For Xloop = 0 To Xpanes - 1
  Line (xstart + Xloop * xoff, ystart)-(xstart + Xloop * xoff + w,
ystart + h), , B
  Next Xloop
End Sub
```

Some readers may think that the use of **meaningful names**, **comments** and **procedure calls** has made the code a lot more difficult. However, consider the following facts.

- It will be very easy to alter any part of the program at a later date, because the code is **well documented** and **well structured**.

- It's now easy to create many different windows in different positions. We simply call the **procedure** whenever it's needed, using different **parameters**.

- Because we are passing **parameters** over to the **procedure** each time it's called, the number of panes and the size and offsets may be altered for each window.

Adding the code for the next row of panes

We currently have only one row of panes, but a quick look at the picture of the house in Figure 6.2 will reveal that a second and third row are needed. This is easily catered for by '**nesting**' the above '**for to next loop**' within another loop that controls how many times the above loop is executed. Each time round the loop we will have to add a 'y offset' called 'yoff'. We also need to pass over the parameter representing the number of panes in the 'y' or vertical direction. This is called 'Ypanes'. The complete window-pane program is as follows:

```
Private Sub Form_Load()
  ScaleMode = vbPixels
  xstart = 50 'Set the x position of the top left window pane
  ystart = 50 'Set the y position of the top left window pane
  xoff = 55   'Set the x offset distance from one pane to the next
  yoff = 55   'Set the y offset distance from one pane to the next
  w = 50      'Set the width of the window pane
  h = 50      'Set the height of the window pane
  Xpanes = 4  'Set the number of windows panes in the horizontal
direction
```

```
    Ypanes = 3    'Set the number of windows panes in the vertical
direction

    Call WindowPanes(xstart, ystart, xoff, yoff, w, h, Xpanes,
Ypanes)
End Sub

Sub WindowPanes(xstart, ystart, xoff, yoff, w, h, Xpanes, Ypanes)

    For Yloop = 0 To Ypanes - 1
      For Xloop = 0 To Xpanes - 1
        Line (xstart + Xloop * xoff, ystart + Yloop * yoff)-(xstart
+ Xloop * xoff + w, ystart + Yloop * yoff + h), , B
      Next Xloop
    Next Yloop
End Sub
```

By the clever use of **procedures**, we have made a routine to draw a set number of window panes in the x direction and a set number of window panes in the y direction. We can specify the width and height of each pane, and we can specify the offset distance which controls the distance between the panes. All this is available by a single procedure call, by passing **parameters** over to it by **reference**.

Most professional programs are made up from a huge number of **procedures**, each usually much more complex than the ones we have shown here. In this way complex programs may be **modularised**, and by using **comments** and **meaningful variable names**, people can understand the code that others have written. It's worth remembering that *in industry, more effort is put into modification of existing code than goes into creating new code*. This is why **structured programming** techniques are so important.

It is left up to the reader to develop the complete program for the house.

Why not write some extra procedures to add other features to the house?

Turning the 'lights' on and off

You should now be able to write all of the code to generate the house shown in Figure 6.2. The 'yellow' panes with the 'lights on' are 'filled in boxes', as are the black panes. In Visual Basic 6, to fill a box we use 'BF' (Block Fill) instead of the 'B' used previously. A simple colour can be inserted by using the command QBcolor(n), where the parameter 'n' is a number between '0' and '15' inclusive. The number '0' is Black and '6' is yellow. The 'Line statement' is therefore modified as follows.

```
Line (50 * x, 50 * y)-((50 * x) + 50, (50 * y) + 50), QBColor(n), BF
```

Our procedures can be modified with (n) being passed over and used in the ways described above to switch the lights 'on' and 'off'.

Self-test questions

1 In a high-level language, control may be passed to different parts of a program based on a Boolean decision. What is a Boolean decision?
2 Most modern high-level languages make use of functions and procedures. Explain what is meant by a function. Give an example of a function, briefly describing how it works from a programming perspective. How does a function differ from a procedure?

3 A variable called 'level' represents the level of water in a tank. Using a high-level language of your choice, or by making suitable use of pseudocode, write code to print out the messages shown in the following table, based on the variable 'level'.

Value of 'level'	Message to be printed out
<= 5 level <= 30	The water level is dangerously low
30 < level <= 80	Water level is satisfactory
80 < level <= 90	The water level is dangerously high
90 < level <= 100	The water level is dangerously high
	The tank has exploded!

Do some investigation to see if the high-level language you are using supports 'case statements'. If it does, code this example again by making use of this new method.

4 Functions may be 'intrinsic' or 'user defined'. What is the difference between these two types of function? Give an example of each, clearly showing how parameters are passed in each of your examples.

5 When using procedures in a high-level language, parameters may be passed either 'by reference' or 'by value'. What is the difference between these two methods? Give an example where each method would be most appropriate.

6 Procedures are useful when programming in a high-level language. Give two different reasons as to why this is so.

7 A program will 'work' even if meaningful variable names, comments and good structure are not used. Why is it important to include these things?

8 The following problem assumes that you have a suitable high-level language capable of drawing simple line graphics. The co-ordinate system for the following problems depends on your computer system setup, but you must make efficient use of loop structures and procedures in your solutions.

(a) Draw 50 horizontal red lines across the screen.

(b) Cover the screen with vertical and horizontal green lines equally spaced 20 pixels apart.

(c) Draw lines across the screen at an angle of 45 degrees. You should cover the entire screen with lines (i.e. no gaps in the extreme corners of the screen).

This problem is quite challenging. Don't forget that there is no substitute for getting a piece of graph paper and manually establishing the patterns for the loops.

9 Consider the following curve-stitching patterns:

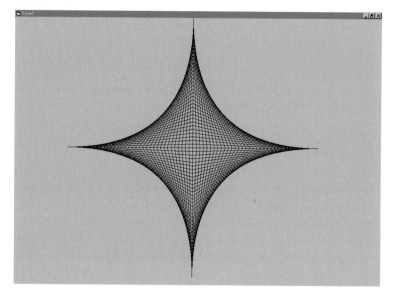

The 'curves' are an optical illusion. The shape is actually made up from four very similar quadrants. Each quadrant is made up by drawing a series of simple straight lines.

(a) Starting in the 1st quadrant (top right-hand side) draw a series of about 25 lines, equally spaced on the axis, to simulate the necessary shape. Hint:

Start working with a vertical line from the top of the y axis to the origin. Keeping the line the same length, move the top down by about 50 graphics units and move the bottom right by about 50 graphics units. Continue in this way until the line is horizontal along the x axis.

(b) Do the same thing for the second quadrant (bottom right-hand side).

(c) Complete the entire shape as shown above.

(d) Write some code to tile (cover) the entire screen with smaller versions of the above shape. You should make use of procedures in your new code. About four shapes horizontally and about three shapes vertically should be enough to demonstrate the techniques.

7 Programming fundamentals 3

In this section you will learn about:

- String functions
- Binary tree data structures
- LIFO stacks and queues
- Array data structures
- Coding simple algorithms making use of pseudocode and a high-level language
- Making use of meaningful variable names and procedures
- The use of structure diagrams

Strings

Numeric examples were used almost exclusively when **structured programming** techniques were covered in Chapter 6. Other data processing is just as important, and some non-numeric techniques are covered in this chapter.

A **string** is a set of **alphanumeric characters** like 'Hello' or 'ABC123'. Processing strings is a common operation. Most high-level programming languages have a large number of string-handling statements. Typically these might enable you to join two strings together (called **concatenation**), extract a substring from the **left**, **middle** or **right** of another string, find out the **length of a string** or to change a **string** into a **numeric** or vice versa.

Some versions of the high-level language Basic require string variables or string data types to end with a '$' sign. This is not a requirement in Visual Basic, but we will use this terminology here because it will work in all versions of Basic, including Visual Basic.

Useful string functions

Strings may be joined quite easily by using the '+' sign. As an example, consider the following code. (*Note that a $ sign is often used to denote a string variable.*)

```
A$ = "Bat"
B$ = "man"
Print A$+B$
```

After being executed, 'Batman' would be printed, because the **string variables** A$ and B$ have been 'concatenated'. Make sure you understand this. If A$ = '2' and B$ = '3' then A$ + B$ would be '23', not 5! You can't do arithmetic with **string data types**, but there are **functions** available in most high-level languages to do the appropriate conversions. The following code shows some of the **string functions** available in Visual Basic 6, together with comments to aid understanding.

```
Test$ = "0123456789"        'Set up a string for demonstration
                             purposes
NewOne$ = Left$(Test$,3)     'New string is built up by copying 3
                             characters
                               from the left of Test$ i.e. NewOne$
                               = "012"
NewTwo$ = Right$(Test$,2)    'New string is built up by copying 2
                             characters
                               from the right of Test$ i.e. NewTwo$
                               = "89"
```

```
NewThree$ = Mid$(Test$,4,3) 'New string is built up by taking 3
                             characters
                             from Test$ starting at the 4th
                             character. i.e.
                             NewThree$ = "345"
HowLong = Len(Test$)         'HowLong is a number whose length is
                             that of Test$
                             i.e. HowLong = 10
```

Examples

By using pseudocode or a high-level language of your choice, write small snippets of code to perform the following functions:

(a) Extract the word 'music' from the string 'The hills are alive with the sound of music'

(b) Extract the first word from the string 'Ten green bottles hanging on the wall'

(c) Extract the 'tooth' from the string 'I have a toothache'.

Solutions

The solutions to parts (a), (b) and (c) are as follows:

```
A$ = "The hills are alive with the sound of music"
B$ = "Ten green bottles hanging on the wall"
C$ = "I have a toothache"
AnswerA$ = Right$(A$,5)
AnswerB$ = Left$(B$,3)
AnswerC$ = Mid$(C$,10,5)
```

String-based algorithms

Armed with the above information, and utilising many of the techniques learned in the previous two chapters, we can now start performing some useful operations. These examples are typical of the standard of pseudocode that you may be required to develop or analyse during an examination.

It's essential that you know enough about the high-level language you are using to develop your own style of writing acceptable pseudocode. Practise this technique often. It becomes easier with more experience.

Examples

Consider the string 'hey diddle diddle the cat had a fiddle'.

By using pseudocode or a high level language of your choice, write some snippets of code to solve the following problems.

(a) Count up the number of vowels and consonants contained within this string.

(b) Print out the words in reverse order.

Solutions

(a) The **algorithm** to find the number of vowels ('a', 'e', 'i', 'o' and 'u' letters) requires that we examine each character in turn and check to see if it is a vowel. If it is a space we ignore it, but if it is a vowel we add it to the vowels count. When the counting has ended, because there is no punctuation, the consonants can be calculated by taking away the 'vowels and spaces' from the total number of characters. The Visual Basic 6 code is as follows:

```
Private Sub Form_Load()
Target$ = "hey diddle diddle the cat had a fiddle"
For x = 1 To Len(Target$)
   Test$ = Mid(Target$, x, 1)
   If Test$ = "a" Then a = a + 1
   If Test$ = "e" Then e = e + 1
   If Test$ = "i" Then i = i + 1
   If Test$ = "o" Then o = o + 1
   If Test$ = "u" Then u = u + 1
   If Test$ = " " Then spaces = spaces + 1
   Vowels = a + e + i + o + u
   Consonants = Len(Target$)- Vowels - spaces
Next x
Print "There are "; Vowels; "Vowels and"; Consonants;" consonants"
End Sub
```

(b) It is very easy to describe the **algorithm** for this problem; we start at the right-hand side of the string, and print out the words in reverse order. However, what constitutes a word? The easy answer is that each word, apart from the first and last words are separated by a space. Therefore, the problem is broken down into finding these spaces. This can be done quite easily as described in part (a) of these examples. The **structure** of the problem can be summed up in the following Visual Basic 6 code, which we then develop further.

```
Test$ = "hey diddle diddle the cat had a fiddle"
For x = Len(Test$) To 1 step - 1
   CODE TO EXTRACT AND PRINT WORDS GOES HERE
Next x
```

To extract a word, we need two **markers** or **flags**. These ideas are shown in Figure 7.1, which concentrates on the word 'had'. Two flags have been set, one to show 'where the word ends' by pointing at the 'letter d', and the other to show 'where the word begins' by pointing at the space in front of 'had'.

These flags can be used as **parameters** for the Mid$ **function** which was explained at the beginning of this chapter. The last word is a special case because the end of the string will have been reached.

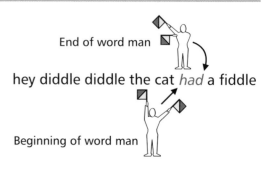

Figure 7.1 Setting up flags ready to extract a word from the string

Our **algorithm** will set both **flags** at the end of the string. This is because we are working from right to left. We work back character by character, testing to see if a space has been found. When a space is found, the end of word flag is put at the end of the previous word. This is done by positioning it one less than the beginning of word flag.

This process is continued until the beginning of the string is reached. We then print out the first word because this will not be done by the previous part of our algorithm.

The code for problem (b) is summed up as follows:

```
Private Sub Form_Load()
  Target$ = "hey diddle diddle the cat had a fiddle"
  End_Flag = Len(Target$)
  Beg_Flag = Len(Target$)
  For x = Len(Target$) To 1 Step -1
    Test$ = Mid$(Target$, x, 1)
    If Test$ = " " Then
      Beg_Flag = x + 1
      Final$ = Final$ + Mid(Target$, Beg_Flag, End_Flag -
      Beg_Flag + 1) + " "
      End_Flag = Beg_Flag - 1
    End If
  Next x
  Print Final$ + Left(Target$, End_Flag)
  'Gets the first word of the string which can't be
  'extracted using the code in the main routine.
End Sub
```

Basic tree structures

A **tree structure** is similar to a family tree, with parents and children, as shown in Figure 7.2.

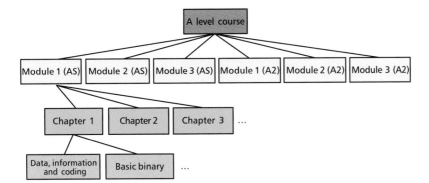

Figure 7.2 A tree structure, showing this modular A level computer science course

In computer science different parts of the tree have different names. Each entry in a tree structure is called a **node**. The red box at the top is the **root node**. The grey boxes at the bottom are examples of **leaf nodes**. Chapter 1 would be an example of a **parent node**, because it has two **children** 'Data, information and coding', and 'Basic binary'. 'Module 1 (AS)' and 'A level course' are also examples of parent nodes. Any node sharing the same parent is called a **brother** or a **sister node**. '**Branches**' from one node to the next are called **pointers**, because these help point to the next item.

Binary trees

A **binary tree** is one in which **parents** are allowed *a maximum of two children*, as shown in Figure 7.3. This particular binary tree is an **ordered binary tree**, which means that it has been constructed (i.e. the nodes inserted) by following pointers in **alphabetical order**. A binary tree is an example of a useful **data structure**, which means that data is arranged so that it can be processed efficiently by a computer.

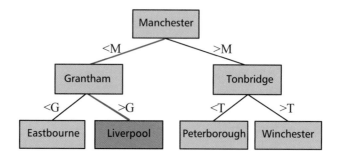

Figure 7.3 An ordered binary tree showing the 'Liverpool' node being inserted

In Figure 7.3 the 'Liverpool' **node** is being added. To insert the 'Liverpool' node we start at the **root node**, comparing 'Liverpool' with 'Manchester'. As 'Liverpool' < 'Manchester' alphabetically, we follow the '< M' pointer (branch). Liverpool is next compared with the 'Grantham' node. Because 'Liverpool' > 'Grantham' alphabetically, the right-hand path is followed. We finally arrive at a spare node, and thus Liverpool is inserted as a **leaf node** in the appropriate place, shown by the red box.

An **ordered binary tree** structure is useful to add things to an alphabetical list without actually moving the other data elements! The mechanism for doing this will be looked at more closely in the second book in the series when A2 work is covered.

FIFO or Queue

A **linear queue** is a **data structure**, taking its name from the type of queue normally associated with a shop. If you are the first person in a queue, you would expect to be served first. The 'first in' is the 'first out', and this type of structure is therefore known as a **FIFO** (**First In First Out**) or **queue**.

Consider Figure 7.4(a). Nine memory locations have been set up for the purpose of implementing a **queue**. At this moment the queue is **empty**. The 'start' and 'stop' **pointers** show the beginning and end of the queue. Because the queue is empty, these **pointers** are both set to zero.

Figure 7.4(b), shows the queue after the data 'Fred' has been added. As there is only one item (or customer!) in the queue, 'Fred' is both the start and end of the queue, and as 'Fred' occupies memory location (1), the start and stop pointers are both set to point to location number (1).

Having established the pattern of data and the **pointer** system, Figure 7.4(c) shows the situation after the data 'Tom' and 'Guy' have been added to the queue. Figure 7.4(d) shows what happens after the data 'Bill', 'Bert', 'Bob', 'Jim', 'Kate' and 'Carol' has been added. There are no more spaces in the queue, and therefore the queue is '**full**'. If we attempt to add another data item to the queue it would **overflow**.

Many different structures in real life can be mirrored with a tree, and many algorithms are developed from these. Some of these algorithms are found in the A2 book.

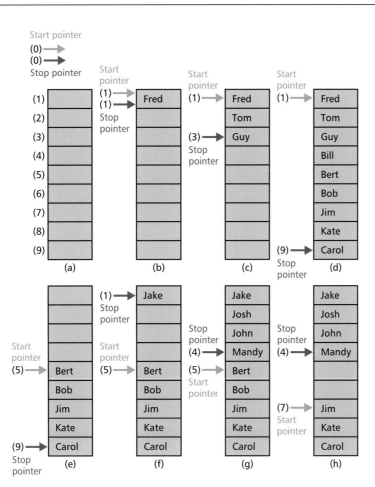

Figure 7.4 A FIFO system implementing a queue in the computer's memory

Figure 7.4(e) shows the situation after 'Fred', 'Tom', 'Guy' and 'Bill' have been served (removed from the data structure). However, if another data item is to be inserted into the queue, there is no memory after memory location (9), and thus we put the next data item 'Jake' in memory location number (1), as can be seen from Figure 7.4(f). Notice how the **pointer** system still maintains the order of the queue. The order in which the data will be processed is 5,6,7,8,9,1, indicating the order in which the items joined the queue.

Figure 7.4(g) shows what happens if 'Josh', 'John' and 'Mandy' join the queue. The queue is again full, and any attempt to add more data would result in an **overflow**.

Finally, Figure 7.4(h) shows what the queue looks like after 'Bert' and 'Bob' have been served. The important thing to notice is that there is not an infinite number of memory locations, and a **round robin** approach is used to manage the pointers, and this is called a **circular queue**. The sequence 1,2,3,4,5,6,7,8,9,1,2,3,4,5,6,7,8,9,1,2 ... is repeatedly used for the pointers, unless the queue is empty, in which case the pointers are set to zero.

LIFO Stacks

A **LIFO** (**Last In First Out**) data structure is similar in principle to the **FIFO** or **queue** covered in the last section. This time it's based on the 'unfair principle' that the last item into the structure is the first item to come out. Think of this using the principle of somebody interrupting you in the middle of doing a job, as explained in the next paragraph.

You are having lunch and the doorbell rings; you then leave your lunch to answer the door. The doorbell ringing was the last thing to happen, but it was the first thing that you sorted out while interrupting your lunch. If, while answering the door the phone rings, you might ask the person at the door to hang on while you sort out who is on the phone. The phone was the last thing to happen, but you sorted this out first while interrupting the person at the door. Being annoyed, you might tell the person to phone back, then go to the door and tell the salesman that you are having your lunch, and finally you get back to eating your lunch.

In each case the last thing to happen was the first thing to get sorted out, and you have a classic example of a **LIFO stack**. This principle is used extensively in **operating systems**, and will be revisited in the book A2.

Arrays

An efficient **data structure** to implement a **LIFO** or **FIFO** is an **array**. It's also useful if you have lots of variables of a similar type. Therefore arrays are covered before going onto the next example. Typically we might have a set of numbers, all of which need a different variable assigned to them. The following list, though small, illustrates the principles.

{73, 52, 74, 56, 32, 78, 87, 19, 24, 35, 43, 76, 34, 45, 37, 78, 19, 64, 72, 88}

It would be inefficient to call these a, b, c, d, e, ... etc. because we would run out of letters. We could use aa, ab, ac, etc. but it gets ridiculous, and you can't remember which is which.

A better method is to make use of an **array**. Let's suppose that these 20 numbers represent temperature, in Celsius, of the water in a tank. The idea is to use a variable like $Temp_1$, $Temp_2$, $Temp_3$, ... $Temp_{20}$. These are called **subscripted variables** because we are making use of the subscripts as shown here. When using a typical high-level language, these would be referred to as Temp(1), Temp(2), Temp(3), ... Temp(20). By using this method, we can refer to each number using a **meaningful variable name**.

There are interactive learning materials available to help you understand more about FIFO and LIFO data structures.

Before we can make use of lists of numbers like these we have to **dimension** the **array**. This is typically done using a **Dim statement** in a high-level language. The following code shows how 20 different numbers may be input into the computer and the subscripted variables assigned as suggested above.

```
Dim Temp(20) As Real
For x = 1 To 20
    Input Temp(x)
Next x
```

Arrays may have more than one **dimension**. Two, three or more dimensions are common in computing, especially when modelling and manipulating graphical images. **Two dimensions** may be visualised as rows and columns of numbers, and accessed using a **subscripted variable** like Array(x, y). **Three dimensions** may be visualised as a stack of **two-dimensional arrays**, placed behind each other, and accessed using variables like Array(x, y, z). Some three-dimensional graphics systems are modelled in this way, where (x, y, z) are the co-ordinates of a point in space. The number of dimensions is usually limited by the size of the array and the amount of memory inside your computer. Many dimensions are usually possible.

Example

By making use of pseudocode, write a routine to add data to a queue having just 5 memory locations. The idea (with 9 locations) is shown in Figure 7.4. You don't need to write the routine to remove any data from the stack, and you also don't need to produce a graphical interface. However, your routine must not allow data to be added to a full queue (i.e. when 5 'names' have been entered, then no others can be added).

Solution

This problem is a little more complex than the ones tackled previously. We therefore need a structured way to solve it. Before developing any high-level language code, we need to develop an overall strategy for adding names to the queue. *Make sure you have read the section on FIFO (queues), and are very familiar with Figure 7.4.*

Our pseudocode strategy will be as follows:

```
REM Structured solution to add names to a queue
Set up data structure and variables
REM The following 'while loop' adds names to a queue unless it is full
REM The process is terminated if a "*" is entered instead of a name
DO While Name <> "*"
            Print "Please enter a name, terminate this process by entering a *"
            Input Name
            Check if Queue is full
            IF Queue is full Then
                    Print "Queue is full"
                    REM Terminate program because queue is full
                    EXIT Procedure
            END IF
            REM Check if Queue is empty
            IF Queue is empty Then
                    Initialise Pointers
                    Store the Name
            ELSE
                    REM Queue is neither empty nor full
                    Update the pointers
                    Store the Name
            END IF
    END While Loop
```

We will now add some meaningful variable names, and the tests to see if the queue is full or empty. We could have done this all in one go (it is O.K. to do this in an exam) but some of the simple structure shown above would have been more difficult to understand.

```
REM Structured solution to add names to a queue
REM Set up the data structure and variables.
Dim Names(9) As String
Dim Name As String
Dim StartPointer, StopPointer As Integer
StartPointer = 0
StopPointer = 0
REM The following 'while loop' adds names to a queue unless it is full
REM The process is terminated if "*" is entered instead of a name
DO While name <> "*"
```

Pseudocode is just one of the strategies that can be used for solving complex problems. It is an important strategy for AS level examinations.

Other strategies, involving hierarchical diagrams are covered later in this chapter.

Writing pseudocode statements like those shown here is a vitally important skill in computer science. It can also be used to help solve high-level language problems if you do an A2 programming project.

```
        Print "Please enter a name, terminate this process by entering '*' "
        Input Name
        Check if Queue is full
        IF (StartPointer = 1 AND StopPointer = 9) OR (StartPointer = StopPointer + 1)
        Then
                Print "Queue is full"
                EXIT Procedure
        END IF
        REM Check if Queue is empty
        IF StartPointer = 0 Then
                StartPointer = 1
                StopPointer = 1
                Names(1) = Name
        ELSE
                REM Queue is neither empty nor full
                StopPointer = StopPointer + 1
                Names(StopPointer) = Name
        END IF
  END While Loop
```

Example

By making use of a high-level language of your own choosing, change the pseudocode algorithm above to work on your computer. Don't forget that you don't need to remove data from the stack, or do a graphical interface. However, you will need some kind of printed data or you won't know if it's working.

Solution

Starting with the pseudocode algorithm already developed, it's easy to change the pseudocode into a suitable high-level language. Visual Basic 6 is used here as an example.

```
Private Sub Form_Load()

  Rem Structured VB 6 Code to add names to a queue
  Rem Set up the data structure and variables.
  Dim Names(9) As String
  Dim Name As String
  Dim StartPointer, StopPointer As Integer
  StartPointer = 0
  StopPointer = 0
  Rem The following 'while loop' adds names to a queue unless it
  is full
  Rem The process is terminated if "*" is entered instead of a
  name
  Do While Name <> "*"
    Print "Please enter a name, terminate this process by
    entering '*' "
    Name = InputBox("Please enter a name, terminate with a '*'")
    Rem Check if Queue is full
    If (StartPointer = 1 And StopPointer = 5) Or (StartPointer =
```

Problems like the FIFO (queue) shown here could be developed into full blown A2 projects. A student who is good at programming could develop an animated teaching aid with a graphical interface.

```
        StopPointer + 1)
    Then
        Print "Queue is full"
        Exit Sub
    End If
    Rem Check if Queue is empty
    If  StartPointer = 0 Then
        StartPointer = 1
        StopPointer = 1
        Names(StopPointer) = Name
    Else
        Rem Queue is neither empty nor full
        StopPointer = StopPointer + 1
        Names(StopPointer) = Name
    End If
    Rem Routine to look at the contents of the stack
    For x = 1 To 5
        Print Names(x)
    Next x
Loop

End Sub
```

Structure diagrams

In the last section we saw how **pseudocode** can be translated into a suitable high-level language very easily, but it's often useful to present a pictorial solution to a problem, and many methods are available for this. One method of breaking up a problem into **modules** is by the use of a **structure diagram**. There are many different types of structure diagram, but for the purposes of AS Computing, a structure diagram is the same as a **hierarchical diagram**, which shows the relationships and grouping of data items in pictorial form. Figure 7.5 shows a typical structure diagram.

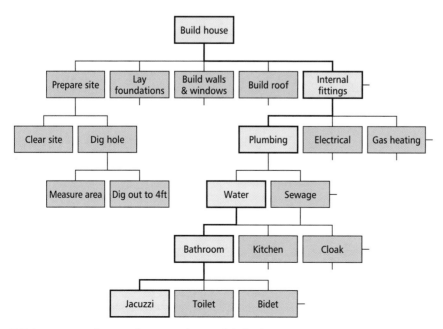

Figure 7.5 An structure diagram demonstrating modularisation

7

The structure diagram Figure 7.5 shows how a house might be constructed. Organising a project in this way enables it to be modularised. Each module, like 'Internal Fittings' can be subdivided into smaller modules like 'Plumbing', 'Electrical' and 'Gas'. The 'Jacuzzi', for example, is part of the 'Bathroom', which is a subsection of the 'Water' system which is also part of the 'Plumbing'. The plumbing belongs to the 'Internal fittings' section which also includes 'Electrical' and 'Gas'. 'Internal fittings' is just one of the main subsections of the 'Build house' project.

Many projects can be organised in this way, especially computing projects involving programming. At A2 level you will learn about object-oriented programming, which is based on a hierarchy of objects. Splitting up **large programs** into **smaller modules** is one of the methods of good **structured program design**.

In Chapter 6 we designed a 'house' which was modularised using similar principles. Each '**box**' in the **structure diagram** could easily correspond to a '**procedure**' in a **modular program**. Very large procedures (just like the internal fittings in Figure 7.5) can be split up into smaller ones until each part of the project becomes manageable. It also has the added advantage that a number of people can work on different modules, because you know the relationships between the **modules** from the **structure diagram**.

Example

Draw a structure diagram showing the relationships and grouping of the following hardware and software components in your computer system. The main categories are 'Hardware' and 'Software', with subcategories of 'Peripheral equipment', 'Components housed in the case', 'Motherboard', 'Graphics card', 'CPU', 'Memory', 'Sound card', 'Floppy disk', 'Hard disk', 'Applications software', 'System software', 'Office suite', 'Word processor', 'Spreadsheet', 'Database', 'Operating system', 'Utilities' and 'CAD package'.

Solution

Most of the above concepts are covered in previous chapters. A possible structure diagram is as shown in Figure 7.6.

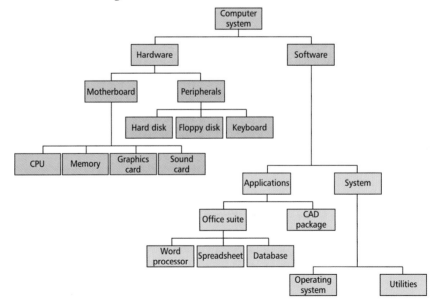

Figure 7.6 A possible structure diagram for hardware and software

Some parts of Figure 7.6 are open to different interpretations. A '**database**', for example, might not be part of the 'office suite'. However, the general principles of the structure diagram can be seen very easily and are quite sound.

A typical **high-level language program** might be divided up using a **structure diagram**. Indeed, this is the way you are meant to design your projects at A2 level. A possible structure diagram to show how the procedures for the house drawing program in Figure 6.2 is shown in Figure 7.7.

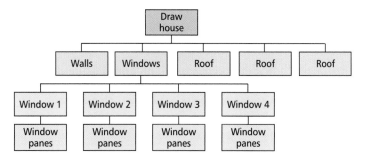

Figure 7.7 A Structure diagram showing procedures for the house program

Self-test questions

1 Explain the terms 'data type' and 'string'.
2 Consider the variable test$ = 'The cat sat on the mat'.
 Using pseudocode or a high-level language, write code to do the following:
 (a) Extract the word 'mat'
 (b) Extract the word 'cat'
 (c) Rebuild test$ replacing 'cat' with 'dog' and 'mat' with 'log'
 (d) Add an option to type any 'animal' and 'object on which to sit'. The string should
     be printed out each time, until terminated by entering dummy data '*'.
3 Using pseudocode or a high-level language of your choice, write a small program to
   invite a user to input a string of words without punctuation. Your program should then
   print out the words in reverse order:
       i.e. if 'there are lies dam lies and statistics' are input, then
       'statistics and lies dam lies are there' should be output.
4 You are going to write a simple Umbongoneese-to-English translator.
   This very limited language is shown in the following table.

Umbongoneese word	English word	Umbongoneese word	English word
toodle	have	urk	a
mushi	I	goop	big
umshi	mouth	jally	don't
targ	nose	oojip	do

   Using pseudocode or a high-level language, write a program to invite a user to input a
   string of valid Umbongoneese words, which then get literally translated into English.
5 By using pseudocode or a high-level language, write a program to scramble an English
   phrase into gobbledygook, and then write the program to translate it back again. (You
   can do this several times to see if your friends can crack your code.)

7

Question 6 in this exercise would be more than is expected in a single examination question.

Question 7 in this exercise will take most candidates a number of hours to program. It will take even longer if you are learning the high-level language as you go along.

6 By using pseudocode or a high-level language, modify the 'FIFO code' in this chapter to remove data from the stack too. Your code should not allow data to be removed from an empty queue, and should cater for a maximum of 9 entries.

7 Using a high-level language, add a graphics interface to question 6. Your aim is to create a graphical interface which shows the entry and updating of data on the stack. You should ensure that no data is added to a full queue and no data can be removed from an empty queue. Your program should mirror the ideas shown in Figure 7.4.

8 Draw a structure diagram to show the relationships and grouping for the following systems. You should choose some suitable categories for each subsection/s, and develop a single subsection to three or four levels of depth (i.e. show typical subsections).

(a) The parts that make up a car

(b) The hierarchical structure for staff in a school, with the head teacher at the top

(c) The food & drink needed for a special celebration dinner party

(d) Things to take on holiday.

8 Communication basics

In this section you will learn about:

- Simple ideas of communication and modulation
- Bit rates and baud rates
- Synchronous and asynchronous communication methods
- Error detection and correction
- Protocols and handshaking

Simple ideas of communication

Different methods can be used to transmit data over long or short distances, with 'radio waves', 'light', 'lasers' and 'electrical signals down copper wires' being common examples. To transmit 'data' a change in the state of the transmitted signal must occur. Changing the signal so that data can be sent is called **modulation**. A simple **Frequency Modulation (FM)** example is shown in Figure 8.1, where digital data from the computer on the left is **modulated** by the modem into an analogue signal for transmission over a standard analogue telephone line. At the other end a modem '**demodulates**' the signal so that the original digital data can be extracted from it.

Modern analogue modems, capable of transmission rates of up to 56 Kbits/sec make use of Quadrature Amplitude Modulation or QAM. More sophisticated methods are explained later in this chapter.

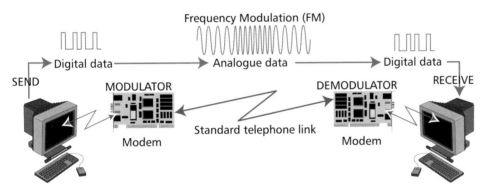

Figure 8.1 Frequency modulation is used for transmission over an analogue link

Other attributes of a signal can also be changed. Instead of altering the frequency we could alter the **amplitude** (as in AM radio stations), or alter the **phase** (an angle relative to some reference), hence the term '**phase modulation**'. We could also code some pulses (**pulse-code modulation**), determine the position of some pulses (**pulse-position modulation**), or determine the width of pulses, which gives us **pulse-width modulation**. In fact, modern systems make full use of all of these methods, plus some others too, and **combinations of these methods** make for some very interesting modulation systems. The actual systems employed (see margin entry) are considerably more complex than the simple principles shown in Figure 8.1, which would be suitable only for very low data transmission rates. This is due to the very limited range of frequencies that can be transmitted down the telephone line, which was designed to cope only with speech.

Classification of simple transmission systems

Simplex is the name given to a system capable of transmitting in one direction only. **Duplex** is a system in which two-way communication is possible, but only one way at any moment in time, and **full duplex** allows for simultaneous two-way communication.

Serial and parallel communications

Transmitting data around the world is fundamental to the way in which society now operates. You already know about **ASCII** and **Unicode**, and should realise that **ASCII** represents a single character by using 1 byte. If we wish to send a character from point A to point B, then 8 wires would be needed, if all the bits were to arrive simultaneously. This method of transmitting data over lots of wires simultaneously is called **parallel data communication**, and is ideal for the bus systems inside a computer.

It is not easy (not to mention the expense!) to run so many individual wires across large distances, and so data has to be sent **serially**, or **one bit after the other**. The individual bits have to be reassembled at the other end, to turn it back into bytes, which represent the actual information. Such a method of data transmission is called **serial data communication**, and is the method used for the vast majority of computer communication systems on **LANs** and the **internet**.

Synchronous and asynchronous data communications

Parallel communication of data usually happens under the direction of a **clock**, and therefore all the timing is **synchronised**. When different computers talk to each other over long distances like the internet, there is no way for them to be able to synchronise in this way. The **serial method** of data transmission is therefore called **asynchronous data transmission**.

When sending data **asynchronously**, we need a method of synchronising the signal at the receiving end, or we will not be able to make sense of what's happening. It is usual to make use of **start bits** and **stop bits** for this purpose. These ideas are shown in Figure 8.2.

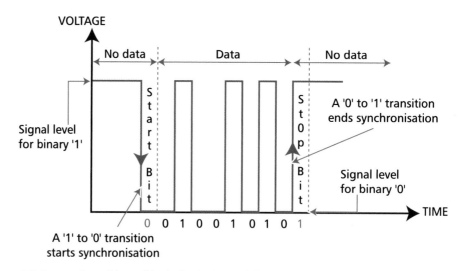

Figure 8.2 Start and stop bits enable the beginning and the end of transmission to be determined

Figure 8.2 shows a signal in which a high level represents a binary '1' and a low level represents a binary '0'. One byte of data consisting of the digits 01001010 is being sent at this time.

When no data is being transmitted the signal remains at a high level. At the beginning of the transmission, a high to low transition or a **start bit** '0' is sent to 'wake up' or synchronise the receiving electronics. The byte of data (01001010) is then clocked in by looking at the data at exactly the right time intervals after the start bit has activated the system. After 8 bits have been clocked in, the **stop bit** returns (or maintains) the signal at a high level ready for the reception of the next start bit which indicates that the next byte of data has arrived.

If the above system is being used, it's essential to agree on how fast the data is being transmitted. If both the receiving and transmitting electronics send data at the appropriate rate, then the level of the signal, as shown in Figure 8.2 will be interpreted correctly.

Example

An asynchronous communication link is receiving gobbledygook. Suggest one possible reason why the data is not being interpreted correctly.

Solution

One possible reason could be that the rate at which the data is being transmitted does not correspond to the same rate at which the data is being interpreted at the receiving end. Binary 0s and 1s are therefore be getting mixed up, misinterpreted or lost completely, thus ensuring that the data is incorrect.

Baud rates and bit rates

Baud rate is *the number of state transitions (signal changes)/sec*, and **bit rate** is *the number of bits/sec*. Although not strictly correct, it has been common in the past to use **bit rate** and **baud rate** to mean the same thing (i.e. bits/sec). Modern encoding methods, using a combination of modulation techniques, mean that more bits/sec can be transmitted than would be indicated by the **baud rate** alone. Hence we need the term **bit rate** to represent the actual number of bits/sec being transmitted. Due to the inclusion of the **start** and **stop bits**, and other possible overheads like **parity** (see later), the actual information transmitted is slightly less than might be assumed by looking at the bit rate alone. Other ways of measuring the speed could be characters/sec, or information rate/unit time.

For A level specifications, remember these definitions and you will not go wrong.

How to get more bits per baud

It is possible to combine different methods of modulation, like different **phases**, **amplitudes** and **frequencies**, for example, to create different states. Each **state transition** (change of state like **voltage**, **frequency** or **phase**) may be used to encode binary information. In this way it is possible to transmit more information than would appear at first sight from a typical signal, and this is why the **baud rate** is defined as a **state transition**, which means a change in the state of the signal like an amplitude change (voltage), frequency change (cycles per second) or a phase change (angle with respect to some reference signal). Clever methods of modulation make use of all of these attributes.

Simple methods of error detection

If the extended **ASCII** character set is not used, then only the least significant 7 digits are needed to represent the data being transmitted. If the top bit is not set, then this leaves us with the ability to use it for error detection purposes. There are two simple systems in operation, called **odd** and **even parity**. We can transmit the message 'hello', using ASCII, as shown in Table 8.2.

If we use the top bit (128s column) as a **parity bit**, then, making sure that there are an even number of 1s in each row determines the setting of this bit. A '1' is added here if we need to make the total number of 1s even. When the message is received, a **parity check** is done on the data to see if there is still an even number of 1s in each byte received. If there are, it is assumed to be correct, if not, an error has occurred during the transmission of the data. **Odd parity** is the same idea, but an odd number of 1s is used instead.

Table 8.2 A message with no parity

	128	64	32	16	8	4	2	1
h	0	1	1	0	1	0	0	0
e	0	1	1	0	0	1	0	1
l	0	1	1	0	1	1	0	0
l	0	1	1	0	1	1	0	0
o	0	1	0	1	1	1	1	1

Table 8.3 A message with even parity

	128	64	32	16	8	4	2	1
h	1	1	1	0	1	0	0	0
e	0	1	1	0	0	1	0	1
l	0	1	1	0	1	1	0	0
l	0	1	1	0	1	1	0	0
o	0	1	0	1	1	1	1	1

Example

Making use of the appropriate ASCII codes shown below, draw tables to show how the message 'Rocky the Dog' can be sent with 'no parity', 'even parity' and 'odd parity. (The *hex values* of the ASCII codes for the characters in 'Rocky the Dog' are as follows:

'R = 52', 'o = 6F', 'c = 63', 'k = 6B', 'y = 79', 'space = 20', 't = 74', 'h = 68', 'e = 65', 'D = 44', 'o = ?' and 'g = 67'.)

Solution

Table 8.4 'Rocky the Dog' sent with a variety of parity mechanisms

	'Rocky the Dog' with NO PARITY								'Rocky the Dog' with EVEN PARITY								'Rocky the Dog' with ODD PARITY							
	128	64	32	16	8	4	2	1	128	64	32	16	8	4	2	1	128	64	32	16	8	4	2	1
R	0	1	0	1	0	0	1	0	1	1	0	1	0	0	1	0	0	1	0	1	0	0	1	0
o	0	1	1	0	1	1	1	1	0	1	1	0	1	1	1	1	1	1	1	0	1	1	1	1
c	0	1	1	0	0	0	1	1	0	1	1	0	0	0	1	1	1	1	1	0	0	0	1	1
k	0	1	1	0	1	0	1	1	1	1	1	0	1	0	1	1	0	1	1	0	1	0	1	1
y	0	1	1	1	1	0	0	1	1	1	1	1	1	0	0	1	0	1	1	1	1	0	0	1
	0	0	1	1	0	0	1	0	1	0	1	1	0	0	1	0	0	0	1	1	0	0	1	0
t	0	1	1	1	0	1	0	0	0	1	1	1	0	1	0	0	1	1	1	1	0	1	0	0
h	0	1	1	0	1	0	0	0	1	1	1	0	1	0	0	0	0	1	1	0	1	0	0	0
e	0	1	1	0	0	1	0	1	0	1	1	0	0	1	0	1	1	1	1	0	0	1	0	1
	0	0	1	1	0	0	1	0	1	0	1	1	0	0	1	0	0	0	1	1	0	0	1	0
D	0	1	0	0	0	1	0	0	0	1	0	0	0	1	0	0	1	1	0	0	0	1	0	0
o	0	1	1	0	1	1	1	1	0	1	1	0	1	1	1	1	1	1	1	0	1	1	1	1
g	0	1	1	0	0	1	1	1	1	1	1	0	0	1	1	1	0	1	1	0	0	1	1	1

Note how the parity bits for odd and even are the inverse of each other.

Communication protocols and handshaking

Many different **protocols** exist – these are the *rules*, which bodies like the **International Standard's Organisation** (**ISO**) agree upon. Some familiar protocols are **HTTP** (the Hyper

Text Transfer Protocol), which enables web browsers to communicate with HTTP servers on the internet, and **FTP** (the File Transfer Protocol), which enables files to be copied from one computer to another over an LAN or the internet. Without protocols you would not be able to send information from one computer to a different type of computer very easily.

Protocols are used to establish the methods of communication between devices like computers and printers, different modems or wireless communications, for example. The process of establishing communication between two different devices is known as **handshaking**. Typically two modems (*see Figure 8.1*) would use handshaking to agree on 'baud rate', 'parity' or 'compression methods'.

More simply, a computer would use handshaking to negotiate with a printer to determine if it's O.K. to send more data. You can imagine the printer 'talking' to the computer, requesting more data as it has finished printing the previous data. The printer might also have to stop the computer sending data because it has run out of paper.

Modems

The name '**modem**' is made up from the words MOdulator and DEModulator. A **modulator** is a device that changes a signal into a different form, usually for the purpose of transmitting over a telecommunications link, like the phone line example shown in Figure 8.1. Don't forget that the standard analogue subscriber line (an ordinary phone line) was intended to transmit audio signals only. The function of an **analogue modem** is to change the signals into audio form so that they can be transmitted over a standard telephone link. At the other end of the link another modem is needed to act as a **demodulator**, which extracts the original digital data. A typical externally connected analogue modem, having a maximum speed of 56 Kbit/sec, is shown in Figure 8.3. A typical connection speed for this type of modem is about 33 Kbit/sec.

Figure 8.3 A Genius 56k Data/Fax modem

Figure 8.4 A US Robotics ADSL modem giving a maxim speed of 1 Mbit/sec

Much of the telephone system in Great Britain has now been upgraded to a digital network, with the exception of the links between the local exchange and consumers' houses. However, special equipment built into the local exchange enables some consumers (where the exchange has been upgraded and where the consumer does not live too far from the exchange) to use a faster communication link. There are various methods of connection, but **ADSL** (**Asymmetric Digital Subscriber Line**) is popular, giving a typical download speed of 500 Kbits/sec and a typical upload speed of 256 Kbits/sec. A different type of modem (an ADSL modem as shown in Figure 8.4) is needed for this type of connection, which although it is a **dial up connection**, remains on all the time. Faster ADSL lines are available, but the cost is greater as the bandwidth increases. It is usual for customers to share this bandwidth with others, and a **contention ratio** of 50 : 1 is typical. This means that 50 different people could theoretically be using the bandwidth at exactly the same moment in time. If this proved to be the case, the response would be awfully slow. In practice, not all people would be surfing the net at the same moment in time, and even if they were, some would be looking at information, and not actually downloading at exactly the same moment in time. In practice, it generally works rather well.

An alternative to a **dial up connection** is a **leased line**. This is a system where you rent a permanent connection (i.e. you don't have to dial in), which is usually a higher bandwidth than a standard 56 kbit/sec link. The cost of a leased line can vary from a few hundred to thousands of pounds per year, depending on the bandwidth required.

Both the **ADSL modems** and **analogue modems** are examples of devices used with **dial up connections**, in which the **TCP/IP** protocols are used to connect to the **internet** via an **internet service provider** (or **ISP**). Students are usually fascinated by how a typical internet service provider can connect so many users to the internet simultaneously. The answer lies with lots of rack-mounted modems of the sort seen in Figure 8.5. These can be strung together in large rooms which have banks of these rack-mounted systems. The ones shown here enable hundreds of people to connect to their ISP simultaneously and hence to connect to the internet.

Figure 8.5 A modem rack used by a typical ISP, enabling hundreds of users to be connected to the phone lines simultaneously

The methods of connecting to the internet, the software, hardware and protocols used are fascinating, but these topics are left to book 2 in this series, when the A2 work is covered.

Self-test questions

1 Briefly, what is the difference between serial and parallel communication methods? Give two different situations in which each method of communication would be preferable over the other, stating why this is so.
2 Explain the difference between asynchronous and synchronous transmission methods.
3 In the context of a communication signal, what is meant by the term 'modulation'? Suggest three different methods that could be used to modulate a signal.
4 The telephone line is capable of transmitting signals at a few KHz only. How is it possible for modern modems to achieve data transfer rates which hitherto would have been impossible?
5 Define the terms 'Bit rate' and 'Baud rate'. Why is the amount of information transmitted usually less than the number of bit/sec in the transmitted signal?
6 Detecting errors in data transmission is important for data integrity. Outline how the use of parity enables the errors to be reduced. Why are more sophisticated methods needed when transmitting over the internet?

7 The trouble with standards is that there are so many of them! Why are there so many communication protocols for transmitting data between computers?

8 Explain the function of a standard analogue modem. Why is a modem necessary to transmit signals over a standard telephone link?

9 An ADSL modem is needed to connect a subscriber to an ADSL line. List two reasons why an analogue modem could not be used.

10 What is the typical maximum speed that can be achieved over an analogue telephone line with a fast modem? How much faster is a typical ADSL link?

9 Networking basics

In this section you will learn about:

- The ideas of networking and shared resources
- Network topologies like star, ring, bus and tree
- The hardware and software needed to connect to a network
- Connecting to the internet
- URLs and domain names
- Intranets
- Accessing the internet and intranets from an LAN

Simple networking

If you have only two computers at home, then you don't need an Ethernet hub (shown in Figure 9.1) to set up a network. However, you may need a special lead called a crossover lead to connect the two computers.

You may also use a hub if you wish, but this is the most expensive component.

If you have three or more computers, then you definitely need a hub to build up an Ethernet network.

A computer **network** is '*a number of computers connected together, enabling common resources such as printers and file servers, etc. to be shared*'. Simple networks are now very cost effective and easy to set up. This means they are common in small offices and even in the home. Large and complex networks are now found in most schools, colleges, offices and factories. Networks like these, covering a local area like a 'house', 'building' or 'campus', are called a **local area network** (or **LAN**). A network also needs an operating system to support this interactivity, and modern **operating systems** like Windows are examples of **network operating systems**. A system of cables link the computers together, and various ways of doing this are covered soon.

A simple network might consist of two or three computers, set up as a **workgroup** so that each person may share the resources of the others. Typically this might be as shown in Figure 9.1, where one of the computers has an **ADSL modem**, and the others share this internet connection via the Ethernet network. All three computers share the **printer** connection.

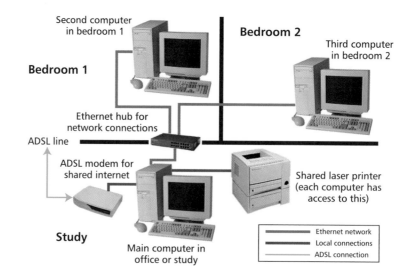

Figure 9.1 A home network set up to share resources

To share computers as a **workgroup** you need a **hub**, and a **network interface card** (**NIC**) in each of the computers. Most operating systems like **Windows** allow computers to be connected like this, but you need a professional operating system like Windows 2000 or Windows XP Professional if you wish to apply any degree of security to the system. This prevents disasters like the kids in bedroom 2 deleting work on Dad's computer in the main office! A machine not connected to a network is known as a **standalone** machine.

More sophisticated networks

More sophisticated systems are needed in schools, colleges and offices, and it's less usual to set up a simple workgroup as shown in Figure 9.1. Security is usually of paramount importance, and one or more **file servers** will provide this. A **file server** is a computer, set up to control access to folders belonging to different users and departments. A **file server** or a **domain name server** (not the same as an internet domain) is usually set up to control 'who can log on' to the network system, and to control 'who has access to which resources'. A **file server** or a **printer server** might control who can print to a variety of different printers available on the network, and a **proxy server** might control which users have access to the **internet** and when. These large and complex networks, usually under the control of a local institution like a university or college, are still examples of **LANs**, even though there may be tens of miles of cables, thousands of computers and several thousand users connected to the system.

At some point we need to make use of networks that service a large geographical area, making use of the public communication networks. Networks such as these, linking cities and spanning continents, are known as **wide area networks** or **WANs**. The **internet** is a huge network of networks, and is obviously the largest example of a **WAN**.

Network topology

Network topology describes the ways in which networks are physically connected. Different technologies make use of different topologies. The most basic (although not the easiest to set up or the most popular) is called a **bus network**. This is shown in Figure 9.2. The file server here is also acting as a **printer server**, and has a laser printer attached locally.

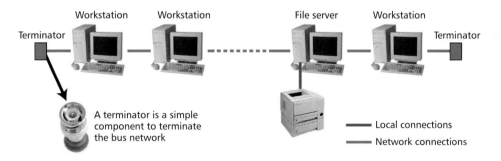

Figure 9.2 A bus network showing a Ethernet connection for a 10 Mbit/sec network

A bus connection, like the one shown in Figure 9.2 is suitable for low bandwidth networks running Ethernet at 10 Mbit/sec. It has the disadvantage that if a network card goes wrong, then the entire network could be out of action, because data intended for one machine must go via all the others. The physical security of the network is also low because data intended for one machine must pass by all the others too.

A more secure network is based on a **star network topology**, as shown in Figure 9.3. It's more secure because it is appropriately arranged; data intended for one machine does not

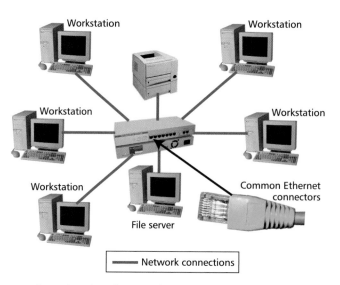

Figure 9.3 A star network topology based on an Ethernet switch

have to pass all of the others. The most secure type of star network would have a main-frame computer at the central point. A star network is also more robust. This is because if any workstations go wrong, then all the others should keep working, because they have their own independent connection. Figure 9.3 also shows a **network printer**. This is a printer with a **network interface card** (**NIC**) inside it. It is not a shared printer belonging to a particular computer, as was the case in Figure 9.1, when simpler networks based on workgroups were considered. Networks based on this type of Ethernet technology typi-cally transmit data at either 100 Mbit/sec (called Fast Ethernet) or 1000 Mbit/sec (called Gbit Ethernet).

Example

(a) **What is meant by standalone operation?**

(b) **Give three reasons why a network might be used instead of standalone operation.**

(c) **What are some of the differences between a 'workgroup' and a network set up making use of a 'file server'? You should consider 'ease of setting up' and 'security' in your answer.**

(d) **When is a star network more secure than a bus or ring network?**

Solution

(a) Standalone operation means that a computer has no network connection.

(b) Three reasons for using a network are 'shared resources like files and other software', 'sharing a printer' and 'to enable collaborative working'.

(c) A workgroup is made up by two or more computers being connected to a network. Each computer can share resources (like files), software and hardware (like printers). The person who is using an individual workstation is in charge of security, and this could lead to chaotic situations if the operating system does not have sufficient security or the users don't know what they are doing. A file server is usually set up by a network administrator, and users would log onto a domain which has been set up for this purpose. Security is usually very high if the system is set up properly. A workgroup is easy to set up, but a file server is very difficult to set up professionally.

(d) A star network is more secure than most others only if the central communications point is set up so as to allow communications between specified machines. You could arrange it so that no machine can talk to any other except for the file server, and this would provide better security.

Lots of rings may be interconnected with other rings to form very complex networks, and ring networks may also be interfaced with bus and star networks if the appropriate hardware is available. You will learn more about how to do this next year, when A2 work is covered.

A third type of **network topology** is based on a **ring**. Computers are connected in a continuous loop, and a message gets passed around the loop until it finds the appropriate computer. One type of ring network, called a **token ring**, is shown in Figure 9.4.

A **token ring network** makes use of an electronic token, which is passed around the network and grabbed by a machine wishing to communicate with others. Only one workstation will therefore have control over the network at any one moment in time. You should compare this with the Ethernet system, where any workstation can transmit information at any moment in time, but clashes will occur if two machines try at the same time.

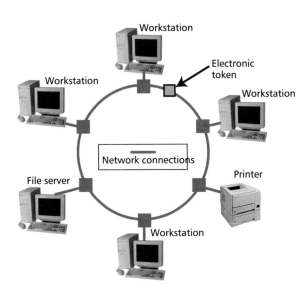

Figure 9.4 A ring network topology based on a token ring network

One final **network topology** (the most common) is called a **tree network**, and is usually made up from Ethernet hubs plugged into others as demonstrated in Figure 9.5.

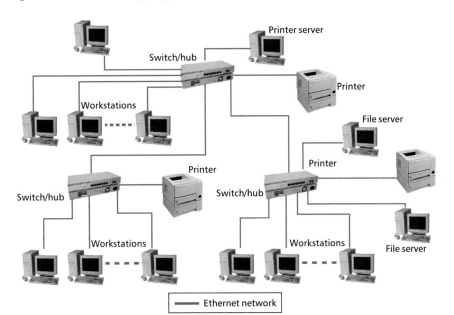

Figure 9.5 A tree network consisting of hubs/switches printers, file servers and and an internet connection via a proxy server

This is typical of what might be found in a large school, a large office or a college. Hundreds of computers may be connected in this way, but there are technical limitations to the number of hubs and switches that can be connected together like this. In practice, companies may have a combination of network topologies. It's a huge job to upgrade networks, and therefore legacy systems like the older 10 Mbit/sec bus networks might have to coexist with star, tree and ring topologies to form an extremely complex set of interrelated networks.

The network interface card

Each machine connected to a network will need a **network interface card** (NIC) or **network adapter**. Typical NICs for Ethernet are shown in Figure 9.6 and Figure 9.7.

Figure 9.6 A 1 Gbit/sec Ethernet card

Figure 9.7 A Combination Ethernet card for 10 Mbit/sec or 100 Mbit/sec

These network interface cards provide for the physical connection between the computer and the network, and the electronics needed to change the network signals into a form that the computer will understand. Fibre optic connections (not shown) are common for 1 Gbit/sec Ethernet, and the RJ-45 connections (the blue connector in Figure 9.3) are common for 1 Gbit/sec and 100 Mbit/sec Ethernet. The BNC connectors (the connectors for the terminators shown in Figure 9.2) are common for 10 Mbit/sec connections.

In addition to this hardware, **drivers** are needed to interface a particular card to a particular operating system like Windows, for example. These **device drivers** contain the detailed machine code necessary to interface the network card to the operating systems. Once the hardware has been installed, and the drivers loaded, the parameters like **IP addresses** (covered later) are set up so that each machine on the network has a unique address. Once this has been done, and the **share** and **security permissions** have been set up, users may **log onto** the system – assuming that they have a valid **account**.

Example

A college has set up a large network system for thousands of students. Answer the following questions, giving the most likely scenarios in each case.

(a) A student has an account on the network. What provides the security for this?

(b) What prevents students from seeing the work of others on the file server?

(c) A student's password has been cracked. Suggest some rules that they could follow to make sure this is less likely to happen in the future.

Solution

(a) A password is usually the only security that a student has against others breaking into the work on a network. The user's account name may be known to others, because it might be easy to guess.

(b) Each directory on the file server has security permissions applied to it. The network administrator would usually set this up so that others could not see any directory to which they should not go.

(c) The following rules give good password advice.
  1 Don't choose a password that's a normal word in a dictionary
  2 Choose a suitably long password (e.g. 10 characters or more)
  3 Put punctuation within words to make it difficult to crack

The internet

The **internet** is a 'worldwide network of networks'. Although people incorrectly use these terms interchangeably, when undertaking A level computing, you should distinguish between the **internet**, which is *the physical collection* of networks, and the **world wide web**, which is *the information delivered* via the internet.

The internet is the biggest possible example of a **wide area network** or **WAN**. You should compare and contrast a **WAN** with a **LAN**, considered earlier in this chapter. A **WAN** usually covers a wide geographical area, making use of systems like the public telecommunications networks, whereas a **LAN** usually covers a small geographical area like a single building or a campus, and is under the control of the institution which set up the network.

Virtually all students will have made extensive use of the internet. One of the author's web sites for helping students with computing revision is shown in Figure 9.8. Here Microsoft's Internet Explorer browser is being used to view the revise computing web site.

There is an extensive set of revision materials on the author's revise computing web site.

The site contains advice on project work, lots of examination questions with answers, many useful portal links and some careers advice for students thinking about a career in a computing based subject.

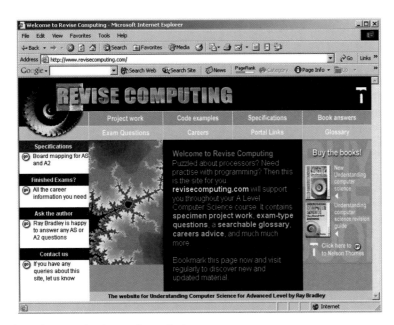

Figure 9.8 The author's Revise Computing web site

The uniform resource locator

To locate a resource on the internet we use a **uniform resource locator** or **URL**. The URL for 'Module 1 examination questions' on the author's revise computing site is as follows:

```
http://www.revisecomputing.com/exam_questions/module1.htm
```

This **URL** consists of several parts, with the **protocol** prefix appearing first. The **http protocol** (**hypertext transfer protocol**) is shown here before the ':' part of the URL. This is because this is the protocol needed to access this particular resource on the web. Other protocols might be **ftp** (**file transfer protocol**) or **https** (a secure version of **http**).

The '**www**' part indicates that this particular site is on the **World Wide Web**. (Some sites might not be available on the web, but via an **intranet** – see later.)

The character string '**//www.revisecomputing.com**' indicates the name of the **server** on which this web site is hosted, and is called the **domain name**. This user-friendly name must be resolved into a 32-bit host address. This is made up from 4 bytes, like '**129.7.1.10**', for example, shown here as decimal numbers separated by full stops. This is also known as the **IP** (**Internet Protocol**) **address**, and uniquely identifies a computer on a network like the internet.

The next parts indicate the 'path to the actual resource' on the **file server**. In this case there is a **subdirectory** called 'exam questions', and in this directory there is a **file** called '**module1.htm**' which indicates the page to display in the web browser.

In practice, the URL can appear quite complex, as the examples in the margin indicate. However, for the purpose of AS computing, the above knowledge is sufficient.

The Domain Name System

The **domain name system** (**DNS**) mentioned above needs extensive organisation. Each user-friendly domain name on the **internet** needs to be *resolved* into an **IP address** used by the communications systems to help perform the actual routing (i.e. making sure that a client gets connected to an appropriate server).

Special **servers** on the internet called **DNS servers** maintain a **database**, which consists of all the **registered** domain names and their corresponding **IP addresses**. These DNS servers are usually held by Internet Service Providers (ISPs), and most requests for domain name resolution from a client will be handled by their ISP's DNS server. If the requested entry is not in their database, a request is made from a special server called a **root server**. There are a limited number of root servers, and these contain the definitive information about all the sites registered for a particular domain.

The most important part of the **internet domain name system** consists of the **top level domains**. Generic names like '**.com**' are most popular, because clients can easily have a guess at the probable URL of a company or organisation. Other examples of generic names are '.org' and '.net', but a prefix representing a country is also used, with '**.uk**', '**.fr**' and '**.jp**' being just one or two obvious examples. The URL for the web site at the author's school, for example, is as follows:

```
http://tonbridge-school.co.uk
```

Here the **top level domain** is '**.uk**', hopefully indicating that the site is about an institution in the United Kingdom. '**.co.uk**' is an example of a **subdomain** of '**.uk**'. Therefore, '**tonbridge-school**' is a subdomain of '**.co.uk**'. We are rapidly running out of sensible domain names, and several new top level domains appear at intervals to try and get over this ever increasing problem.

Example

Consider the following URL and answer the questions.

```
https://registration.ft.com/registration/
login.jsp?FTSite=FTCOM&location=http://mwportfolio.ft.com/
custom/ft-com/portfolio/view.asp%3FFTSite=FTCOM
```

(a) What protocol is being used to access this site?

(b) What it the top level domain?

(c) What is the name of the server on which the site is hosted?

(d) There is lots of other information shown here. In general, what is the function of this information?

(e) Try to work out what is happening!

Solution

(a) The protocol being used is the secure version of the hypertext transfer protocol.

(b) The top level domain is '.com'.

(c) The name of the server on which this site is hosted is '//registration.ft.com'.

(d) These are parameters, used to customise what is happening to a particular individual using the site. In this particular case an active server page (asp) is being used.

(e) ft.com is the Financial Times web site. A registered user is logging into a secure part of the site, which is running a page prompting for a username and password. (*Astute readers might type in the above information and have a look!*)

Intranets

An **intranet** consists of one or more in-house web sites built up for internal consumption by organisations like schools, colleges and public or private companies. The web sites on an intranet are intended only for the employees of the company or the students in a school, and are not usually available to the general public. The Computer Department intranet web site at the author's school is shown in Figure 9.9.

The **URL** in this case is simply `http://ict`. As this is not available on the World Wide Web, no 'www' part appears in this address. However, the site is available from anywhere in the world via our **VPN**, and this is covered later. The site contains links to booking the computer labs, the departmental library and information

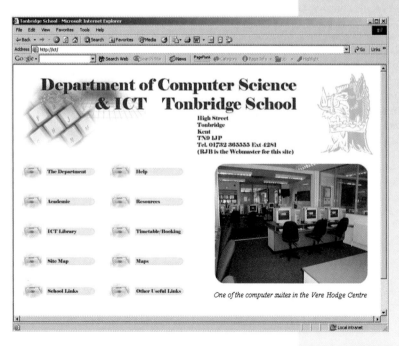

Figure 9.9 The author's departmental intranet site

about homework for each year. There are extensive sets of training materials for a huge number of courses, and links to student databases where hundreds of e-mail addresses are stored. There is also an extensive set of links to the rest of the school intranet site, with many academic departments having their own entries. Because this web site contains much private information, you would not normally want the general public to see it, and this is the whole point of an **intranet**.

Example

Suggest some typical hardware and software that would be needed to set up an intranet site for a school or college. You may assume that a network infrastructure similar to that shown in Figure 9.5 exists already.

Solution

You should note that sharing a folder on a network into which you place your site is not the same as publishing it on a file server. If you simply share a site you will find that some of the functionality of the site will not be available – uploading a site onto your web server gives you facilities similar to when you upload your site to a server on the World Wide Web.

To set up a proper intranet you need a web server. This is a file server on your network, running software like Microsoft's Internet Information Server, for example. This is a server that will host the web sites, and provide other functionality like links to databases. If properly set up, the users of your site will notice no difference from using the World Wide Web, with the exception that the 'www' part of the URL will be omitted.

Each machine will obviously need an appropriate browser, and a DNS server may be needed to resolve any internal web site names if there are more than one.

It would probably be desirable to include software to construct the web site, and Macromedia's Studio MX is a good example of this, containing 'Flash' for animations, 'Art package' for construction and manipulation of images for the web, and a whole variety of useful utilities.

The internet and intranet on a LAN

Organisations like schools and businesses require their students or workers to be able to surf both the **internet** and the **intranet** from their **LAN**. They would expect their clients or pupils to have access to both **internal** and **external** e-mail, the company or school **database** and other resources like **software** and **hardware** too.

Figure 9.10 outlines the main resources that would need setting up to be able to do this effectively. There are three internet connections shown here, but in practice this could be managed by a single connection if necessary.

The first internet connection shown in Figure 9.10 enables users of the LAN to access external sites on the World Wide Web via a proxy server. It is the job of the proxy server to deliver the web pages to the appropriate workstation on the LAN. In practice, there needs to be a firewall to help prevent hackers from gaining access to the LAN from the outside world.

The second internet connection shown in Figure 9.10 enables users of the LAN to access internal e-mail from the mail server. This mail server is also connected to the internet so that internally generated e-mail for the outside world can be sent, and mail from the outside world may be received.

A third internet connection enables users from the outside world to gain access to the facilities available on the **LAN** via a **VPN** (*see next section*).

The web server can be seen on the left of Figure 9.8. This is the server on which the intranet site/s can be hosted. Any URLs resolved for the internal web sites go via this (or

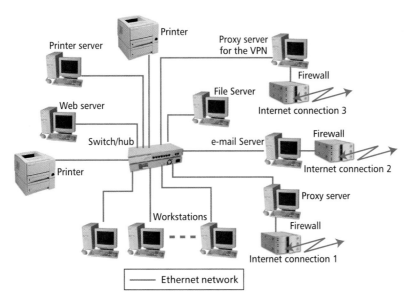

Figure 9.10 A system for implementing an intranet, e-mail and access to the internet and other resources via a LAN

other internal web servers), and any request for outside sites go via the proxy server to the World Wide Web.

If well set up, the system should be transparent for the users of the LAN, who may not even realise that they are getting e-mail from a server within the organisation, or are getting the intranet resources from inside the company instead of from an external source.

Intranets and extranets

Clients may have access to the internet from either work or at home, and have access to the intranet from work. However, it's likely that clients might want access to the private intranet from home, and this can be done by setting up a **virtual private network** or **VPN**.

Students at the author's school, for example, have access to their private directories (where project and other work is stored) the school e-mail server and the school intranet via a **VPN**. The ideas are shown in Figure 9.11. The intranet is hosted on one of the school's file servers, and made available to anyone surfing the web, provided they have access to the VPN, which is encrypted and protected by user names, passwords and firewalls.

The **intranet** is the name used for web resources from within a local organisation, but the term **extranet** is used when an intranet is available from anywhere in the world via a system like the VPN shown in Figure 9.11. An extranet is therefore an intranet available via the web, usually only to private customers with the appropriate authentication.

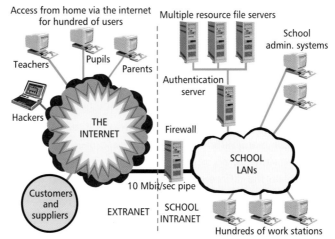

Figure 9.11 A typical view via a virtual private network

9

Example

School resources are to be made available from home via a VPN. Suggest some of the things that could be useful to pupils, parents and teachers. Why should the system differentiate between these users and how is this done in practice.

Solution

Some useful things that can be made available to each class of user are as follows:

(a) Pupils – access to school work; access to homework; access to information on clubs and societies; access to staff and other pupil e-mail addresses, etc,

(b) Parents – access to homework schedules; access to 'what's on at the school'; access to examination results and reports for their sons or daughters, etc.

(c) Teachers – access to school database containing names, addresses and telephone numbers of pupils, parents and staff; access to systems for report writing, examination entry and booking forms for rooms and other resources.

Each group will have a unique user name and password. It is these attributes that would be used to allow users access to different parts of the web server and administrative systems like the school database.

Self-test questions

1 What is meant by a network and why is it useful?
2 A small school requires a classroom where 25 pupils can make use of computers (PCs) simultaneously. Two hundred and fifty different pupils and staff will make use of this system, and special areas are needed to store the individual work for pupils and staff.
    (a) How many PCs will be needed altogether? Give reasons for your answer.
    (b) Suggest a suitable network topology for this system.
    (c) Suggest a suitable network bandwidth for this classroom.
    (d) Two printers are required such that each pupil may print to either one of them. Suggest two different ways of doing this.
    (e) Where will the pupils' work be stored at the end of each day?
    (f) Suggest a structure that would be suitable for storing the pupils' work, and a system of user names that might be useful when logging on.
3 What is meant by network topology, and why is it important to consider the implications of which topology to use?
4 What is the difference between a LAN and a WAN? Outline a typical scenario in which each type of network would be most useful.
5 A LAN has an internet connection via a proxy server. What is this and how does this enable many different users to simultaneously access the net? Suggest a typical bandwidth for an internet connection for the users in question 2.
6 Explain the difference between the internet and the World Wide Web.
7 Different resources on the internet can be accessed by using different protocols. Make a list of five different protocols on the internet, indicating a typical use for each one.

8 Explain the domain name system for retrieving information on the web.

9 What is a URL? Give an example of a typical URL, clearly indicating which protocol is being used, the server address, the directory paths and the resource to be loaded.

10 Outline in principle what happens when a domain name is resolved into an IP address. What scenario is undertaken if the ISP does not have the appropriate address in its database?

11 How might users on a LAN access both internal and external e-mail?

12 Explain the terms internet, intranet and extranet.

13 A virtual private network (VPN) enables users outside of an organisation to access information contained in private intranets and other resources on the LAN. What security precautions are usually taken to enable them to do this?

14 What extra software and hardware is needed to set up an intranet on a LAN?

15 Name four different types of server that it's possible to have on a local area network, indicating what particular function is performed in each case.

Module 1 examination questions

AQA examination questions

1 (a) Two classifications of software are *System Software* and *Applications Software*. What is meant by:

    (i)   System Software   *(1 mark)*

    (ii) Application Software?   *(1 mark)*

    (iii) Give an example of System Software (not a product name).   *(1 mark)*

  (b) Application software can be subdivided into *general purpose*, *special purpose* and *bespoke* software.

    (i)   Give a type of general-purpose application software package.   *(1 mark)*

    (ii) What is meant by a special-purpose application software package?   *(1 mark)*

  (c) A school is planning to introduce an electronic registration system. The management have the choice of buying a readily available software package or having bespoke software written for them.

    (i)   What is meant by bespoke software?   (1 mark)

    (ii) Give **one** advantage and **two** disadvantages of bespoke software over readily available software.

          Advantage   *(1 mark)*

          Disadvantages   *(2 marks)*

[AQA Unit 1 (CPT1) Computer Systems, Programming and Network Concepts June 2003 Q(1)]

2 The following code is part of a high-level program to manipulate text:

```
Var S1: String
Var S2: String
Var Ptr: Integer
Var L: String
S1:="PAT"
S2=""                    {"" denotes an empty string}
For Ptr:=1 To 3 Do
        L:=Copy (S1, Ptr)
        S2:=Concat(L, S2)
EndFor
If S1 = S2
        Then Print ("True")
        Else Print ("False")
EndIf
```

  (a) By copying **one** relevant line from the above code, give an example of:

    (i)   variable declaration   *(1 mark)*

    (ii) selection statement   *(1 mark)*

    (iii) iteration.   *(1 mark)*

  (b) The built-in subroutines **Copy**, **Concat** and **Print** have been used in the above code.

Copy (S, n) returns the nth character of string S

example: Copy ("ABCED", 2) returns the character 'B'

Concat (S1, S2) concatenates the two strings S1 and S2 and returns a single string

example: Concat ("ABCD", "EF") returns the string 'ABCDEF'

Print (S) prints the string S as output

Subroutines are either functions or procedures. Indicate, by ticking the correct boxes, what each of the above subroutines is.

subroutine	procedure	function
copy		
concat		
print		

(3 marks)

(c) Dry run the above code by completing the table below.

S1	Ptr	L	S2
"PAT"			" "
	1	"P"	"P"

(8 marks)

[AQA Unit 1 (CPT1) Computer Systems, Programming and Network Concepts June 2003 Q(7)]

3 (a) How many bytes are in a Kilobyte?   (1 mark)

(b) A computer system uses 2 bytes to store a number.

(i) What is the largest pure binary integer it can store?   (1 mark)

What is the bit pattern if the number 37 is to be stored as:

(ii) a pure binary integer

(1 mark)

(iii) a BCD (Binary Coded Decimal)?

(1 mark)

(c) The ASCII coding system uses seven bits to code a character.

The digits 0 to 9 are assigned the decimal number codes 48 to 57.

An extra bit is used as a parity bit.

A computer system uses the most significant bit (MSB) as a parity bit for each byte and works with even parity.

(i) What is the bit pattern if the digits 37 are to be stored as characters?

(3 marks)

(ii) Explain how the parity bit is used by this computer system.   (2 marks)

[AQA Unit 1 (CPT1) Computer Systems, Programming and Network Concepts June 2003 Q(2)]

4 A small organisation has several computers in an office connected to form a network as shown:

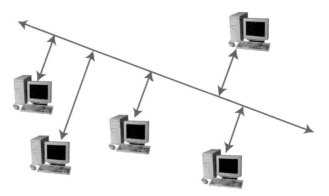

(a) What is the name of this network topology? *(1 mark)*

(b) The network could instead be connected as a star topology.

   (i) Draw the connections between the computers in a star topology in the diagram below.

   (ii) State one advantage of a star connection compared with the network you have named in (a) above, and give a reason. *(2 marks)*

(c) The organisation would like to connect to the internet. The management has to decide whether to use *leased line* or *dial-up networking*.
   What is meant by:

   (i) leased line networking *(1 mark)*

   (ii) dial-up networking? *(1 mark)*

[AQA Unit 1 (CPT1) Computer Systems, Programming and Network Concepts June 2002 Q(1)]

5 Some of the internal components of a computer system are: processor, main memory, control bus, address bus, data bus, keyboard controller, VDU controller and disk controller.

The diagram below shows how these are connected.

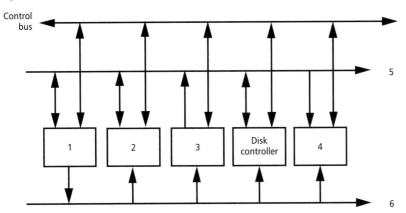

(a) Give the correct name for parts 1–6 labelled in the diagram.   (*6 marks*)

(b) If the data bus consists of 8 lines, what is the largest denary value which could be transferred in one go?   (*1 mark*)

(c) Computer systems built using the von Neumann architecture use the stored program concept.

   (i)   Where is the stored program while it is being executed?   (*1 mark*)

   (ii) Where is the data stored?   (*1 mark*)

[AQA Unit 1 (CPT1) Computer Systems, Programming and Network Concepts June 2002 Q(4)]

6 (a) Machine code is the first generation of programming languages. All other generations of programming languages need a program translator before the program can be executed. Name a type of translator suitable for:

   (i)   second-generation language programs   (*1 mark*)

   (ii) third-generation language programs.   (*1 mark*)

(b) Imperative high-level languages are third generation.
Give **two** characteristics of high-level languages that distinguish them from second-generation languages.   (*2 marks*)

(c) In one high-level language an example of a constant definition would be:

```
CONST VatRate = 17.5
```

State one advantage of using a named constant, like VatRate, rather that the actual value (17.5) in a high-level language program.   (*1 mark*)

(d) (i)   Name an imperative high-level language that you have studied.   (*1 mark*)

For the language you have named in (d) (i) above, give an example, using the correct syntax, of:

   (ii) iteration   (*2 marks*)

   (iii) selection.   (*2 marks*)

[AQA Unit 1 (CPT1) Computer Systems, Programming and Network Concepts June 2002 Q(3)]

7 A binary search tree is a data structure where items of data are held such that they can be searched quickly and easily.
The following data items are to be entered into a binary search tree in the order given:

   London, Paris, Rome, Berlin, Amsterdam, Lisbon, Madrid.

   (a) Draw a diagram to show how these values will be stored.   (*4 marks*)

   (b) Circle the root node of your diagram.   (*1 mark*)

   (c) If Madrid is being searched for in this binary tree, list the data items which would have to be accessed.   (*1 mark*)

   [AQA Unit 1 (CPT1) Computer Systems, Programming and Network Concepts June 2001 Q(8)]

8 (a) A computer system is made up of hardware and software. What is meant by:

   (i) hardware   (*1 mark*)

   (ii) software?   (*1 mark*)

   (b) A home user wants to link up a stand-alone personal computer to the internet.

   (i) What computer hardware is required?   (*1 mark*)

   (ii) What is the function of this hardware?   (*2 marks*)

   (c) Once connected to the internet, the user can access a whole range of information, including the World Wide Web.

   (i) What type of application software is required to access a web site?   (*1 mark*)

   A Uniform Resource Locator (URL) is the address for the data on the internet. For example, http://www.bbc.co.uk is the address of the BBC home page. Explain the two different parts of this address.

   (ii) http://   (*1 mark*)

   (iii) www.bbc.co.uk   (*1 mark*)

   (d) The internet is one example of a WAN (Wide Area Network),

   (i) Describe a WAN.   (*2 marks*)

   (ii) Why is a protocol needed?   (*1 mark*)

   [AQA Unit 1 (CPT1) Computer Systems, Programming and Network Concepts June 2001 Q(1)]

9 Computer systems do not just store information representing numbers and characters. Sound and graphics are also frequently stored.

   (a) When sound from a microphone is recorded, how is it converted into a form which can be stored on a computer?   (*2 marks*)

   (b) (i) How can a black and white image be represented as a bit-mapped graphic?   (*2 marks*)

   (ii) What change needs to be made to (b) (i) to represent a coloured image?   (*1 mark*)

   [AQA Unit 1 (CPT1) Computer Systems, Programming and Network Concepts June 2001 Q(9)]

10 Applications and effects

In this section you will learn about:

- Planning to implement a major information processing application
- The possibilities of 'bespoke', 'in-house' and 'off-the-shelf' solutions
- A major information processing application
- The information requirements of a system
- The communication requirements of a system
- The ethical, legal, social and economic effects of the application

Introduction

A major **information processing** application must be studied in order to be able to understand concepts like the 'information requirements of a system' and the 'communication requirements of a system'. The **social**, **legal**, **ethical** and **economic** consequences of the application must also be considered.

It's difficult to carry out the above things hypothetically, so a real application needs be studied. There are thousands from which we could choose, but an administration and management system for a large secondary school has been selected, mainly because it's easy for students to identify with the requirements of this particular system. You have all had experience studying in schools, and the project is complex enough to highlight typical problems that usually arise when looking at the requirements for any large application.

You are to assume the role of an administrator at a school with 1500 pupils and 100 teaching and administrative staff. It's your job to set up a new computer system to run the school administration. The magnitude of this task is enormous, and the school has probably got a large number of 'legacy systems' (*see margin entry*) with which you will have to contend.

You will obviously need to know why the existing system is to be changed. For the sake of argument, let's assume that a long-standing and dedicated teacher has run the administrative system for years by writing custom software designed for a variety of tasks. This key member of staff is about to retire, and nobody else knows how to operate or modify the system to keep it up to date! This scenario is an all too familiar one in many schools.

Before looking at any new system in detail, it's useful to set up some background information. Over the next few pages we indicate actions that would need to be undertaken by any school before committing to a particular application. It's useful to do this for two reasons:

1 It puts the application we are going to study into context.

2 If you study computing at A2 level, you will need to carry out scenarios like this.

The information requirements of the system

Most major projects start off by '*defining what the system has to do*'. In practice a committee would probably be set up, chaired by the administrator (you!), consisting of a representative range of personnel. Typical of these might be one person chosen from each of the 'teaching staff', the 'pastoral staff', 'administrative staff', a 'head of department', the 'examination's entry officer' and a 'parent/governor representative'. The exact mix will

Many schools have a large number of 'legacy systems' running their administration systems. This means that systems have been developed in an ad-hoc way, usually by clever and dedicated teachers who have an interest in computing.

With the vast increase in school administration, this approach is becoming virtually impossible to maintain, and the school is at a disadvantage when the person who set up a system like this leaves.

depend on the school. Over the next few meetings a set of **general objectives** should be agreed by the committee, which might contain statements like the following:

- to provide a system that is maintainable, irrespective of the personnel at school
- to provide a system which is customisable, that can be adapted quickly, if necessary, to the changing needs of the school
- to provide a greatly improved administrative system, cutting down the amount of time taken to undertake typical administrative tasks
- to provide a wide range of information and administrative functions via the school LAN, the school intranet and from home via a virtual private network.

As the chairperson you delegate responsibility, requesting that each person performs the task of finding out what people need/want in their particular areas. Typical methods used to gather information during this critical phase would be **questionnaires**, **interviews** and **e-mail**. The mass of data received should be correlated, and the *major requirements* for each section written down to build up a **system specification**. The **system specification** should detail the nature, objectives and details of the project, and should include things like those shown in the following list:

- the functions to be performed by the system should be made extremely clear
- the data-input specifications to the system, including any special features and forms that may be needed should be documented
- the data-output specifications from the system, including any special features and the purpose of the output, with examples, need to be considered
- links between this and other programs should be identified.

This document would form part of the **systems analysis** of the project. Systems analysis is covered in more detail in the A2 book.

It's important to put a problem into context, and see why a particular application might be chosen to solve a complex task.

The first couple of pages in this chapter are outlining the background to the likely choice of this particular application.

Example

Make a simple list of headings (e.g. examination statistics) that correspond to the sort of things this administration system must do. (Don't list more than ten things.)

Solution

The possible list of things is vast. Typical entries include 'Option choices', 'Attendance records', 'Examination entries', 'Internal and external examination results', 'Registration', 'Timetabling for pupils', 'Timetabling for staff', 'Personal information for students (name, address, parents/guardians, etc.), 'Personal information for staff', 'Assessments', and 'Reporting', etc. Other categories, unlikely to be guessed by students, are the statistical returns undertaken each year for the DfES (Department for Education and Skills).

The communication requirements of the system

The **communication requirements** of the system are things like *modelling the interfaces required by the users*. For each major module, careful consideration needs to be given to the type of **user interface** that might be optimum, both in terms of the software required and extra peripheral devices. Typical examples might be as follows:

- Would it be an advantage to have data entered into the system via the internet or an intranet?
- Will information downloaded into a PDA be preferable in addition to accessing the same information on a desktop PC?

A good example of a possible **communication requirement** for our school-based system might be to consider a **tablet PC** or **portable** for class teachers, linked via a **radio-based LAN** to the central school office for *registration of classes*. Perhaps the teacher need only tick 'students who are absent from class', and our new information processing system does the rest. One of the general objectives in our original specification is 'cutting down the time taken to do common administrative tasks' – ticking one or two boxes to register a class would certainly achieve this objective for this particular part of the system.

Different ways of solving the problem

The task of developing this administration system from scratch would be enormous, and there are basically three major options.

1 Employing one or more professional programmers to build up a custom system from our specifications, keeping the best parts of the legacy systems intact.
2 Employing a company to write a bespoke system from our specifications.
3 Using an off-the-shelf application from a company that specialises in school administration.

Each of the above methods has pros and cons. To help us make the right decision the companies concerned would probably give presentations regarding what they can offer. There should be two presentations from each company; one for non-technical users who wish only to make use of the system, and one for technical people who will be involved in maintaining the system, including repairing it when it goes wrong.

Not forgetting the **economics**, the likely costs of each of the above solutions depends on many factors, including the technical personnel who will be at the school to operate it.

Example

Consider the three different ways of solving the problem outlined above. In consultation with others in your class, make notes as to the likely pros and cons of each option. (*There are no right or wrong answers here, just intelligent observations.*)

Solution

Option 1 – A professional programmer would be on a set salary, which might have to be substantial to get someone of the right calibre. However, if this person leaves, you are probably in the same position as now, especially as is likely in education, they have little time to build up the vital project documentation. (This is documentation showing enough technical detail about the system to enable others to carry on with the project if necessary.) This option maintains the status quo.

Option 2 – This is quite easy to set up, because others are doing it for you. However, the specification you have produced is vital. Modifications to the system by the software company that develops it for you could prove very expensive. They will inevitably blame your specification if you want to make slight changes to the original system which you may not have thought about at design time. Schools are dynamic institutions with rapidly changing requirements, and new additions to the system are likely to be needed at frequent intervals.

Option 3 – The third option is to buy an off-the-shelf package. This can be quite expensive initially, but the system is proven, having been used in many other schools. It is also something that can usually be managed more easily, because the system does not depend too much on the personnel that you have at your school. You will recall that this was one of our general objectives. However, don't underestimate the amount of time that it takes to get the enormous amount of data into the system, and don't expect it to do everything that you want it to do without considerable effort on the part of personnel within the school.

Other sources of information

The DfES information can be found on the web at http:// www.dfes.gov.uk/ ims

Although obviously not the case for competing commercial institutions, organisations should not consider their problems in isolation from others. Hundreds of schools have similar problems to solve. As with any major **information processing application**, you should look, if possible, at the ways in which everybody else is coping. The DfES (Department for Education and Skills), for example, provides guidelines and advice on the electronic collection, management and transfer of pupil and other school management information. This is called their **Information Management Strategy** (*IMS – See margin entry*), and is to do with the collection of statistical information from schools.

If possible you should make visits to other schools who have used the three options outlined above. There are also a variety of different off-the-shelf options, and you will obviously want to look at more than one. The **World Wide Web** is also a vast resource for information regarding school administration systems, with hundreds of resources available for teachers and managers in schools.

The above introductory material has put the problem into context, and you now have familiarity with at least some of the things that an administration system will have to do. We now go onto look at a particular solution.

The Facility CMIS system

Facility CMIS can be found on the web by typing www.ccmsoftware. com/schools.

All AS students are required to study a major **information processing application**; we will assume an off-the-shelf solution meets our general objectives better than the other two options.

CCM software (*see margin entry*) develops and markets an advanced set of off-the-shelf solutions for administration and management in schools, colleges and universities. They also cater for government agencies and corporate institutions. The appropriate system from CCM software to help solve our problem is the schools option within **Facility CMIS** (**Computer Management Information System**). The system is modularised, but data is stored once only in a **centralised data source** (*the* main **database**). The general idea of CMIS is shown in Figure 10.1.

As can be seen from Figure 10.1, CMIS uses the **modular structure**. A brief description outlining the function of some of the modules is considered later, in Table 10.1.

A strategic overview

CCM software needed to visualise how the overall system relates to individual 'objects' like 'times', 'dates', 'employees', 'rooms' and 'equipment'. They also needed a strategy showing how 'constraining influences' and the 'organisation's rules' would interact with particular modules within the system. As with most projects of great complexity, teasing out the **information and communication requirements** from the initial **specifications** is hard to do, and a diagram showing the broad interactions is very useful.

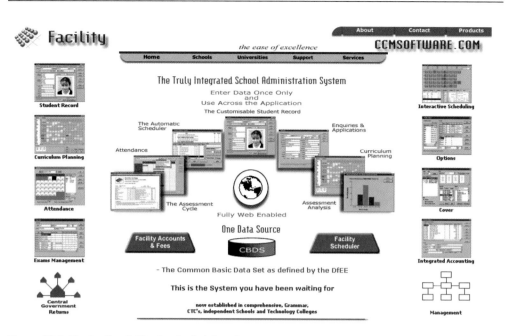

Figure 10.1 The Facility CMIS school administration system

CCM software came up with the concept of an 'event', and placed this idea at the core of their system design. An event is defined in terms of 'human' or 'physical resources', 'times', 'dates' and 'places'. These **events** can be manipulated according to certain **rules** and other **logic** to produce the required **output**. These ideas are neatly summed up in Figure 10.2, where this generalised system applies also to the corporate defence and health sectors too.

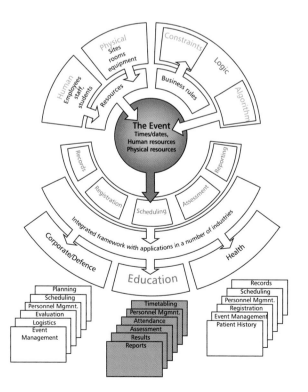

Figure 10.2 The importance of an 'event' in Facility CMIS

We are concerned only with the application of Facility CMIS to the education sector, and examples of **output** from this sector are shown at the base of the diagram in red. At AS level we are concerned only with the **information and communication requirements** of this system, together with the **economic**, **social**, **legal** and **ethical** issues.

Example

Consider the Facility CMIS diagram shown in Figure 10.2. Concentrate on three different areas of the school administration system, and then make a list of *five* different constraints for *each of the areas* that you have chosen to mention.

Solution

Area 1 – Timetabling: Typical constraints would probably be 'staff numbers', 'subject specialist numbers', 'number of rooms', 'time' and 'facilities' (e.g. the computer room would probably be needed for an ICT lesson). etc.

Area 2 – Option choices: Typical constraints would probably be 'ability of students', 'staff availability', 'facilities' (as above), 'forbidden combinations' and 'compulsory subjects', etc.

Area 3 – Cover for staff absence: Typical constraints would probably be 'availability of other staff', 'number of times a particular member of staff has been asked to cover', 'can a subject specialist be found?', 'can the lesson be covered from within a particular department?', 'is work set for the lesson to be covered?' etc.

A modular structure

Facility CMIS is highly modularised, but all modules need not be purchased initially. 'Timetabling', 'financing' and the 'e-portal' could be purchased later. Modules, like 'timetabling', need not purchased at all if a school prefers to do this manually. The **economics** are therefore quite flexible. The main modules are described briefly in Table 10.1.

It would take too long to analyse the **information and communication requirements** of the entire system, therefore typical examples will be used for the purpose of illustration.

An 'information requirement' example

The **management reporting module** is an interesting place to start. Schools need to provide information for a range of people including governors, the senior management team, heads of departments and subject teachers. A few of the **information requirements** for people likely to use the management reporting module are outlined below.

The **board of management** (*school governors*) need summary reports on a variety of issues. These should be printed in a precise format, enabling effective management decisions for future planning to be made.

The **senior management** team (*Head teacher, Director of Curriculum, etc.*) will require detailed statistics and reports on all subject areas, and need to be able to view how departments and individual teachers and pupils are performing relative to others.

Table 10.1 The modular structure of Facility CMIS

Module name	A brief description of some of the functionality of each module
Student record	This is a fully customisable student record, containing both personal and statistical data. It is integrated with other systems like the 'timetable' and 'cover' modules, and contains health and emergency procedure notes too.
Applications and enquiries	This is for gathering information about students who wish to enter the school. It allows the school to use statistics generated from this module to help with targeted marketing.
Curriculum planning	A planning module enabling the school to manage teachers, students, classes, rooms and other resources. The timetable can be produced in a variety of different formats, enabling different departments to view the information in a variety of different ways.
Assessment analysis	This helps with statistical analysis of assessments by providing detailed information regarding individual students or classes, etc. It also provides mechanisms by which the school can calculate 'added values' (how well a student is currently doing compared to the time when they entered the school).
Student attendance	This module creates records for student attendance, and can generate statistics based on a variety of criteria like 'lateness', 'absence', 'study leave' and 'family bereavement', etc.
Management reporting	Information can be produced for a variety of personnel ranging, from senior management to ordinary members of the academic and administrative staff.
Central government returns	Using this module the school can make statistical returns to the government by electronic means. It will be generated from the data already in the system. It conforms to the Common Basic Data Set required by the DfES (The Department for Education and Skills.)
Examinations management	This module can 'read data from' and 'send data to' all examination boards in electronic format. It allows for any examination components and assignment of examinations on the basis of teacher, teaching groups and external candidates, etc.
School finance	A complete set of routines for LEA (Local Education Authority) financial management of schools, including the links via e-portal to the local authority.
Facility e-portal	This gives access to most of the functionality of the CMIS database via the intranet or the World Wide Web. It works in real time, producing dynamic information content.

Heads of departments (*e.g. 'Head of Maths', 'Head of English', etc.*) need statistical reports regarding the progress of each class and pupil taught in their department. Summary information will be needed for departmental meetings, and inter-departmental summary information can also be provided (Physics, Chemistry and Biology, for example).

The **subject teacher** (*a normal class teacher*) should have access to detailed profiles on each of the pupils they teach. This should include performance summaries and standard reports for both pupils and parents.

The **timetabler** will require help with the production of the timetable, including subject options, staff cover and curriculum planning. This is integrated into CMIS.

Special needs are catered for. Records of events that have happened can be recorded, and special events (like needing to see a dyslexia specialist or the school psychologist) can be triggered automatically.

Communications with the LEA (Local Educational Authority) need to be handled. Transfer of information from the school to the LEA should be accomplished seamlessly.

The **administrator** of the system should be able to set up a variety of permissions, enabling different information and different modules to be used by the appropriate people. (A subject teacher should not necessarily be able to view a psychologist's report for a particular student, unless, of course, they are involved as a form tutor.)

Each of the above users should be able to create their own **queries** and **reports**, assuming they have permissions to view the information. The management system allows users to create customised **queries** in this way. A wide variety of customised **templates** should be available which can be used 'as is', or as a starting point for a new type of query or report specific to a particular educational institution.

Example

Regarding the 'information and management module' outlined above, consider the information requirements from a parent's perspective. Outline a list of information that you feel should be made available to parents.

Solution

Things to include from a parent's perspective might be 'academic reports', 'special needs reports', 'examination statistics', 'value added statistics', 'tutor's reports', 'special achievements', 'particular problems', 'punishments given out', 'test results', 'individual teacher's marks for homework', 'ICT skills acquired' and 'sporting skills', etc.

A communication requirement example

Continuing with the **management reporting module** considered in the last section, we now look at the main user interface. An **integrated interface** enables users to control the entire management reporting module, and this is shown in Figure 10.3.

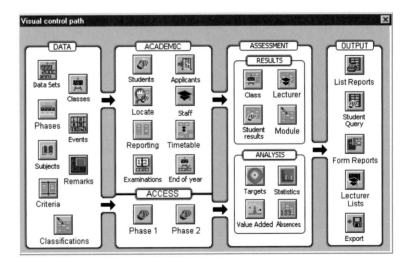

Figure 10.3 The management reporting module's main user interface

As can be seen, the integrated interface is split up into several logical categories, namely 'data', 'academic', 'assessment', 'analysis' and 'output', giving a variety of different users the option of carrying out a number of alternative activities.

Example

Considering the communication requirements of the management information module from a parent's perspective, outline two desirable features that you feel would be of benefit the parents.

Solution

1 It's essential that parents are not excluded from information because they don't have access to the appropriate technology. Therefore, the ability to produce professional standard output in printed form and then send it home via the conventional post will be essential.

2 Many students and parents now have access to computers at home. It's a desirable feature of the system for these people to be able to access this information via the internet. For security reasons this would probably be done via a VPN (virtual private network), which gives parents access to certain information available from the management module. Security would be via a valid user name and password.

The timetable

As another brief example, we now consider some of the **communication requirements** for the timetabling module. Building up a timetable means juggling resources like 'students', 'staff', 'rooms' and 'time', then mixing these up with constraints like 'this subject can't be taught in that room', 'this can't happen at the same time as that' or 'this must happen before that', etc. Part of the interface to program these constraints can be seen in Figure 10.4.

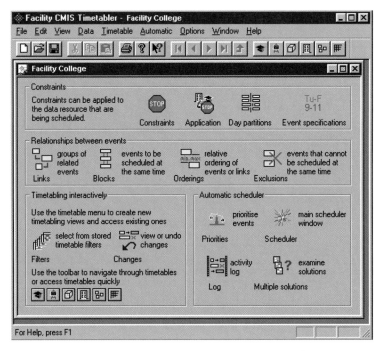

Figure 10.4 The timetable interface showing constraints and other relationships

The timetabling interface shows how users may set up individual constraints and specify events, including those that must happen at the same time and those that can't happen at the same time. It also allows the timetabler to define relationships, create a multiplicity of different views on the data within the timetable, to assign priorities, examine the solutions, to examine impossibilities and view the activities being carried out by the system.

The **communication requirements** for this particular system have obviously been built up over years with a tremendous amount of feedback obtained from prototypes and frequent users of Facility CMIS. If you design your own system, it's unlikely that you would come up with an ideal solution straight away. This is another advantage of an off-the-shelf system compared to a bespoke system built up from your initial specifications.

If you were to specify the communication requirements of the general administrative system, it's likely that you may use a separate timetabling package, or manually draft the timetable. Facility CMIS enables you to integrate these into a single entity, and thus derive benefits from the single-entry data model. If, for example, you have already entered the teaching staff into the administrative system, then you don't have to enter them again into the timetable system. The power of any timetabling system depends on the sophistication of the **algorithmic logic** behind the decision making, and the versatility of the communications interface. Timetabling software has had a bad reputation in the past, but modern systems like Facility CMIS cope with virtually all eventualities.

Web awareness

The Facility CMIS system can be made web aware (can be used via an **intranet** or the **internet**) if the **e-portal module** is purchased. Properly set up, this would enable all the basic **information and communication system requirements** for ordinary users to be satisfied via a web-based interface. You may recall that this was one of the requirements in our original specification. Figure 10.5 shows part of a typical student report viewed via the internet.

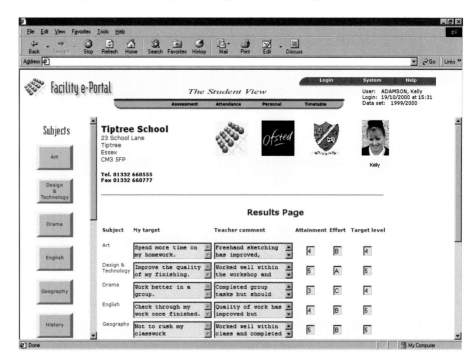

Figure 10.5 A student report accessed via the Facility CMIS web-based interface

The information shown at the top right-hand side of Figure 10.5 shows that Kelly Adamson is viewing her report at 15:31 on 19/10/2000. Typically this could be achieved by logging onto the school **LAN**, or via her home using a **VPN**.

It may seem that using an **intranet** or the **internet** for delivery of some of these systems is a luxury. However, nothing could be further from the truth. Teachers spend a considerable amount of time doing administrative tasks at school. If tasks such as 'examinations entry', 'entering homework marks' or 'writing reports' can be done from home, without the need to transfer this data into the administrative system when the teacher gets back to school, the saving in time alone is considerable.

Other issues

Major **information processing systems** raise **social**, **legal** and **ethical** issues in abundance. Facility CMIS, for example, enables teaching staff to spend more time at home with their families *if* they make use of the e-portal described above. Levels of stress can thus be reduced using this particular method of working, and this is good from a social perspective.

The **economic issues** relating to Facility CMIS may not be as far reaching as other major applications like 'computers in banking' or 'computers in the police force', but the economics of using Facility CMIS from the organisation's perspective is important. Moral, ethical and social issues are more appropriately covered by looking at particular applications similar to those covered in Chapter 12. Nevertheless, the subject specification requires that we consider these issues for *a* major application that you have studied, and we now look briefly at some of the issues raised from the point of view of using Facility CMIS.

Legal ethical and moral issues

Any system which stores **personal data** on a computer is subject to strict **legal controls** under the **Data Protection Act** of 1998 (*see Chapter 12*). The school should ensure that all relevant parts of the Data Protection Act are followed, and staff should be made aware of the consequences of mishandling the system. Some typical **legal**, **ethical** and **moral** issues for **Facility** CMIS (or indeed any database in which pupil information is stored) are as follows:

1 It would be **illegal** for a member of staff to let his or her user name and/or password be known outside of the teaching and administrative staff. This contravenes the **Data Protection Act** as the data must be protected from unauthorised access at all times.

2 A scenario which occasionally happens is that of a pupil asking to use a 'teacher's account' because the pupil has forgotten his or her password. He or she might plead with the teacher because urgent coursework must be printed out. Doing this unsupervised would give this pupil unrestricted access up to the level of security held by this particular teacher. It is **unethical** for the teacher to do this, because he or she is contravening the **Data Protection Act**, which protects data from unauthorised access.

3 A pupil may discover that a member of staff has left a computer system logged on unattended, and failed to lock their machine. The pupil could use this account to access data on the system, up to the level of security held by this errant member of staff. It would be **morally wrong** for the pupil to take this action, and the teacher is at fault because they are contravening the **Data Protection Act**, which protects data from unauthorised access.

4 A member of staff might give a colleague at a different school a copy of the CMIS software so that their school may use it too. This is stealing, and is a breach of the **Copyright Designs and Patents Act** of 1998. All intellectual property is protected in this way, and software is particularly easy to steal especially if it is given away in the way being described here.

5 It is a requirement of the school to store only data that is relevant to the activities being carried out by the school. Data deemed to be in excess of this requirement is unlawful. This includes valid data held on pupils for unusually long periods of time.

6 Parents and pupils have the right, under the **Data Protection Act**, to see information that is stored about them on any computer. They have probably consented to allow the school to use the data stored about them in particular ways when they sign the application forms to join the school.

There are numerous other implications, but the above are adequate for illustrative purposes. The CCM software company is aware of the legal implications of storage of data on its systems, and this is one more reason why using an off-the-shelf package may be preferable compared with writing your own system from scratch. If you are employing a third-party programmer, or getting a company to build a database to your specifications, would they be aware of all the legal implications from the point of view of an educational establishment?

Example

A pupil has deliberately written and injected a new virus into the school computer system, which has now rendered the main database inoperative.

1 **What legislation has the pupil contravened?**

2 **What must the administrator do to recover the situation?**

3 **Should the pupil be expelled for doing this?**

Solution

1 Deliberately injecting a virus into a computer system is in contravention of the Computer Misuse Act (*see Chapter 12*).

2 The administrator should remove the virus from the system, and then restore the database to its pre-virus state using the most recent backup copy. A backup of the system should be made at least once a day, and therefore not too much information will be lost.

3 The pupil has acted in a morally indefensible way. He or she has caused a lot of damage, a vast amount of unnecessary work and broken the law. Expulsion is usually a last resort, used only when all other possible avenues have been explored. However, as a deterrent to others, expulsion would be a serious consideration. It would be catastrophic if others thought they could get away with such a serious offence without receiving the ultimate punishment from the school.

Economic issues

Facility CMIS has economic implications for the school, and some are briefly considered below.

1 **Staff training** in the use of the system must be considered. This might involve some considerable initial expense, not least in terms of the time taken for the person or people who will be responsible for running the system. The skills needed by the technicians, the administrators and the administrative staff should not be underestimated either. Many hours of work will be needed to fully understand any system to the point of being able to use it effectively.

Much information on the development of internet policies can be found on http://www. foruminternet. org/en/ (The/en/ensures that you view the English version of the French-based site.)

2 Has the school considered how the present system will be changed over to the new one? It's most likely that a **parallel system** needs to be run for some time until the school is happy that the new system is working properly. It would be embarrassing for the school to have its main administrative system go down for any length of time. Key areas of the school may be rendered inoperative. The extra expense of running a parallel system should be considered.

3 A **phased implementation** of the new system is most likely. However, if the old member of staff is about to retire, how can we run the old system along with the new one? Perhaps the old member of staff will need to be kept on for a little longer, and a new member of staff might have to be hired to help set up the new system. This could mean that two salaries will have to be paid for a period of time, involving considerable extra expense.

4 If the old system was **manually intensive** (e.g. secretaries typing, correlating, addressing envelopes and printing documents, etc.) there may not be a need for so many administrative staff in the future!

5 If a **standard system** is used, it's likely to be easier to find a manager for maintaining the system. The level of computer literacy (and hence the salary) needed by this person would be considerably less than for an in-house programmer, who may also understand little about the education system.

Self-test questions

1 What is meant by the 'information requirements' and the 'communication requirements' of an information processing application?

2 Consider a typical school administration system, similar to Facility CMIS studied in this chapter.
   (a) Write down five different information requirements for the 'attendance module' (i.e. the module which monitors, records and processes the information on student punctuality and attendance).
   (b) Write down five different communication requirements for the 'attendance module'.
   (c) Suggest ways in which the parents can be informed about continued absence or other problems like lateness.
   (d) How might the communication requirements for the 'attendance module' differ between different target audiences? (How might a teacher's view be different from the view needed by a parent or by a governor?)

3 A typical curriculum at any secondary school should ensure that all pupils achieve a balanced education.
   (a) How might a computerised timetable help to achieve this?
   (b) Typically, what information requirements would need to be fed into the system to achieve a balanced curriculum?
   (c) Let's assume that pupils opt for subjects by filling in a form via the internet. How might the communication requirements of this be affected by the balanced curriculum?

4 An end-of-term reporting system is to be set up for 'parents', 'pupils', 'subject teachers', and 'senior management'.
   (a) Outline some differences that need to be considered when dealing with the information requirements of each class of user.
   (b) How might the communication requirements differ between 'senior management' and a 'subject teacher'?

5 Consider a computer system set up for use in a local medical practice.
  (a) Write down five different information requirements that will need to be considered by the designers of the system.
  (b) Suggest two ways in which the communication requirements of the system might be set up to help print out prescriptions in the reception area automatically (i.e. consider the user-interface needs of this particular system).
  (c) Suggest two social, moral and ethical issues raised by the use of computers in a medical practice.

6 Consider a computer system set up for criminal investigative purposes by the police.
  (a) Assuming that the system is modularised, like the application studied in this chapter, suggest five different modules, outlining the purpose of each.
  (b) Outline two different information system requirements for each of the modules suggested in part (a).
  (c) Suggest two different communication system requirements for each of the modules you have suggested in (a) (i.e. user-interface needs).
  (d) Suggest one advantage and one disadvantage that might apply to this system from a legal, social and ethical perspective.

11 General purpose packages

In this section you will learn about:

- A general purpose package
- Advantages and limitations of a database
- Advantages and limitations of a word processor
- Advantages and limitations of a spreadsheet
- Advantages and limitations of a presentation package
- Advantages and limitations of e-mail

What is a general purpose package?

A general purpose package is a **software application** in which tasks, common to the majority of users are carried out. Typical examples are **word processors**, **databases**, and **spreadsheets**. *All students should be familiar with these packages*. Detailed theory, like relational databases, for example, is covered elsewhere. We now concentrate only on typical uses of these packages, their advantages and limitations. You will then be able to make judgments about the suitability of these applications to any particular task.

It's important to realise the significance of **general purpose packages**. Without computers running these packages, the huge volume of work undertaken each day would not be possible. Indeed, without computers there would probably be a manpower shortage, even if all available workers are employed.

This chapter covers only the principles of general purpose packages. During your course you should make use of these different packages to obtain the skills needed to answer the questions posed in examinations.

Many of the tasks undertaken by a general purpose package are repetitive in nature; such repetition, boring for humans, is ideal to be carried out by a machine. Compared with humans, a computer is often more accurate, has the ability to perform checks automatically, and thus provides a high degree of consistency. The ability of computers to cross-reference data and make use of centrally stored databases makes them a cost effective option. You should not forget that most businesses exist to make a profit; using these packages helps them to do this.

Databases

A database is one of *the* most important general purpose packages. A **database** is crucial to most organisations, mainly because it often *is* the organisation. If a company were to lose information about its customers, lose payment records or lose information about its products, then the company would not survive for long.

A **database** is a collection of data, arranged in such a way as to aid quick and easy storage and retrieval of information. Common operations like 'searching', 'conducting queries' and 'reporting' can be carried out with ease. Databases can range from holding simple information about a, say, 'video collection' to complex information like 'mapping the human genome'.

Small and medium sized databases can be set up with ease making use of software like Microsoft's Access.

General purpose packages make businesses more cost effective. If this were not the case then few companies would make use of them.

Figure 11.1 A Terabyte database stored on disks inside the two large cabinets in the background

Huge databases in industry and commerce, holding staggering amounts of data, are usually set up making use of **SQL servers** available via **LANs**. Very large databases sometimes exceed 1 Tbyte (1 000 000 000 000 bytes) of information, and large SQL servers are able to handle this volume of data. An example is shown in Figure 11.1, where access to the database is via a thin client computer on a local area network running an internet browser.

Information stored in a **database** is not limited to **text** and **numbers**. **Bit–mapped** and **vector** based **graphics**, **audio**, **video** and virtually any other computer-based information can be handled. The database can also link to other general purpose packages like **word processors** and **spreadsheets**. Databases may be customised by using **macro languages** (Microsoft's Access has a macro language called VBA which is very similar to **Visual Basic**), and data from many advanced databases may be processed in a variety of ways using different **high-level languages**.

It is possible to set up many different views of the same database. This is important because different users will have different requirements. Only the accountants, for example, might be granted access to the 'payroll' part of the database and only the personnel officers might be granted access to sensitive 'personal information'. The information viewable by different users would normally be controlled by '**user name**' and '**password**' giving access to resources.

Information may need to be accessed in a variety of forms. We could process data via the **internet** or an **intranet** (via **forms** on a **web browser** like the system being shown in Figure 11.1), via **application packages** like 'office suites', via **PDAs** (Personal Digital Assistants – the small hand-held computers), **Tablet PCs** (like a notebook with a writing pad) and via suitably sophisticated **mobile phones**. Companies regularly make use of databases in this way, keeping their employees in touch with their customers' requirements, even if they are far away from the main office.

Database limitations

It's a complex task to set up a large database, and usually *disastrous* if it goes wrong. Part of good database design should include **disaster recovery**, and **backups** of the database should be instantly available to aid recovery. The disks which store the database are often arranged as a **RAID array** (Redundant Array of Independent Drives). If mirroring is used, this means that a catastrophic failure of a hard drive might not affect the database, and a replacement disk could be swapped over while the computer is still running. However, such techniques do not get over errors caused by the database software or many human errors.

The **information requirements** needed to specify a large database is a daunting task, and building up **specifications** for a company database usually takes a very long time. If the specifications are not produced correctly, certain parts of the database will not operate in the intended ways. Changing fundamental things at a later date, although possible, is usually time consuming and expensive (*see Chapter 10*).

The personnel operating the database perform a crucial role, and organisations are clearly in the hands of these people. Enormous power is given to the **database administrator** who designs and maintains the database. He or she will have the ability to view any information, personal or confidential, that is held in the database, and must therefore be a person of the highest integrity. The potential to misuse the information held in databases is enormous, and legislation (*see Chapter 12*) has been around for some time to protect individuals from this potential threat.

A thin-client computer is one which acts as a terminal on a network. It usually has no local hard disks, no floppy disks and little local processing power other than the ability to display things on the screen. All processing is done via a remote server. These machines are very easy to maintain.

Word processing

The **word processor** is the de-facto standard for the production of text in the home, office, school, college or in industry. Unfortunately, most students are too young to appreciate the hassle of producing type-written text in any other way. In fact students are so used to using a word processor that they think they know everything about them; this is not usually the case. This can be demonstrated by asking a class to write down 30 or 40 different operations that a typical word processor can perform!

A word processor gives an obvious increase in productivity compared to other methods like a 'typewriter' or 'pen and paper'. **Editing** is easier, mistakes can be corrected, **spelling** and **grammar checks** can be undertaken, **thesauruses** consulted and the text is already in **electronic form**, enabling further processing by a variety of other **computer applications**.

As well as the obvious **text formatting** and **text layout** capabilities, modern **word processors** enable you to produce **diagrams**, insert **mathematical equations**, perform **mail merges**, print labels and output to a variety of different media in full colour.

Users of word processors don't appreciate the degree to which systems are customised for a particular organisation. Tasks may be automated using **macro languages** (Microsoft Word uses the **VBA** language for this) and complex **templates** may be set up by experts, ensuring that commonly used documents are instantly available in the appropriate form. Figure 11.2 shows part of a template constructed for designing a postcard and business card. It is available as a download from the Microsoft Word template gallery on the internet.

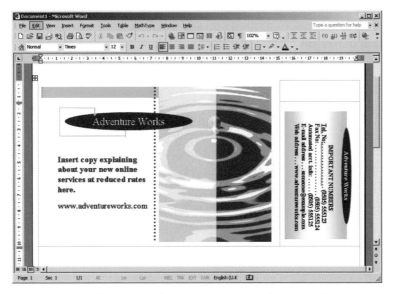

Figure 11.2 Part of a template from Microsoft, set up to produce a form for a shipping company

Visit the Microsoft site, (www.microsoft.com) and look in the Office template gallery.

You will see a variety of different templates for word processors and other general purpose applications.

Never download work from the internet and present it as if it were your own. If you are caught doing this for important examination coursework you are likely to be disqualified from taking all your AS examinations in all subjects.

By making use of **word processors** it's easier to collaborate with others in the production of large documents, even if you are in different parts of the world. A word processor can be linked to information contained in **spreadsheets** and **databases**. It's often possible to hot-link these applications too. An example of this might be somebody changing an entry in a spreadsheet, which automatically changes the data available to a word processor which has a picture of a graph linked to the data. Innovative features like **voice recognition** work rather well, but **language translation** is still in its infancy.

Word processing limitations

A modern word processor is not yet capable of competing with a good **desktop publishing** (or **DTP**) package for laying out complex pages similar to those found in glossy magazines and text books. Try setting up a poster 48 inches by 48 inches in your word processor and you will probably see this particular limitation. Quark Express, for example, one of the top of the range **DTP** packages is able to do this. If you are creating books, glossy magazines, large high-quality posters and the like, then a word processor is usually used to produce the text, which is then imported into a more suitable package to make up the final layout.

You can't expect the simple diagram tools within a typical word processor to compete with a **CAD package** like AutoCad or an **Art package** like Adobe PhotoShop, but you can import these diagrams into a word processor if you export them from the Art or CAD package in an appropriate form.

One major limitation of word processing in schools, colleges and universities is that they encourage students to 'cut and paste' articles and present them as if they were their own. This problem is becoming so common that a national computer has been set up to help lecturers marking coursework to check for possible **plagiarism**. Northumbria University has set up a service (the JISC Plagiarism Service) which helps check work against material on the internet and other electronic sources, and also against material produced by other students!

Spreadsheets

Spend a brief time sufing the internet looking for 'Spreadsheet simulations' or 'Excel Simulations' and you will gain a small insight into the vast number of simulations that are possible making use of this incredibly versatile general purpose package.

Spreadsheet simulations are useful in Science, Engineering, Economics and Mathematics.

All students should make extensive use of a spreadsheet. A **spreadsheet** functions as a tabular arrangement of **cells** into which **labels**, **numbers** and **formulae** may be typed. There are extensive **functions** for **financial**, **statistical** and **mathematical** analysis. The power of a spreadsheet lies in its ability to recalculate when a user changes data, so that powerful **'what if?' scenarios** may be **modelled**. Nevertheless, a spreadsheet is much more powerful than this (see simulations and modelling covered shortly), and is just as important as a database or word processor. Computers are often sold solely for their ability to run a particular spreadsheet.

The spreadsheet has liberated workers from manually calculating accounts, working out solutions to some mathematical problems, and producing graphs and statistics from a variety of data sources. Data may be imported from **word processors**, **databases** and other **electronic sources**, processed and then exported back to the original application and to other applications.

The spreadsheet can generate **pseudo random numbers**, and can thus be set up to perform a variety of simulations ranging from a 'one-arm bandit' (fruit machine) via simulating a 'queuing system in a large retail outlet' to 'modelling stellar densities throughout the cosmos'.

The user interface on a spreadsheet can be customised with graphics so that novice users may not be aware that a spreadsheet is being used. Figure 11.3 shows a simulation, set up by the author, making use of Microsoft's Excel. It is an interactive system showing how fundamental electronic circuits can be set up to add together groups of binary digits. If you have the imagination, a spreadsheet is a versatile **general purpose application**.

Spreadsheet limitations

You must never forget that a spreadsheet is only as good as the mathematical model that you have chosen to use. If the theories on which you are basing your arguments are flawed, then the results will be incorrect. Students unfortunately have a tendency to believe the

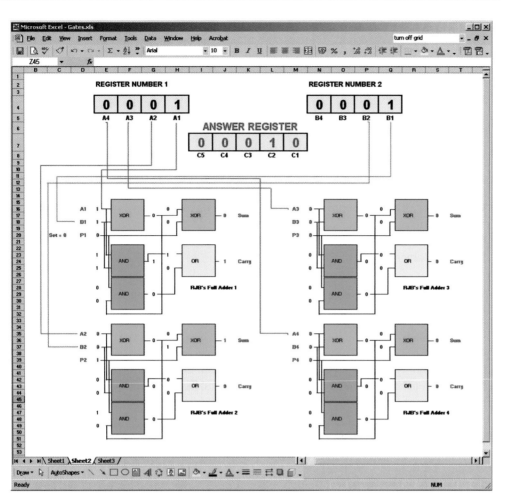

Figure 11.3 An Excel spreadsheet set up to simulate the addition of binary numbers making use of simple electronic circuits

results they get *because* they were obtained 'scientifically' from a spreadsheet. Enormous spreadsheets are possible, but there are obviously physical limits to the size of sheet that can be sensibly used. Also, the precision with which you wish to work out the numbers (number of decimal places, etc.) might not be available, and errors due to limitations of number representations are common.

Example

Different ways exist to exchange data between a word processor, a spreadsheet and a database. Explain several ways of exporting data from *each* package, outlining some advantages and limitations of the use of each of your chosen methods.

Solution

Data from most general purpose packages can be exported to other packages by using a variety of formats. The following are typical ways in which this might be achieved

1 **Word processors**
   Text only may be exported as a text file. This is basically text stored as ASCII or Unicode characters, without any styles and very limited formatting. Although the

text does not get laid out like the original, virtually all packages can handle this simple format.

RTF or Rich Text Format might be available to export text only, together with a variety of styles and formatting. As long as the package receiving the data supports this format and has all the available fonts, a good likeness should result.

Export to other similar applications. The main word processors like Microsoft Word, Lotus Notes and Corel's Word Perfect will often support the exchange of files between each application. However, the version of the software you are using may not be supported by the other package, unless you have the most up-to-date version.

2 **Spreadsheets**

CSV Format – Comma Separated Value format. This format allows values (data items within each cell) to be exported to other applications that support this format. Most spreadsheets and databases do support this and a variety of others like Tab separated values.

Export to other similar applications. The main spreadsheets like Microsoft Excel and Lotus 123 can exchange data in native form, but the version you are using needs to be supported by the other package, or new features used in one package might not be available in the others.

3 **Databases**

CSV Format – Comma Separated Value. This format allows data values (data items held within each field) to be exported to other databases that support this format. Most do.

ODBC – Open Database Connectivity. This format allows data from one database to be directly linked with data in a different type of database. This is more convenient if keeping a link up to date is important. If a CSV export is used, the data must be exported again if the original data changes in any way, with ODBC you don't have to do this.

Presentation packages

Most office suites will normally contain a **presentation package**. Microsoft has PowerPoint and Lotus has Freelance Graphics. Each package enables you to present a dynamic set of *slides* with any type of computer information including **pictures**, **sound**, **video** and **animated media clips**. This general purpose package has largely replaced the Overhead Projector acetate sheets for important lectures at places where a **Projection TV** system is available. It is now rare to see a major business presentation which does not make use of this type of technology.

Sets of **style sheets** (**templates**) enable users to create professional-looking slide shows, which can be customised to have a common corporate look. It's easy to type in text, to cut and paste from the clipboard or to import text and pictures from other applications. Slide presentations may be linked to the **internet** or an **intranet** and to other packages like **spreadsheets**, **databases** and **word processors**.

If you are unhappy with the look of the presentation, it's usually possible to change the style instantly. A number of **effects** for **slide transitions** and **animations** are usually available, many of which can be timed to coincide with music and other effects. It's also possible for the lecturer to make use of infra-red devices to control the presentation. It is useful for a teacher or lecturer to have his or her presentation checked by a colleague, and this can be done very easily by e-mailing the presentation as an attachment.

One possible way of getting a taste of what life might be like at your chosen university is to surf the university site and look at some of the lectures that are available.

Most universities have lectures, produced by a presentation package available on the net.

Many **presentation packages** can be viewed over the **internet** or an **intranet** via a suitable **web browser**. Lectures may be delivered to remote locations, or viewed by students at a later date. Lectures may be delivered to different locations simultaneously, and if an audio link is established the recipients can hear the lecturer too. **Video conferencing** is also possible to get two-way interaction between the lecturer and the students in a class. Many such lectures can be viewed on the internet, as universities have set up thousands in this particular way.

Limitations of presentation packages

With so many people using these packages there is a tendency to see the same style used at many different presentations, and this could lead to boredom. It's therefore essential for a professional company to develop their own **templates** to avoid this major pitfall, which, ironically, is due to the success of these products.

Example

A sales team has a presentation to give to 100 people using a computer-based presentation package. However, the organisation hosting the lecture does not have the necessary equipment to support this method of working. Suggest a suitable list of hardware and software that must be taken in order to ensure success.

Solution

A portable computer, portable projection TV system and a portable screen will be required. From experience, a long mains extension lead is also necessary! The portable will need appropriate software like Lotus Freelance Graphics or Microsoft's PowerPoint, together with the actual slide show installed on the machine.

E-mail packages and schedule organisation

E-mail is now the *preferred method of communication* for many organisations. This change to the 'normal' way of working has had a staggering impact on the efficiency with which internal and external memos and communications can be sent. A general purpose e-mail package like Microsoft's Outlook Express enables novices to create accounts and send or receive e-mail to and from anywhere in the world. **Address books** into which contacts are put are easily maintained, and user-friendly names can be used as **aliases** for real **e-mail addresses**.

By making use of e-mail it's much easier to keep track of who has asked you to do what, and also to keep track of the replies that you have sent. Most e-mail users would not want to return to the days of keeping photocopies of letters sent to colleagues to verify that you have said or done a particular thing. E-mail **inboxes** and **sent folders** can be used as **filing cabinets**, with the e-mail software able to search on real e-mail addresses, aliases or e-mails containing certain text. Each e-mail is time and date stamped too.

Attachments ranging from 'pictures', 'text' and 'videos' via 'application documents' and even 'applications themselves' can be sent. We are thus able to share anything on our computer at the touch of a button with anyone else anywhere in the world, assuming they have a computer and access to the **internet**. This degree of communication was not available before the advent of e-mail. E-mail is an enormously useful general **purpose application** package used by tens of millions of people worldwide.

Authentication of e-mail

A **digital identification** (**ID**) can be obtained from an authority like VeriSign. A digital ID is made up from three parts – a **public key** and a **private key** (see **encryption** methods in Chapter 12), plus a **digital signature**. You can digitally sign an e-mail (called a digital signature) making use of a package like Microsoft's Outlook. Your **digital signature** and **public key** combine to make what's called a **digital certificate**.

Others may use your digital certificate to verify your e-mails. They can use your public key to send encrypted e-mail messages to you. Only you can read these messages because only you have the private key needed to unlock the encryption. If you wish to make extensive use of digital certificates you will obviously need a different digital certificate from each person with whom you wish to communicate in this way, and these certificates are usually stored in your address book along with the person's e-mail address. If you have set this system up, it's still possible to compose e-mail messages without using digital signatures.

Limitations of e-mail

If you want more sophistication in the corporate environment, Microsoft Outlook is far superior to Outlook Express, in which it is harder to set up things like '**simultaneous e-mails**' to large groups of people. Many basic e-mail packages also don't support a corporate way of working in which **diary** and **calendar information** can be shared among groups of people in different departments within an organisation.

Some **ISPs** will put a **limit** on the amount of information that can be sent in an **e-mail attachment**, with several Mbytes being the norm. Messages above this limit can be rejected by the server, and returned to the sender. Any large files might therefore have to be sent using the **FTP** (file transfer protocol) system.

A system of **authentication** making use of certificates is needed to be sure that the e-mail you are receiving is actually from the person who appears to be sending it.

The amount of **spam** (unwanted e-mail or junk mail) can be enormous, especially if pupils at school visit sites on the web set up by unscrupulous people (*see Chapter 12*).

Limitations on all general purpose packages

All **software**, including **databases**, **word processors** and **spreadsheets**, will have limitations. Without an infinite amount of primary and secondary storage in your computer you are limited regarding the size of file that you can process at any one time. Each package will have limitations, for example the maximum number of rows and columns in a spreadsheet or the maximum page size in a word processor. You might be limited by the number of colours that can be used simultaneously, or with several niggling little problems which might mean that the software does not allow you to do what you want in the exact way that you would wish to do it.

The above problems don't include the thousands of **bugs** (errors in the programming) normally resident within any large application suite. Some of these bugs may be so esoteric that the majority of users will never encounter them. **Service packs** are usually available for most applications, and these cure most known bugs.

Many application packages like **word processors**, **spreadsheets**, **desk top publishing packages** and **presentation packages** can export files in a form suitable for the **web** (**html files**), but the code produced by these exports, although clever, is not usually as good as pages created in a proper web site creation package.

Self-test questions

1 List ten different things that each of the following packages can do. Make sure that you don't list things that are common to all packages like 'saving work to disk', or trivially obvious like 'entering text'. Don't use the same thing more than once (e.g. if a spelling checker has been used for a word processor, don't use it again).
   (a) Database
   (b) Word processor
   (c) Spreadsheet
   (d) Presentation package
   (e) e-mail

2 Describe what is meant by the term 'mail merge' when using a word processing package. How might data be extracted from a database so that a mail merge operation could be carried out using a word processor?

3 Using a template is common when word processing. Suggest a typical use for a template in an office. What attributes are likely to be controlled by a template?

4 Spreadsheets can be used to model a variety of 'what if?' scenarios. What is meant by this statement? Give a typical example of something that could be modelled in this way.

5 A one arm bandit or fruit machine with three windows is to be simulated using a spreadsheet. Explain how some of the features like showing different pictures in the windows, generating 'what combinations of fruit will win' and simulating 'pulling a handle' might be achieved in practice.

6 Queries and reports are common database operations. Give an example of each for a hypothetical database of your choice.

7 Explain how it's possible to give different users different views of the same database. How are they prevented from accessing parts of the database to which they should have no access?

8 Teachers at a school want to set up a system of writing reports using a word processor. However, the reports must be viewable only by the appropriate parents over the internet. Explain, in principle, how a database might be used to help solve this problem.

9 Suggest the type of hardware and software that would be needed to deliver an interactive lecture simultaneously to groups of students in different parts of the world.

10 Give three reasons why e-mail has revolutionised the ways in which some people communicate. More e-mails are now sent each day than conventional letters. Will e-mail ever replace the normal post?

11 Software purchase on-line is now common. It's possible, by using a credit card, to purchase, install and use a new software package within minutes of making the decision. Explain the crucial part e-mail often plays in using this particular method of purchase.

12 Explain why some people may want to digitally sign e-mail communications. How might they be open to forgery if this is not done?

13 Consider the following tasks. State, with reasons, which general purpose package/s you would use to undertake each one, clearly stating any assumptions that you make.
   (a) The analysis and production of end-of-term examination statistics for a school containing 1000 pupils. Separate sets of statistics are needed for each parent, and a complete set for the 75 staff at the school.
   (b) Sending out a personalised Christmas card to all customers who have eaten a meal in a particular restaurant.
   (c) Arrange a critical software update for 7000 employees who work all over the world.

12 Social, economic and ethical consequences

In this section you will learn about:

- What is meant by ethics and morality regarding the use of computers
- Responsible computer use policies in the workplace and at school
- Developing ethical and moral arguments using brainstorming and bubble charts
- Encryption, privacy and the use of computers
- Monitoring software and privacy
- Legislation governing the use of computers

Introduction

In computing you are expected to be able to make reasoned judgements about the **moral**, **social**, **ethical** and **economic** consequences of the *current use* of computers. You should be able to do this in relation to **employment**, **government**, **education** and **leisure**. You are also expected to be up to date with some of the legal implications, especially in terms of 'ownership of information', 'protection of data', and 'privacy'. One of the best ways to do this is by having discussions with your colleagues in class, and the following sections outline many of the topics which may be taken much further as a group activity.

Ethics and morality

Morality is basically 'standards of behaviour' or 'concrete activities' that are regarded as 'acceptable' by civilised people. You should appreciate that 'standards of morality' or 'what is right or wrong' in one country may not apply in another, and this provides for a rich source of discussion (*see ethics*). In computing examinations you should not make the assumption that Western standards of morality are necessarily right, and other standards are necessarily wrong. General humanitarian standards of morality would normally be assumed as a good starting point. It is assumed that you uphold the values of human welfare; namely things like 'not murdering people', 'not stealing', 'respecting other people's privacy' or 'respecting other people's different points of view'.

Ethics is the science of moral order. It is a philosophical study of how morality affects people's behaviour. It is thus the theory of moral values or moral philosophy, or what the moral order ought to be. Computer scientists, doctors, engineers and many other professions have ethical obligations to make sure that the work they are doing does not contravene the rules governing their profession. It's unethical for a doctor, for example, to divulge confidential patient information, or for a database administrator to divulge information to which he or she has access. In either case the person concerned would probably be sacked for such an offence, because it is a breach of confidentiality.

Social and economic consequences

It's relatively easy to outline social and economic consequences of the use of computers. Don't fall into the trap of making bland statements like 'Computers are taking over the World' or 'Computers are putting everybody out of work' because these will get you no marks. There are always points for and against the use of computers, and the best way to carry out the group activities described above is to practise both sides of an argument.

The best way to get group discussions going is to set up two teams per topic. One team argues for a particular idea and the other argues against it. It's good practice to argue for something with which you disagree!

Where to start?

Whole books are written on these topics, but you need concentrate only on the use of computers, and how they relate to the topics just covered. Some ideal topics for fruitful discussions are shown in Table 12.1.

Table 12.1 Some possible discussion topics on ethics, morality, economic and social consequences

Possible topics	Areas likely to be covered	Typical routes that can be taken
(1) Have computers helped or hindered children's education in the UK?	Education	Social, economic
(2) Has the internet been a power for good or for evil?	Leisure, education	Social, economic, moral, ethical
(3) Should encryption be generally available to all?	Government	Social, moral, ethical
(4) Computers – have they caused unemployment or created more employment?	Employment	Social, economic, moral, ethical
(5) Computer games – should children be allowed to play them or not?	Leisure, education	Social, moral, ethical, economic
(6) Computers are a threat to our privacy. Is this statement true or false?	Government	Social, moral, ethical
(7) People are under increasing stress because they can easily be reached using e-mail.	Leisure	Social, moral, ethical
(8) Computer viruses, hacking and spam are making computers more difficult to use. What can be done about this problem?	Leisure, government, education	Social, moral, ethical

Making a plan

When presenting an argument you need to make a **plan**. I suggest that each group or individual undertakes a **brainstorming session**, where all things related to a topic can be jotted down, irrespective of whether they will be used or not.

Computer gaming as an example

Taking topic number 5 in Table 12.1 as an example, we could brainstorm the **social**, **moral**, **ethical** and **economic** consequences of **computer games** in **leisure** and **education**. The **bubble diagram** in Figure 12.1 outlines some possible ideas.

To develop the discussion further, we take a couple of bubbles at random. Starting with 'Addiction', it's clear that computer games can be addictive, as anyone who has played a game in which they are interested will confirm. Addiction means 'a total dependence on something', and this probably means that the individuals concerned are gaming to the detriment of other parts of their lives. Is their work suffering? Are they being excluded socially? Are they living a suitably balanced life? This can lead to a discussion upholding moral values, usually those held by the society in which the student lives.

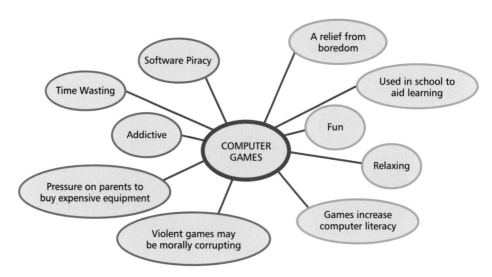

Figure 12.1 A brainstorm related to the topic of computer games

On the positive side of gaming there is a massive leisure industry, worth billions of pounds each year, employing thousands of people in various industries involved in the development, production and distribution industries. You have only to look at the credits for a major game to see that many people, ranging from artists to programmers are intimately involved. Games also have a beneficial effect, and can actually enhance a student's ability to work well. Most students will have experienced being fatigued after studying for hours. An hour of intense computer gaming can refresh and revitalise, because the mind is totally removed from any problems with the work you were undertaking.

Whole essays with arguments and counter arguments can be developed for each of the topics listed in Table 12.1. It is suggested that you develop the games ideas outlined above in more depth, and try to come to some conclusion regarding the original question 'Should children be allowed to play them?' You will probably end up putting conditions under which they should be allowed to play, and should thus have developed a well balanced argument.

Encryption technology

A popular strong encryption algorithm is Phil Zimmerman's PGP or Pretty Good Privacy. It's available from pgp.com on the web.

For thousands of years humans have tried to get secret messages from point A to point B without others intercepting them. The main problem was getting the key used to decipher the message to the recipient without it being intercepted. This problem was solved relatively recently using the **public key encryption system** shown in Figure 12.2.

Cryptographers like to use people called '**Alice**' at point A, '**Bob**' at point B and '**Eve**' as the person who likes to **eavesdrop** on messages being sent from A to B. Figure 12.2 shows that Eve has illegally intercepted the encrypted message from Alice to Bob, and also has a copy of Bob's **public key**. This does not matter, however, because the message to Bob can only be decrypted by using Bob's **private key**. Only Bob has a copy of this, and he has never sent it to anyone else. This clever system got over the age old problem of the distribution of the keys necessary to decrypt the message.

Encryption and privacy

To the casual observer, the **public key encryption** system shown in Figure 12.2 does not seem too revolutionary, but nothing could be further from the truth. The problem arises

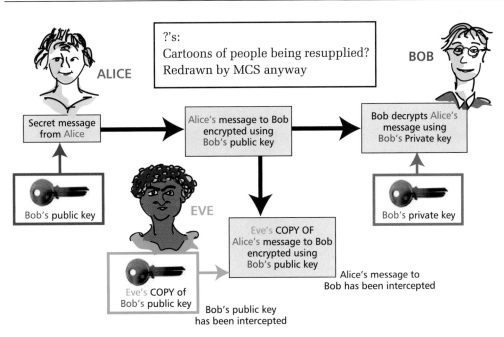

Figure 12.2 The public key encryption system in operation

from using **strong encryption** that is now easily available to all. **Strong encryption** means that it's virtually impossible to crack the codes, even if you have access to banks of powerful supercomputers like those available to the CIA or MI5. These computers, guessing possible codes at rates of millions of guesses each second, could take longer than the universe has been in existence to crack **strong encryption** algorithms.

We therefore end up with a system where anybody, including criminals, terrorists and legitimate users can send secret messages to each other which can't be deciphered by any government organisation. This is absolutely fabulous for privacy, but unfortunately hinders the fight against terrorists, drug traffickers, child pornographers and others who make use of computers to carry out illegal activities. On the positive side, oppressed people living in countries under dictatorships could use this method of communication, and the brutal governments would not be able to decipher the message. Don't forget the guiding principles under which we should be operating regarding moral judgements. One person's terrorist might be regarded as a freedom fighter in the eyes of others.

Until very recently **strong encryption** was regarded as a '**munition**' (a weapon of war) by the US government, and is still illegal in many countries, including France. If you are caught using encryption in some countries you could be imprisoned. The British government have also considered legislation as to whether it should be outlawed, and the outcome of this is unknown at the time of writing. When mobile phones were in the development stages, the British government prevented strong encryption methods from being used inside them, instead opting for use of weaker encryption methods. The big problem with legislation on this matter is that criminals, already in possession of strong encryption methods, would obviously not stop using them because it's illegal.

Privacy and the general use of computers

There are always two sides to an argument, and using computers from within a school environment offers a rich source of suitable material on which these arguments can be based. For example, should students be allowed total privacy at school when using computers? From a student's perspective the answer is obviously yes. However, from a legal perspective, teachers are in 'loco parentis'. This means that they are in charge of the pupils while they are at school, and are therefore ethically obliged to act as a responsible parent would if an under-age pupil is using a computer at home. We have a moral obligation to make sure that we block access to chat rooms and other sites where adults can lure children into inappropriate relationships.

It's physically impossible for teachers to observe what pupils are doing, especially with hundreds of computers and thousands of users. It's therefore necessary to have an **agreed policy** and make sure that the students stick to it. The policy at the author's school is as follows, but most responsible schools would have something very similar.

Table 12.2 The computer-use regulations in force at the author's school

Topic	Specific advice
(1) Personal safety	You should not post contact information about yourself or other people to public forums. Contact information includes school and home addresses, telephone and pager numbers.
	You should promptly tell your teacher about any message you receive that contains inappropriate language or enclosures or makes you feel uncomfortable in any way.
(2) Illegal activities	You should not attempt to go beyond your authorised access. This includes attempting to log in through another person's account, sending e-mail while masquerading as another person, or accessing another person's files in their directory.
	You should not make deliberate attempts to disrupt the computer system or destroy data by, for example, spreading computer viruses or altering the configuration of the system.
(3) System security	You are responsible for your individual account and should take all reasonable precautions to prevent others from being able to use your account. Under no circumstances should you provide your password to another person, and if you suspect that someone knows your password, change it immediately. In any circumstances, you should change your password at least once a term.
(4) Inappropriate language	Restrictions against inappropriate language apply equally to e-mail messages, newsgroup messages, and material posted onto and downloaded from Web pages.
	You should not use indecent, obscene, offensive, or threatening language.
	You should not post information that could cause damage or a danger of disruption.
	You should not engage in personal, prejudicial, or discriminatory attacks.
	You should not harass another person. Harassment is persistently acting in a manner that distresses or annoys another person. If you are told by a person to stop sending messages to them, you must immediately stop.
	You should not knowingly or recklessly send or post false or defamatory information about a person.
(5) Respect for privacy	You should not re-post a message that was sent to you privately without permission of the person who sent you the message.
	You should not post private information about another person.

Table 12.2 *Continued*

Topic	Specific advice
(6) Respecting resource limits	You should not download large files unless absolutely necessary. If necessary, you should download the file at a time when the system is not being heavily used.
	You should not send annoying or unnecessary messages to a large number of people. This is sometimes called spamming, and usually consists of pages of jokes or virus warnings, which are widely circulated. Dealing with these messages wastes time and system resources.
	You should check your e-mail frequently and delete unwanted messages promptly.
(7) Plagiarism and copyright	You should not plagiarise works that you find on the internet. Plagiarism is taking the ideas or writings of others and presenting them as if they were your own.
	You should respect copyright. Copyright infringement occurs when you inappropriately reproduce a work that is protected by a copyright. If you are unsure whether or not you can use a work, you should request permission from the copyright owner.
(8) Access to inappropriate material	You should not use school computers to access material that is profane or obscene, that advocates illegal acts, violence, or discrimination towards other people.
	If you mistakenly access inappropriate information, you should immediately tell your teacher. This will protect you against the accusation that you have intentionally accessed this material.
	Your parents or guardians should instruct you if there is other material that they think it would be inappropriate for you to access. The school fully expects that you will follow your parents' or guardians' instructions in this matter.
(9) Privacy	You should expect only limited privacy in the contents of your personal files on the school system. The system administrators, your Housemaster, and your parents or guardians have the right at any time to request access to your school directory. As a general rule, keep nothing on the system you would feel uncomfortable justifying in front of your parents, your Housemaster, or the Headmaster.
	Routine monitoring of the school's system or a search of your files conducted on reasonable suspicion may lead to the discovery that you have infringed this Policy, the school rules, or the law. In such cases appropriate action will be taken. (*This is on a separate document* – the author does not wish to publish school policies on this issue.)
(10) Personal responsibility	When you are using the school's system, you may think that it is easy to break these rules without the risk of detection. You should realise that whenever you use a network you leave an electronic trace that can subsequently be followed.
(11) Software piracy	The School has a responsibility under the terms of its software contracts to make sure that no unlicensed software is used on the school machines. Such software can contain damaging viruses, and software companies, aware that pupils in schools steal millions of pounds worth of applications and games every year, have been prepared to prosecute both schools and individuals.

Implementation of these policies in practice

Because of **legal** and **moral** obligations to the pupils and parents, schools should take reasonable precautions by **filtering internet sites** that are deemed **illegal** or **unsuitable** for pupils under 18 years old. You can also control 'where', 'when' and 'who' has access to the internet.

Any machine on a **LAN** can be granted access or denied access to the **internet** by IP address, and any pupil may be granted or denied access to the internet by **user name**. Both of these functions can be timed, and whole clusters of machines can be granted or denied access to the internet during lessons at the flick of a switch. At the bottom of Figure 12.3 are the controls for '**SurfControl's SuperScout**' running on an **ISA server** over a **LAN**. This allows the school to make use of a 'list of internet sites', produced by this company, which most schools would deem unsuitable. Any site on this list will not display, and the user is prompted with a message that they have been blocked by SuperScout. In addition to this an *entry is made in a log*, listing the **site**, **user name**, **time** and **machine number**. The invasion of privacy issue must be weighed against the responsibility in law to protect pupils from accessing unsuitable material and making sure pupils are adhering to the rules.

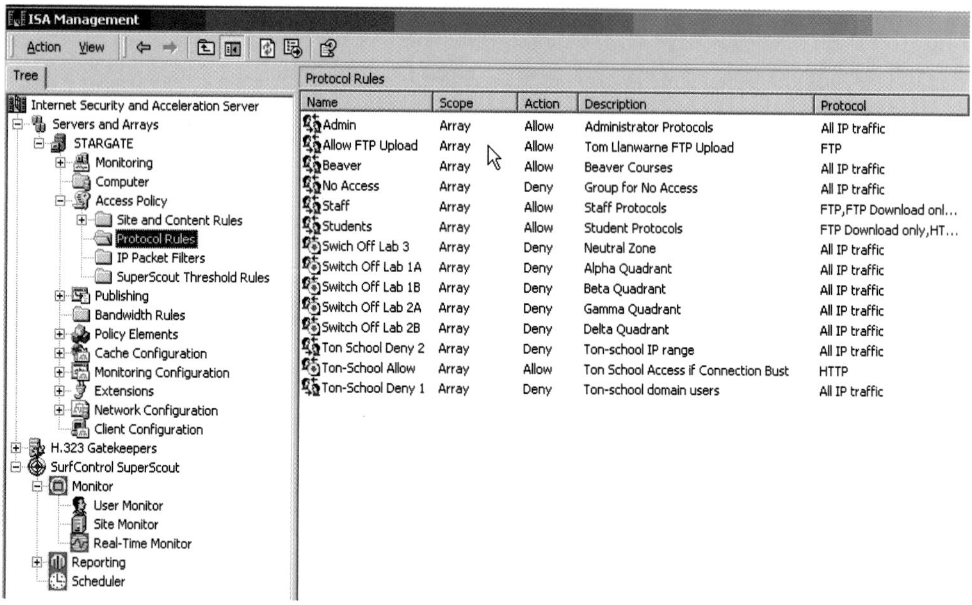

Figure 12.3 Microsoft's Internet Security and Acceleration (ISA) Server with SurfControl SuperScout

The system is not foolproof, and the list produced by the company is updated frequently. However, any school brought to a court of law could justifiably say that they have done all that's sensibly and economically possible.

Example

Many parents know little about using computers, and are blissfully unaware of what their children might have been doing on the internet. Make a short list of a few simple things that a parent could do to view recent information.

Solution

A variety of simple things can be done from pressing the 'back button' on the browser, to looking at the browser's history files or searching in the 'temporary internet files' directory.

SurfControl is available from http://www. surfcontrol.com.

Take a look to see typical features and the issues raised.

Privacy and Policy Central

The internet misuse issue is largely handled by the ISA server and **SurfControl's SuperScout**, but other rules remain that should not be breached. The rules about 'inappropriate language' not being used on school machines, is a good example. **Policy Central** monitors all **keyboard strokes**, **incoming e-mail** and **other material**. It reports 'words', 'sentences' or 'phrases' that are deemed unsuitable. The odd swear word is probably inevitable, but gross misconduct and continued use of bad language can easily be picked up in this way.

It could be argued that organisations using **Policy Central** are spying on every single thing that users do. However, this is not the case, because *only illegal activities are logged*. Users who are using the system appropriately have no record of what they have done, but those who use it inappropriately have large entries in the log files.

The system has to be used with care and attention, and needs close integration with **anti spam software** (*see later*). Some students inevitably get signed up for inappropriate sites by 'friends' using computers at home because they think it's amusing to do so. Some unscrupulous sites operate polices that come into action if users attempt to click on a button that is supposed to unsubscribe you from a list. Instead of unsubscribing, you get subscribed to many other similar ones instead! If students have hundreds of inappropriate e-mails, then this is usually what's happened.

What about human rights?

At the same time as the **Human Rights Act** came into force in the UK, the **Regulation of Investigatory Powers Act** made it unlawful to intercept e-mails and other communications over public or private networks without lawful authority, or without the permission of both parties sending the communications. However, the government recognised that this would prevent monitoring misuse of facilities in the workplace and similar institutions, and thus gave employers and schools the right to monitor communications in the workplace *without the consent of the people concerned*, provided that it is for a variety of reasons, which as far as schools are concerned, include the following:

- preventing unauthorised use of computers and the telephone system
- ensuring that the employees or students are not breaching the policies on the use of computers, the internet or e-mail.

It is up to the employer or school to inform the employees or pupils that the computers and e-mails might be monitored. This is made clear in the computing rules (*rule 9 in Table 12.1*), which are signed by the students and parents. It is also made clear on the school's intranet site. Few parents would disagree with this process, and the **Policy Central software** outlined in the last section ensures that only illegal or abusive activities are monitored. Such software is essential because staff neither have the time nor the inclination to look at e-mail or other communications belonging to other people. However, we have **moral** and **legal** obligations to make sure that reasonable polices are enforced, and to ensure that the system is not being misused in a variety of ways.

Using unlicensed applications

So far we have not covered the illegal use of software applications within an institution. Software called **AppSense** can monitor all software being run, and if the software is not on an approved list, then users will be denied access to it. This is useful for schools and colleges wishing to prevent students from downloading software from the internet, installing

Policy Central is available from http://www. securitysoft.com.

There are many legal issues covered on this site which are worth reading.

The Regulation of Investigatory Powers act can be found at http:// www.hmso.gov.uk/ acts/acts2000/ 20000023.htm.

However, it's far easier to read the legal implications parts of the Policy Central web site.

The Copyright, Designs and Patents Act can also be found on http://www. hmso.gov.uk.

it and illegally running it on their machines. It also prevents software from being illegally installed from a floppy disk, CD-ROM, memory sticks or DVD, etc. If students have not paid for the software this is contrary to the **Copyright Designs and Patents Act of 1998**, which protects intellectual property rights.

The standard security found in operating systems is usually concerned only with protecting data, and is thus lacking the necessary features to prevent users from installing and running games and other software not intended to be part of the system. Users often breach security by attempting to install things into the temporary directories. Network managers can't deny users access to these directories, because many applications would not run if this was done.

The **Policy Central software** outlined previously can also be set up to monitor **illegal software installation** (i.e. installation of software by anyone other than a bone fide administrator). Therefore, if a student *is* successful in installing an illegal application, an entry is made in one of our logs, and the student is chased up by the computer department at a later stage.

Viruses

A **computer virus** is a computer program written specifically to infect a computer once the virus code is executed. If a computer becomes infected, the program attaches itself to other programs and **replicates** itself to other computers via the **internet, e-mail, macros** in application software, **boot sectors** on disks and a variety of other mechanisms. A good topic for moral and ethical values might be to consider the reasons why people write viruses. What would be a suitable punishment for causing billions of pounds worth of expenditure on virus protection and repairing infected machines?

The effect of a computer virus can range from 'silly messages on the screen' to 'annoying effects' to 'catastrophic deletion of important data'. There are even **hoax viruses** causing unsuspecting people to unnecessarily delete important files! Much hassle is caused to computer users, both by the effects of the viruses and the precautions that must be taken to ensure that your computer is less likely to become infected. Good advice includes the following:

- Install an **anti-virus package** on your computer and scan your computer regularly
- Keep your anti-virus software up to date – check frequently for updates
- When downloading from the internet, make sure you only use reputable sites
- Never open an e-mail attachment from an unknown source
- Never reply to spam e-mails
- Always keep a backup of your important work in case you do get infected.

Spam

Spam is the equivalent to **junk mail**. This might not sound too much of a social problem but it is becoming so. Vast quantities of unsolicited mail are sent out each day, many of them containing **viruses** and some subscribing you to **illegal** or inappropriate activities. When you purchase goods on the net or when you visit a variety of sites, never sign up to receiving junk mail *unless* you really are interested in being updated about what you are reading. Unscrupulous sites will pass these lists onto others and you could find that you are receiving hundreds of spam mails each day, many of which are difficult, if not impossible to block, even if your e-mail system allows you to do this. The problem is now becoming so great that companies like Microsoft are spending huge amounts of money in trying to block spam from e-mail systems like MSN hotmail.

Example

The computer policies in operation at many schools might seem restrictive, and some pupils think they impinge on their personal privacy far too much. Write a *short* account *from the school's perspective* as to why it's sensible to have a policy like that at the author's school (*shown in Table 12.1*).

Solution

Institutions failing to control systems are open to a wide range of abuse. Failing to limit the amount of space allocated to each user would render the system inoperative when disks become full. Failing to monitor internet activities could lead to possible criminal prosecution if pupils are carrying out illegal activities from within the school. Failure to monitor installation of illegal software may lead to fines imposed on the school, and failure to monitor incoming e-mails for viruses could render the system inoperative.

Failure to monitor for misuse of computers in more general ways could lead to complaints from parents making embarrassing accusations that the school seems to have little or no knowledge of what pupils get up to when making use of the school system. In short, any school that fails to have a suitable written policy, effectively implemented leaves itself open to civil and criminal prosecutions.

Legislation

You need to be aware of **legal documentation** regarding the use and abuse of computer systems. This should include the **protection of data** and **programs**. The legal system finds it difficult to keep pace with the fast changing technologies, but over the last ten years many legal structures have been put in place to protect individuals and companies.

The Data Protection Act 1998

Originally introduced in 1987, and revised in 1998, the **Data Protection Act** legislates to protect information about individuals held on a computer system. In a nutshell the act provides for the following:

- The data should be processed fairly and lawfully.
- The data should not be used for any other purpose.
- The data shall be adequate and relevant.
- The data shall be accurate and kept up to date.
- The data shall not be kept for longer than necessary.
- The data shall be protected from unauthorised access.
- The data shall not be transferred outside the EEC unless the country concerned complies with the act.
- The person about whom the data is stored must have given their consent.

In addition to the above, the user about whom the data has been stored has the right to examine the data and demand it to be changed if there are errors.

The UK Patents Office can be found at the following web address:

http:// www.patent.gov.uk/ links/index.htm

Information about intellectual property can be found at the following address:

http:// www.intellectual- property.gov.uk/

Example

Why is it necessary to have an act like the Data Protection Act 1998? Give an example of a right that a user has under this act, and how this legal right might be useful in practice.

Solution

Before the Data Protection Act people had no legal redress as to how information stored about them in computer systems was used. Before the use of large-scale data processing and the internet, information held about individuals in filing cabinets in different locations was difficult to process and correlate. With computer systems this is now easy, and large dossiers can be built up on individuals and transferred to other organisations. Financial institutions might refuse to grant funding based on incorrect information stored on a computer by a credit reference agency. For a small fee, an individual now has a right to examine the information, and get it changed if it happens to be in error.

The Computer Misuse Act

Until the **Computer Misuse Act** was passed, the only crime committed by **hackers** was that of stealing electricity from the company into which they might have hacked. This act formally makes it a crime to illegally gain access to information held in computer systems to which you should have no access. The act also makes it illegal to deliberately inject a **virus** into a computer system.

The Copyright Designs and Patents act

Software and **multimedia** are regarded as **Intellectual Property** (**IP**). This means that those who write computer programs or design games, etc. have the same rights as those who have invented a physical object. **Copyright** means granting rights to those who have written software, thus allowing it to be used only in certain well defined ways, and subject to restrictions regarding making illegal copies. Anyone who wishes to make copies must get permission from the person who owns the copyright. A **patent** can also be filed to prevent others manufacturing virtually identical products, including hardware and software. However, a patent only applies to the territories in which it is granted. Thus separate patents will have to be taken out in the UK and USA, for example. A patent will only last for a limited period of time, but this is quite long.

European Legislation

Much information on the development of internet policies can be found on http:// www.foruminternet. org/en/ (The /en/ ensures that you view the English version of the French-based site.)

There is now a surfeit of **European legislation** on **computers** and **e-commerce**. With electronic commerce taking off, a huge amount of legislation is needed to make sure that everything from the protection of credit-card numbers to the privacy of the individual using the internet is covered. The web site shown in the margin entry is a mine of information on this issue, with hundreds of links to relevant sites. Some of the issues covered by part of the site dealing with law and e-commerce are as follows:

Distance selling	Electronic signatures	IPR software
Internet management	Electronic contract	Taxation
IPR copyright	IPR databases	
IPR semiconductors	Privacy	
Legal documents	IPR (Intellectual Property Rights)	

As you can see from the shortened list, hundreds of documents on European Legislation exist, and you should be aware of the main points covered, such as **security of information**, **intellectual property rights**, privacy, **taxation issues**, and **validation of authentication** (electronic signatures in e-mail – *see Chapter 11*).

Example

Suggest three legal issues that may arise when using e-commerce.

Solution

1 Goods, legally obtained in one country, may not be legal in another. Typical examples might include pornography, illegal imports such as ivory, and the acquisition of firearms or illegal software.

2 Intellectual property rights may not be observed in some countries. For example, in the Far East, pirated software can be obtained illegally and ordered via the net.

3 Much software needs serial numbers to be entered. Unscrupulous web sites publish the serial numbers for thousands of items of software. If you have an illegal copy of the software, some of these numbers might enable you to operate it illegally.

Make sure that you keep reading the computer press, and are aware of current legislation and ethical issues.

Self-test questions

1 Why might it not be a good idea to introduce high-tech solutions in a third-world country? Give arguments for and against this view.
2 What ethical issues might have to be argued if computers ever become intelligent?
3 Computers are addictive. Outline a typical scenario in which this could be true, saying what you would possibly do to overcome the problem.
4 Pupils learn more effectively by using computers. Outline a case for keeping teachers.
5 Suggest six different ways in which computers might be misused in the workplace.
6 What legislation is in place to protect individuals from the misuse of data held about them on computers?
7 How might it be possible to collect tax from internet transactions?
8 List some areas in which modern European legislation affects computers and their use.
9 Suggest three areas of ethical concern regarding computers.
10 Can privacy be maintained without compromising security?

13 File organisation and structure

In this section you will learn about:

- What a file is, and different types of files, like binary or text files
- Serial, sequential, indexed sequential and direct (or random) access files
- Fixed and variable length records, and estimating the size of a file
- Hierarchical file structures
- Using hashing to calculate the addresses at which data may be stored

Files and information

A **file** is a *collection of related information*. The name derives from an office filing cabinet. Computer files come in different forms, some can be read by humans (called **text files**), but many cannot (called **binary files**). Binary files usually consist of computer data, coded such that they are easily read by a computer. A file can be a computer program, or it might be data in an appropriate form that can be read by a computer program. *Files form the basic units of storage* on **secondary** media like **disks** and **tape**.

Files used for **data processing** are made up from a collection of **records**. It is easy to visualise a 'record', and one from Microsoft's demonstration database is shown in Figure 13.1. It contains personal information like 'Address', 'City' and some general comments. Take note of the controls at the bottom of Figure 13.1, enabling the user to manually sequence through all of the records in the file. Each record is further divided into sections called **fields**. In the record-card layout shown here, different boxes contain field information like 'City' and 'Phone'. A field is subdivided into **individual characters**.

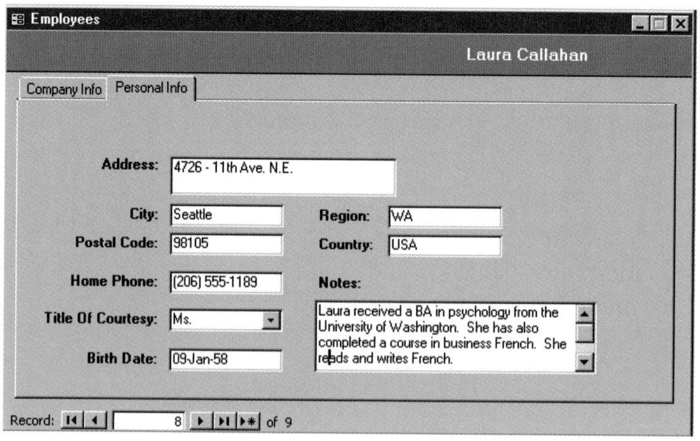

Figure 13.1 Example record card.

A **key field** identifies a record. For an employee database, employee ID is a good choice. The use of 'name' as key field is not as good, because the key field has to be unique. This unique field is often called the **primary key field**. This is to distinguish it from other key fields, which need not necessarily be unique. These other fields are called **secondary key fields**, and may be used to identify people in different departments, for example. A primary **key field** may be used as an **index**, so that records may be quickly located. Secondary key fields could be used to index other information, or used to sort subsets of data. Names, for example, could be sorted alphabetically within each department.

Example

A file is to be set up containing ID number, surname, first name, middle name, six-line address, telephone number, e-mail address, fax number and personal picture. Estimate the size of the file, given a maximum of 1000 records. *Give reasons for any of the estimations that you make*.

Table 13.1 Estimation of field size

Field information	Size (char.)
ID number	10
Surname	20
First name	20
Middle name	20
Address 1 (Line 1)	20
Address 2 (Line 2)	20
Address 3 (Line 3)	20
Address 4 (Town)	20
Address 5 (County/State)	20
Address 6 (Post code)	10
Telephone number	25
e-mail address	40
Fax number	25
Picture	1000
Total for each record	1270

Solution

Assumptions about the maximum number of characters that will accommodate each of the criteria are shown in Table 13.1. These are possible values only, and are a compromise between having to cope with unusually long entries (hence wasting storage space), and making sure that most ordinary data can be entered with little truncation. The picture at the bottom of the list will need to be captured and saved in jpeg form. 1 Kbyte is enough for a reasonable size and quality image, given that it will be viewed on a computer screen.

If there are 1000 records, then we need 1000 × 1270 = 1 270 000 bytes of space. However, there are overheads associated with files and databases. If the above information were to be stored in text file, then little extra would need to be added on. The only extra information would be the headers and end-of-file markers, etc. A sensible estimate of the file size (always make it a little larger than needed) would be 1.5 Mbytes.

Estimating size with a database

If we construct the last example using a **database** application package, then estimation of the amount of space taken up by the data is also quite straightforward. To do this, first create a database with blank records and then measure the size of the database file. Next enter information into a single record, and measure the size again. The *difference* is an estimate of the amount of space needed to hold the information you have just entered.

Fixed and variable length records

The last example assumed the field length is fixed. **Fixed-length fields** give rise to **fixed-length records**. These are easier to process because the software routines that access the information may count a known number of characters. With fixed-length records, altering the contents will not alter the length of the record. It is also useful to have **variable-length fields**. For example, a free-flowing text field, where users can put extended comments. Although efficient from a storage space point of view, **variable-length records** are more difficult to maintain than fixed-length ones.

File structure

The *anatomy of a file* includes layout, like the logical organisation of the **records** within a file, and organisation of the **fields** within each record. A **hierarchical data structure** may be used for this purpose, as shown in Figure 13.2. The fields are subordinate to the records, which are subordinate to the file. This data structure represents the **logical structure** of the file, and not the way a file would be stored. Each piece of data is identified by the name of the field, and the **key field** identifies each record.

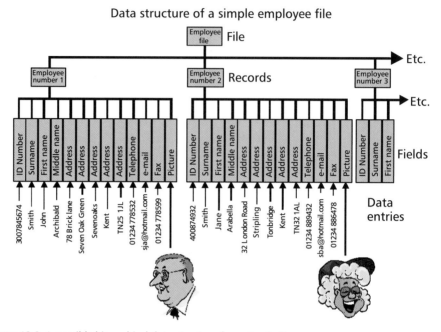

Figure 13.2 A possible hierarchical data structure for a simple file

File organisation

There are four main access methods, described as follows: **serial access**, **sequential access**, **direct access** (same as **random access**) and **indexed sequential access**.

Serial access refers to storing records, one after the other, *with no regard to order*. **Sequential access** means storing information in a particular sequence, such as alphabetical or ID number. **Serial-access storage media** only support these two access methods.

Direct access is the ability to go straight to a record or interest, without having to serially work though all of the previous records. This is done by using **hashing** (*see below*).

Another way to find records quickly is to build up an **index** of **pointers**, which point to important positions within the file. This is called **indexed sequential access**, as the index is used to access part of the file, which is then searched sequentially for the item of interest. Typically an index might point to places like 'the beginning of names starting with A' or 'the beginning of names starting with B', etc. If this alphabetical index is used, 26 pointers would be needed. If a name like 'Gazebo' is being requested, then the G pointer is followed to the beginning of the 'Gs', and the G list is sequentially searched.

Direct-access (or **random access**) **storage media** like disks can support all access methods, both **serial** and **direct**. You must realise that serial access methods are ideal for batch processing operations like the production of utility bills or processing a pay roll, for example.

Hashing

A **hash function** is a **mathematical formula**. The point of using this is to gain *rapid access* to where the data is stored, or to *map data* onto specific locations, as shown later in this section.

A **hash function** may be applied to data within a record to generate an **address** at which the data will be stored. Consider the **key fields** in Figure 13.2. 'John Smith' has an ID number '3007845674'. This number might contain coded information about the department in which he works, and his security rating. However, it's unlikely that this would be a good number to use to store his data because it's too big to be used as a convenient address.

A common method to generate an appropriate range of addresses (*mapping*) is to use **modulo arithmetic** (*see margin entry*). Suppose that we have a maximum of 50 employees, and wish to map these into an address range of 1 to 50. A possible hash function to do this is:

```
Address = Key Field (Mod 50) + 1
```

For 'John Smith' this would work out as

```
Address = 3007845674(Mod 50) + 1 = 17 + 1 (John Smith is stored
at location 18)
```

Hash functions sometimes generate the same address for different records! To get over this problem we use a pointer system which points to an area of memory called an **overflow table** in which records with the same hash address are stored. We then use a **linear search** (i.e. search each item one after the other) of the records with the same hash number until we find the desired record. Generating a **hash function**, even if **overflow tables** are used, is very rapid compared to searching a vast file by other means, and is ideal for a **direct access** file.

Modulo arithmetic is simple. A number, modulo N, is simply the remainder after division by N.

Therefore, 23(Mod5) would be worked out as 3, because 5 goes into 23 four times with 3 left over. The remainder is 3 and thus 3 is the answer to 23(Mod5).

Most high-level languages support a MOD (modulo) command.

Example

Suppose the company whose employee database is shown in Figure 13.2 has a maximum of 400 employees. We wish to store the data at locations 1 to 400. Suggest a suitable hashing function to do this, and work out where Jane Smith's (employee ID 400874932) data would be stored.

Solution

A suitable hashing function for 400 employees would be:

```
Address = Key Field (Mod 400) + 1
```

Jane Smith would be stored at

```
Address 400874932(Mod 400) + 1 = 132 = 1 = 133
```

Self-test questions

1 A data file on a computer may be split up into records, fields and characters. Explain these terms.
2 A shop keeps details of stock in a single file held on computer. They have a maximum of 10 000 items in stock. Estimate the size of the file given that the following fields are stored for each item. (State any assumptions that you make.)
   (a) Name of item   (b) Product description code
   (c) Price   (d) Description of item
   (e) Page number in the catalogue

3 What is the difference between a 'serial file' and a 'sequential file'?

4 Name two different types of secondary storage media that support serial access files.

5 What does an indexed-sequential file mean? Illustrate your answer by using an example involving searching for people's names.

6 Explain why hashing is sometimes used when storing information in files.

7 A company has used 'surname' as a key field when designing a file. What might go wrong with this? What would you change in order to rectify the situation?

8 A particular branch of a bank makes use of 8-digit account numbers. They will not accept more than 1500 customers at this branch.

   (a) Suggest a suitable hashing function to store data for each customer, quickly accessible from their account number.

   (b) Show how two different account numbers can generate the same hash address.

   (c) What is done to overcome a clash of hash addresses?

14 Security, integrity and management of data

In this section you will learn about:

- The difference between data integrity and data security
- Methods of checking data integrity, such as hash totals, check digits and CRC checks
- Methods for keeping data secure
- Privacy and security issues
- Strategies for backing up data
- Master and transaction file processing
- Strategies for disaster recovery
- File management techniques

Security and data integrity

Security means keeping data safe from hackers. **Integrity** means making sure that data is not corrupted, either by human error or by hardware or software problems.

Maintaining data integrity

The most important part of any computer system is the data. If a system is destroyed we can buy a new one, but the new computer will not have our precious data stored on it. Much effort therefore goes into making sure that data is transmitted, processed and stored safely, and backups are taken frequently. An enormous number of bytes of data are transmitted between computers each and every day. If a single byte of this data is transmitted or processed in error, then someone's data is corrupted.

Batch totals

A **batch total** is one method of checking the **integrity** of data. A batch total can be used as a check to make sure that a *batch of data* has been entered into the computer system correctly. Customers' account numbers, for example, could be added together to form a number which is the batch total. The data-entry clerk then enters all the data for each of the accounts, and the computer automatically calculates the batch total based on the data just entered. If it is different from the original batch total, the clerk may have forgotten to enter data from one or more of the accounts.

Hash totals (control totals)

A **hash total** is made by performing a suitable operation on a batch of data, and is therefore similar in principle to the **batch total** outlined above. As an example, consider a typical **transaction file**, generated after trading for a day in a shop. Each transaction will have a cost associated with it. A good **hash total** in this case might be to add up the total cost of all the transactions contained within the file. This total cost would then be the **hash total** or **control total**, which is the extra number transmitted along with the file for **data integrity** purposes.

When the transaction file is received at the other end, a new **hash total** or **control total** is calculated using the same methods. If it is different to the hash or control total sent along with the file, the data can be assumed to be in error, in which case the transaction file can be retransmitted.

Example

By using a simple file, consisting of just three records, each with two fields, containing a 'surname' and 'first name' respectively, show how you could generate a suitable control total, not greater than '199', that can be transmitted along with the file for data integrity purposes. You must explain your methods and calculate a suitable control (hash) total for the names that you have assumed to be in the file.

Solution

Consider the record structure shown in the left two columns of Table 14.1. The algorithm being used is to add the ASCII codes together of the first character in the 'surname' field. The results are shown in the right-hand column. Next we total the numbers in the right hand column to get 223. We only want numbers in the range 0 to 199 inclusive, and so Modulo 200 is used, giving an answer of 23, which is the control total used to check data integrity.

Table 14.1 Generation of a suitable control total

Surname	First name	ASCII code for first letter of 'Surname' only
Bradley	Ray	66
Martin	Guy	77
Prakash	Jared	80
	Total	223
Control total = Total(Mod 200)		23

Check digits and checksums

Modulo arithmetic is covered in Chapter 13.

A **check digit** is similar in principle to a **hash total**, but *only a single digit is produced*. It is particularly useful when verifying a single account or stock number, where a **transcription error** (the wrong number is entered) or a **transposition error** (two digits or letters are swapped over) may have occurred.

To calculate a **check digit**, a **weighting** is applied to each digit, based on the position of the number. The **least significant bit** is usually reserved for the check digit, and is assigned a weighting of 1. All the other digits in the number have a weighting of 2 to 9, repeating if necessary. The idea is shown in Table 14.2. CD is where the **check digit** is to be placed. The new number, with the check digit added, is shown at the bottom of Table 14.2.

Table 14.2 How to calculate a check digit

	Calculation of a check digit for the number 447546231								
Number	4	4	7	5	4	6	2	3	1	CD
Weighting	2	9	8	7	6	5	4	3	2	1
Product of number and weighting	8	36	56	35	24	30	8	9	2	–
Sum	8 + 36 + 56 + 35 + 24 + 30 + 8 + 9 + 2 = 208									
Mod 7 division	208/7 = 29 remainder 5 – Therefore '5' is added on at the end									
New number	4	4	7	5	4	6	2	3	1	5

You will also come across the term **checksum**. ASCII codes of each alphanumeric character can be added together to produce a sum, which is transmitted or stored, along with the original message. Consider the message 'Is this OK?' as shown in Table 14.3. The ASCII codes are shown in the right-hand column.

The digits '909' form the checksum to be sent along with the message 'Is this OK?' As you can see from the above, a **check digit** is used for a single number or alphanumeric entry, and a **checksum** is used as an integrity check on a batch of data. However, it is not as effective in detecting and correcting errors compared with the CRC methods covered in the next section.

Table 14.3 How to calculate a check sum

Calculating a check sum	
Data	ASCII code
I	73
s	115
	32
t	116
h	104
i	105
s	115
	32
O	79
K	75
?	63
Sum	909

Cyclic redundancy checks (CRCs)

The **CRC mechanism** is ideally suited to the errors encountered when transmitting data over a network. The message to be sent is split up into predetermined lengths. The binary data to be transmitted is used to generate **coefficients** of a **polynomial**. A polynomial is the name given to a mathematical function with increasing powers of x, like the one shown below. The coefficients are simply the numbers in front of each x within the polynomial. If, for example, the digits 10110011 are to be sent, then this generates the following polynomial:

$$1x^7 + 0x^2 + 1x^5 + 1x^4 + 0x^3 + 0x^2 + 1x^1 + 1x^0$$

This is now used, together with another standard polynomial (not shown here) in a division sum, to produce an answer and a remainder. The remainder, which is also a polynomial, is used to generate the bits in the **CRC check digits**. If, for example, the remainder polynomial were as follows:

$$1x^3 + 0x^2 + 1x^1 + 1x^0$$

The digits for the CRC check would be 1011 (*the coefficients of this remainder polynomial*).

This **CRC method** is useful in that *small numbers of digits are produced for large numbers of digits checked*. The error detection rate is also one of the best that is available, but only the principles need be known. For all of the data integrity checks covered here, if an error is detected, then the message should be transmitted again.

Note the pattern of the 0s and 1s compared to the digits to be sent.

Computer viruses

You will recall that a **virus** is a **program** which *illegally enters* and **infects** your computer system, then **replicates** itself, with the intention to annoy or cause damage. The effects of a virus can range from 'annoying messages on the screen' to 'frustrating technical "faults" such as running out of memory' to 'catastrophic deletion of data' or 'denial of service'.

Computer viruses are a major threat to *both* **data integrity** and **data security**. They are a threat to **data integrity** because data can be changed and destroyed without the knowledge or permission of the user. They are also a threat to **data security**, because some Trojan viruses can sniff out passwords or credit-card numbers from a system.

The only defence against a virus, (aside from the unrealistic restriction that you *don't share any data*) is to install **virus-protection software**. You must also ensure that your

14

virus protection software virus definition files are *kept up to date*, but any new virus may not be dealt with; at least not for a day or two, while the virus protection people get to work and produce an update to combat the new threat.

To recover lost data after being infected with a virus you need to use your **backup** which was made made at frequent intervals. The source of a computer virus may be an infected floppy disk, Zip disk, CD-ROM, DVD or tape, but the internet is also a major source, because viruses can arrive with downloaded programs, pictures or e-mail. There are also macro viruses, which attach themselves to some of your applications, like word processors, or spreadsheets.

Keeping the data secure

Data security means keeping your data away from prying eyes. This is particularly important in industry, commerce and government, where sensitive data needs to be transmitted over secure networks. You will also need to ensure that your data is **backed up**, so that you may recover it in the event of a hardware failure, fire, or other natural catastrophe.

You should not overlook **physical security**. This means making sure that unauthorised personnel have no access to the rooms in which computers are housed to store sensitive data. It also means making sure that authorised personnel don't leave computers logged on. A careless system administrator and an opportunist are all that's needed to overcome the best of security systems. As is often the case, humans are the weakest link.

File privacy

The most common protection is a **password**. *Passwords should be easy to remember, but difficult to crack.* A 'simple' password like 'discombobulating' could be subject to a dictionary attack because it is a word in the English language. A Password like 'Sausage_Chips_Beans' is difficult to crack because the 'word' is not in the dictionary, and other characters (like numbers or punctuation) have also been used. It is also very easy to remember. The password is used, in conjunction with **operating system security** to grant privileges to users, depending on their status. The only thing that protects users from logging onto a network as an administrator is the administrator's user name and password. It is vital that passwords are kept secure, and changed at regular intervals.

Encryption

The passwords must obviously be stored on the computer system in a file, but must not be in a form that can be read, even if the system is hacked into. This is achieved by **encrypting** the passwords. **Encryption** (*see Chapter 12*) is a method of keeping data safe, based on keys, or codes, which are needed to decrypt the encrypted data. Without the key, it would be virtually impossible to crack the code by guesswork alone.

Example

A computer system has been protected from viruses, passwords have been used and the data is encrypted. However, a disgruntled employee, sacked a few weeks ago has got in through a back door. Explain what has happened.

Solution

Computer programmers often leave a 'way in' which bypasses security. This is useful to fix bugs on new systems as they are being developed. If anyone leaves and this loophole is not plugged, then a disgruntled employee may easily hack into the system and cause malicious damage. Some programmers deliberately put a back door into systems unbeknown to the employer! If important programmers are sacked, their passwords are instantly changed and they may not be allowed to use their computer before leaving!

Strategies for disaster recovery

As well as protecting data from hackers, viruses and human error, we must also protect data from **natural hazards** such as **fire**, **hardware failures** or **software crashes**.

Companies might have significant problems due to the vast quantities of data they process, and the urgency with which this data may be needed in the event of a system crash. An airline booking system, for example, needs to be running efficiently on a 24/7 basis, even in the event of a hard disk crash. Some **file servers** operate what's called **disk mirroring**. This is one example of a **RAID system (Redundant Array of Independent Drives)** in which identical copies are made on two independent disks. This does not provide any protection against human error, hackers or viruses, but often provides protection against hardware failures like a hard disk crash.

Any system *will go wrong eventually*, so you must look at what can be done to minimise any inconvenience? The data held in a computer system may be split into two major parts:

- **data** belonging to the business
- the **application software** and **system software** needed to process the data and run the computers

It's common to store important **data** on **file servers**, accessible via **LANs** or **WANs**. This not only allows data to be accessed from anywhere in the world, but also allows for *central control of the data by a system administrator*. He or she can make sure that **backups** of the data are taken at suitably frequent time intervals.

At the end of each day, or more frequently if necessary, a **tape backup** can be made of the appropriate directories. One strategy might be to back up data at the end of each day, and to label the tapes 'Monday', 'Tuesday', etc. until 'Sunday'. Next week the tape labelled 'Monday' could be overwritten with the new data if this would provide an appropriate recovery route. These backups can either be **incremental** (*only the files which have been updated will change*), or **total**, in which case *all files* will be backed up, irrespective of whether they have been altered.

The above tape backup strategies would not cater for people who create new work and delete it on the same day, before the actual backup has been made. In the above scenario it would only be possible to revert to the previous day's work. However, special **utility software** like a **file undeletion program** may be used to recover the newly created data *if it is used soon after the data has been deleted*. It won't, for example, be able to recover a deleted file if the operating system uses the free space released by the deletion of the file, or a user has run a **defragmentation** program.

Other institutions might need for a different backup strategy. At the author's school, for example, we operate a ten-day cycle. Therefore, we have ten tapes, one corresponding to each day of the academic cycle. We also make monthly backups and end-of-term backups too. Don't confuse the term **backup** with an **archive**, which means *taking little used data off line so that it may be used at a later date*.

Other backup strategies

Lots of businesses generate a **transaction file** (transactions for a particular day). At the end of the day, this file is used to update the information on a **master file**, which then becomes the new master file, as shown in Figure 14.1. The **new master file** is called the **'son' file**, because the **old master file**, shown on the left, is the **'father' file**. For the next update, the new master file becomes the 'son', the old master file becomes the 'father' and the oldest master file, from the day before, becomes the **'grandfather' file**. In this way, three generations of files have been created.

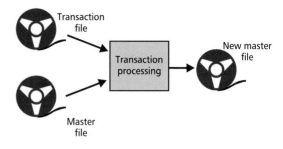

Figure 14.1 Updating a master file

The computer may generate a **transaction log** during this process, containing information about changes that have taken place. This is often useful to **backtrack** and sort out errors.

Updating serial-access files

The **serial access files** (tape or files on disk organised to operate in this way) must be **ordered** for the system shown in Figure 14.1 to work properly. Typical arrangements might be 'alphabetical' or 'customer ID' number. It's easy if you think of a serial-access file being stored on tape, even though it might actually be stored on disk. From Figure 14.2 we can see that we can't simply insert the record for 'Betty' into the appropriate place in the ordered file, because you can't physically cut the tape.

Instead we have to go through an update process similar to that shown in Figure 14.1.

Imagine both the **transaction file** (containing Betty's data) and the **master file** (containing all the other data) to be at the beginning of the tape. The 'Betty' record is compared with the 'Alice' record. Because 'Alice' comes before 'Betty', 'Alice' is copied to the **new master file**. The 'Betty' record is next

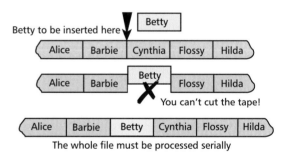

Figure 14.2 Problems updating a serial-access file

compared to 'Barbie'. As 'Barbie' comes before 'Betty', 'Barbie' is copied to the **new master file**. The 'Betty' record is next compared to 'Cynthia'. As 'Betty' comes before 'Cynthia', 'Betty' is copied to the **new master file**. The remainder of the **old master file** is copied, in order, to the **new master file**, resulting in a **new master file** with the 'Betty' record inserted in the appropriate place. This process would obviously work for many transaction file updates, assuming that *both files are in the appropriate order*.

File management and hierarchical structure

A Windows-based **directory structure**, showing part of a Windows 2000 directory, can be seen in Figure 14.3. Folders exist so that the system is managed in a **hierarchical** way.

Each folder may contain 'other folders' and 'files', allowing you to manage the system more efficiently than if all the files had to be stored in the same directory. The position of the **directories** (shown by the yellow folders) and **files** (shown by the other icons) in Figure 14.3 is on the C drive, in the **WINNT** directory, as indicated by the directory path name on the title bar of the window. Therefore, the exe (executable) file called 'Play32.exe' is in this directory. The **NTFS** (similar to DOS) **file pathname** is therefore

```
'C:\Winnt\Play32.exe'
```

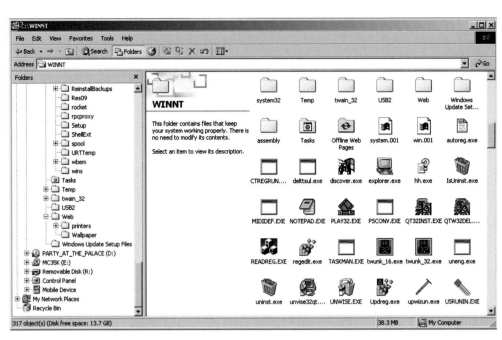

Figure 14.3 A typical hierarchical file management structure in Windows 2000

Notice the format, which is 'Drive letter:' followed by '\' followed by all the directories separated by '\', and terminated by the leaf **file name**.

Figure 14.3 shows a hierarchical file structure. A **logical drive**, labelled K, is set up to store data files. The root directory on this particular disk has subdirectories labelled 'Art course', 'Word processing' and 'Finances'. The word processing directory is divided into two subdirectories, called 'Home' and 'School'. There are also other sub directories not shown. Finally, the files are put at the **leaf** position in the tree, and represent the end of a particular path structure. Therefore, the geography project, labelled 'Geog.doc' would have the following path name.

```
K:\Word Processing\School\Geog.doc
```

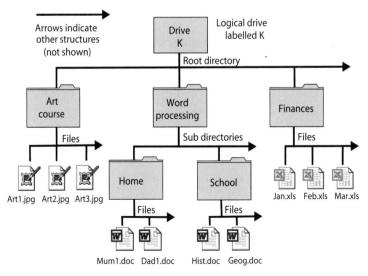

Figure 14.4 Directories showing hierarchical file organisation

This hierarchical system allows use of the same file names in different directories. This knowledge also enables you to understand the commands needed for **batch operations**. From Figure 14.4 you can see that drive K has been called a **logical drive**. This is to distinguish it from a physical drive, which is the drive actually present in the machine. A logical drive is, therefore, a drive simulated by software. A **physical drive** is the disk drive which is inside the machine. Very large drives are usually **partitioned** into smaller **logical drives** to make the storage of information more efficient. From a user's view a logical drive acts as though it were a physical drive in the machine.

Example

You are the network manager in a school that organises resources on several networked file servers. There are 1500 users, split up into staff and students (Years 1 to 7). Each pupil is allowed disk space on a server. Resources like word processors are loaded from a local hard disk to cut down on the network bandwidth required. Other resources, such as clipart, web design tools and other common utilities are to be found on one of several resource servers. Suggest a file structure, including the naming of any logical and physical drives presented to the users, and the role that these drives might play in the logical organisation of the system.

Solution

We will assume an individual file server for each year, and one for the staff. To gain access to private areas on the appropriate file server, a logical drive (labelled Z for convenience here) would be mapped to that area on the file server to which the student or member of staff has read/write permissions. If, for example, the file server allocated to the upper sixth (Year 7) is called Enterprise, and one of the students is called James T. Kirk, then the physical directory in which James may save his work might be:

    :\\Enterprise\students\KirkJT

This indicates that the U6th (Year 7) student called Kirk has his work stored on the Enterprise file server in a directory called students in a subdirectory called Kirk J. T. This would be on one of the main disks in the file server called 'Enterprise'. (':\\Enterprise' is a server on a network.) This file path name would have to be unique within the organisation. Another student in a different year could have the same leaf directory name because the file server name will be different. The network manager may automatically map a logical drive for this student. When the student logs on, he or she will see 'drive Z', and any other mapped drives to which he or she may be entitled. The student may then attach a label (shortcut) to the Z drive like 'My Work'. Other resources, like the clipart mentioned above, might be assigned a different drive letter like Y, and be labelled 'Clipart'. The student would see this drive also, and other drives showing other resources as seen fit to assign by the network manager. As far as the user is concerned, it appears identical to the physical disk drives in their own workstation, but the files are actually loaded from the network file servers or other resources.

Sharing files on a network

Most resources can be shared in the ways described above. If you have permission to do so, you could put a CD into the drive of your local workstation, and **share** it so that all people on the network can have access to it. Indeed, on **local area networks** you have to be very careful about sharing resources, and should not do so without your network manager's permission. It would be possible in a badly protected network to wipe the files from somebody else's hard drive, just because they have shared it.

Self-test questions

1 Explain the difference between the terms 'data integrity' and 'data security'. Give an example of a typical breach of each of these terms.
2 Explain what is meant by a batch total, giving an example of where such a system might be used.
3 How might a 'hash total' or 'control total' be used to check the data integrity of a batch of school reports?
4 What is a checksum?
5 Calculate the check digit that would be transmitted along with the account number 795436. Write down the new account number with the check digit included.
6 Explain why a cyclic redundancy check is one of the best methods to detect errors in the storage or transmission of data.
7 Outline a suitable strategy for keeping the data held in a file secure.
8 Why could a computer virus be a threat to both data security and data integrity? Give an example of a scenario showing how a virus could do this in each of these situations.
9 Outline four different physical security methods that might be used to counter a threat to data security.
10 Explain what is meant by a master file and a transaction file.
11 A chain of shops creates several transaction files, one for each branch. At the end of the day these files are transmitted via the internet to head office, where the master file, containing up-to-date information about all the shops, is handled. Explain the batch processing that goes on each day at head office, making sure that you include the grandfather, father and son files in your explanation.
12 Explain, in detail, how serial transaction file records can be used to update a serially based master file to produce a new master file. Write some pseudocode to control this process, stating any assumptions that you need to make to ensure that your code will work under all conditions.
13 Both data files and programs (application files and system files) need to be backed-up to recover in the event of a system crash. Outline the different techniques that might be put in place to deal with these two very different types of file.
14 Explain the difference between a backup and an archive. Give a good example of where archived data might have to be used in the future.
15 What is the difference between a physical and a logical drive? Why are both used extensively in practice?
16 A college has many networked workstations connected to LANs and several file servers containing important data. Outline backup strategies that could be used in the following situations:
(a) fat clients on the networks
(b) thin clients on the networks.

15 Databases

In this section you will learn about:

- The difference between a flat file and a relational database
- Splitting up a relational database into suitable tables
- Creating a simple database using Microsoft Access
- Creating relationships like one to one, one to many and many to one
- Indexing, validation and look up columns
- Creating database queries and reports
- Accessing data from other applications and exporting via CSV format

Databases

A **database** is a collection of related information, possibly contained in just one **file**, but usually consisting of many files, often related in special ways. These files are organised for efficient processing, like **searching** and **sorting**. If a database consists of one file, it is called a **flat-file database**. Modern databases are often **relational** (*see later*) and are accompanied by utilities to perform functions from '**reporting**' or printing out the results of **queries**, to managing security for users. As shown in the next section, a database can be viewed as a table (or tables) of **rows** and **columns** which contain information.

Database concepts

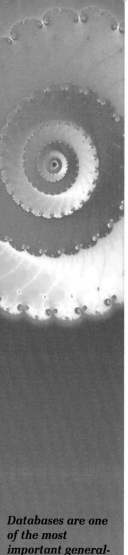

Databases are one of the most important general-purpose applications (see Chapter 11), and you should work hard to understand this material.

We start off with a simple example. Table 15.1 shows some information stored about books in a library database. At present this information is not stored efficiently.

Table 15.1 Table for a library database

ISBN	Author	Title	Publisher	Price	Etc.
0-7487-4046-5	Bradley	Computer Science	Nelson Thornes, Delta Place, 27 Bath Road ...	24.00	...
0-7833-8822-7	Farmer	NT 4 Server Secrets	Nelson Thornes, Delta Place, 27 Bath Road ...	39.00	...
0-6324-2817-6	Martin	Radio Techniques	Nelson Thornes, Delta Place, 27 Bath Road ...	36.00	...
0-5834-9921-7	Bradley	Quantum Computers	Nelson Thornes, Delta Place, 27 Bath Road ...	57.00	...
0-3844-8463-8	Bradley	Modulation	Peter Gibbs, Gibbon Road, Tunbridge Wells ...	45.00	...
0-3523-7668-2	Prakash	Java Programming	Peter Gibbs, Gibbon Road, Tunbridge Wells ...	23.00	...
0-6543-9332-8	Burgin	CD-ROM Servers	Castle House, High Street, Windsor ...	20.00	...
Etc.	...	...	...		...

The table is not large, but we see **duplication**, like the 'publisher information' shown in the highlighted column. In practice, these **attributes** (**fields** that go to make up a **record**) like 'name', 'street name', etc. would be stored in separate columns, but we have shown the 'publisher information' as a single column for simplicity. Duplication of information is inefficient, so the 'publisher information' is taken out and put into a separate table, as shown in Table 15.2. We now have much less **redundancy**, which is one of the aims of good database design. With a couple of million books in a very large library, you can imagine how much storage space would be wasted if we did not remove obvious data duplication. Although we have removed the 'publisher information', we still need the 'name of the publisher' left behind to **link** these two tables; otherwise they would *not* be **related**. What remains of Table 15.1 is shown in Table 15.3. We now have two **related tables** instead of the original. Although more improvements can be made, you can see the advantage of moving information to a different table. If there were 2000 Nelson Thornes books in this library, then using Table 15.1 would mean storing Nelson Thornes' address 2000 times. In the **relational** scheme of things, this address is stored once only.

In a **relational database**, a **table** corresponds to a **file**, a **row** corresponds to a **record**, and a **column** contains the entries corresponding to a **field** (*see Chapter 13*). The highlighted columns contain the **relational information** which relates Table 15.2 to Table 15.3.

The processes covered here are just some of the things that go into relational database design, and are covered in much more detail in the A2 book.

Table 15.2 A second table for the library database – the new publisher information table

Publisher	Address (multiple columns in practice)	Phone	Fax	...
Nelson Thornes	Delta Place 27 Bath Road Cheltenham Glos. GL53 7TH	01242 267100	01242 221914	...
Peter Gibbs	Gibbon Road Tunbridge Wells Kent TN99 1JP	01732 889563	01732 994352	...
Castle House	High Street Windsor Berkshire SL78 1TG	01753 765427	01753 895532	...
Etc.	...	...	...	...

Table 15.3 The modified Table 15.1 – after removing much of the duplicated publisher information

ISBN	Author	Title	Publisher	Price	Etc.
0-7487-4046-5	Bradley	Computer Science	Nelson Thornes	24.00	...
0-7833-8822-7	Farmer	NT 4 Server Secrets	Nelson Thornes	39.00	...
0-6324-2817-6	Martin	Radio Techniques	Nelson Thornes	36.00	...
0-5834-9921-7	Bradley	Quantum Computers	Nelson Thornes	57.00	...
0-3844-8463-8	Bradley	Modulation	Peter Gibbs	45.00	...
0-3523-7668-2	Prakash	Java Programming	Peter Gibbs	23.00	...
0-6543-9332-8	Burgin	CD-ROM Servers	Castle House	20.00	...
Etc.	...	...	...	...	...

Example

Consider the library database described in the last section.

(a) If the tables were not related in the ways described, but were held on several independent files, data inconsistency may occur. Explain what this means.

(b) Suggest a better way of storing publisher information such that if changes were needed, like a change of publisher name, this would have to be altered once only.

Solution

(a) Data inconsistency means that data stored in different places may not be consistent (i.e. entries that should be identical might not be). If independent files are used to store information, then the likelihood of data inconsistency is high. If the name of a publisher contains an error, then this will, in effect, be regarded as a different publisher by the system. These errors can be minimised in a relational database.

(b) It is more efficient to replace publisher names with a publisher ID. The publisher ID information can then be used to link the two tables, just like the publisher name did previously. This new method is better as there is less chance of data inconsistency.

The tables related on publisher ID

If we replace 'publisher name' with 'publisher ID' as suggested above, 'Publisher ID' now becomes the **primary key**, shown in Table 15.4. Table 15.3 also needs changing to reflect the new 'Publisher ID' information, and this is shown in Table 15.5. The two highlighted

Table 15.4 The modified Table 15.3 – replacing publisher name with publisher ID

Publisher ID	Publisher name	Address *(multiple columns in practice)*	Phone	Fax	...
1	Nelson Thornes	Delta Place 27 Bath Road Cheltenham Glos. GL53 7TH	01242 267100	01242 221914	...
2	Peter Gibbs	Gibbon Road Tunbridge Wells Kent TN99 1JP	01732 889563	01732 994352	...
3	Castle House	High Street Windsor Berkshire SL78 1TG	01753 765427	01753 895532	...
4	Etc.	...	...	...	...

columns now provide the **relational information**, linking the two tables. The publisher now appears once only. If 'Nelson Thornes' were to be changed to 'Nelson Thornes & Sons', only one field would have to be altered, although the entire database, possibly containing thousands of references to this publisher, have all been updated. The chances of **data inconsistency** have therefore been reduced considerably.

The above example illustrates just one of the many advantages that a **relational database** has over a **flat-file database**.

Table 15.5 Publisher name replaced by 'Publisher ID'

ISBN	Author	Title	Publisher ID	Price	...
0-7487-4046-5	Bradley	Computer Science	1	24.00	...
0-7833-8822-7	Farmer	NT 4 Server Secrets	1	39.00	...
0-6324-2817-6	Martin	Radio Techniques	1	36.00	...
0-5834-9921-7	Bradley	Quantum Computers	1	57.00	...
0-3844-8463-8	Bradley	Modulation	2	45.00	...
0-3523-7668-2	Prakash	Java Programming	2	23.00	...
0-6543-9332-8	Burgin	CD-ROM Servers	3	20.00	...
Etc.	...	...		...	...

Library example using Microsoft Access

We are now going to set up the library database shown above using Microsoft Access. To do this, load Access and, using the Wizards, create a **new database**, entering the fields as shown in Figure 15.1 You are reminded about **data types** (*see Chapter 5*) or **field types**. A **text data type** (i.e. alphanumeric characters) is suitable for most of the fields, but 'number' is used for the 'publisher ID' and 'currency' is used for the 'price'. Prudent use of data types ensures few errors are made when databases are being designed.

Make **ISBN** the **key field**, shown in Access by the key next to the ISBN field name in Figure 15.1. Next use the form wizard to get a convenient data-entry method. Add all the fields and accept the default templates. You should end up with a data entry **form** (**record card**) similar to that shown in Figure 15.2. Data can be entered directly onto the datasheet, but special forms make data entry particularly easy for novice users. In practice, you would use more sophisticated methods to limit data entry errors, but these have been omitted here for the sake of clarity. The **labels** used on the forms do not have to correspond to the **field names**, but need to reflect the needs of the people who will actually enter the data.

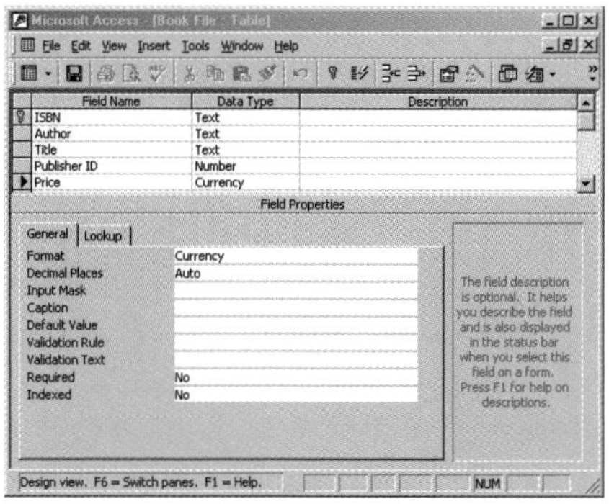

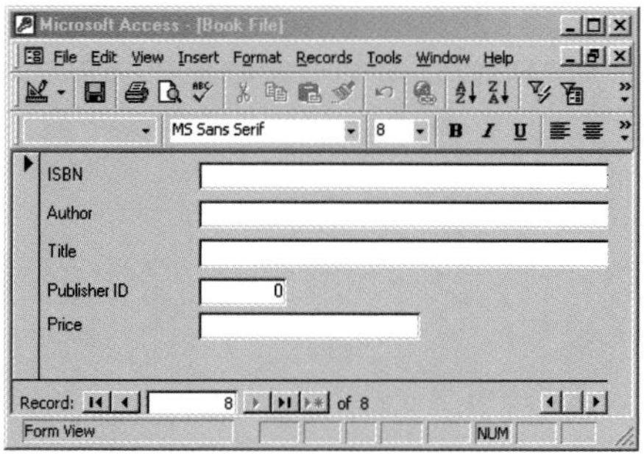

Figure 15.2 A form created in Access

Figure 15.1 Table built up from Access

Next add the data in Table 15.3. After entering the data, view the table containing the data using the datasheet viewing option, as shown in Figure 15.3. Finally, create the publishers table. Create a new table (**not** a new database), and set up the table, as shown in Figure 15.4.

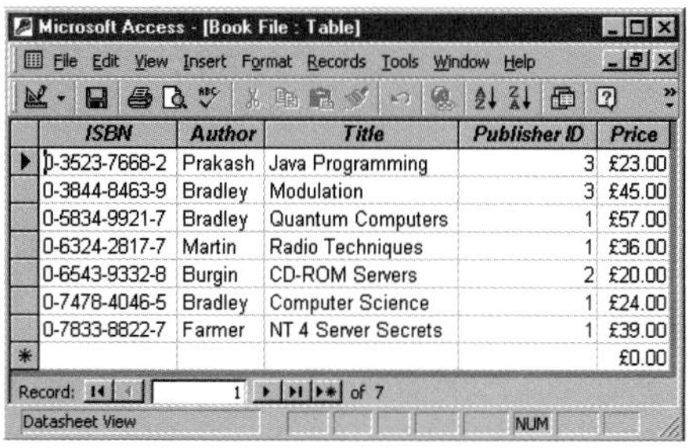

Figure 15.3 The data has now been entered into the book table

As noted at the beginning of this chapter, we now allocate six different text fields for the address information. (This will replace the single field shown in Table 15.4.) This is more efficient than putting the whole address into a single field. Doing this enables easier searching on criteria such as 'postcode' or 'county'. As an example of this, the sixth address field contains the country of origin of the publisher. We could therefore search for country of origin very quickly by establishing a match on this particular field. We have also assigned the **key field** to publisher ID as shown in Table 15.4.

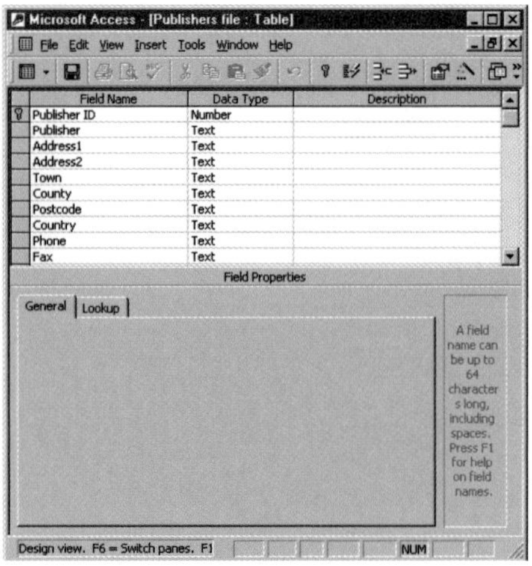

Figure 15.4 The publisher's table

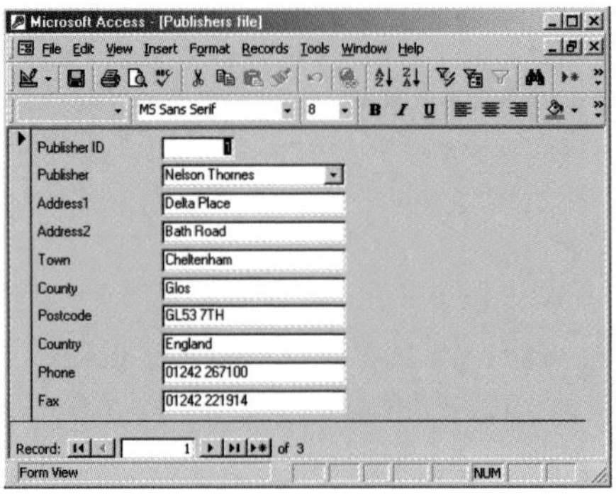

Figure 15.5 The publisher's table

Finally create a form for entry of data into the publisher's table, as shown in Figure 15.5. After the data has been entered, confirm that all is correct by looking at the three records in datasheet view, as shown in Figure 15.6.

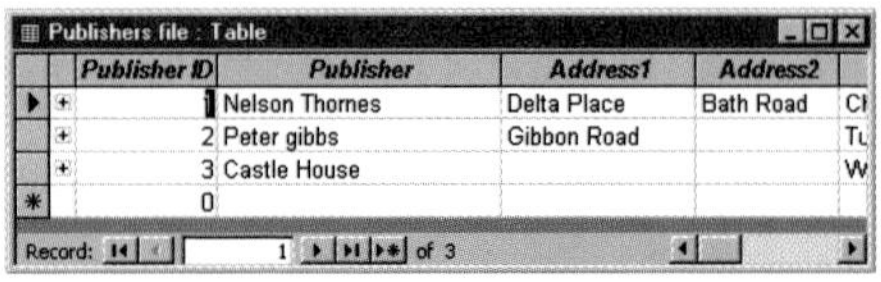

Figure 15.6 The records in datasheet view

Creating a relationship using Access

We now create a **relationship** between Table 15.4 and Table 15.5, based on the 'Publisher ID' (i.e. link the highlighted columns). You can create a **one-to-one**, **one-to-many** or **many-to-one relationship**. Here, the relationship between the 'Book table Publisher ID' and 'Publisher table Publisher ID' is **many-to-one**, because many entries in the book file or table are mapped onto just one entry in the publisher file or table.

To set up a relationship using Access, click over the relationship button on the tool bar, and make sure that both tables can be seen. Choosing the appropriate tables and clicking 'show table' in the view tool can achieve this. To create a **many-to-one relationship**, drag the Publisher ID field in the publishers file to the Publisher ID field in the Book file. You will then get the screen shown in Figure 15.7. Figure 15.7 confirms the relationship is between the Publisher IDs in both tables, but the relationship is one-to-many, not many-to-one. However, don't forget that this is with respect to the Publishers table. From the point of view of the Book file table, it is the many-to-one relationship we required, and this is confirmed by inspection of Figure 15.8. This is because the infinity sign (many) is tagged to the Book file. You should enforce **referential integrity**, as this will check that you have no references to entries that do not exist. Also, make sure that the 'cascade update related fields' box is checked, so that Access automatically updates corresponding values in the related table. To confirm the appropriate relationship is set up, your tables, and the relationship between them, should be as shown in Figure 15.8.

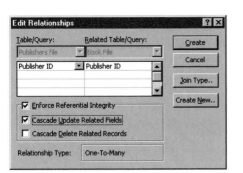

Figure 15.7 Setting up a relationship

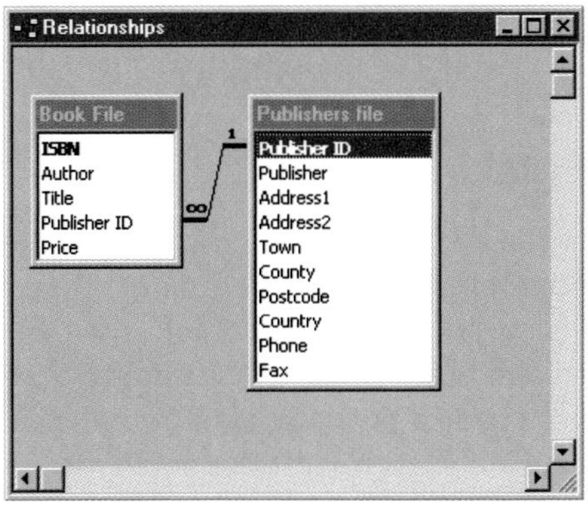

Figure 15.8 A many-to-one relationship

Other relational database terminology

The **key field**, which identifies a record in a table, is called the **primary key. ISBN number** is the **primary key** in Table 15.5, and **Publisher ID** is the **primary key** in Table 15.4. Any other key not used as the primary key is called an **alternate key**.

We could produce a list of books by Nelson Thornes by matching the **primary key** to Nelson Thornes in the Publishers table. We need to decide how the results are to be sorted, as all primary-key entries are the same. We might choose 'Title', for example, so all books published by 'Nelson Thornes' are listed in ascending order of title. In this case, 'Title' is called a **secondary key**. In Figure 15.8, the **primary key field** was dragged to the **foreign key field** in another table. Taking Figure 15.8 as an example, the **primary field** 'Publisher ID' in the 'Publishers table' is dragged to the **foreign key** 'Publisher ID' in the 'Book table'. This creates a **one-to-many relationship** from 'Publishers table' to 'Book table'.

Example

(a) **List four different data types that may typically be used when setting up a database. For each data type, suggest why it might be used. Why are data types important when designing a database?**

(b) **Briefly explain the following terms when applied to database design: 'flat-file database', 'relational database', 'table', 'primary key' and 'foreign key'.**

Solution

(a) Four different data types are 'text', 'integer', 'date' and 'Boolean'.
The text data type is suitable for entering alphanumeric characters. The integer data type will ensure that only whole numbers are entered. The date data type will ensure that valid dates only are entered. The Boolean data type is a true/false or yes/no field. If suitable data types are used at the design stage, there is less need for complex validation techniques.

(b) Each term is defined as follows:
A flat-file database is one in which the whole database is contained in a single file or table. A relational database is one in which a number of linked related tables are set up to store the data. A table represents an individual file, whose rows represent the records and whose columns represent the fields. A primary key is one that identifies

a table. A foreign key is the target key used when identifying a relationship. The relationship is usually between the primary and foreign key.

Indexing

In Chapter 13 you saw how **indexes** can be used to efficiently locate information stored in **files**. A database is little different from a sophisticated collection of files, and it's therefore not surprising to find that indexes are used to good effect here too. Most database software will automatically create an index on the **primary key**, which is called the **primary index**, but you can set up **secondary indexes** too, based on any other key. Not all fields can be indexed, because of their data type. The use of these indexes speeds up operations like **searching** and **sorting**. If the field is indexed, then the time taken to find an item of data will be reduced. However, you should not index everything, or the overheads and complexity will become great. If you frequently make a search on 'Publisher name', for example, then this field would be worth indexing.

To view an **index** in Access the table needs to be loaded and design view must be selected. Next view the indexes by making use of a submenu under the view option on the toolbar. The indexes set up for the 'Book table' for our library example can be seen in Figure 15.9. Here you can see the **primary index**, created automatically for the **primary key** ISBN number, and a **secondary index**, for publisher ID. You can add extra indexes, and may alter attributes of each index.

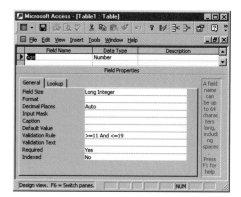

Figure 15.9 Viewing the indexes in Access

Validation techniques

Creating rules that must be obeyed before data is entered into the system will **validate** the data. For example, a pupil at a secondary school may have his or her age validated to be in the range $11 \leqslant age \leqslant 19$. Therefore, if a data-entry clerk was to enter '51' instead of '15' (called a **transposition error** because the two digits have been transposed) then the **validation rule** would ensure that this data does not get entered. Assuming you can think up a suitable set of rules, then validation is very easy to achieve. Using the above age example, we can set up this rule on an age field in Microsoft's Access as shown in Figure 15.10. Here the validation rule for the age field has been set to:

Figure 15.10 Some validation parameters

```
>=11 And <=19
```

Note the **syntax**. We do not need the field name 'age' anywhere because this is the validation rule for the age field. This method will ensure that only those values between 11 and 19 inclusive are accepted.

When doing AS projects (*see the module 3 work*) thinking up lots of validation rules is vital if you wish to achieve a good grade.

Example

(a) **Suggest a sensible way of validating the following data using any acceptable syntax:**

   (i) a date, (ii) weekdays only, (iii) a two or three digit number, (iv) a person's name.

(b) **What is meant by data verification?**

Solution

(a) (i) It is not necessary to design a set of complex validation rules to check if a date is entered correctly. Set the data type to a date field. Further validation may be required if dates need restricting further.

   (ii) If days of the week are to be entered in full, a function like the following is required.

   ```
   Monday OR Tuesday OR Wednesday OR Thursday OR Friday
   ```

   (iii) Assuming that the # sign is the wildcard for a number (i.e. the sign that represents any digit 0 to 9 inclusive), then the validation rule may be something like:

   ```
   '##' OR '###'
   ```

   (iv) Names cannot usually be validated. There is no way of telling whether they are right or wrong (e.g. should a surname be Clark or Clarke?). Verification is usually used instead.

(b) Although validation can't usually be used to determine the correctness of a person's name, it is possible to verify that the name has been entered 'correctly'. Verification can be achieved by entering the same data again. The computer then checks to see if the new data is the same as the original data. If the two data sets are in agreement, it is assumed that the data is correct. If there are differences, it is brought to the attention of the operators, who check the data again. This reduces the likelihood of error, but cannot eliminate it completely, especially if the data on the data capture form is wrong. The validation rules can be of enormous complexity. If there are not enough functions within Access to perform what is required, then you may write your own validation methods making use of the programming language VBA (Visual Basic for Applications).

Look-up columns

Although there are other ways to enter data, one worthy of note, if you are developing a database in the window's environment, is the **look-up column**, (on the Publisher field) shown in Figure 15.11. This is useful if a **defined set of data** must be entered into a particular field. Here a user may choose a name from a column of possibilities presented to them. If a new publisher were to be entered, then the list must be extended by the designer of the system. This helps with **validation** of the data too.

Queries and reports

A **query** is extracting data from a database, and presenting it to the user. A query is easy to create using the query wizard. Let's extract records from the library database containing the authors 'Bradley' or 'Farmer'. We specify which fields are to be included in the search, as shown in Figure 15.12.

The 'Book file' (table) has been chosen, and we have included the fields called 'Author', 'Title' and 'ISBN'. Access will then run the query and find records, if they exist, where the field 'Author' has a value of 'Bradley' or the field 'Author' has a value of 'Farmer'. The results are shown in Figure 15.13.

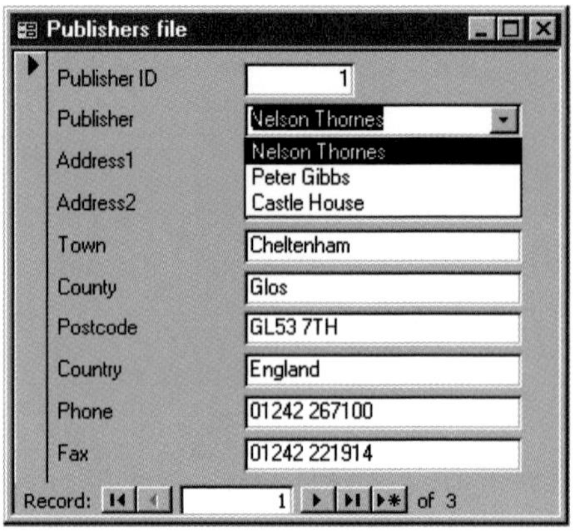

Figure 15.11 A look up column shown on the Publisher Name field

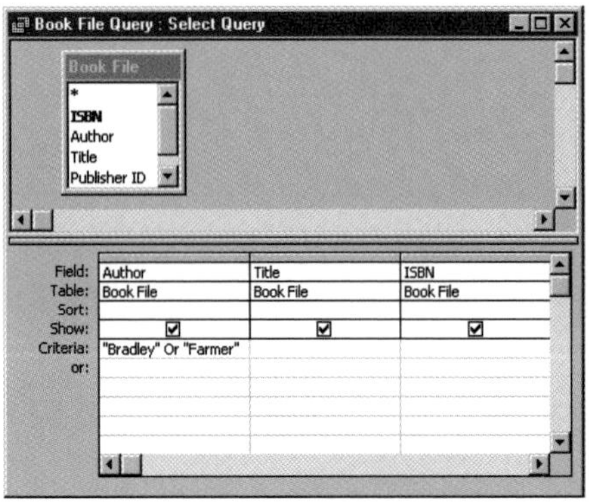

Figure 15.12 Setting up a query

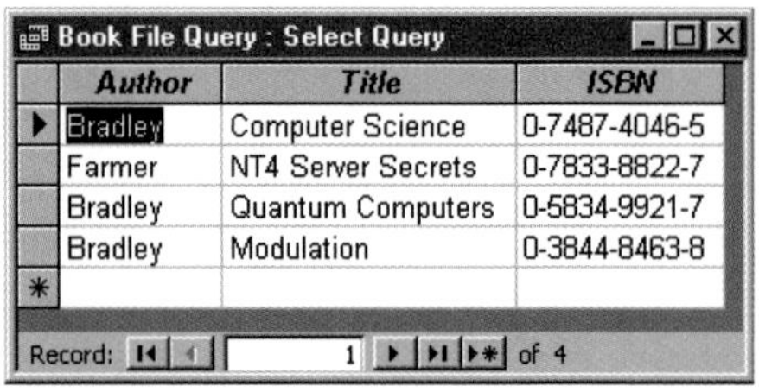

Figure 15.13 The result of the query

The query found four records matching the entries given in Table 15.5. The information in the fields 'Author', 'Title' and 'ISBN' are displayed. Queries can span multiple tables, and contain complex search criteria, with combinations of **Boolean operations** such as 'OR', 'AND', 'NOT', '<>', etc.

Example

Write a query to list the 'Author', 'Title' and 'Publisher' of books in the library database, which contain the word 'Computer' or 'Computers' in the title.

Solution

Run the query wizard. Choose the fields 'Author' and 'Title' from the Book file, and 'Publisher' from the Publisher file. Set up the Title to contain the words 'Computer' or 'Computers' as shown in Figure 15.14. From Figure 15.14 you can see that both tables have been used, because the fields requested are a combination of fields from each of the tables.

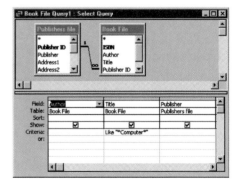

Figure 15.14 Setting up a query

If we search for the string 'Computer' in the title, we will also find 'Computers'. Therefore, we use the following test:

```
LIKE "*Computer*"
```

The command LIKE (placed in the title field) asks Access to find any number of characters (*) followed by the word computer, followed by any other number of other characters (*).

Running the query confirms the required results are obtained, shown in Figure 15.15.

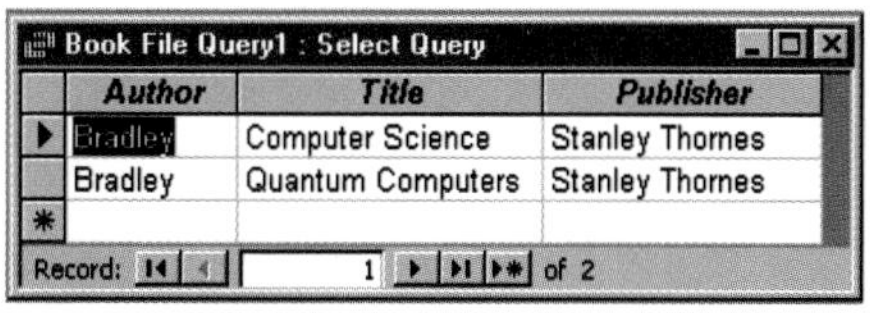

The simple ways of expressing queries, like those shown above are often called **query by example** or **QBE**, because the novice user can tick boxes and enter data with relative ease, compared to the **SQL language** which is explained in more detail when A2 work is covered in the second book in this series.

Figure 15.15 The results of the query

Reporting

Results need to be presented in an acceptable format, with **headings**, **subheadings**, **headers** and **footers**, etc. This makes the data more usable, attractive and professional.

Microsoft's Access provides a wizard that guides you through the processes of choosing which fields will appear in the report, and how the fields will be formatted in the final layout. It allows the fields to be sorted into ascending or descending order and allows specification of headers and footers, both within sections of a report and at the top of the individual pages. It allows you to define the style of the report by the provision of set templates, and allows you to specify headings and sub-headings. You may also design reports from scratch using design view. A report is shown in Figure 15.16 and the Access screen for design is shown in Figure 15.17.

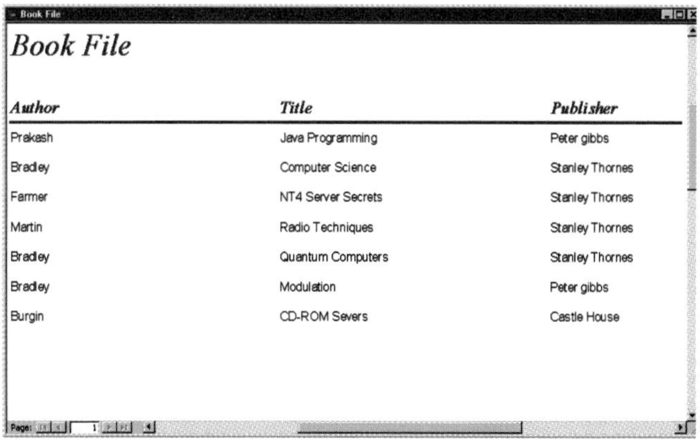

Figure 15.16 A simple report layout

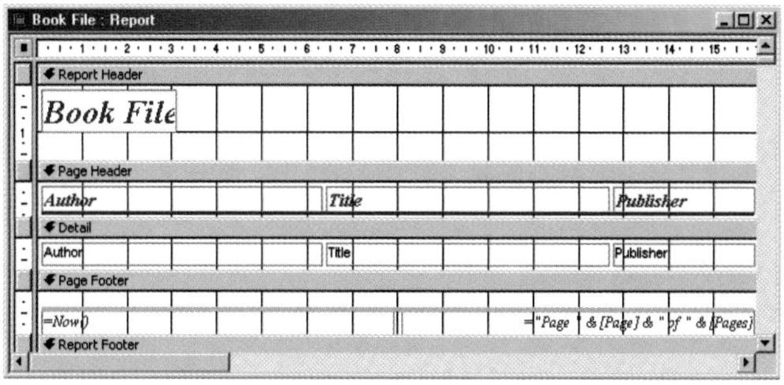

Figure 15.17 The design view of a report

Note how the title and the 'page headers and footers' are designed. The detail of the report contains the 'Author', 'Title' and 'Publisher' fields, which list each record underneath each other in a column. The data contained in the report can be **exported** to other applications like **word processors**, **spreadsheets** and **databases**.

Example

(a) **Explain what is meant by a database report. Why does a query have to be produced first?**

(b) **The production of reports is often said to be the reason for producing a database. Why is this likely to be the case in large and complex databases?**

Solution

(a) A database report is a formatted output (headers, footers and heading, etc.) showing information that is related to criteria which have been used to search a database. Without a suitable query it would not be possible to produce a report, with the exception of a printout of the entire database!

(b) Most companies produce a variety of reports. Things like 'current orders', 'profitability', 'back orders', 'best customers', 'customers owing money', 'best salespeople' and 'current stock position' to name but a few. This is the point of maintaining a database, to produce these statistics at the touch of a button.

Producing a report from a query

You can print out the entire database as a report, but it is more usual to specify some **query** to which the data must adhere. In the library file you may, for example, want a query which outputs to a report only those books with a value over £25. If you are using Access, for example, you can specify that the report is to operate on a query, rather than on a table. You can do this by changing the option as shown in Figure 15.18.

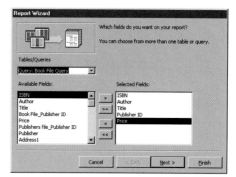

Figure 15.18 Producing a report from a query

Accessing the data from other applications

One of the powerful features of modern databases is the fact that they can be accessed directly from other applications. For example, in Microsoft's Office suite, data from the Access database system can be accessed from **Word**, **Excel**, **PowerPoint** and **Visual Basic**, to name but a few. This gives programmers the ability to do powerful data processing, using facilities in an environment with which they may be more familiar.

Example

A medical database has been set up to store the results of experiments. It is your job to extract the experimental data from the database, analyse it making use of a

spreadsheet, and then use both the original data from the database and the calculated statistics to produce a word-processed report. You need to explain how to do the following operations:

- How is the data from the database imported into the spreadsheet?
- How might the statistics be calculated and stored in the spreadsheet?
- How might the original data from the database be imported into the final report?
- How are the statistics from the spreadsheet imported into the final report?

Solution

An easy way to export data from one application to another is by using a Comma Separated Value file, in which commas separate the values representing the data. To create a CSV file, a query is defined, and the output of the query is saved in CSV format. Suppose we have five records, with each record containing just two fields as follows.

'A,1' 'B,2' 'C,3' 'D,4' and 'E,5'

When importing the data into a spreadsheet, 'A' would be imported into cell 'A1' and 1 would be imported into cell B1. Being a new record, 'B' would be imported into cell A2 and '2' would be imported into cell B2, etc. The whole import can be seen in Figure 15.19.

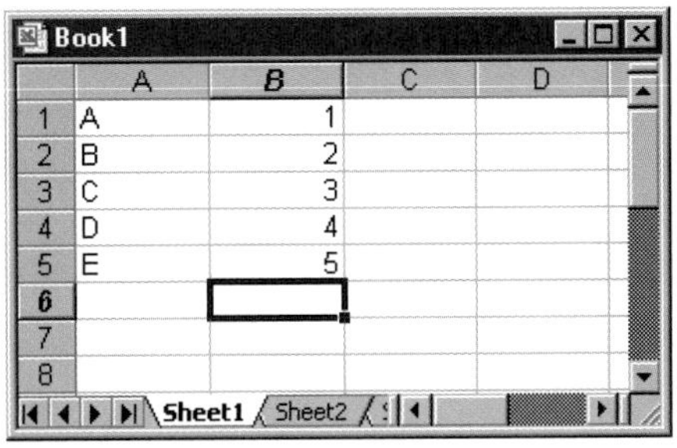

For the medical database, we define a query that will extract the data and output the results of the query as a file in CSV form. Once saved, the CSV file can be imported into the spreadsheet and then changed to the native format of the spreadsheet for further analysis.

Figure 15.19 CSV data imported into the Microsoft Excel spreadsheet

If we are using Excel, for example, we might want to save the CSV data in 'xls' format. The required statistics and other analysis may now be carried out. The layout of the generated statistics will have to be carefully thought out, and the results of calculated formulae may have to be changed to numbers. This too can then be saved in a file in CSV format.

The final stage with the word processor depends on how the statistical data is to be processed. If, for example, data from queries is needed in the word processor, then the CSV file may be loaded directly as a table. Figure 15.20 shows the previous simple CSV data imported directly into Microsoft Word and displayed as a table. It may be more appropriate to the report being created to mail merge individual records. This can also be done from the database, and the data placed in tables embedded into Word in ways similar to that shown in Figure 15.20.

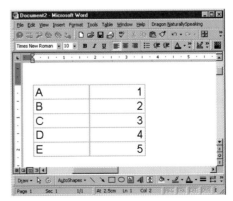

Figure 15.20 CSV data imported into Microsoft Word

Application of database theory to the AS practical exercises

At the beginning of this chapter it was stated that you should work hard to understand the material covered here. Another reason for doing this is that work covered in this chapter can be vitally important for the **AS practical exercise** created by the **AQA board** (Module 3). These **practical exercises**, typically solved by a database or high-level language program, are covered in Chapters 20 to 23 inclusive. It is up to the student to choose an appropriate method, and a database has been used as an example when module 3 is covered in this book. Typically you will be asked to consider many things, including the following:

- Data security (*Passwords, file security and physical security*)
- Data types (*Boolean, integer, text or date, etc.*)
- Which items of the data are the key fields?
- Records, file organisation and processing (*i.e. tables, rows and columns, how different tables are related, etc.*)
- The system design (*including splitting up the data into appropriate tables and the relationships between the tables, etc.*)
- Data integrity (*i.e. data validation rules and methods*)
- The user interface (*the design of the database forms, including the queries and reports*)
- Setting up suitable queries to solve problems
- Creating suitable reports to present data to the user
- Proof of testing the system with extremes of data
- Annotated listings of your database tables and reports.

The above list is not exhaustive, and should not be used as a check list for your practical exercise project. It is simply to show how the work covered in this chapter could be vitally important, not only for module 2, but for module 3 also.

Self-test questions

1 What is the difference between a flat-file database and a relational database?
2 How is the data in a database table related to the data stored in the file on disk?
3 What do the rows and columns represent in a relational database table?
4 (a) What is meant by the term 'data inconsistency' when applied to a database?
   (b) Give an example of data inconsistency.
   (c) Reducing data redundancy is important when designing a database. How does a reduction in data redundancy help with minimising data inconsistency?
5 What is a primary key and why is this concept important in database design?
6 Different data types may be chosen for representing the information stored in each field. Suggest a data type for each of the following, giving reasons for your choice:
   (a) Surname
   (b) Age
   (c) Male or female?
   (d) A picture
   (e) A telephone number.
7 Explain the terms primary key and foreign key.
8 What is meant by a relationship with regard to a relational database? Give three different examples of the types of relationship it is possible to have.
9 Explain what primary and secondary indexes are with respect to a relational database, giving an example of each.
10 What is data validation? Suggest a suitable validation rule for the following:

(a) the age of a male old-age pensioner

(b) the price of an item in a shop.

11 Data must be chosen from a pre-defined list of possibilities. Suggest a way of doing this when designing a form to enter data into a database.

12 Suggest two different ways in which facilities in a typical database may be used to help prevent tired data-entry staff making errors.

13 What is meant by a database query?

14 Boolean operations are often used when querying a database. What is a Boolean operation? List three different Boolean operators, giving an example where one of them could be used in a database.

15 It is probably necessary to maintain referral integrity when designing a database. What does referential integrity mean?

16 Design a suitable report layout to list the pupils in a school by house, with each house being listed by year and then form.

17 Some data contained in a database needs to be analysed using statistics not available within the database package. However, the appropriate mathematical functions are available in a spreadsheet. Outline the principles of what has to be done to analyse the data.

18 Macro languages like VBA, for example, can be used to extend the functionality of a database like Access. Explain how this might have overcome the problem outlined in question 17.

16 Operating systems

In this section you will learn about:

- What an operating system is and what an operating system does
- Different types of operating system like batch, interactive, network and real time
- Different operating system interfaces like command-line and GUI
- Operating system utilites
- Operating system security, resource management and auditing
- Specialist operating systems like process control

The role of an operating system

The **operating system** is an *extremely complex* piece of **software**, which turns the raw hardware of the computer into a useful and easy-to-use system. Without the operating system there would be no software to interpret and process the characters typed in at the keyboard, or to display the graphics on the screen; without the operating system you would not even be able to format a disk, or drive a printer attached to your computer.

Operating systems like the early versions of **DOS (Disk Operating System)** were rudimentary and **command-line** driven. Users had to remember codes typed in at the command line prompt, with the object of performing functions similar to those performed using a mouse in a windows environment.

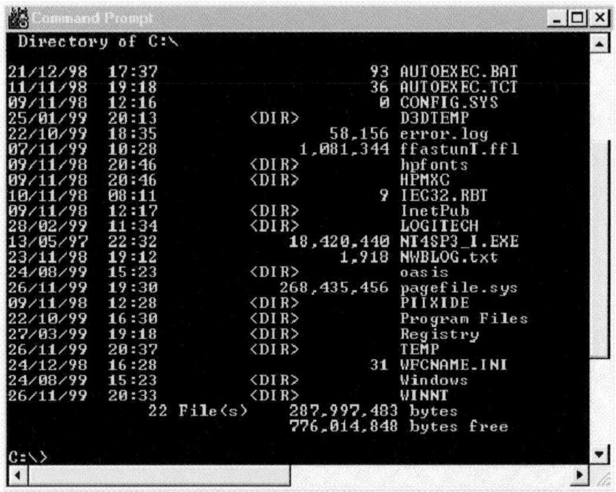

A typical DOS screen, listing some files and directories, is shown in Figure 16.1. After the command 'DIR' has been issued at the **DOS prompt** (i.e.'**C: \\>**'), the folders and files in the root of the C drive are displayed. Contrast this with the Windows display seen in Figure 16.2.

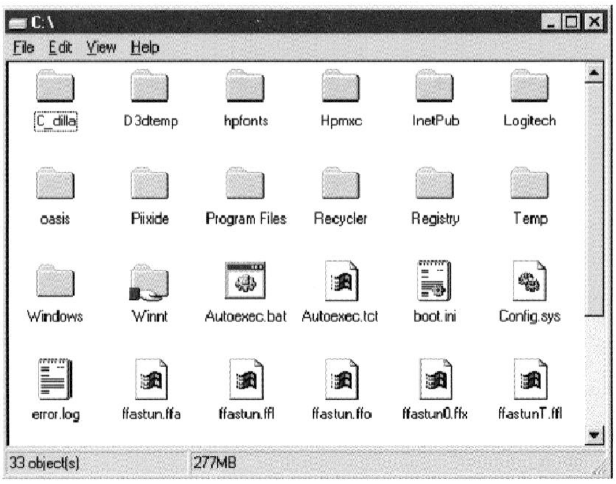

Figure 16.1 The root of a C drive displayed via DOS

Figure 16.2 shows a **GUI (Graphical User Interface)** presented by **Windows**. **MSDOS** is an example of a **command line** system, and **Windows** is an example of a **GUI**. Do not dismiss DOS or other command-line based operating systems as old fashioned and useless; *they are essential*, even in a modern operating system.

As you can see from the above, the *operating* system not only performs vital functions like listing the files on

Figure 16.2 Part of the same C drive displayed via Windows

the drive, but also *gives the computer characteristics like a GUI or command-line environment*. The all-important operating system is this fundamental, and this important concept is called a **virtual machine** (a virtual environment created for a specific purpose).

Example

Give an example of why it's necessary to keep the command-driven aspects of an operating system, even when you have access to a powerful GUI-based system.

Solution

It is useful for a network administrator to carry out similar sets of commands in a batch. Creating new users on a file server would be a particularly good example. Figure 16.3 shows a typical windows-based screen, into which information like 'username', 'password', and other information may be typed.

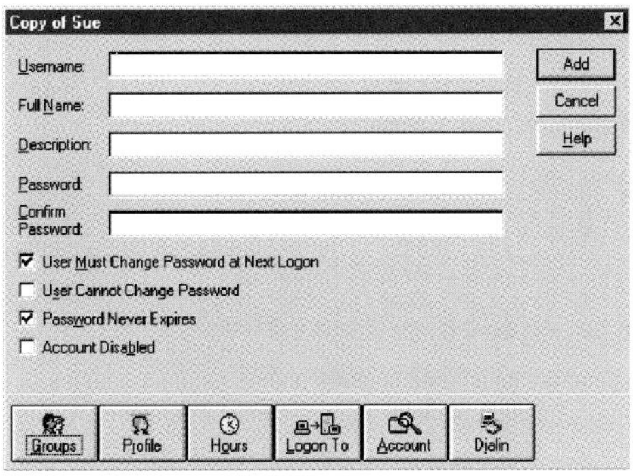

It is very easy to perform the above operations, but can you imagine doing this for 2500 different pupils in a school? It would take many days for a person to enter the data in this way! It would be far better to extract the pupils' names from the school database, and merge them with appropriate batch commands to perform the above operations automatically. This is the power of an operating system that supports command lines, and this is just one of the many good reasons why batch operating systems are still needed in modern GUI systems.

Figure 16.3 Creating users on a file server

A spreadsheet package like Mircosoft's Excel can be used to build up the batch files described here.

Data may be imported into Excel by CSV format, and the cut and paste facilities can be used to add the batch commands.

A batch file (.bat) can be created from the data held in the spreadsheet, which would then execute the appropriate commands in DOS when run as a batch file.

Operating system classification

The main categories, into which operating systems may be classified, are as follows:

- batch
- interactive
- network
- real time.

The word '**batch**' typifies an operating system where a number of jobs may be run one after the other. A **batch operating system** allows a computer operator to control **jobs** (*tasks to be run*) by issuing a set of batch **commands** via what's called a job control language. Operating systems which predominantly work by scheduling a set of pre-determined tasks, and then providing the results at some later stage are said to be running in **batch-processing mode**. This is typical of the **BACS** (the Bank Automated Clearing System) system which processes cheques, or for systems designed to process utility bills like electricity and gas, for example.

You should compare batch operations with the **interactive** nature of **Windows**, where users get an 'instant' response. If you are using an interactive operating system, you are engaged in a dialogue with the operating system. The user controls what's going to happen next by clicking the mouse or by loading particular software packages. In a batch operating system, the system would decide what job to do next, based on the most efficient use of available resources like processors and peripherals. Windows or indeed any **GUI operating system** used on typical PCs are good examples of **interactive operating systems**.

A **network operating system** supports the activities necessary to log onto file servers, share printers with colleagues over a network or get access to the internet via a proxy server (*see Chapter 9*). Most modern operating systems like **Windows**, **Linux** and the later versions of **DOS** are examples of network operating systems. Network operating systems have to provide an interface to hardware like network interface cards, and support the protocols like **TCP/IP** needed to access **LANs** and **WANs** (*see Chapter 9*).

Finally, there are **real-time operating systems**, which are often used in *mission-critical applications*, where a response is essential within a specific period of time. Mission critical operating systems usually have a large amount of redundancy built in, make use of the most expensive hardware and have no compromise regarding the design of the software. It is also most likely that a real-time operating system would concentrate only on the specific tasks for which the system has been designed. **Interactive operating systems** like **Windows** are always a compromise between the hardware available to run it and the cost of the systems. They also have thousands of general purpose software packages to run, and are therefore not optimised for any specific task.

Real-time operating systems are also used in situations like booking airline tickets, where absolute speed is not vital, but a *sensible response time is*. You must appreciate that 'real time' does *not necessarily* mean a lightning fast response, but the fast-response examples quoted earlier are the easiest ones to understand in the context of a real time operating system. **Process-control systems** (*see later*) are also good examples of **real-time operating systems**, where the response time has to be appropriate for the task of controlling a process like a chemical production line or a nuclear power station.

Resource management

One of the major tasks of an operating system is to manage the available resources such as **memory**, or **processor** time. If you are loading a picture into an art package, for example, the size of which is larger than the available amount of RAM inside your computer, the operating system will try to cope by pretending that parts of your hard disk are available RAM (called **virtual memory**). You may be using a word processor at the same time as printing out one of your spreadsheet documents – how is the processor time allocated between these two tasks? If insufficient processing power is allocated to the word processing task, you will find that you will not be able to type very fast!

Example

How does an operating system manage the computer's memory to help organise hardware attached to the system? How might this memory be organised to run programs like DTP systems and spreadsheets at apparently the same time?

Solution

The available ROM and RAM must be mapped out into specific areas. This is called a memory map. Some areas will be for the storage of the operating system itself and others will be allocated to application programs. It is essential that areas be dedicated to graphics and sound, or for the interface of peripheral devices such as printers. Figure 16.4 shows some of the operating-system settings for a sound card on a PC.

These numbers act as pointers to other places in memory where parts of the operating system (code), which actually handle these devices, are located. Application programs must be allocated their own areas of memory. Failure to do this would mean that memory space in use by one application would corrupt memory space being used by another, and the computer would fail to operate correctly. It is the job of the operating system to allocate memory on the fly, so that when memory being used by one application is released, it is automatically available to be used by another.

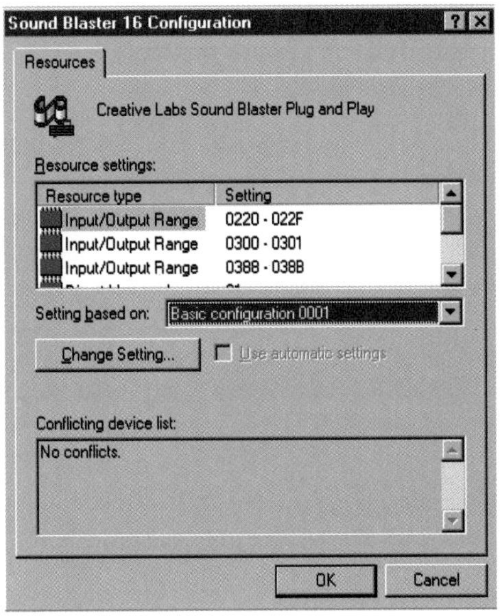

Figure 16.4 Memory map settings

Multi-user operating systems

Operating systems may be **single-user**, like a typical PC at home, or **multi-user**, where more than one person (*usually many more*) can use the **same computer** at apparently the same time. Sometimes it is confusing for students to determine if an operating system is multi-user or not. If, a network uses **fat-clients** (*i.e. a typical PC being attached to a network*) then the user of this PC has exclusive use of the operating system on his or her PC. The fact that you have a network connection means that you can share data with others, but others are not sharing your operating system inside your machine.

The term **multi-user** is *not* normally reserved for different people using the PCs in the ways described above. It is reserved for lots of people making simultaneous use of a larger system. For example, if you are running a **thin-client** system, where the local machines attached to the network have no local drives, and a large file server processes the requests from all of the users 'simultaneously', then this is an example of a **multi-user operating system**. On this sort of system, if there are 20 users, each user will have to wait in turn until the operating system gets round to dealing with them.

Example

Explain the difference between a thin-client system and a fat-client system, indicating some relative advantages and disadvantages of each type of architecture.

Solution

A fat client is the name given to a standard PC attached to a network. The PC will have a network operating system like Windows, have its own local hard disks, and its own local processor, etc. It is usual to load applications from the local hard disk, although the file server can be used for application delivery too, and the network is used only for sharing common resources like printers, and for storing the users' files and other information on a file server. The biggest disadvantage with this system is that it is harder to maintain because all the local hard disks throughout the organisation have to be updated when changes are made.

The alternative is to use a thin-client operating system. Here there is little local processing power, other than the ability to interpret characters at the keyboard, and drive the display on the monitor. There are no local hard disks, and often there is no floppy disk either! All processing is done by sending information back to the operating system on the file server, which in turn processes it and sends it back to the client workstation to be displayed on the screen. This system is very easy indeed to maintain, as there is virtually nothing that can go wrong with the thin-client workstation. However, a large bandwidth is needed for complex work, and graphics processing can often bring the system to a halt.

File security

Secure operating systems like 'Windows 2000' or 'Windows XP Professional' allow you to **control access** to resources and **audit** the systems in real time. In a **multi-user environment** it is essential for security reasons to control access to files, or everybody would be able to read and delete the work belonging to everybody else! In the Windows 2000 operating system, this is achieved by setting attributes for each file on the system.

Figure 16.5 shows that permissions may be set on selected files or folders. This might be a single file, or hundreds of Mbytes of directories and sub-directories within the hierarchical data structure on the file-server disks. You can specify who may **read** or **change** the files, who may **delete** the files, or who may **run executables**, for example. You can get the **operating system** to build up a **log** of who does what, where and when! You can also **audit events** such as printing, so that charges may be made on the number of printouts that are done, or you may charge for the time that a particular person is logged onto the system. Indeed, you can control the exact time when people may use the system, all from similar panels in the operating system.

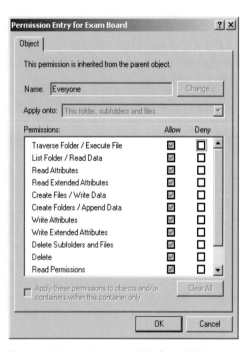

Figure 16.5 Permissions in Windows 2000

Such **permissions**, applied to the C drive of a workstation, can be used to make sure that users do not inadvertently (or deliberately!) delete files or programs that would render the system unusable. **Less secure** operating systems like 'Windows 98' or 'Windows XP', for example, could be rendered ineffective very quickly in environments like schools, colleges and businesses, where careless or reckless users may destroy the system.

Example

Pupils in a school environment use the internet on a daily basis. What facilities provided by the operating system might prove useful in enabling the network administrator to monitor internet activity?

Solution

The network administrator could set up a log, which monitors all network activity regarding the internet. This is easy to set up if all students on the network log into the internet via a proxy server. (This is now common in many schools.) If each student has to log on to use the system, then they have identified themselves to the proxy server, and the sites that they visit can be entered into a log and saved on the proxy server by the operating system. The network administrator can then inspect the log and electronically search for any items of interest.

Time management

You can **account** for the use of **resources** such as **printing**, the **internet** and the **times** at which people may log onto the system. Access times can be controlled as shown in Figure 16.6. This shows an NT4 file server being set up to allow a user called Sue to log onto the system between 9.00 am and 5.00 pm only. If she attempted to log on outside of these hours the system would deny her access. It is also possible to disable an account completely. More sophisticated monitoring and control of access times can be applied to individual resources like the internet and other applications. You should also consider this with material which is covered in detail in Chapter 13.

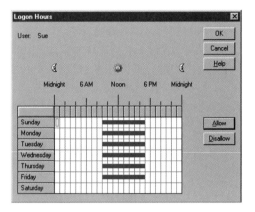

Figure 16.6 Control of log-on hours

Further resource management

Other resources besides time are equally important. Printing, for example, can be audited with the help of the operating system. Each time a user uses a **network printer**, the job is **spooled** via the **file server** and the number of pages printed is incremented in a **database**. Hundreds of users can be monitored printing to a huge variety of printers. Students could be charged for printing, and the statistics automatically exported to a database for efficient processing. In larger organisations it is more usual to charge **departments**.

Example

Suggest a way that an operating system might allow some pupils access to the internet while not allowing others access, even if they are using the same computer.

Solution

You could define the departments they are in, the year in the school to which they belong, or any other similar information. By inventing an internet group, it is possible to deny access to the programs or proxy servers needed to run the internet via a local area network. Making users members of a group, as shown in Figure 16.7, can give them access to certain resources. Defining characteristics of a group can take a long time if the criteria are complex, but users can belong to many groups, and receive a mixture of privileges.

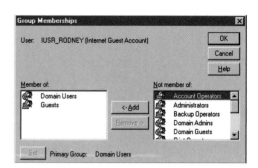

Figure 16.7 Control of groups

Access to resource management

By using a combination of **group** and **time management** outlined in the last couple of sections, it's possible to control what is allowed at any particular time. This is ideal in an educational environment where you may want to deny pupils access to the internet or other software like games during lessons, but allow them to do these things during break.

Access to disk space

It is essential that **disk space** is **managed** effectively, and users are not allowed to save as much data as they wish. The operating system or third party software like 'Quota Manager', for example will manage this effectively. It's possible to allocate users a **fixed quota** of disk space, or allocate certain quotas to different groups within an organisation.

Example

Outline a scenario in which it is possible for an inexperienced user to fill up the hard drives on a network file server. What would be the consequences of this actually being carried out, and what can be done to prevent this happening?

Solution

A novice user might easily input an A4 high-quality (1200 dpi) 24-bit coloured image from a scanner, and attempt to save this huge file onto the network file server. This image could be several Gbytes in size (*see Chapter 2*), and would therefore help to fill up the disk on the main file server.

If this were to happen, then no other person on the network would be able to save any work, and the whole system would be rendered virtually useless until the network manager or the pupil deleted the offending file.

Operating a quota for each user can prevent this happening. It is unlikely that the user would have several Gbytes of personal space on the network, and would therefore be prevented from saving this huge bitmap file.

Auditing the use of files

Occasionally it might be necessary to track down who is making use of a particular piece of software or accessing a particular file. It is possible to put an **audit tag** onto any **file**, which means that if the file is accessed, then the user, the **time** and the **date** is noted in a log generated by the operating system. When the log is inspected, it is possible for the network manager to see which users have been using a particular resource.

Figure 16.8 shows a user called Sue being monitored for applying a permission change to a particular file. As you can see from the settings, a log entry will only be generated if she successfully changes the file permissions on this particular file.

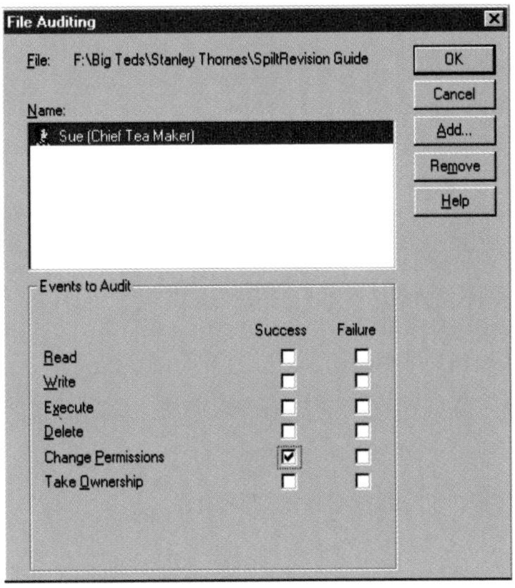

Archives and backups

No matter how much sophisticated security is applied to the system you must never lose sight of the fact that important data could be destroyed by accident. An administrator might delete important files, or a system crash might render a file unreadable. In Chapter 14, when disaster recovery was being considered, you saw how **backups** need to be made of all important files on the system. Don't forget also that little-used data might need to be taken off line, and this is known as an **archive**. Candidates sometimes confuse the terms backup and archive, and the following example should help you to distinguish between the two.

Figure 16.8 Auditing files

Example

Explain the difference between a backup and an archive. Outline a typical scenario which shows that you understand the difference between these two concepts.

Solution

A backup is making copies of important files and folders in your system. The purpose of doing this is to enable you to recover from a catastrophic event like a system malfunction, recovery from a virus infection, or accidental deletion of important data.

An archive means taking little-used data off line. Unlike a backup, an archive removes the data from the system, and places the data onto a suitable medium like a CD-ROM or DVD, for example. A typical example of this might be a company who builds houses. House plans that are years old might not be needed too often, and could therefore be removed to tape. However, an enquiry from an old customer might require that some very old plans are loaded into the computer. It would be inefficient to keep tens of years of work on the current computer system, and so the data is recovered from the archive. It will take longer to do this compared to data on line, but this is a small price to pay for freeing up space on your system to be used by more important data.

Process-control operating systems

Some specialist operating systems are used in the **process-control** industry. These are the systems used to control processes like **manufacturing**, **power plant**, **chemical processes** and utilities such as **water treatment**. These operating systems must usually respond in real time, but these times need not necessarily be lightning fast. As long at the data being received by the sensors is processed in time to be useful then this will be sufficient.

Typical **real-time systems** of the sort described here are to be found in **missile control systems**, in **aircraft control** and other time-critical computer-controlled systems. In these systems **reliability** is of extreme importance, and this usually outweighs the consequences of cost. The term **real-time operating system** is also used in less demanding scenarios. The best definition of a real-time operating system is, therefore, *one that can respond to externally dictated inputs and provide outputs in a satisfactory amount of time.* Many real-time process-control systems are embedded into devices from cruise missiles to digital cameras. These systems, which are usually implanted into a variety of electronic devices, are known as **embedded systems**.

Self-test questions

1 What is meant by the term 'command-line operating system'? Give an example.
2 Distinguish between batch and real-time operating systems, giving an example of each.
3 Give three different examples of resources that are managed by the operating system.
4 How might an operating system manage the security of files on a file server?
5 What is meant by a multi-user system?
6 State two advantages of a fat client over a thin client.
7 State two advantages of a thin client over a fat client.
8 A user with a single processor inside his computer is arguing that he can do more than one thing at a time because many things are happening on screen 'at the same time'. Why is this logic flawed?
9 Why is running a batch of commands useful for network administration?
10 Explain the need for file security in a network environment.
11 Outline three different things that you may be able to do to enhance the security of a file. Give a practical example of where each of your file-security measures may be useful.
12 When dealing with time-management aspects, it is sometimes useful for the operating system to allow log on only between set times. However, if you are already logged on, most systems will not automatically log people off. If this proved to be unsatisfactory, what else could you do to make sure that the users were safely logged off under controlled conditions?
13 A large company wants members of different departments to have different security and access rights on the network. What features of the operating system might enable a network manager to accomplish this task?
14 Even though all the security permissions have been set correctly, information from a file seems to have been accessed illegally from time to time. What features of the operating system might enable a network manager to track down who is getting illegal access to this file?
15 A legal problem has arisen regarding who made alterations to a word processor document. Assuming that auditing is carried out on all accesses to files, how might this enable the company to resolve who actually carried out the alterations?
16 A process-control or real-time operating system often has to have added features and reliability. Give two examples of a real-time system where reliability would be of paramount importance.
17 A real-time operating system does not necessarily have to respond quickly. Give three examples of real time systems where a lightning fast response is not an issue.

17 Input and output devices

In this section you will learn about:

- A variety of contemporary input and output devices and typical uses
- Typical uses of and statistics about keyboards, mice and trackballs
- Typical uses of and statistics about graphics tablets, joysticks and bar codes
- Typical uses of and statistics about OCR, OMR and MICR
- Typical uses of and statistics about video speech and MIDI
- Typical uses of and statistics about capturing scientific data and data from the web
- Typical uses of and statistics about CRTs, LCD and other displays
- Typical uses of and statistics about graphics and sound cards

Input devices

A large range of **input devices** are available. You *don't* need to know the technical details of how they work, but you *should be aware of the characteristics of each device*, and *be able to make an informed choice* regarding their suitability for any given task. You will be expected to choose input devices in the context of different examples. For each range of **peripheral devices**, a table of characteristics is presented, and you would be wise to remember these.

Figure 17.1 A Maltron Keyboard

New input and output devices appear at frequent intervals. Keep up to date with these latest peripheral devices by using the internet or by looking at current computer magazines.

This will help to keep your answers topical.

The keyboard

A variety of different **keyboards** exist, ranging from **QWERTY** layouts (the standard Western keyboard), through **natural keyboards** (helps prevent RSI or **repetitive strain injury**), to specialist keyboards (**concept keyboards**) used for controlling industrialised plant. Keyboards may be linked optically via infrared or via a radio signal to save the need for a cable.

Table 17.1 Important characteristics about keyboards

Device	Typical cost	Main characteristics/speed of use, etc.
Standard keyboards	£5–£50	Main data entry method – a competent typist can enter data between 80 and 120 words/minute.
Natural keyboards	£35–£100	Useful for touch typists only – a competent typist can enter data between 80 and 120 words/minute. Helps to prevent RSI.
Concept keyboards	£150–£500	Overlays may be used to help define the function of each key on a special keyboard. A graphics tablet is sometimes used for this.
Specialist keyboards	£350–£500	These are ideal for people with special needs. Examples are single-handed keyboards and mouth-operated keyboards, etc.

Maltron is a specialist keyboard manufacturer. Take a look at their website at www.maltron.com.

Other keyboard layouts exist, like the 'azerty' keyboard used in France, or the specialist keyboards for use with Far Eastern languages.

Example

Outline a situation in which a specialist keyboard would be essential, saying why it is useful in your given scenario.

Solution

TV, like that used by Sky-Digital viewers, requires a specialist keyboard for surfing and e-mail. Most people will use this keyboard in front of the TV, and a cable would be inconvenient. Therefore, this particular keyboard has an infrared link to the set-top box. The keyboard has been designed with on-line shopping and e-mail in mind, and is also able to double up as the remote control for the TV.

Mice, trackballs and touchpads

Mice and associated input devices have been around for a considerable time. Do not forget the many incarnations of these devices that make them particularly applicable to some situations. It might be inconvenient to use a mouse with a portable computer or PDA; therefore, an ordinary mouse would be inappropriate for data entry here. You must always think in terms of **ergonomics** and the **GUI**. In other words, what user

Figure 17.2 A trackball designed for data entry by young children

interface is most appropriate? Mice may be optically linked via infrared or linked via a radio signal to a PC to save the need for a connecting cable. A variey of buttons exist on many mice.

Table 17.2 Important information about mice, trackballs and touch pads

Device	Typical cost	Main characteristics/speed of use, etc.
Standard mice	£5–£25	Two-button device, possibly with a wheel. Main GUI input mechanism.
Infrared mice	£10–£50	Useful because the device has no rollers which can get clogged up.
Trackballs	£20–£100	Useful where desk space is at a premium or on portables. (see Figure 17.2)
Touchpads	£35–£100	Some touchpads have keys which simulate the operation of the buttons on a mouse. Touchpads are useful on portable computers.

Touch screens, pen-based input and PDAs

Mice, **keyboards, touchpads** and **trackballs** may be dispensed with altogether if a **touch screen** is used. Menu selections may be made with either a pen or the finger pointing at a special screen. Larger touch-screen monitors tend to have a crisscross of infrared links, whereas smaller **PDAs** (**personal digital assistants**) tend to have pen-based input methods. Menu selections and handwriting may be input using a pen-based system. A huge range of applications software is available for PDAs, and most will hotlink to a computer, typically via a **USB port** or the **serial port**. This makes for easy transfer of data between the PDA and the desktop computer.

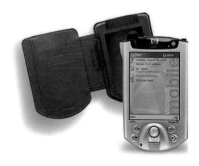

Figure 17.3 A HP IPAQ PDA

Example

A building firm issues its employees with a device for logging the materials used and the progress made each day. This device is to be used in a harsh environment. Suggest a suitable method of inputting data at a building site.

Solution

A specialist portable computer or PDA with a touch screen and pen would be effective, but only if it was rugged enough to be dropped. An effective membrane barrier from the corrosive effects of building materials must be provided, and it should operate in the freezing temperatures likely to be encountered. In such a harsh environment, it is unlikely that the users would want to carry out any keystrokes, especially as they might be using a gloved hand. A pen-based system making use of a touch screen would therefore be very effective here. A gloved hand could easily hold the pen, and appropriate on-screen menus could provide the necessary options.

Table 17.3 Important information about PDAs and touch-screens

Device	Typical cost	Main characteristics/speed of use, etc.
PDA	£120–£800	Typically can run applications like cut down versions of word processors, spreadsheets, databases and presentation packages. E-mail and internet browsing, tasks, notes and diaries, handwriting recognition via stylus input. Can synch with a PC or Mac, typically via a USB, serial port, infrared or wireless (Bluetooth).
Touch screen	£600–£1000+	Useful in situation where an input device like a mouse might be stolen. Typically these are used in bank teller machines and public information centres like museums and shopping centres.

Graphics tablets

Artists are able to use this device as a more natural form of input compared to the mouse. Strokes made with a pen on a touch-sensitive pad can be used to mirror drawing on the screen. **Graphics tablets** are available in sizes ranging from A5 to A3 and beyond.

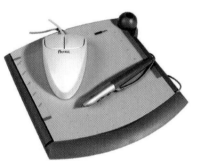

Figure 17.4 A small graphics tablet

Joysticks and consoles

Do not dismiss **joysticks** as simply a method of playing games. There are many industrial uses, like controlling industrial plant, or manipulating molecular structures in a virtual environment, for example. There are many other incarnations of the joystick, and specialist consoles vary from interfaces for games to specialist equipment to train pilots.

Bar codes

You need to know few details other than that different systems are used in the USA and Europe, and many different bar codes exist for different purposes, including some reserved for use within individual businesses. **Bar code systems** are also internationally recognised, like the ISBN number on a book. Bar codes are important for stock control, and speed up the queues at **EFTPOS** terminals. Various methods exist for reading bar codes, including **optical wands** (like a pen), **bar code scanners** (like a gun), and **scanning mechanisms** embedded into supermarket checkouts. **Bar codes** give *error-free input* if the scan is accepted, due to the extensive error checking.

Table 17.4 Important information about Graphics tablets, joysticks and bar code readers

Device	Typical cost	Main characteristics/speed of use, etc.
Graphics tablets	£60–£800	Typically operated with a cordless pen. Position of pen on tablet relates to position on screen. Therefore ideal for artists and designers to draw. Units typically have 150 lines per inch resolution.
Joysticks	£10–£150	Used for serious applications (pilot and military training) as well as games. Force feedback joysticks add realism to flight training.
Bar code readers	£50–£1000+	These range from small hand-held pen devices to hand-held laser scanners to large units housed in supermarket POS (Point Of Sale) terminals.

Example

How might bar codes be used to assign books and other media like video and music CDs to students when they are using a school library?

Solution

If books have bar codes, these can be used, together with the database on the computer to identify the book being borrowed or returned. A bar code could also be used on a student ID card to identify the student who is undertaking the transaction.

Other media like CDs and videos will probably have bar codes too, but if any item, like a map or a fossil, does not have a bar code, then the school can use special software to invent their own bar code for use with this system. Figure 17.2 shows Corel's 'Barcode Wizard' start up screen. Using this software, you can easily make your own bar codes.

OCR systems and scanners

A flatbed **scanner** is normally used for **optical character recognition** (or **OCR**), often with a paper feed, so that multiple documents can be handled easily. Some software can handle multiple column pages, and will even navigate around pictures automatically. Typical software is shown in Figure 17.6.

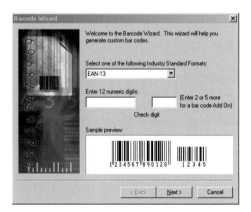

Figure 17.5 Making your own bar codes

Example

Explain the processes that have to be undertaken to turn a sheet of pre-typed text into computer-readable format.

Solution

The paper to be scanned is put into the scanner, and appropriate software is activated. (The HP software start up screen is shown in Figure 17.6.) After scanning the page it is usually in bit-mapped form, meaning that the whole page is treated like a picture. Next, select the appropriate area of the page for processing. Having selected the area, this is operated upon by pattern recognition software, which attempts to correlate the patterns in the picture with known text fonts. It is unlikely that all the text has been perfectly interpreted, and some text will need to be put though a spell-checking process. The user will be prompted to help the system if some of the text is unrecognisable. Manual intervention is normal when using OCR methods.

Figure 17.6 OCR scanning software

Scanners are the main methods for transferring **images** from the printed page into the computer. Remember that huge amounts of memory are required to store large **bit-mapped coloured images** at high resolutions (*see Chapter 2*).

Other OCR systems

Other systems like **turnaround documents** exist, in which **optical character recognition** is used in quite different ways. The turnaround document is ideal for bill payment systems, where information regarding a customer is coded onto the bill, and used for data input at the time of payment. (Hence the name turnaround document.)

MICR systems

Magnetic ink character recognition (MICR) is the standard system used at the bottom of bank cheques. The clearing banks process millions of cheques each day (**Bank Automated Clearing System**). Extra magnetic ink characters are usually put onto the cheques representing the amount and other information, so the batch operation of clearing the cheques can be carried out automatically and quickly.

OMR systems

Multiple choice type answer sheets in examinations typify **optical mark reader** (or OMR) systems, also called **mark sense readers**. Marks, using an HB pencil or other suitable pen,

OMR alternatively stands for Optical Mark Recognition. Using this alternative the device to read the characters would therefore be an OMR reader.

are made in pre-set positions on a specially prepared sheet of paper. Do not forget that this form of input might be ideal for many forms of data capture in which answers to pre-set questions are required.

Key-to-disk systems

Some very large data-processing organisations need to enter huge amounts of data by manual methods. This technique enables many people to enter data at a computer terminal (hence the term **key**) straight onto **disk**, ready for processing at a later stage when all the data has been entered and correlated. It is possible to have the data **validated** or **verified** before being processed by the main computer system.

Table 17.5 Important information about OCR, OMR and MICR devices

Device	Typical cost	Main characteristics/speed of use, etc.
OCR machine	£50–£10 000+	A small scanner is all that's necessary for OCR of normal text into a home or office PC. Specialist high-volume batch jobs on a mainframe reading characters optically from utility bills cost thousands.
OCR software	£40–£200	Software for interpreting characters varies in sophistication. Useful features include multiple columns and ignoring picture areas.
OMR	£300–£5000+	Small volume machines for marking a few A4 sheets at a time are inexpensive. Large high-volume machines for batch marking of multiple-choice examination scripts cost thousands.
MICR	£10 000+	These are specialist machines, used by the banking industry for the BACS system.

Video input of data

Input of video images is now common. We can use a conventional **video camera**, but **digital video cameras** now mean we can download and process video images with little, if any, loss of quality. We also have an arsenal of **digital cameras**, and there are yet still more video image sources such as **DVDs**, **CD-ROMs** and the **internet**.

Powerful **microcomputers** are rewriting the book with regard to what users with modest amounts of money can do with **digital editing**. Whilst 'ordinary' micros are not yet up to the standard achieved by programs such as 'Walking with Dinosaurs' or films like 'Titanic' or 'The Matrix', one day these facilities will be available on powerful home micros. The **post-production** list of software is equally impressive, varying from **non-linear editing** (i.e. assembling sequences of shots into any order), through the addition of **graphics** to the creation of **panoramic 360° shots**.

Example

A firm of estate agents have set up a database to help them sell houses. Explain how the use of 'video-capture techniques' might be helpful in maintaining information on this database.

Solution

A good-quality digital camera or a digital video camera may be used as a mechanism for creating the pictures of the houses and inside rooms. This is ideal for an estate agent because there is no film processing involved in this exercise. Apart from static shots, video footage may be used to give a guided tour of the house, which may be replayed on a computer with a video player like Apple's QuickTime. With a suitable number of still images taken and stuck together, a '360° panoramic view' of a room or the garden, for example, may be created.

Speech input

Speech input is a perfectly usable system, provided that you have trained the software to recognise your voice, a task that usually takes a few hours. It is a bonus for disabled people, and effective for those who cannot type. Nevertheless, many people find it an unnatural form of input for many aspects of their work. For example, when writing this book, I spent much time thinking what to say, and changed my mind frequently. This methodology is more suited to the keyboard than speech input, especially when it comes to complex formatting of documents.

Speech input is an ideal form of **command-driven language**, leaving the operator with his or her hands free. In situations in which a computer must be controlled at the same time that manual tasks are being carried out, it is a vital form of data entry, and will certainly be used more extensively in the future.

MIDI

MIDI, the **Musical Instrument Digital Interface** is, of course, of use only to musicians, but if you are a musician, then this is the musical equivalent of your 'word processor'. The ability to play into a keyboard and get the data into the computer in **real time** is a bonus. The ability to join together scores you have played yourself is fun, and the ability to *print out the music* is impressive.

Example

Explain how several session musicians in different parts of the world might compose a song at the same time, and then make the music instantly available for distribution to members of the public.

Solution

A MIDI-equipped keyboard, connected to the computer via a suitable MIDI interface, could be used to play music into specialist music software like 'Cakewalk Express', for example. If the computer is connected to the internet, then the MIDI data could also be sent to the other sites, where the other musicians, using the same software, could hear what the first musician is playing, and therefore join in with the session. It would be convenient to make use of video conferencing so they could see each other, and hear verbal comments in real time. Finally, when they are happy with the digital recording that they have made, it can be saved on their internet site, ready to be streamed to the masses via suitable software that can play MP3 files, giving almost CD quality audio streaming to their eager fans!

Other forms of computer input

There are many other specialist forms of computer input, with the **data glove** being just one good example. Indeed, **whole-body suits** can have sensors that detect the position of the wearer so that they can interact with **virtual worlds** created on the computer. The data glove would enable you to control electronic systems like **robots** in a hostile environment like a nuclear reactor, or control a submarine moving along the depths of the ocean. The movements of the hand (or body in the case of the suit) are transformed into digital information by the computer, and then transmitted in the appropriate form to the computer that is controlling the action of the robot or submarine.

Example

An advanced sporting simulator is being developed in which a virtual-reality helmet is used to deliver information to the player, and data gloves and whole-body suits are computer input devices. The simulator is to be used for tennis players to improve their skills, and enable analysis of their movements during a typical game. Explain how the two input devices could be used in this way.

Solution

The player is immersed in the virtual world, by observing the 3D images that would be projected into his or her eyes via the virtual reality helmet. The feedback from the data glove and whole body suit would enable the computer to build up a real-time 3D model of the player's body position and hand movements, which could then be translated to predict what is happening to the virtual ball when struck by the player's virtual bat.

A typical scenario, like a computer-controlled player serving the ball could be programmed, and the reaction of the simulator player could be monitored by recording the exact positions of their body, arms and legs, etc. in relation to the delivery of the virtual ball. At a later stage the player could enter the simulator control room, and watch a recorded version of the return of serve played back on the computer monitor. The coach may then be able to calculate a variety of statistics, enabling him or her to analyse the player's movements. From this data it might be possible to predict what the player did wrong if the service was not returned, or how the return could be improved. Being a simulator, the degree of difficulty is under the control of the coach, and beginners and experts alike could use this simulator to improve their game.

Capturing scientific and engineering data

In the scientific and engineering world much data in the form of **quantities**, such as '**radiation**' or '**pollution levels**' needs to be captured, and this is why it is mentioned here for

Table 17.6 Important information about Video, speech, MIDI and data logging

Device	Typical cost	Main characteristics/speed of use, etc.
Video input	£30–£5000+	Simple web cams are ideal for domestic and casual use. Broadcast quality video input is more expensive.
Speech input	£80–£300+	Speech input systems of the sort used for dictation into a word processor are inexpensive and very effective.
MIDI	£50–£200	Hardware interfaces for the computers are inexpensive. The software to control the MIDI interface varies considerably in price.
Data logging	£50–£10 000+	Simple data loggers for use in school are inexpensive. Commercial data logging devices are expensive pieces of professional kit. A large expense for the data logging equipment is the sensors needed to convert the quantity into appropriate electrical signals.

completeness. In an examination it is unlikely that questions regarding **data logging** would be mixed up with the general data-capture methods outlined in this unit.

Capturing data from the web

The **world wide web** has become an enormous **data-capture vehicle** for many companies. Figure 17.7 shows a typical form, filled in by users when booking a hotel.

The user is being prompted to input data regarding the dates, number of adults, and room type (smoking or non-smoking). They are then prompted to confirm the reservation by typing in their name, address, e-mail address and any other information required. After typing in his or her credit-card number over a **secure internet link**, he or she would be given

Figure 17.7 Typical data capture from the web

a confirmation number, and e-mail would be sent with further confirmation if an e-mail address were entered onto the **data capture form**. Much data is now collected in this way, where the information input onto the form would be stored in the **central reservations database** for the hotel concerned. A **scripting language** like **PERL** or an **ASP** (**Active Server Page**) might be used to process the data, and store it in an **SQL database** ready for further analysis by the hotel chain's computer systems.

Manual data collection methods

For the purposes of the examination you might be required to use your discretion about which **input device** is appropriate in a given situation. This is why so many examples have been given involving real-life scenarios. It is likely that the input devices and methods of data collection would be wrapped up in some context, probably in conjunction with output and storage devices too.

Example

An opinion poll is to be undertaken for a television company in which 10 000 people are to be sampled, gathering their political opinions prior to an election. All the data captured that day is required for the evening news bulletin. Suggest a suitable means of data capture for this project. Explain how your method would work in practice.

Solution

Assuming preset questions, a special data-capture form is designed, on which the pollsters place a tick in boxes. A very small sample of the form could be as shown in Figure 17.8. One data capture form can be used for each client interview, and marks made in the box could be used to automatically sense the answers using an optical mark reader.

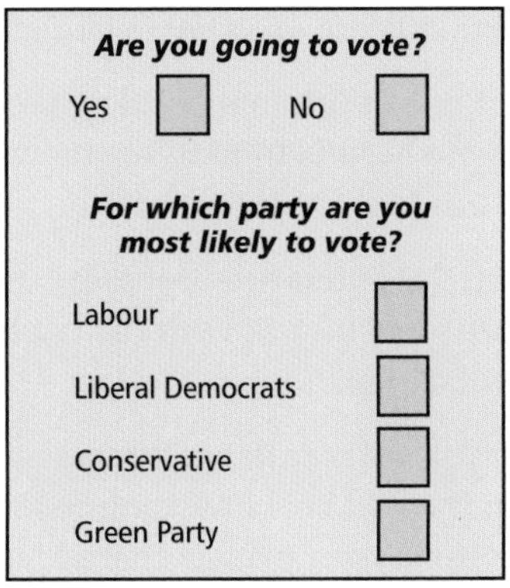

Figure 17.8 A simple layout

Typically, the OMR machine could be set up to enter the data directly into a file, which could then be transferred into a database or spreadsheet, thus getting 10 000 forms processed in a sensible amount of time, probably within a couple of hours, which is sensible to get the statistics out the same day.

To keep the data entry on schedule, it is best if there are no questions requiring written responses for the sample. This would involve manually entering this data, and the results are unlikely to be available on time. You may be expected to design your own **data-capture forms**. Simple effective layouts, like the form shown in Figure 17.8 above, are all that is required in an examination.

Output devices

A very large range of **output devices** is available. We will concentrate not on the technical characteristics of each device, but on their usefulness in different scenarios, which is typical of what to expect in AS computing examinations.

Printers

Colour ink jet printers are popular in the home and small business market, and the **laser printer** reigns supreme in the larger business and corporate market. There is a place for **dot matrix printers**, even though this is one of the older technologies on the market. You can also print to **film** (**microform**). Any printed output, in whatever form, is known as **hard copy**.

Example

(a) Why is an ink jet printer much more suitable for colour printing in the home?

(b) Why would an ink jet printer probably be unsuitable for a network printer?

(c) Why are dot matrix printers still used in shops and some offices?

(d) Which printer is most suitable for use by a secretary for correspondence?

(e) Which printer is most suitable for the production of a glossy magazine? Explain why this printer would be most suitable.

Solution

(a) Ink jet printing is suitable for home use because it is very cheap to buy, and the running costs are unlikely to be too great for very low volume colour printing.

(b) Current ink jet printers are slow compared to laser printers. An ink jet printer is unlikely to be able to produce the volume of printouts in an acceptable time if many people are to share the printer on a network.

(c) Dot matrix printers are useful for the production of stock reports in the retail trade. They are ideal for use with the continuous fan-fold paper, typical of that needed in this application.

(d) A laser printer is suitable for use by a secretary, as the quality of the correspondence is high. It could be a low volume laser printer connected to a local machine, or a high-volume laser printer shared between several secretaries.

(e) Conventional printers are not up to the job of magazine production. Offset litho technology, or expensive laser printers used by the printing industry would be needed to cope with exceptional quality and volumes in a sensible time span.

Other printing technologies

Conventional printers are not adequate for larger jobs of the sort needed by architects and engineers. Larger scale drawings are needed, and a **flatbed X-Y plotter** or a **drum plotter** fits the bill. The drum plotter is most useful if floor space is at a premium. **Line printers** are also useful in the very high volume utility billing industry. This would include batch-processing operations such as printing names and addresses for electricity or gas bills.

Photographic printing technologies

The need to store huge volumes of printed material led to the advent of **microfilm** and **microfiche**. Rolls of film or rectangular-card systems are used to store printed material such that special machines called **COM readers** can read them. **COM** stands for **Computer Output on Microform**, where microform is the collective name for microfilm and microfiche.

Example

Give two typical places in which COM readers are common, suggesting why they are useful in one of your chosen scenarios. What new technologies are likely to replace these devices in the long term? Why?

Solution

COM readers are used in libraries and establishments like garage servicing departments. In the automobile servicing industry they are used extensively because much detailed information like pictures and text can be distributed and viewed very cheaply. The older way to view the same information was to send out thousands of manually printed pages. This is very expensive in terms of delivery to the garages, and also takes up a huge

Table 17.7 Important information about various printing technologies

Device	Typical cost	Main characteristics/speed of use etc.
Dot matrix printers	£50–£500+	Very small dot matrix printers are used for printing out invoices in a shop. Large dot matrix printers are used for printing out continuous form stationery with carbon copies.
Ink jet printers	£50–£300+	Ink jet printers are popular in the home and in schools. They have superb quality output and are cheap to buy, but the cartridges are expensive thus making them expensive to run if larger volumes are required.
Laser printers	£150–£10 000+	This is the workhorse for the office and education environments. The larger printers are designed to print many thousands of copies each day.
Microfiche	£200–£5000+	The microfiche readers are inexpensive to buy, and can be found in libraries and garages, etc. where a large amount of data in text and pictorial form needs to be referenced. This technology is rapidly being overtaken by cheap PCs and CD-ROMs and DVDs, etc.

amount of space, compared to the COM readers and microforms. The users do not have to have access to a computer to view the information. It is also highly reliable. The COM readers are very much cheaper to buy than computers, although in comparison to very low cost PCs, this is no longer the case. Also, the introduction of very low cost CDs and DVDs will probably mean that information printed onto microform will be replaced with viewing similar information from these disks in the future.

Display technologies

Displays are categorised by considering the technologies used to implement them. A conventional video monitor uses a **CRT** display. Typically these range from about 14 in. to 26 in. for high-resolution colour monitors, although smaller and larger screens are available. Monitors now work in resolutions ranging from 800 by 600, to well in excess of 1280 by 1024. The larger monitors are needed to display these very high resolutions ergonomically.

Liquid crystal displays (LCD) are thin screens, which appear on portables. Much larger LCD displays are available, up to 48 in. and beyond. LCD displays will probably become the norm for all computers in the future.

Recent innovations are light emitting plastic (LEP) or light emitting polymer displays, which are paper thin, and theoretically can be of any size. Some of the dreams of science fiction are coming true, as can be seen from the innovative ideas produced by the CDT company, in Figures 17.9 and 17.10.

Figure 17.9 A phone using an LEP display

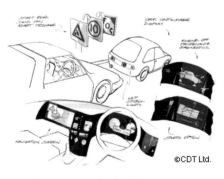

©CDT Ltd.

Figure 17.10 Some LEP display ideas

Example

Why is it likely that LCD and LEP displays will take over from conventional CRT displays?

Solution

LCDs are much lighter than the equivalent size CRT display. The LCD display uses far less energy than the equivalent CRT display, and this is why they are used in portables, where battery power is critical. It is likely that LEP displays will be available at some time in the future, and these will be cheap to produce compared to the LCD display. It may also allow you to roll up the screen for greater flexibility!

Other display technologies

There is an increasing need to display information to large audiences. Currently the projection TV system fits the bill admirably, although the LEP displays might provide a serious challenge in permanent venues like exhibition spaces and educational lecture theatres, for example. The cost of a projection TV is constantly being reduced, and 1024 by 768 displays are now affordable in many classrooms at typical schools. There are other very specialist displays, like the **3D holographic displays** used in the design environment to visualise manufactured artefacts. Such displays might be presented using a **head-up display** like a **virtual reality helmet**, or projected into a special area set up for the purpose. Displays that fit over conventional pairs of glasses are also being developed, and these could be useful for portable computers, or surfing the net via your third generation mobile phone.

Example

A museum of history is to build an interactive display for the public. They are considering a variety of display technologies. Explain how the use of a computer display methods and virtual reality might make for a more memorable experience.

Solution

Touch-sensitive CRT or LCD screens might present the visitor with a menu, which could be used to set up an appropriate environment. LEP displays can be wrapped to any shape. One option would be to build up a model of a human face, and cover it with LEP. This could create the illusion of movement. For example, the manikin would appear to be able to talk, smile or perform other facial expressions. When synchronised with animatronic movements of the body, and sound that appears to come out of the dummy's mouth, this could add a new dimension to an otherwise static display. For the ultimate experience the visitor could put on a virtual reality helmet. This would give the visitor the illusion of being immersed in a computerised world. Other technologies such as data gloves and whole body suits could all add to the illusion of being transported to a completely different place.

Graphics cards

An important role is played by the **graphics card** inside a PC. Without a powerful graphics card, containing a suitable amount of memory it is not possible to refresh the massive amount of information at a rate which is acceptable to the human eye. The higher the resolution, and the more colours that are used, the more strain is put on the graphics card. Some graphics cards are now designed to have a particularly good 3D performance, and this means that computer games and simulations, like 'Microsoft's Flight Simulator 2004', for example, look particularly stunning.

Computer sound

Sound plays an increasingly important part regarding output from a computer. State of the art sound cards now have multiple channels. Many now have surround sound, based on **Dolby Pro Logic** or **THX**. Not only do you have the front left and right speakers, but a central speaker, two rear speakers, and probably a large sub-woofer to boost the base. Such systems are useful not only to play games, but also to listen to movies on DVD systems, where sound is often encoded making use of one of the Dolby systems. These systems create a sound stage, which can make the users feel as if they are immersed in the action. Not only can you have sound going from left to right, but from back to front also. Recent systems, like **Dolby Digital** provide a completely circular sound stage.

Other forms of computer output

Computers can generate **smells**, by an injection of the appropriate chemical into the atmosphere. This is used to great effect in displays like those that can be found in the London Dungeons, for example, where mediaeval atmospheres can be created! This can further add to the realism of computer output in the entertainment and education industries. You should not forget **computer-generated speech** as an output medium. It is relatively easy to generate computer speech, compared to the infinitely more complex task of being able to understand speech. It is, however, still difficult to get natural sounding speech.

Table 17.8 Important information about sound and graphics cards and other display technologies

Device	Typical cost	Main characteristics/speed of use, etc.
Graphics card	£20–£300+	Some motherboards have built-in graphics capability. Specialist graphics cards are needed for demanding applications like CAD and gaming. Top of the range graphics cards have hundreds of Mbytes of very fast graphics RAM, making them more expensive.
Sound card	£10–£200+	A simple stereo sound card is inexpensive. The more expensive sound cards have capability for Dolby Digital and Dolby THX.
CRT	£70–£1500+	Conventional computer monitors – price depends on size.
LCD	£150–£3500+	Flat thin screens–space savings but currently more expensive than CRTs.
LEPs	£pence–£100+	Small displays used in equipment from mobile phones to very large wall displays. Can be wrapped around shapes to form interesting output possibilities.

Self-test questions

1. Will the keyboard ever be completely replaced by voice input?
2. Suggest some typical input peripherals for a PDA.
3. A WAP-enabled mobile phone is used for e-mail. What input device/s would make entry of text more convenient?
4. Outline two completely different uses of OCR techniques, suggesting where the use of each would be particularly appropriate.
5. OMR systems are used for examinations. Suggest two other uses to which these OMR systems can be put.
6. How is it possible for typed text to be input into a computer system so that it is in machine-readable format?
7. A joystick could play an important part in a flight simulator. Suggest three other input devices that might be useful in this context, outlining the role that would be played by each of your chosen devices.
8. What is the modern equivalent of a key-to-disk terminal?
9. Suggest three different systems in which video input of data could play a vital role.
10. Suggest two different applications that can make effective use of speech input, giving your reasons in each case.
11. Explain MIDI as a form of computer input. What data is easily input in this way?

12 Suggest three different forms of computer input that would be ideal for a robot dog or cat. How might each of your inputs be put to effective use in the device.

13 Explain why data capture forms are often important ways of gathering data.

14 How might information be gathered from internet users?

15 Design a data-capture form for gathering information needed when a pupil goes to a new school. What other forms of data capture are likely to be needed in this case?

16 Design a data-capture form for use by a university regarding student applications for undergraduate courses.

17 Design an on-line form to capture data about surfers using a retail site that sells CDs, music cassettes, videotapes and DVDs.

18 Suggest a typical use for a flatbed plotter.

19 Describe what LCD and LEP displays are.

20 Why is a graphics card needed?

21 What are the main differences in performance and use between laser printers and ink jet printers?

22 What is a COM reader?

23 What is an offset litho machine?

24 Dot-matrix printers are still being used – why?

25 How many pages/minute are typical for a modern laser printer?

26 Suggest a use for LEPs.

27 What name is usually given to the devices based on CRT technology?

18 Primary and secondary storage devices

In this section you will learn about:

- Primary storage devices like RAM
- Other types of ROM and RAM
- Secondary storage devices like floppy disks and hard disks
- Optical drives like CD and DVD
- Magneto-optical drives
- Tapes and tape backup systems
- Large Terabyte disk farms and tape backup for very large amounts of data

Storage devices

A large range of storage devices is available. You *don't* need to know the technical details of how they work, but *you should be aware of the characteristics of each, and be able to make an informed choice regarding the suitability of each device for any given task.* In your examinations you will be expected to choose storage devices in the context of given examples and this is why lots of examples have been included in this chapter. For each range of storage device a table of characteristics to be learnt is presented.

Primary storage devices

The most important objective of **primary storage** is speed of operation. **RAM (random access memory)** on the main motherboard is one of *the* determining factors regarding how fast your computer can operate. The word 'random' derives from the fact that you can access any memory location without having to go through all the previous locations. (Compare this with **serial access** and **direct** or **random access files** in Chapter 13.)

Figure 18.1 One Gigabyte of DDR SDRAM in two Direct In-line Memory Modules

The current generations of semiconductor RAM are **volatile**. This means that if power is removed from the system, the contents of memory are lost. This is why it is important to save data onto a secondary storage device before switching the computer off. An alternative name for **RAM** is **IAS** or **immediate access store**.

ROM (read only memory) is non-volatile, but you obviously cannot change the contents of this primary-storage device. This is therefore useful to store programs that do not change very often, like the computer **BIOS**, or parts of the operating system, for example. In modern computers the BIOS is stored in a special type of **ROM** called **flash memory** which means it can be upgraded in situ.

Both **RAM** and **ROM** are examples of **direct-access** devices. This means that it is possible to go directly to the data in memory, without having to read any previous data. You should compare this method with **serial access**, where previous data does have to be read, like reading a tape, for example.

Cache

Different technologies used to implement RAM vary in expense and speed of operation. Very fast access chips, currently having access times less than 10 **nsec** are used as a **buffer** between the main memory and the fast processor. If the instructions that the processor needs are stored inside this fast memory (called **cache**), then the program instructions will be executed even more quickly, leading to an overall improvement to the system.

Other types of RAM and ROM

A huge variety of memory types exist, and this range has been increased considerably due to the introduction of devices like **digital cameras**, **MP3 players**, sophisticated **mobile phones** and **PDAs** (Personal Digital Assistants.) Many of these devices use **flash ROM**. This technology was developed from **EPROM** (Erasable Programmable Read Only Memory), which enabled the contents of a ROM chip to be programmed by a special machine. The next device to be developed was an EEPROM (Electrically Erasable Programmable Read Only Memory), which enabled devices to be programmed electrically. Finally, **Flash ROM** enabled ROM devices to be programmed in situ.

The latest devices enable ROM to be programmed so quickly that it can act as a **solid state disk drive** (a disk drive with no moving parts). Typical of these are the USB Flash ROMs of which one is shown in Figure 18.2. The top comes off to reveal a USB connector which can be plugged into any computer with a USB port. These devices currently range in memory capacity from about 64 Mbytes up to 2 Gbytes. They are ideal for transferring data between computers and for carrying your data around in your pocket.

Figure 18.2 A 128 Mbyte USB Flash ROM

Example

Different RAM-based technologies exist, like EPROM, Flash ROM and Static RAM. They are used in different ways in a computer system. Describe these different devices, and give a typical use for each.

Solution

EPROM stands for electrically programmable read only memory. With a special machine called an EPROM programmer, it is possible to permanently store programs inside this chip and then use them as though they are ordinary ROM. This enables companies or individuals to program embedded systems with ease and is useful for development purposes. Flash ROM is a special ROM chip that can be programmed in situ. Using this chip you could do an automatic BIOS upgrade for your motherboard via the internet, for example. Static RAM is currently the fastest semiconductor memory available, and is used for very fast cache between the processor and the main RAM.

Table 18.1 Important characteristics about primary storage devices

Device	Typical cost	Main characteristics/speed of use, etc.
Dynamic RAM	£10–£250	The main primary storage device. There are many different types like SDRAM, DDR SDRAM and EDORAM, etc. The speed of RAM increases frequently. Typical speeds are 60 nsec or less. Typical costs depend on type or RAM and speed, but SDRAM is currently about £50 for 128 Mbytes. You may need to upgrade your motherboard to support the latest types of RAM.
Static RAM	£35–£200	Fast RAM used for cache memory. It is more expensive than the equivalent amount of DRAM (£35 for 256 K or £125 for 6 Mbytes). Fast SRAM is currently about 5 nsec. SRAM tends to come in smaller sizes (e.g. 128 K or 256 Kbytes) for cache and specialist applications like A to D converters.
ROM	£35–£100	Useful for permanent storage of data. Now used mainly for embedded systems. Modern computers use flash memory chips so that the BIOS may be upgraded in situ.
Flash memory	£20–£250	Used on the motherboards of modern computers to store the BIOS. This type of ROM is also used in devices like digital cameras, music players and mobile phones. Typical price is £50 for 128 Mbytes, but the price depends on the format.

Secondary storage devices

The primary objectives for **secondary storage devices** are **data integrity**, **reliability** and a large **mass-storage capability**. Obviously very fast data access is an objective too, but mechanical devices like hard drives or floppies cannot compete with the speed of access of electronic primary storage devices like semiconductor memory.

The floppy disk

The modern double-sided high-density disks can hold 1.44 Mbyte of uncompressed data. Although small by today's standards, floppies are still useful, especially when combined with **compression utilities** like **WinZip**, for example, which gives the option of saving a single large file on multiple floppies. A floppy disk can also be used to boot up a computer where the hard disk has failed. The **LS-120 disk format**, which is compatible with the current 1.44 Mb format mentioned above, is a **magneto-optical device** (*see later*), capable of storing 120 Mb and the more recent HiFD, gives us 200 Mbytes. This is a better size capacity, but the 100 Mb and 250 Mb **Zip disks** are currently the most popular, as is the 1 Gb **Jazz** format. Standard floppies are very slow and often unreliable. It also takes a relatively long time to find the data on these devices, because they don't usually spin when no data is being read.

Example

State the relative advantages and disadvantages when transferring data between different computers of using removable media like floppies, Zip and Jazz disks.

Solution

Virtually all computers are able to read a floppy disk. The file size is small, and the data transfer rate is very slow (about 500 Kbits/sec). A compression utility can be used to place larger files onto several disks. Floppies tend to be the least reliable method of transferring data. Although quite popular, not everybody will have access to a Zip drive, and therefore this method might not be available. Larger files, typically 100 or 250 Mbytes (more if a compression utility is used) can be transferred and the system is more reliable than a floppy. The data-transfer rate is also better (about 1.4 Mbyte/sec).

Hard disk drives

Hard drives are currently the main **secondary storage** systems for all types of computer. Typically a hard drive would be 120 Gbytes or more for a modern microcomputer. The speed of access varies with the technology, with fast SCSII drives currently giving an access time of a few **msec**, with data-transfer rates currently up to about 40 Mbytes/sec. This is hundreds of times faster than the data transfer rate of the humble 3.5 inch floppy disk. Don't forget that disk drives allow **direct access** or **random access** to the data stored on them.

Hard drives are much more reliable than floppies and typically have a life span of 5 years or more. However, you can guarantee that the system will crash eventually and ruin much if not all of your precious data. A hard drive spins round all the time that the system is switched on and the disk head floats above the magnetic surface of the disk. If this head inadvertently touches the surface of the disk on which data is stored, then the surface is scratched and the intricate pattern of **sectors** and **tracks**, placed there when the disk was **formatted**, are lost, together with the valuable data that the sectors contained.

Example

Access to data on a hard drive has become very slow, compared to when the computer was new. Suggest a reason for this, and say what might be done to overcome this problem. How might we increase the amount of information that could be stored on the hard disk?

Solution

When a disk has just been formatted, information is stored on the disk, one piece after the other in an efficient way, making use of the track and sector patterns. Over time, as files are deleted, gaps appear in the middle of other files. Smaller files can then be stored in these gaps, but are unlikely to fill the available space. Files quickly get split up and this means that it is more difficult to locate all the bits of a file, compared to when similar files used to be stored more efficiently. Access times for the same information will thus be drastically increased.

When the above scenario happens, the disk is said to be fragmented, because fragments of files appear all over the disk, as shown by the red sections in Figure 18.3(a). However, run a defragment utility several times and the same disk, containing the same data, now looks like the picture shown in Figure 18.3(b).

It is possible to use a compression utility to compress files on the disk, and this will probably allow significantly more information to be stored on the disk compared to the original data. However, access will be slowed down because the data has to be uncompressed before it can be read.

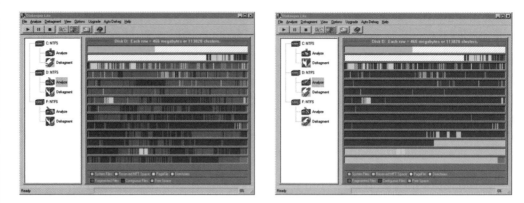

Figure 18.3 The before and after screen shots showing (a) a badly defragmented disk and (b) the disk after a defragment utility has been run

Virtual memory

A computer system might not have enough RAM to run certain programs, or to store the data for immediate use. One way to get round this is to make use of the **hard disk memory** as an extension to **RAM**. This means that data, normally held in fast RAM, would be temporarily stored on the hard disk. This is an effective way of overcoming the problem, but is obviously very slow compared to the normal speed if the data were to be held in RAM.

Disk arrays

Although hard disks are now able to store tens of Gbytes on a single disk, this may not be enough for the data-storage requirements of many organisations. Therefore, large cabinets of disks, called **Terabyte Disk Farms** are used to string together an array of disks.

RAID systems

A **Redundant Array of Independent Drives** used to be referred to as a Redundant Array of Inexpensive Drives. This system, usually used on network file servers, has advantages over using a single drive. There are **five levels** of **RAID systems**, but put simply, these disks can keep the system going in the event of a hard-disk crash (by mirroring data on a different drive), or increase the speed of access (more accesses in a given amount of time) because data stored on different drives can be accessed at the same time.

Example

How is it possible to increase the reliability of a network file server by the use of a RAID array? Does the system have any other advantages?

Solution

If a RAID array is used, then identical data from one hard disk may be stored on another. Under normal conditions this mirroring process may not be noticeable. However, if one of the drives were to crash, then the other could take over immediately, with no noticeable delay to the users. The manager would have to replace the errant disk drive (it would usually be swappable even though the system is still running), and the system would build up the new disk to the point where the mirroring is again functional. If the data is spread over a couple of different drives, then both disks may be used to read the data 'twice as quickly', because we have two independent drives, each capable of mopping up the data. Complex controllers and software are needed to manage this system so that no mix-ups can occur.

Table 18.2 Important characteristics about magnetic-disk-based secondary storage devices

Device	Typical cost	Main characteristics/speed of use, etc.
Floppy disk	£0.20 or less	Although it can only store 1.44 Mbytes of data the humble floppy is still commonly used to transfer data between PCs. The advent of compression utilities such WinZip have ensured that they will be around for many years to come, even though CD-ROMs and DVDs can store much more.
Removable storage	£8–£20	Iomega's ZIP drive has become one of the de-facto standards for removable storage. They are available in 100 Mbyte and 250 Mbyte versions. Media costs depend on capacity. The data transfer rate depends on the interface, with about 6.6 Mbytes/sec being the best available.
Hard disk	£40–£500+	This is the mainstay of secondary storage in the PC industry. Typically the smallest disk drive you can now buy is about 20 Gbytes. Larger hard disks go up to about 250 Gbytes, although this capacity is increasing all the time. The cost depends on size and speed of access, which is typically 5.1 msec for a 10 000 r.p.m drive. Different interfaces like IDE, SATA and SCSI also affect the speed and price.
Disk farms	£1000–£20 000+	A disk farm is (usually) a large number of disks arranged such that it acts as a very large storage unit housed in one or more cabinets. Companies like Boeing or Airbus industries would use storage devices like this to store and archive huge amounts of information. Disk farms currently cope with several hundred Tbyte each.
RAID systems	£150–£1000+	These are disks arranged in a variety of ways to enhance performance or reliability or both. Disks may be arranged to increase speed by writing to more than one disk simultaneously, or to increase reliability by writing the same data to more than one disk. If you have enough disks connected to the system you can do both of these things at the same time.

Optical drives

Optical technology works with LASERS instead of magnetic heads. Typical of this sort of device are the **CD-ROM (Compact Disk Read Only Memory)** drives and **DVD (Digital Versatile Disk** or **Digital Video Disk)** drives. A standard CD-ROM can hold about 650 Mbytes of read-only data.

The data transfer rate of a single-speed CD-ROM is 150 Kbytes/sec. Double-speed is twice this and so on. Other limits, like the software that is being used, will ensure that a 52-speed CD-ROM drive will not actually give you 52 times the speed of a single-speed device! You can record data onto a special type of CD-ROM called **CD-R (Compact Disk Recordable)** and may erase and write the data again on a **CD-RW (Compact Disk Rewritable)** disk.

A single-layer single-sided DVD can store about 4.7 Gbytes of data, considerably more than conventional CD-ROM drives. The current maximum capacity for a double-sided DVD is 17 Gbytes. You might also be able to re-record data by using the **DVD-R** and **DVD+R** formats.

Magneto-optical drives

These **MO (magneto-optical)** devices use a combination of LASER and magnetic heads to reduce the size needed to store the data on the disk. These drives are currently not quite as good as the conventional magnetic disk drive in terms of access time (time to access any item of random data) and data transfer rate. They are particularly suited as a backup storage medium. A magneto-optical drive is sometimes removable, in which case it is called a **floptical disk**. Some floptical disks are of the $3\frac{1}{2}$-inch disk format, and these drives can be read by conventional floppies too. MO drives are also used in large organisations for storage and archiving of massive amounts of data. The storage library shown in Figure 18.4 uses a number of 5.25 inch MO drives, giving a maximum storage capacity of 5.8 Tbytes of data for this particular system.

Figure 18.4 Plasmon's 5.8 Tbyte MO drive storage and archive solution for large enterprises

At the other end of the scale the media for much smaller MO drives, which can also read conventional 3.5 inch **floppy disks** are shown in Figure 18.5.

Figure 18.5 A selection of Verbatim's 3.5 inch MO drives

Example

The advent of new types of secondary-storage media such as DVD and CD-RW has caused many headaches for the music, film and software industries. What are these problems, and what might be done to combat rampant piracy? What extra problems might the internet pose?

Solution

Software is distributed on CDs, and used to require special factories to make the disks. However, using recordable CD-ROMs, the consumer can make copies of CDs, and it is thus easy to pirate software or music. Recordable DVD formats mean that it is easy to pirate high-quality copies of films too, but media costs are a little more expensive.

Codes need to be typed in to activate software, but internet sites provide thousands of illegal codes that have been hacked for hundreds of software products. Illegal market stalls, often selling thousands of pounds worth of software for about £5 or £10 are also a problem. You get no manuals or technical support if you obtain software via this illegal route, and stand a chance of being arrested too. At the moment there are few technical solutions to software piracy, other than the use of a dongle or hardware key. This is a device, which plugs into the computer, without which the software will not run.

The internet is posing a great threat because software, music and films can be downloaded with ease, although it might take quite a few hours to download a large software package. However, as some ISPs now give free internet access, and some even give free phone calls at certain times of the week, a long phone call would be of little consequence.

Tapes

A huge variety of tape formats exist, ranging from **DLT (Digital Linear Tape)** drives on large computer systems (*see Figure 18.6*), to the smaller 4 mm **DAT (Digital Audio Tape)** systems used as backup devices on small and medium size file servers, for example. The speed with which data can be accessed from the tape varies from system to system, but the **serial nature** of the storage media means that you will probably have to wind the tape a long way until you find the item of interest. Therefore, a few tens of minutes or even longer is not uncommon for data retrieval from a serially based tape. Typical 4 mm-DAT systems can store up to about 26 Gbytes, and typical tapes are shown in Figure 18.7.

Figure 18.7 A selection of Maxell data tapes, capable of backing up or archiving data

Figure 18.6 40 Gbyte and 80 Gbyte DLT tape drives and DLT tape

Table 18.2 Important characteristics about optical storage devices

Device	Media costs	Main characteristics/speed of use, etc.
CD-ROM	£1	It is now common to distribute software on CD-ROM. CD-R and CD-RW drives are now also commonly used for backup and archive purposes. A typical CD stores about 650 Mbytes of information, and the speed of access depends on the speed of the drive (e.g. 40× or 60×, etc). A single-speed CD-ROM reads data at about 150 Kbytes/sec.
DVDs	£2–£20	DVDs are now becoming popular as media costs decline. DVD-R is now possible. Media cost is between £2 and £20 depending on type of DVD disk.
MO Drives	£35–£100	Typically Magneto-optical drive capacities range from about 100 Mbytes to several Gbytes. Typical access speeds for a MO drive are about 40 msec. Typical removable media costs are £35.

DLT tapes can store up to about 35 Gbytes, but you obviously can have many tape drives in a single system to increase the effective **backup** or **archive** storage capacity considerably.

Some students may think, quite rightly, that you could buy a second 80 Gbyte hard drive for less than the cost of an 80 Gbyte tape system. Therefore you could back up your 80 Gbytes of data very cost effectively. However, you must not forget that tapes are relatively inexpensive (about £20 or £30 each) and thus you can back up many disk drives on many different tapes using a single tape drive unit. You must also not forget that generations of backups of the same data are taken at suitably frequent intervals (*see Chapter 14*).

Example

Tapes are often used as a system for backup or archive purposes. Explain the fundamental difference between these two terms. What other systems might be used instead of tapes for backing up or archiving?

Solution

A backup is a copy of the original files to be used in an emergency, such as accidental deletion or a system failure. Such backups would be taken at suitably frequent intervals, such as the end of each day.

An archive is taking little-used parts of your system or data files off line so that they may be retrieved at a later data if needed. Material in the archive cannot usually be accessed quickly. Removable storage media such as CD-RW, DVD+R, MO disks and ZIP disks are also ideal for archive purposes.

Large tape systems

Larger tape systems can be found in the **mainframe** and **supercomputer** environments. Some DLT tape machines can store up to 1630 DLT cartridges and have a native data transfer rate of 1.44 Tbytes/hour. Now that's some archive! The Compaq SDLT drive shown in Figure 18.8 has 326 slots giving a performance of 633 Gbytes/hour. Notice the robot arm which is capable of replacing different tapes under the command of the computer. It is therefore possible to get the computer to automatically select

Figure 18.8 Compaq SDLT drives and 326 slots, offering 35.86 Tb of backup capacity (native) storage in a 1.03 sq. metre of foot print, and native backup performance of 633.6 Gb/hr

a tape from the rack and insert it into one of the drives. With systems like this you should now appreciate how Tbytes of archived material can be accessed atuomatically.

Table 18.3 Important characteristics about tape storage devices

Device	Typical cost	Main characteristics/speed of use, etc.
DAT tapes	£30	DAT or Digital Audio Tapes are commonly used for backup and archive purposes on file servers in a network environment. DAT tapes store about 40 or 80 Gbytes, depending on whether compression is used or not.
DLT tapes	£50	DLT or Digital Linear Tapes store about 40 or 80 Gbytes, depending on the type. They cost about £50 for each tape.
Large tape systems	£35–£100	Useful for archiving the massive amounts of data to be found in large commercial organisations. The cost of the original robot-controlled machines is tens of thousands of pounds.

Storage-based examples

You may be required to suggest certain types of secondary storage devices and estimate their size based on a given application.

Example

An agency produces glossy brochures, and employs four people in the technical department. Most brochures are colour, and may run to 50 pages. On each page there will usually be four high-quality photos, each being a maximum of 3 inches × 2 inches in size. The rest of the material on each page is text based, although there may be a coloured logo. The company produces a maximum of 20 brochures each year, and a maximum of 6 brochures may need updating at any one time, meaning that 14 brochures may be archived. Estimate the amount of primary and secondary storage that would be needed to store the material using the following information:

- The average size of brochure is 30 pages.
- Colour photos are stored as 24-bit bitmaps and each photo has a resolution of 300 dpi.
- The magazine material may be archived once the magazine has been produced.
- No more than 16 pages will need to be held in memory at any one time.
- You need to include some storage capacity for the applications that would typically be needed by this company.
- You also need to allow storage space for correspondence and other administrative material.
- The system must be very reliable, as brochures are produced to tight deadlines, and any delay due to technical faults is unacceptable.
- You should allow for recovery in the event of a system failure.

Your answer should include facilities for storage that is accessible by all four workstations simultaneously, and allow for backup and archiving of the material.

Solution

First estimate the size of each photo, stored at a resolution of 300 dpi, having a size of 3 in by 2 in. The number of bits for 24-bit colour is $3 \times 2 \times 24 \times 300 \times 300 = 12\,960\,000$ bits, thus giving us 13 Mbits per image.

There are 4 images on each page; therefore, each page will require $13 \times 4 = 52$ Mbits. Text based storage requirements for each page would be much less demanding than this. For estimation purposes, we will assume 7 Mbytes are needed per page in total.

A maximum of 16 pages need to be stored in memory at any one time. Therefore, 16×7 or 112 Mbytes of RAM would be needed to store the document in memory. Not forgetting the operating system, DTP and art package requirements, which will probably take up a similar amount of RAM, I would suggest that a minimum of 256 Mbytes is needed for each workstation, and preferably 512 Mbytes. On average, the brochure page extent is 30 pages. On average, each brochure would take up $7 \times 30 = 210$ Mbytes of secondary storage.

As 6 brochures may need to be worked on at any one time, $6 \times 210 = 1.26$ Gbytes of secondary storage would be needed on the file server to store these documents. A file server is the most efficient way of storing the brochure work and other resources as the workstations can be connected to it by means of an LAN. Assuming that software like the DTP packages and art packages are stored on the file server too, then an extra 2 Gbytes would be adequate for this, as temporary files and local backups would take some considerable space. The administrative work would need considerably less storage than this, and therefore 6 Gbytes would seem to be adequate for all foreseen purposes. I would suggest 10 Gbyte to act as a margin of safety.

The reliability should be high, and downtime should be kept to a minimum. A RAID system with mirroring would seem necessary to overcome a possible hard-disk crash. The mirroring would double the disk capacity to 20 Gbytes, arranged in 2 lots of 10 Gbytes. Practically, it would be more cost effective to buy two 40 Gbyte drives. Therefore, the disk capacity on the file server would be 80 Gbytes, ensuring a generous margin for expansion. The archiving of material for each year would involve the storage of 20 brochures. This would require, on average 20×210 Mbytes $= 4.2$ Gbytes of space. Therefore, an 8 Gbyte tape streamer would seem adequate for this purpose, which could also be used for recovery of the system in the event of a system failure. The archive system could, therefore, be an 8 Gbyte DLT tape streamer. One tape would probably be needed for each year, and therefore several tapes capable of holding 8 Gbytes each would need to be purchased.

Other storage considerations

When deciding on what devices to use for storage you should consider things like reliability and the length of time that the data is expected to last on a particular medium. Some of this data is unknown at the time of writing, because some of the latest technologies have not been around long enough to find out! You should be aware that all computer storage devices will eventually lose data after a number of years. Any archive that may have to last for more than 20 or 30 years needs considerable thought. It will probably be the case that any archived data will have to be archived again to different media which has yet to be invented. Don't forget also that all devices used to store data will fail eventually. A hard drive will last between 5 and 10 years depending on use and quality. This is why it's essential to have a plan for **backing up** and **archiving** data.

Self-test questions

1 RAM and ROM are both needed in computer systems. Why is this so?
2 RAM is volatile. Explain what this statement means. What can be done to prevent loss of data in the event of a power cut?
3 Explain what 'disk caching' means. How might the technique of caching enable you to have more RAM than might physically be available?
4 Explain the difference between primary and secondary storage, giving a typical use for each type of storage system.
5 Why are hard-disk drives faster and more reliable than floppy disk drives?
6 After frequent use a disk may become fragmented. Why is this a problem, and what can be done to overcome this?
7 There are various types (levels) of RAID array. Explain two problems that different types of RAID systems would help you to overcome.

8 A home computer user has just brought a computer system with 60 Gbytes of hard disk space. His old computer had only 200 Mbytes. Why is this new disk likely to get filled up sooner than he or she may think?

9 Explain what is meant by serial access and direct access. What type of access is supported by floppy and hard disk drives?

10 Suggest a suitable sized hard disk for use in a file server for a school that has 2000 pupils. The disk is to store data for the pupils only (i.e. no applications software). Explain exactly how you arrive at your conclusion.

11 A user has a 100× speed CD-ROM drive. Why is he or she unlikely to see a 100 times increase in speed over and above a single-speed drive?

12 What other technologies are threatening the CD-ROM as the 'distribution medium of choice' for software packages like applications and games?

13 What is CD-R? Give three different legitimate uses for this technology.

14 Compare and contrast the CD-R and MO devices as a backup storage medium.

15 What is meant by an archive, and how does this differ from a backup? A company wishes to create a large (many Gbytes) archive on CD-ROM. Is this a good idea? Comment on this compared to other suitable media.

16 A company backs up about 50 Gbytes of data each day. State, giving reasons for your choice, whether you would put this on a single large tape or several smaller ones.

17 A company uses computers to control a critical real-time process. The computer must be able to recover from a disaster like a disk crash without adversely affecting the control process. What secondary storage devices might help in this situation?

Module 2 examination questions

AQA examination questions

1 A desktop PC has access to a local disk drive, C: and a networked drive, N:

  (a) What is meant by:

      (i)   local disk drive   *(1 mark)*

      (ii) networked disk drive?   *(1 mark)*

  (b) The command 'Type' lists the contents of a specified file on the desktop PC's VDU screen as shown in Figure 1.

```
C:\>Type C:\Project\Source\MyFirst.Pas

     Program MyFirst;
     Begin
            Writeln('Hello World');
     End;

C:\> Type C:\Project\BuildMyFirst.Arc
```

Figure 1

Using only the information contained in Figure 1, give one example of each of the following:

      (i)   a logical drive   *(1 mark)*

      (ii) a file pathname   *(1 mark)*

      (iii) a sub directory   *(1 mark)*

      (iv) the filename of a text file   *(1 mark)*

      (v) the file name of a non-text file.   *(1 mark)*

  (c) Using the information contained in Figure 1 complete the directory structure diagram shown in Figure 2 for the desktop PC's local drive, C:

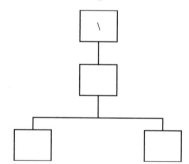

Figure 2

[AQA Unit 2 (CPT1) Principles of Hardware, Software and Applications May 2003 Q(2)]

2 Mobile phone systems rely upon a smart card called a Subscriber Identity Module or SIM in a mobile phone to identify the subscriber to the mobile phone network. Each SIM card is allocated a unique number that is stored in the SIM and which is

continually sent to the nearest base station in the mobile phone network whilst the mobile phone is switched on. Each base station is able to access a central relational database consisting of several relations (tables), two of which **LocationRegister** and **CallRegister** are constructed as follows:

> **LocationRegister** (SIMCardNo, MobileTelephoneNo, MobilePhoneSerial No, ActivationDate, ServiceType, CurrentBaseStationID)
> **CallRegister** (CallID, SIMCardNo, Date, Time, Duration, CalledTelephoneNo, Charge)

Each mobile telephone call is assigned a unique CallID.

(a) What is a smart card?   (*1 mark*)

(b) State a suitable primary key for the **CallRegister** relation.   (*1 mark*)

(c) (i)   Explain what is meant by a foreign key.   (*1 mark*)

    (ii) Name the attribute which is the foreign key in the relation **CallRegister**.

                                             (*1 mark*)

(d) Relation **LocationRegister** is *updated in real time* whereas **CallRegister** is updated in a *batch processing* system which uses records collected from the network's base stations every 24 hours.
    What is meant by:

    (i)   updated in real time   (*1 mark*)

    (ii) batch processing?   (*1 mark*)

    (iii) Give **one** reason why relation **LocationRegister** should be updated in real time.   (*1 mark*)

(e) Indexes are created on **CallID** and **SIMCardNo** attributes in relation **CallRegister**.

    (i)   Why is an index used?   (*1 mark*)

    (ii) Which of the two attribute indexes is a secondary index?   (*1 mark*)

Table 1 shows a sample of the CallRegister table and Table 2 shows a sample of the LocationRegister table.

Table 1 CallRegister table

CallID	SIMCardNo	Date	Time	Duration Telephone No	Called	Charge
:	:	:	:	:	:	:
:	:	:	:	:	:	:
1204200227	310-68-4451003	12/04/2002	8:01:00	360	07713411027	300
1204200228	310-68-4451005	12/04/2002	8:02:00	420	01296552341	210
1204200229	310-68-4451003	12/04/2002	8:08:10	120	07713631281	100
1204200230	310-68-4451008	12/04/2002	8:02:20	240	07934433016	80
1204201200	310-68-4451003	13/04/2002	9:32:35	120	07934433016	40
1204201201	310-68-4451008	13/04/2002	9:35:35	240	0235670023	160
:	:	:	:	:	:	:
:	:	:	:	:	:	:

Table 2 LocationRegister table

SIMCardNo	Mobile Telephone no	Mobile Phone SerialNo	Activation Date	Service Type	Current BaseStationID
310-68-4451000	07713631281	4990600	10/02/2001	A	10211
310-68-4451001	07713421224	4990613	07/10/2001	A	20231
310-68-4451002	07713411927	4990628	13/07/2001	B	11367
310-68-4451003	07718491221	4990632	12/09/2001	B	-
310-68-4451004	07714621289	4990644	23/11/2001	A	-
310-68-4451005	07713421123	4990656	24/12/2001	C	34111
310-68-4451006	07713482414	4990661	01/02/2002	C	32178
310-68-4451007	07713421582	4990673	10/03/2002	C	22987
310-68-4451008	07715621276	4990689	29/04/2002	D	10345

(f)   The following show a Query By Example (QBE) applied to the **LocationRegister** and **CallRegister** tables.

MobileTelephoneNo	Date	Time
077118491221	12/04/2002	>8:00:00

QBE

(i)   What will be the minimum number of records returned by the QBE?

(*1 mark*)

(ii)   Complete the following QBE to extract the SimCardNo and ServiceType of all the mobile phone accounts activated before 01/03/2002.

MobileTelephoneNo	Date	Time
077118491221	12/04/2002	>8:00:00

(*3 marks*)

(g)   The last digit of the MobilePhoneSerialNo is a check digit.

(i)   What is a check digit?   (*1 mark*)

(ii)   What is its purpose?   (*1 mark*)

[AQA Unit 2 (CPT1) Principles of Hardware, Software and Applications May 2003 Q(8)]

3 The following is an extract from a spreadsheet that shows how many supermarket loyalty points a customer would earn by spending different amounts of money on supermarket goods. The supermarket is currently operating a bonus scheme which adds a fixed percentage of points to the points earned. The fixed percentage is 10%.

	B	C	D	E	F	G
1	Bonus%	10		Pounds spent	Points earned without bonus	Points earned with bonus
2	Points earned per pound if £10.00 or less spent					
3	Points earned per pound if more than £10.00 but not more than £30.00 spent					
4	Points earned per pound if more than £30.00 or less spent					
5				5	10	11
6				15	45	50
7				30	90	99
8				60	240	264
9				90	360	396
:				:	:	:
:				:	:	:
20				240	960	1056
21				270	1080	1188
22				300	1200	1320

(a) The formulae in G5 is F5*(1 + C1/100) where $ denotes absolute cell referencing. What is the formula in cell G8? *(3 marks)*

(b) The value in cell G6 is calculated from $45 \times (1 + 10/100)$ which equals 49.5. However, the value displayed in cell G6 is 50. How might this happen? *(1 mark)*

(c) Write the formula that was entered in F5 and copied into cells F6 to F22. Your formula should perform an automatic recalculation if the value in cell C2, or the value in C3, or the value in C4 is changed. *(6 marks)*

[AQA Unit 2 (CPT1) Principles of Hardware, Software and Applications May 2002 Q(8)]

4 A new copy of a sequentially organised master file is made whenever records are added.

(a) A program is written to add a single record to this master file. List the processing steps for this program that generates an amended copy of this master file. *(5 marks)*

(b) When many records need to be inserted, these records are stored in a transaction file. The program is modified so that it reads the transaction records from the transaction file.

(i)   What file organisation should be used for this transaction file? *(1 mark)*

(ii) In what order should the transaction records be stored in the transaction file? Justify your answer *(2 marks)*

[AQA Unit 2 (CPT1) Principles of Hardware, Software and Applications May 2002 Q(9)]

5 A file of 80 records has the following record structure:

ProductID, **ProductDescription**, **QuantityInStock**

ProductID is a four-byte integer, ProductDescription is a fifty-six byte fixed-length string, QuantityInStock is a four-byte integer.

(a) What is the size of this file in bytes? Show your working. *(2 marks)*

(b) Suggest a suitable primary key for this file. Justify your choice. (*2 marks*)

(c) On closer examination, it is found that 30% of the file storage space is wasted.

   (i) Explain why this may occur with the current record structure. (*1 mark*)

   (ii) How could the record structure be changed whilst retaining three-fields per record so that this problem is overcome? (*1 mark*)

   (iii) Give one disadvantage of the restructured solution. (*1 mark*)

[AQA Unit 2 (CPT1) Principles of Hardware, Software and Applications May 2002 Q(2)]

6 Many people now communicate via e-mail. Excluding cost, state three other reasons why people use e-mail rather than the conventional postal service. (*3 marks*)

[AQA Unit 2 (CPT1) Principles of Hardware, Software and Applications May 2001 Q(1)]

7 Name the most suitable storage medium for each of the following.

(a) Backing up a 30 Kb file. (*1 mark*)

(b) Backing up 2 Gb of data. (*1 mark*)

(c) Distributing a software package requiring 500 Mb of storage space. (*1 mark*)

[AQA Unit 2 (CPT1) Principles of Hardware, Software and Applications May 2001 Q(2)]

8 A student on work experience in the payroll department of Widgets plc, when left alone, successfully logged into the company's computer system by guessing the administrator's user ID and password. The student changed the hourly rate of several employees by accessing the company's payroll file.

(a) The Computer Misuse Act defined three types of offence. What two offences did the student commit according to this act? (*2 marks*)

(b) Given that the student was left alone in the computer room, the company could have prevented or detected what happened. Describe three methods of security that the company should have used. (*3 marks*)

[AQA Unit 2 (CPT1) Principles of Hardware, Software and Applications May 2001 Q(5)]

9 Users sharing a disk may access their own and other files.

(a) State two disadvantages of using a multi-level directory system for these files. (*2 marks*)

(b) Users are granted various *file access rights*. Give **two** examples of file access rights. (*2 marks*)

[AQA Unit 2 (CPT1) Principles of Hardware, Software and Applications May 2001 Q(4)]

10 For each of the following, name a suitable type of operating system. Give **one** reason for your choice.

(a) A computer system consisting of several desktop PCs sharing each others files. (*2 marks*)

(b) A compute system dedicated to controlling the flow of chemicals in a chemical processing plant. (*2 marks*)

(c) A computer system dedicated to processing, at the end of each day, a bank's transactions stored on magnetic disk. (*2 marks*)

[AQA Unit 2 (CPT1) Principles of Hardware, Software and Applications May 2002 Q(3)]

19 Systems development and testing

In this section you will learn about:

- The development of projects using the classical system life cycle
- Methods of collecting information and analysis using data flow diagrams
- Program flow charts and systems flow charts
- Entity relationship diagrams and entity attribute relationship diagrams
- Hierachical diagrams, pseudocode, prototyping and dry running
- The human computer interface, unit testing, integration testing and system maintenance

The classical system life cycle

The classical **system life cycle** is the accumulated wisdom applied to the development of computer-based projects. Useful **stages**, useful for project development are shown in Table 19.1.

Table 19.1 Stages of the system life cycle

(1) Definition of the problem	(5) Design
(2) Feasibility study	(6) Implementation
(3) Information collection	(7) Evaluation
(4) Analysis	(8) Maintenance

Definition of the problem

The following are typical of activities undertaken by a **systems analyst** (*the person who analyses and designs new computer systems*), whose job it is to define the problem.

- He or she would have a number of **interviews** with potential clients – notes should be taken, or taped interviews can be used.
- If the system replaces a **manual** or older computer system, you need a detailed look at how the older system operates.
- Look at other **similar systems**. There are few new projects, the like of which has not been seen before, but commercial pressures may make this difficult.
- A **detailed written specification** needs to be drawn up. This must describe exactly what the project has to do. A bulleted list is usually suitable for this.

The material here is intimately tied up with the **information** and **communication requirements** of a system, covered when **applications** and **effects** were studied.

The feasibility study

The problem is looked at in detail *before* any work is commissioned. It may not be technically feasible, parts may not be improved by a computer-based solution, or it may be too expensive. Proposals will impact on staff, possibly in the form of training, and hiring or even firing of staff. Systems analysts will be aware of the financial costs of similar systems, but these are ballpark figures and many projects do go over time and budget. The **feasibility study** is crucial, as much money is wasted if the conclusions are wrong.

The work in module 3 represents the synoptic element of your AS course. This means that it brings together all your knowledge so far, and enables you to apply your knowledge to a variety of computer projects.

The Facility CMIS application in Chapter 10 is a good example of the analysis of a real system. You should look at Chapter 10 if you have not covered this work.

Collecting information

If the report produced by the systems analyst is favourable and if the company decides that they wish to go ahead, the **information-gathering phase** is triggered. The following is typical of activities that are carried out during this phase.

- **Devise questionnaires** – give them to people who will use the proposed system.
- **Interview clients** and other interested parties like customers, if applicable.
- Take a detailed look at the existing system, if applicable. **Existing methods need a very critical analysis**.

It is likely that ideas not considered before may come to light, and this could mean going back and redefining certain parts of the problem. The users of the system often have the best ideas for potential improvement, and wise managers will take note of sensible suggestions. The development of systems is dynamic, and modifications at this stage are the norm. The further the project is towards completion, the more difficult it is to implement even minor changes. If good ideas are thought up at a later stage, it may not be possible to implement them because of time delays or other financial considerations.

Analysis of the problem

A common language needs to be developed between the designers of the system and the people who will implement it. Common methods like **systems flowcharts, data flow diagrams** or **Entity-Relationship diagrams** might typically be employed here. You would be wise to use these methods in your projects. **Data flow diagrams** are useful for describing the movement of data, both

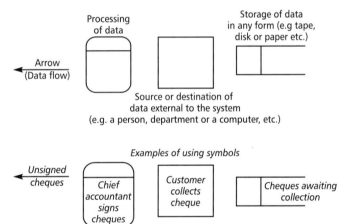

Figure 19.1 Data-flow symbols

You will lose marks in your module 3 project if you do not use appropriate diagrams during your analysis and design phases. Chapter 22 shows a typical project write up in which this is done.

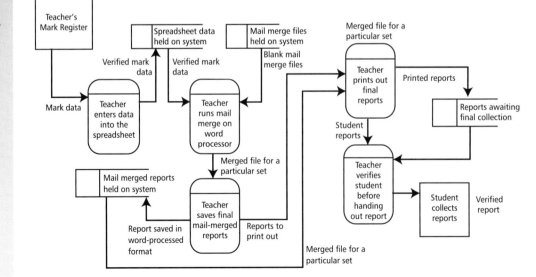

Figure 19.2 A scenario for student reporting (*see the example below*)

within the computer or elsewhere. They are ideal for tracing the route of paperwork through an office or factory, etc. but could also be used to trace the sequences and the physical forms of data from one application to the next. There are just four different symbols in use, as shown in Figure 19.1.

Example

A mail-merge document that uses a spreadsheet as the source of data is to generate student reports for a teacher. Draw a data-flow diagram showing a typical scenario for the flow of data, from entering it into the spreadsheet to production of the reports.

Make sure that you are able to use a suitable software package for the creation of diagrams like data flow diagrams and systems flowcharts.

Solution

A data flow diagram is shown in Figure 19.2. This solves the problem by making use of the symbols outlined in Figure 19.1, and is explained in more detail here. This diagram allows you to analyse the flow of data, in detail, and to highlight possible problems. For example, students should not be given a report belonging to someone else, and thus the teacher verifies the report before handing it back to you. If you are using Microsoft Office, some of the files will need to be in Excel format, some of the files in Word format. The transition between these two forms will therefore have to be managed. This type of diagram makes it possible to identify these problems.

Flowcharts

There are two main types of flowchart called **program flowcharts** and **system flowcharts** (see next section). Program flowcharts are an alternative to **pseudocode** (*see Chapter 5*), and are mainly used to express **algorithms** (*sequences of instructions to solve a problem*). Program flowcharts use the symbols shown in Figure 19.3.

Well presented computer generated diagrams look best in your final report project.

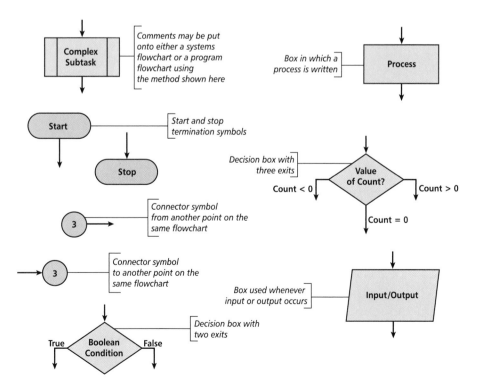

Figure 19.3 The main symbols used for program flowcharts

The use of these symbols is quite straightforward, but you should *not* attempt to create massive flowcharts because the logic is too easily obscured once a problem becomes complicated. It would be far better to **modularise** the problem into suitable **sub-problems**, and then do a **flowchart** for each. Under these conditions the flowcharts can be connected making use of the off-page connectors shown in the systems flowchart symbols of Figure 19.5. Complex sub-task boxes can also refer to other flowcharts or to other large parts of the project. **Program flowcharts** describe the solution to problems at a **microscopic** (or program code) **level**, hence the name **program flowchart**. The decision boxes, for example, mirror the IF 'Boolean condition' THEN 'do something' exactly. To solve a problem at a **macroscopic (system) level**, we use **system flowcharts**.

Example

Draw a program flowchart to input an unspecified quantity of positive and negative numbers whose range is checked to be between −500 and +500 inclusive. The data is to be terminated by using a rogue value of −999. Your solution should output how many positive, negative and zero numbers are in the list.

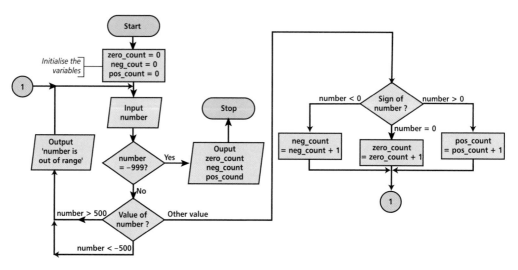

Figure 19.4 An algorithm for finding positive and negative numbers

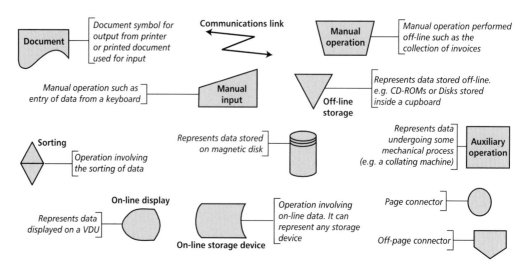

Figure 19.5 System Flowchart symbols

Solution

This solves the problem by making use of the symbols outlined in Figure 19.3. Flowcharts can be any shape, but the solution here is drawn horizontally. A flow line could have been drawn to connect the two points labelled (1), but an interconnection symbol has been shown here as an example.

Systems Flowcharts

System flowcharts use all the symbols shown in Figure 19.3, but some extra ones are added, and these are shown in Figure 19.5. These extra symbols are ideal for **project design**. As you can see, a good variety of symbols are available covering many of the things that you may have to do in your project work.

Example

Draw a system flowchart showing a method to describe the manual entry of data from a keyboard. The data, obtained from invoices, is to be validated, and then saved to a transaction file if no errors are found. An error report is to be generated and printed for the system manager if there are any errors detected by the data-entry routines.

Solution

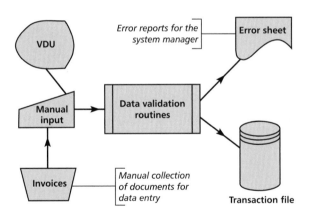

Figure 19.6 A very simple system flowchart for validating invoices

The system flowchart is shown in Figure 19.6. It is assumed that the data is going to be manually typed in from paper-based invoices, and the error report will also be placed on a printed sheet (i.e. no error report will be saved to disk).

Entity relationship diagrams

Entity-relationship diagrams (**ER diagrams**) help with the design of a **database** (*see Chapter 15*). An Access representation of entities and relationships is shown in Figure 19.7, which uses Microsoft's 'NorthWind Traders' Database as an example. However, *you should not use this in the design stage of your project, because it can't possibly exist before you have designed the database!* Therefore you should use the type of ER diagrams shown in Figure 19.8.

Some relationships shown in Microsoft Access image:

Figure 19.7 Some relationships shown in Microsoft Access

Before going any further you are reminded about the following types of relationship.

- One to one
- One to many
- Many to one

An **entity** can be thought of as an object within a system. If you are designing a library, then **entities** may include '**books**', '**authors**' and '**publishers**'. Entity relationship diagrams help to clarify the **links** between **entities** and the **types of relationship** that join them. Sometimes Entity Relationship diagrams are called **Entity Attribute Relationship** diagrams or **EAR diagrams** and these alternatives are shown later in this section. The **attributes** represent the 'information stored about each entity'. For example, a 'book' entity might have some attributes like 'title', 'author' and 'ISBN', etc.

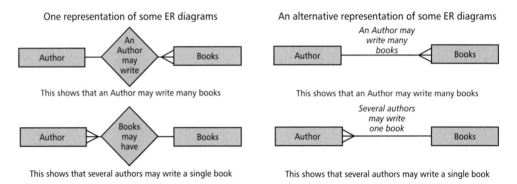

One representation of some ER diagrams

Author — An Author may write ⊃— Books

This shows that an Author may write many books

Author —⊃ Books may have — Books

This shows that several authors may write a single book

An alternative representation of some ER diagrams

An Author may write many books

Author ————⊃— Books

This shows that an Author may write many books

Several authors may write one book

Author —⊂———— Books

This shows that several authors may write a single book

Figure 19.8 Two types of ER diagram useful for AS projects

The **entity** 'books', outlined in Figure 19.8, for example, might refer to a **table** in an Access database, similar to those shown in Figure 19.7. The attributes like 'title', 'author' and 'ISBN' would be listed in the entries that represents the tables. Here each **entity** corresponds to a **table** and each **attribute** corresponds to a **field** within a table. Using diagrams like those shown in Figure 19.8 at the design stage of your project, you can work out what mappings will be needed when you implement your database using software like Microsoft Access, for example.

These diagrams may be extended into what are called **Entity Attribute Relationship** diagrams, and an example of this is shown in Figure 19.9. The attributes are tagged onto the entities.

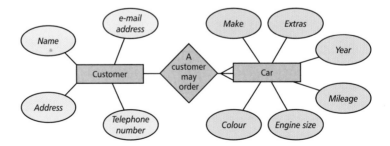

Figure 19.9 A simple example of an EAR diagram

Design methods

Many different methods exist to explain how to solve problems. The **top-down design** method is common for giving the overall solution in terms of the sub-problems that need to be solved. This should be contrasted to **bottom-up design**, which is particularly suited to programming, for example, where small modules of code are developed and tested before being joined onto other modules for making up larger systems. If this latter method were used then it would be referred to as **bottom-up programming**.

Example

You are to write a user guide explaining how to draw a grandfather clock using a typical computer art package. Show how it is possible to split up the construction of a suitable clock using a top-down design method. Don't go into too much detail.

Solution

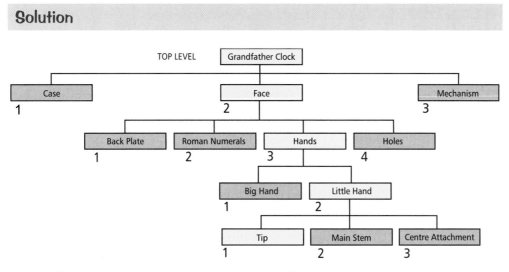

Figure 19.10 One possible representation of a hierarchical diagram

The clock needs to be split up into suitable components – case, face and mechanism (pendulum, etc.) is a good start. The face might consist of a circular back plate, some Roman numerals, some hands and the holes into which we put the key. The ideas, expanded a little further, are shown in Figure 19.10. Here you can see that the design of the little hand, for example, consists of three subsections, namely the tip, stem and centre attachment. The little hand is a part of the hands section, which itself belongs to the face, a major subsection of the clock project. Using this method you can see that the user manual could be divided up into three major chapters. Chapter 2, on the face, could then be split up into four sections. The hands, being section 3, are split up into little and big hand sections. Using this diagram you could refer to an individual part of the project by a number, and once arranged like this, you can work on the project from the bottom up, explaining how each section of the little hand might be constructed using the package.

The user interface

A good **user interface** is **essential**. If it is wrong, it might be difficult or unintuitive to use. Learn a lot from looking at programs like Microsoft Office. The **tools** on the **tool bars** have similar functions and the way that the **drop-down menus** work is the same in all cases. Microsoft has tried to ensure **consistency** across a range of applications.

The following may be applied when designing a user interface:

- Has the user been consulted about what he or she wants?
- Is it to be graphical or text based?
- Is it clear how to enter the data?
- Can the data be edited easily before being saved?
- Do you need to provide any help?
- Is the feedback to the user adequate if something goes wrong?
- Is there a security issue?
- Should a prototype be built to test the new user interface?
- Is the interface going to be used in a life or death situation like an intensive-care ward, for example?
- Is the user experienced or a novice?
- Will any special hardware be useful?

Strive to make sure that users undertake only valid events at appropriate times. If a button can be clicked to transmit information, make sure that inadvertent or deliberate clicking of the button does nothing if the information has not been entered, or some of the information is missing. Be aware of appropriate **input** and **output devices**. Use these as necessary, but don't be afraid to develop custom solutions. For example, how might you ensure that a parcel collection and delivery service keeps track of parcels during their journey? Your solutions might include running software from a PDA connected to a mobile phone in a delivery van, which could be coupled with GPS readouts to identify position. This could be used to keep a customer database updated.

Example

Outline techniques that might be used when designing a good user interface for a tired telephone operator entering data regarding credit-card enquiries. You may assume that the following information needs to be input or retrieved from the system:

'Customer card ID', 'Customer name', 'Address' and 'Details of transactions for any month', which may include the following: 'Date', 'Reference number', 'Description', 'Price', 'Balance' and 'Special notes'.

You are not required to design the input screen, but should make sensible suggestions.

Solution

It is essential that information is validated on entry. For example, an illegal account number cannot be entered. This could be accomplished by means of a check digit (*see Chapter 14*). If a valid account number is entered, the customer's name and address and all relevant details should be to hand. If the customer does not know the account number, then other information, such as address, postcode and some extra security data like 'special place' or mother's maiden name, could help.

If a specific transaction is required, this should be searchable by number and name of the shop, if possible. If not, the price of the transaction could be used to locate it if necessary. The system should not rely on the operator manually searching for information, although this option too must still be available. Any standard enquiry such as 'current balance', 'credit limit' and 'special requests' should be available via look up columns.

Security is important when dealing with credit card information. Therefore the operators must log on using individual passwords. The workstations must be lockable if the operator wishes to take a break and transactions should be logged, both for the protection of the operator and the peace of mind of the customers. The interface should be tested extensively, using valid, invalid and extreme data.

Pseudocode

It's convenient to express ideas in a form that can be changed into a high-level language easily, and **pseudocode** is ideal for this. If, for example, we were to validate the customer card number as used in the last example, we might apply a **check-digit** routine, like the one outlined in Chapter 14. The **pseudocode** could be as follows:

```
REM Account number checking routine
Input Account_number
Procedure Check_digit(Account_number)
If Result = FALSE
  THEN
    Display error message
    IF try_again = TRUE
      THEN Procedure
            Check_digit(Account_number)
      ELSE
        Display "Apologies message"
        Exit Procedure
        End if
  ELSE
  Load the account information
  End if
End Procedure
NEXT PART OF PROGRAM
```

The account number is entered, and the check digit routine called. If the result is false, the operator is prompted to try again, else the system can be exited without successfully entering the account. If Check_digit passed back a valid result, then Result = TRUE, and the account information is therefore loaded. **Pseudocode** is not in any particular language, but uses good **program structure**, and can be coded into a high-level language quite easily. *Use pseudocode to make the technical documentation of your project clearer.*

Before using pseudocode you should plan a project. A **hierarchical diagram** like that shown in Figure 19.10, for example, shows how modules fit together. *It is very bad practice if the moderator of your project has to wade through a series of code (even pseudocode) to try and understand the overall project.* There *must* be an abstract view of the system first, and this is why a **hierarchical diagram** or a **system flowchart** is essential.

Prototyping

You should **prototype** any new user interface or code that you develop. Check it out with the user to see if 'it is fit for its intended purpose', is 'easy to use' and 'actually works'! Note the constructive criticism that you may receive, but inform the user that he or she is using a prototype for the purpose of testing, and the real thing may not respond in quite the same way (*it might be slower if the real system has to load files or other data*).

One purpose of **prototyping** is to see if your ideas are **technically feasible**. You could simulate part of your project interacting with another. This might help you to see if it is technically possible to get the real interaction working? Use information obtained from developing the prototype to help write the final **specifications**. The process of achieving a final interface may involve going back to the users to refine what you have done.

The human computer interface

The way that people interact with machines is called the **human computer interface** (HCI) or human machine interface. You should be able to look at the HCI in a wider context. Users must be comfortable with the interface provided, and this includes consideration of **ergonomic** and **psychological** factors, like 'the use of colour'.

Simple testing strategies

It is rare for a system of great complexity to be delivered bug free. Testing of individual modules is therefore a good place to start on the road to checking out the entire system, and the following sections outline typical practices used to get closer to a fully functioning system. *Make sure that you test your project thoroughly, many marks can be lost if you fail to document this important part of your project.*

Dry run testing

A **dry run** is a simulation of the execution of a program on paper, or running the program on the computer making use of appropriate test data. This is useful if you have found an error in your code. By inserting appropriate **break points**, you can examine variables to see if they have the right values at a particular moment in time.

Table 19.2 Test data for temperature conversion

Test data for F to C and C to F conversion			
Test data (*expected results*)		Actual data obtained after a dry run	
C	F	C	F
0	32	0	23
−40	−40	−40	−49
100	212	–	–

As an example, consider debugging a small module, which converts temperatures from Celsius to Fahrenheit. The formulae used to do the conversions are as follows:

$$c = \frac{5(f-32)}{9} \quad \text{and} \quad f = \frac{9c}{5} + 32$$

After making up **test data**, shown in Table 19.2, the first test fails, because 32 Fahrenheit does not get produced as an answer when 0 Celsius has been entered. The second test also fails, as −49 is produced when −40 is expected. As we are converting from C to F, the part of the program that deals with the second formula needs investigation. The Visual Basic code for this program is being debugged in Figure 19.11. The input variable representing C is correct, but the variable representing F is wrong. Inspection of the formula reveals a **logical programming error**, (*a mistake in the logic of the program*) as '23' has been typed in instead of '32' at the end of the line above the **break point** (shown by the **Stop**).

Environments like **Visual Basic**, **C++**, **Delphi** and **Visual Java** all provide a rich variety of tools for **debugging** (*getting the bugs out*) your programs. Make use of these in your projects to show that you have tested various scenarios. You will often have to put in extra lines of code if the errors you are trying to track down are proving elusive. Such code might print out the values of important variables at various stages during execution.

The test data used for the temperature conversion program was chosen because it represents common values. However, what about −273°C? This is absolute zero, the lowest temperature; beyond which you cannot go. Therefore, if you type in −300 for a Celsius

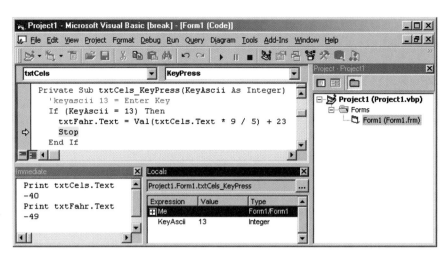

Figure 19.11 A breakpoint is set to help debug part of the code being tested

temperature, do you want your program to produce the number –508, or generate an error? This is a very simple example of possible **bad specification**.

Module (unit) testing

Each **module** should be tested individually. You can use the **black-box approach** to do this. The module can be considered as a unit with **inputs** and **outputs**. It's called the black-box testing method because you are not concerned with how the outputs are generated from the inputs (*the mechanism to do this is hidden, like being inside a black box*). If you put certain data into the system, you expect certain data out from the system. Any data not intended to be valid input should be rejected. As an example, we will write a routine to create a record which accepts only positive integers between 100 and 1000 inclusive. In this case, fractions, negative numbers, letters and other special characters input should all be rejected as shown in Table 19.3.

Important numbers to use as test data in this case could be as shown in Table 19.4.

Although the above is not exhaustive, if the system passed these tests it would indicate a high degree of confidence in the system. You should realise that '*when writing software, more effort goes into validating the data than goes into writing the code to solve some of the problems!*'

If the above module accepted all positive integers, then you need to specify the largest positive number that the system can handle. This can usually be found in the manual for the language you are using, or in the manual for the database you are setting up, etc.

Table 19.3 Black-box testing method

Conditions devised for unit testing	
Input	**Result**
Integers < 100	Error
100 <= Integers <=1000	OK
Integers > 100	Error
Negative whole numbers	Error
Fractions	Error
All other characters	Error

Table 19.4 Some black-box test data

Test data for unit testing	
Input	**Reason for use**
99	Integers < 100
100, 500, 1000	Valid numbers in range
–150	Negative integer
1001, 5000	Integers > 1000
0.75, –0.75	+ve and –ve fractions
A, %, +	Other characters

Example

Devise some black-box test data to check that a routine written to validate dates in the form 'dd/mm/yyyy' works satisfactorily.

Solution

Table 19.5 Black-box test data

Test	Invalid data for tests	Test	Invalid data for tests
All numeric	23/Jan/1999 24th/12/1998	Month is Sept, Apr, Jun or Nov – Therefore day not > 30.	31/9/2000 31/4/1999 31/6/1999 31/11/1999
Numeric < digits for the year	23/2/99	Leap Year	30/2/1997 30/2/1998 30/2/1999
1 <= month <= 12	12/13/2000	1 <= day <= 31	32/2/1998

The black box test data in Table 19.5 should reveal obvious errors in the validation routines. Testing just outside the limits of the range will usually reveal much more than testing lots of valid data within the range. Don't forget to check that the system works for valid data too!

Integration testing

Once individual modules have been tested, sub-modules need to be joined together and the system tested again. It is essential to carry out this test so that no inadvertent effect between the modules is revealed. When two or more modules are tested together, this is referred to as **integration testing**. The final stage of integration testing is when each and every module in the project has been joined to all the others. It is only by doing this that you can minimise unexpected errors due to integration of all the modules into one.

Testing the solution

When the programmers are satisfied that the entire system is working to the best of their ability, or at least the last few known **bugs** are being worked on, then the system undergoes what is called **beta testing**. This means that trusted customers and other similar people will test the new system under real conditions and report any problems encountered back to the programming team. When the project has undergone rigorous **beta testing**, version 1.0 of the final product is released. Again, on large projects, the real customers will also find errors that have not been detected, and newer versions of the software (like 1.01, 1.02, etc.) are released.

Construction and implementation

This phase of your practical systems exercise will depend on your chosen method of solution, e.g. **database**, **programming** or a combination of these (*see the next few chapters in this book*). Whichever method you chose, you should explain why you have implemented the project like this, and why, in your opinion, your chosen method is better than other alternatives. Limitations of your system will influence your chosen design. Do plenty of screen shots and place these in your report with explanations of the methods used, which should refer back to diagrams you have produced in your project design section.

Maintenance

After completion of a project, a vital part of appropriate customer service in the real world is to maintain the system in peak performance. This will involve providing '**bug** fixes' outlined in the last section, but also to make modifications to the system in the light of requests from customers after using the system in the field for some considerable time.

All software will become obsolete if not maintained properly, or not brought up to date periodically. As computer systems change and as customer requirements become ever more demanding, **maintenance** has become a vital part of any project activity. In industry there are more programmers engaged on maintaining systems than in developing new ones. This should be an important lesson regarding the importance of adequate **documentation**. The **technical documentation** that should accompany any well-developed product, is a key part of this maintenance function. Without good documentation, people who need to modify the system at a later stage may not even be able to understand it!

Technical documentation usually consists of **analysis** and **specifications**, making use of diagrams such as **system** and **program flowcharts** or **hierarchical diagrams**. The project would be split up into major sections, **pseudocode** might be used to provide broad outlines, and actual code listings, together with suitable comments would be provided using the high-level language in which the system is implemented.

The same sort of argument applies when applications like databases and spreadsheets are used to provide the solutions to major problems. Do not forget also that **macrocode** like VBA, for example, would often accompany complex solutions to problems making use of such applications.

User guide

Unless a project is trivial there should be a **user guide**. This is a relatively simple document explaining how to use your system. This user guide should be non-technical in nature. It is intended for the *user* of the system, and not for the designer of the system. It should contain background information like the **hardware** and **software** to run your system, the **minimum specification** of a computer (operating system and processor, etc.) and instructions on how to set up the system from scratch. It should contain information about what to do in the event of errors, and information about backing up data to recover from any disasters. It should preferably have screen shots of the system to help explain how it operates, and preferably be put in a separate booklet to your main project. It is also usual to put the author and **version number** of the software into this document.

You should be aware that a user guide is essential for most commercial software. However, you don't need to produce a user guide for your AQA module 3 project.

Evaluation

How well does your project work? Don't just say it's wonderful, even if it is! Instead say that it works to specification, as is demonstrated by the extensive testing that has been carried out and the **user feedback** which you have received. There may be some parts of your project that do not work well. Mention this, and you will get more marks if you supply constructive criticism. Your evaluation should reflect the standard of technical documentation that accompanies your project. Without sufficient technical documentation the system will not be maintainable, and may not be able to respond to the changing needs of the user.

Unless you are very clever and very lucky, it is unlikely that you will be able to solve all problems within the timeframe that you have been given by the examination board. The benefit of hindsight is a wonderful thing. You should always be able to think up better ways of doing your project, and this should be mentioned in your evaluation section. You will get marks for being honest, stating what works well and what does not, compared to a bland statement saying that 'all is well', which is worth virtually nothing.

Some sound project advice

Much of the information in this chapter has been general in nature, and applies to projects in industry and commerce. This last section provides information which is specific to computing projects for examination purposes. Unlike conventional examinations, getting a good mark in your project is entirely under *your* control. Always remember that other people will be marking your project.

Take note of the following important points:

1 *Always follow the mark scheme exactly* – If possible keep to the number of words advised for the implementation of the project – this does not usually include any code listings, which may be put into an appendix.

2 *Split your project up into identifiable sections which correspond to the mark scheme* – You will be advised of the sections for a particular practical exercise, but typically these include an 'analysis', 'design', 'implementation', 'testing' and 'evaluation'. The design, implementation and testing should include methods like those shown in this chapter.

3 *Always put a contents list at the front of your project* – Your contents should include the major sections (like design, implementation, etc.) and should include the sub-headings. Your teacher and the moderator should always be able to find a section quickly. Always remember that much effort gets wasted by staff trying to find things. This is unproductive work, and does not inspire confidence in your project.

4 *Put a page number on each page of your project, together with a suitable header/footer* – This not only gives the impression that you know how to use a word processor, but it aids finding all the sections very quickly, especially if the major section title is embedded into the header or footer.

5 *Create a suitable style for your project* – use a word processor and a computer to generate the 'hierarchical', 'data flow', 'systems flowcharts' and other suitable material. Always learn a suitable CAD package early on in your course.

6 *Keep your project write up concise* – put detailed code into an appendix. If there is a 4000 word limit, for example, stick to it.

7 *Don't rely on simple screen shots to show validation; have documentary evidence to show the actual validation formulae you have used* – Students are disappointed when a screen shot showing some data being rejected is not sufficient evidence of validation. To get full marks you will need to produce documentary evidence of how the validation works.

8 *Include diagrams, with titles, and make sure you refer to these diagrams in the text* – It is bad practice to have diagrams without titles. How is the moderator expected to know what he or she is looking at? Refer to these diagrams in your write up.

9 *Include documentary evidence of testing – use black-box testing methods.* Use the appropriate methods for testing and justify your test data. It's easiest to design the test data before you have implemented the project!

10 *Check spelling and grammar and get a different person to read through your work* – The odd spelling error or typo is inevitable. We have all used the spelling and grammar checker only to do a final minute alteration and then forget to check it again. However, many obvious spelling and grammatical errors will cost you marks.

11 *Fill in the check list provided by the board – help your teacher (and the moderator) by listing the pages numbers of the places in your project in which the appropriate material can be found* – You are the only person who knows were everything is in your project. It's tremendously helpful to your teacher and moderator if you include the page references at which important material can be found.

12 *Don't plagiarise material. If you find something useful, get permission from the author of the material and acknowledge it.* There is legitimate material that may enhance your project. If you use it without acknowledgement you could be accused of cheating.

Self-test questions

1 What is meant by a feasibility study?
2 During the design of a data processing system it is usual to collect information by using a variety of methods. Outline three different methods, suggesting a typical scenario in which each would be particularly appropriate.
3 What is a data flow diagram? In what situations is a data flow diagram useful?
4 When setting up a database, relationships between attributes in the database can be modelled by using an **ER** diagram. Show how an **ER** diagram may be used to model one-to-one and many-to-one relationships by choosing a suitable example.
5 Draw a program flowchart to determine the largest and smallest numbers from a list of ten numbers which are to be input by the user. Your flowchart should automatically output the value of the largest and smallest number in the list.
6 Draw a program flowchart to read in an unspecified number of examination marks where pupils are allowed to score between 0 and 100 inclusive. Make sure that any data outside of this range is ignored and an appropriate message is printed out. Work out the average examination mark for the correct number of examination entries, and make sure your algorithm does not crash if no marks are entered.
7 Draw a program flowchart to create a four-function calculator. The user should enter an operator (+, -, / or *) followed by two numbers to be used in the calculation using the convention that the top number or first number in the calculation should be entered first. After checking for a valid operator and performing the correct calculation, the correct answer should be output. The calculations should terminate when a $ is entered.
8 Draw a system flowchart for helping to manage the arrivals, collation and distribution of newspapers and periodicals that arrive at a local newsagent.
9 Draw a system flowchart to check if students are present using a computerised registration system. Assume it is linked to the school office by a radio-based network.
10 You are designing the front end to a database. Outline some of the features that you might include when the users are entering data.
11 Outline what factors could influence the design of the human computer interface when undertaking computer-based projects.
12 What is dry run testing? Why is this particularly important when testing program segments? Give an example of a dry run on a routine of your choice.
13 Explain why prototyping is often an important part of systems development. Outline a typical scenario in which prototyping might be useful.

14 Why might extensive testing of a system not find all the bugs contained within it? Is the computer industry doing anything about this problem?

15 You are helping to test the interface on a new **WAP** enabled third generation mobile phone. The phone interface is to be simulated on the computer.

(a) Suggest three different tasks that the phone might have to perform.

(b) For one of your tasks, suggest some suitable testing method.

16 Outline the difference between module testing and integration testing. Why are both important parts of testing a modern system?

17 Design a suitable interface to enable a person who has impaired vision to operate a simple 4-function calculator on the computer.

(a) What method will you use to enable the user to enter numbers?

(b) What type of display have you chosen?

(c) Are then any special features that you have used to enhance the interface?

18 You are going to test the calculator designed in question 17 for integer arithmetic addition. Suggest some suitable test data and describe how you arrived at the numbers and methods you will use. You must state any assumptions that you make.

19 You have to evaluate one of your colleagues' projects. Outline what strategies you would set up to undertake a fair evaluation.

20 The maintenance phase of the system life cycle is important. What is 'system maintenance', why is it needed and how is it carried out?

21 Outline two different situations that may lead to system maintenance being carried out on a software system that has been successfully in operation for some time. What resources should the software engineers have at their disposal to undertake effective system maintenance?

20 A module 3 project – the analysis phase

In this section you will learn about:

- The background to project development at AS level
- A typical project specification
- How to proceed with the analysis phase of a typical AS project

Introduction

The AQA board will set an **exercise**, considerably in advance of the actual examination. It is published along with other information contained in the subject specification. You are expected to use your knowledge of the development of **systems** (*see Chapter 19*), together with your practical experience in learning applications like **databases**. Mix this with your knowledge of other parts of the AS syllabus, and then add a sprinkling of your **programming skills**. This chapter continues the **synoptic element** (*bringing your knowledge together*) of the AS Computing course, and armed with this experience you should be able to provide suitable solutions to a wide range of different problems, from 'payroll', though 'stock-market simulations', to 'video-rental databases'.

All systems-analysis problems require similar techniques, and many of the necessary skills are outlined in the next few chapters, which concentrate exclusively on module 3 AS project work for the AQA board. Ensure that you have read Chapter 19 before starting this work.

The AS Practical Exercise – a re-mark system for the UKAB

The project used here is a **real AQA project** taken from the **2003 examination**. We are grateful to the board for allowing us to publish this specification, and to use 50% of the real examination paper shown in Chapter 24. The examination-board specification is shown in green, to distinguish it from other material provided in this book.

Background

The (imaginary) United Kingdom Awarding Body (UKAB) has asked you to design a system for the monitoring of its post-examination re-marks.

If a centre feels that the grade awarded to a candidate for an examination is much lower than expected, the centre can ask for that script to be re-marked. The UKAB expects all re-marks to be completed within three weeks.

The system described in the following specification has been considerably simplified. For example, few subject examinations consist of only one paper. In reality, many details are stored for the purpose of analysis and monitoring.

Specification

1 For any script for which a re-mark is requested, the following details are stored:
- Candidate name
- Candidate number

You are advised to look at the module 3 project near the beginning of your AS course.

At the author's school, we let candidates know about this project from the very first lesson. This adds particular urgency to the lessons on databases and the lessons on systems analysis, both of which can be taught quite early on in the course, enabling students to start thinking about their project in good time.

- Centre number
- Subject reference code
- Original mark
- Re-mark mark (whether changed or unchanged)
- Whether the centre has requested the return of the script.

You will find it necessary to store other details.

2 For a subject, the following details are to be stored:
- Subject reference code
- Grade boundaries for grades A–E and U.

For the purpose of this exercise, only the following subjects need to be considered:

Subject reference code	Grade boundaries (%)				
	A	B	C	D	E
01325	75	67	60	54	48
20094	70	60	50	40	30
28181	90	78	66	54	42
54821	85	79	74	64	55
64773	68	60	52	46	40

3 The solution must be able to produce a hard copy of the following:
- A daily list of any re-marks completed where a mark change has affected the grade
- A daily list of any re-marks still outstanding, i.e. that have not been completed within a three-week period
- A list of re-marks that have been requested for a particular subject
- A list of re-marks that have been requested from a particular centre.

4 The solution must produce a document to be returned to the centre giving the results of the re-mark. This document should display the UKAB logo. The following details should be included in this document:
- Centre number
- Candidate name
- Candidate number
- Subject reference code
- Original mark
- Original grade
- Either the re-mark mark and grade, if changed, or a sentence to say that there has been no change.

5 Test data for at least five candidates from four centres and the subjects listed above should cover situations in which marks are both increased and decreased.

6 (i)   Candidate numbers are of four digits and will be unique within any centre, but not between two centres. The solution should ensure that this is allowed for.
   (ii) Centre numbers are allocated within the range 10000 to 80000 and are unique.
   (iii) Subject Reference Codes are five numeric digits.

Requirements of the Practical Exercise

Candidates are expected to design and implement an appropriate computing system and provide sufficient documentation to demonstrate the following practical skills:

- Design
- Implement/test

You should note that a spreadsheet is no longer an acceptable method of solution for this component of the AQA course from the 2004 examination onwards.

A database is probably the best solution, but a programming (high-level language) solution is also acceptable.

Most students would not implement these projects using a high-level language. However, small snippets of code, like VBA if you are using Microsoft Access, for example, might be needed to solve some parts of the problem in an elegant way.

The task may be undertaken by:

either   writing a program in a chosen high-level language
or   using a suitable rational database.

Candidates are expected to produce brief documentation including some of all of the following, as appropriate:

Design

- Definition of data requirements
- User interface design, including output, forms and reports
- Method of data entry, including validation
- Record structure, file organisation and processing
- Security and integrity of data
- System design

Implementation/testing

This part changes every year.

This documentation is to be brought to the examination and handed in with the candidate's answer script for Unit 3 (CPT3) at the end of the examination. A Cover Sheet, signed by the teacher and the candidate, authenticating the work of the candidate, must be attached to the documentation.

Where to start?

From 2004 onwards, the only methods of solution acceptable to AQA for module 3 AS projects are 'databases' and 'high-level languages'. The brightest students might choose to implement a system using a programming language like 'Visual Basic' or 'Visual C++', but for the majority of students, including very bright students who have better things to do with their time, a database will probably be the easiest and best solution of all!

This is a **practical exercise**, and you will therefore be limited to using the particular database package you have at your centre. With the Microsoft Office suite being '*the* standard' used in most schools and colleges, the author will implement this model solution using **Microsoft's Access database**. Although many hints and tips will be given, this book will not attempt to teach you the basic principles of using Microsoft Access. There are many separate textbooks, web-based training courses and CD-ROMs, etc. dedicated to this task. You can't expect to sit at the computer, start Access and instantly do the project from scratch. *There is a lot of work that needs to be done before using the computer* and this initial **analysis** and **design** work is therefore covered first in Chapters 20 and 21.

Know the requirements of the exercise

First, make sure you are familiar with the **Requirements of the Practical Exercise** as shown above (last few parts of the green text). By observation we see that the **design** of the **system** must be considered first. Don't forget also that you are expected to produce **brief documentation**. However, the detailed explanations in this chapter will make the documentation in this book seem much longer. Chapter 23 will give an example of the final documentation, and this will be used for examination purposes in Chapter 24 when a

It does not matter if you do not have Microsoft Access at your school. You should be able to implement this solution using any competent relational database program.

Note that a simple flat-file database system (see Chapter 15) will not have the necessary sophistication needed to tackle a project of this complexity.

An advantage of using Microsoft Access is that most markers are familiar with it.

mock examination can be taken on this particular module. As the design is to be considered first, this is where we will make a start, as shown in the next section.

Design of the system – details for re-mark requests

From the Requirements of the Practical Exercise we see that a '**definition of data requirements**' is needed. A **data dictionary** is ideal for this, and is simply a table (or tables) of data about the data (sometimes called **metadata**). A data dictionary contains information like the **names** used for each item of data, the **data types** and **number of characters**, a **description** of the data and possibly some typical examples.

First, concentrate on part (1) of the UKAB specification. We can see that any scripts being re-marked require the following information to be stored about them:

- Candidate name
- Candidate number
- Centre number
- Subject reference code
- Original mark
- Re-mark mark (whether changed or unchanged)
- Whether the centre has requested the return of the script.

Therefore, we need to decide on a suitable name, data type, number of characters and a description of the above data. Part of a typical **data dictionary**, including some examples from the possible sets of data, is shown in Table 20.1.

Table 20.1 A typical data dictionary for the re-marks

Name	Data type	No. of characters	Typical example	Description
Candidate surname	Text	30 characters	Ponsonby-Smythe	The name of the candidate, not unique.
Candidate initials	Text	10 characters	R.I.P.	Capitals only, separated by dots with a dot at the end.
Candidate title	Text	10 characters	Ms.	Mr, Mrs, Ms, Dr, Rev., etc. (These would be typical for the purpose of this exercise.)
Candidate number	Integer	4 digits	7845	Candidate number, not unique (but unique within a particular centre) Within the range 0001 to 9999. (*See note below.*)
Centre number	Integer	5 digits	61679	Within the range 10000 to 80000 inclusive. This is unique.
Subject reference code	Integer	5 digits	28181	Subject reference code, unique. Within the range 00001 to 99999 inclusive.
Original mark	Integer	3 digits	25	Range from 0 to 100% inclusive.
Re-mark mark	Integer	3 digits	75	Range form 0 to 100% inclusive.
Return script?	Boolean	1 character	Y	Yes or No only.

You should note that *there are no absolutely right or wrong answers* to some of these data requirements. Take 'candidate number' for example; the specification says it should consist of four digits, and be unique within a centre. No range information is given. Is '0000' a valid candidate number? The answer is probably not. In the absence of any other

There is a lot of design work to undertake before you sit down at the computer and make a start on the project.

Start making an attempt at writing your final report at an early stage. There is no reason why the data dictionaries shown here can't be changed into the final ones used in your report. You can always add things later because your write up should be done on a word processor.

information, you will have to make a decision. You could have a range from 0001 to 9999, but leading zeros will cause a problem (candidate '0001' will get displayed as '1') if you store this data as an integer, unless you use a custom numeric format ensuring leading zeros are inserted. You could store it as text, but you would then need fancy validation techniques to ensure data integrity. An easy way is to limit the 4-digit candidate numbers to the range 1000 to 9999! The candidate number can then be stored as an integer, and still obey the specification regarding each candidate having a unique four-digit number within a centre. However, *if you make assumptions like this*, you should state in your report the *reasons* why you have done it. You could try applying the same principles to the subject reference code, but you would come unstuck when you enter 'centre number 01325' (*explicitly required by the specification*) in the subject table!

The UKAB specification does not request any specific format for the storage of names, and therefore 'Title', 'Surname' and 'Initials', stored as separate fields, will be used in this project. When you make decisions like these you must *scan through the specification to ensure that your decisions will not prevent you from implementing a required feature at some later stage.*

The other details

The specification suggests that you will need to store 'other details' about the re-mark scripts, and we now need to think about this.

Looking at the **UKAB requirements** in detail (green text at the beginning of this chapter), you can see that they expect all the re-marks to be completed within a three-week period. As there is no date information present, this request would be impossible to fulfil unless we had stored the **date on which the request was received**, and after the re-mark has been done, **the date on which the re-mark information is dispatched to the centre**. Two extra attributes about dates therefore need to be added to the data dictionary shown in Table 20.1. Additional information that would be useful would include **subject name**, and **examiner name** (or **ID**).

Looking at the **UKAB requirements** in detail again, (green text at the beginning of this chapter), we can see that there is no provision for information about a possible grade change. The system could, therefore, not generate this information automatically. One way of solving this problem would be to have two extra attributes, namely '**Grade before re-mark**' and '**Grade after re-mark**'. One final piece of information needed is whether a **grade change** has actually taken place. This is shown at the bottom of Table 20.2.

A unique 4-digit code (ID) for each marker could be linked to more information about them, stored in another table containing 'Title', 'Surname', 'Initials' and possibly their 'addresses' and 'phone numbers', etc. However, this would complicate the database further, and was not *specifically requested* in this simplified system. However, it's important to identify this sort of extra information, and the codes shown above are an easy way to satisfy this requirement.

From the specification (shown in green at the beginning of this chapter) we see that a real system would store a lot of other detail for analysis and monitoring purposes. There are many other attributes which could be added (e.g. the name of the original marker and the name of the person who did the re-mark, etc.) but only the above information is needed to implement the project according to the simplified UKAB specification; don't make life too complex by adding others which will get you few, if any, extra marks. A particular date format has been chosen in Table 20.2, in the absence of any preference from the UKAB specification.

Table 20.1 and Table 20.2 would now be joined together to form the data dictionary about the re-mark scripts, and this has been done in the final module 3 project write up shown in Chapter 23.

Think carefully about the detail before going ahead with the database design.

For example, it would be nice to put in the exam markers' names when the re-mark list is printed for a particular subject. This might identify markers who have been too harsh. This has been added to Table 20.2, by inventing a new 4-digit code for each examiner.

Table 20.2 The data dictionary for the extra requirements

Name	Data Type	No. of characters	Typical example	Description and notes
Date request received	Date	9	30/8/2004	The date on which the request for a re-mark was made. Format limited to that shown (e.g. no dates like 30th August 2004).
Date request processed	Date	9	19/9/2004	The date on which the appropriate re-mark information was sent to the centre. Format limited to that shown.
Subject name	Text	50	Computing	Title of the examination paper.
Grade before re-mark	Text	1	U	A, B, C, D, E, F and U only.
Grade after re-mark	Text	1	A	A, B, C, D, E, F and U only.
Grade changed	Boolean	1	Y	Yes or No only.
Original marker ID	Integer	4 digits	2176	Range from 1000 to 9999. Unique ID for UKAB marker.
Re-mark marker ID	Integer	4 digits	2873	Range from 1000 to 9999. Unique ID for a UKAB marker.
Grade changed?	Boolean	1	N	Yes or No only.

Analysis of the system – details for subjects

Next we concentrate on part (2) of the specification shown in green at the beginning of this chapter, namely the information about each of the **subjects** that can be examined. For convenience, the appropriate information from UKAB is shown in the next table.

Subject reference code	Grade boundaries (%)				
	A	B	C	D	E
01325	75	67	60	54	48
20094	70	60	50	40	30
28181	90	78	66	54	42
54821	85	79	74	64	55
64773	68	60	52	46	40

We now build up a **data dictionary** for the information above; this is shown in Table 20.3.

Table 20.3 The data dictionary for the subject information

Name	Data type	No of. characters	Example	Description and notes
Subject reference code	Integer	5 digits	01325	Subject reference code, unique. Within the range 00001 to 99999 inclusive.
Subject name	Text	50 char.	Computing	Name of subject as used by UKAB.
Grade boundary A	Integer	3 digits	78	Range 0–100 inclusive.
Grade boundary B	Integer	2 digits	67	Range 0–99 inclusive.
Grade boundary C	Integer	2 digits	60	Range 0–99 inclusive.
Grade boundary D	Integer	2 digits	53	Range 0–99 inclusive.
Grade boundary E	Integer	2 digits	46	Range 0–99 inclusive.

No other information is needed about each subject for the purpose of this UKAB exercise, and the **subject name** mentioned earlier has been grouped with the above data. However, do have at look at the margin entry! Can you notice anything important that's missing? It will not matter if you can't because we will check the entire system again *before* proceeding to the detailed design and implementation.

Modelling the solution

Having got a good idea of the **data requirements** from the **data dictionaries** in Tables 20.1, 20.2 and 20.3, we now develop a strategy for solving the problem. We know what information we have, and from the UKAB specification part (3), shown in green at the beginning of this chapter, we know what information needs to be produced. For convenience the outputs from the system are shown here:

- A daily list of any re-marks completed where a mark change has affected the grade
- A daily list of any re-marks still outstanding, i.e. that have not been completed within a three-week period
- A list or re-marks that have been requested for a particular subject
- A list of re-marks that have been requested from a particular centre.

Next we need a generalised method of solution which links the data input to the system, the data output from the system (shown above in green) and hence the sort of processing that needs to go onto produce these statistics. A **data flow diagram** (DFD) is ideal to show these processes pictorially, and will display your thoughts to the examiners in a very convenient and standard form. You will recall from Chapter 19 that a **data flow diagram** is ideal not only for showing processing carried out by a computer, but also the flow of data like paper through an office. The DFD will therefore be ideal for tracing the flow of data from requests being made for re-marks through the actual marking of the scripts to the letters being sent out to the centre informing them of the decision.

How to produce a suitable data flow diagram

We now need to think our way through a typical scenario, by imagining we are working at the UKAB. All the examinations have been marked, all the statistics about centres, candidates, marks and grade boundaries for each subject are already stored in the Board's database, and you have your first request from a centre requesting a re-mark. How is it to be processed? In general terms, what does our system need to do to produce the letter sent out to the centre informing them of the decision made by the board?

The advantage of a **data flow diagram** at this stage is that it does not depend on any particular method of solution, and would be the same irrespective of whether a database or programming solution is chosen to implement this project. A typical **DFD** is shown in Figure 20.1. Remember that you don't need to consider details which are not central to your system. The actual mechanism for getting the papers to the examiner and re-marking them, for example, is not shown here. We merely show the data being sent off and the statistics being returned.

You should note from Figure 20.1 that there is no unique **data flow diagram**. If you come up with a completely different system that works, then it should do just as well. Don't expect to come up with the same ideas as all of your colleagues, even if you are solving exactly the same problem. This is where your creative ability comes in handy. If your colleagues do have the same data flow diagram as you, this would indicate a considerable degree of cheating!

Some important data has been deliberately missed out from the data dictionaries used here to make a point of checking the system at a later stage!

Can you think of anything extra that would be needed at this stage?

Generating a good DFD on a suitable CAD package like the diagrams shown on the next page will take a long time, but it needs to be done professionally for your final report.

Start off with a pencil, paper and rubber, gradually changing the DFD into the final form.

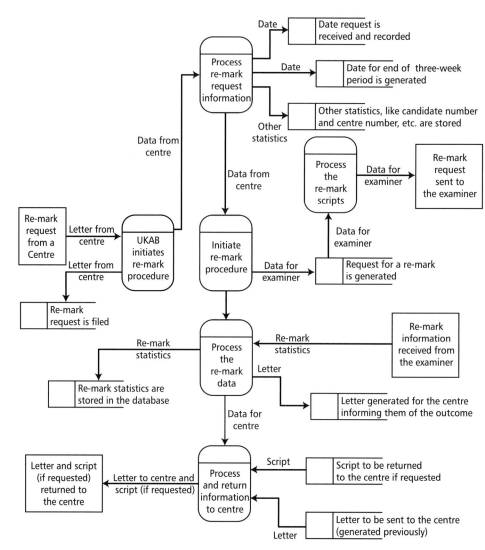

Figure 20.1 A possible data flow diagram for the main processing

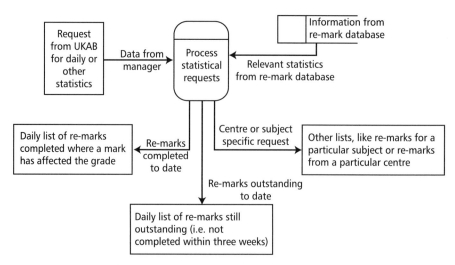

Figure 20.2 A possible data flow diagram for the UKAB statistical requests

In addition to the processing of the re-mark requests, UKAB requires that statistics be generated on a daily basis regarding a variety of other information. A separate data flow diagram shown in Figure 20.2 has been generated for this.

Check the detail before going any further

Having got some suitable **data dictionaries** and **data flow diagrams**, *we need to stop and take stock before going any further*. I would strongly suggest that you tick off each piece of data that will be needed according to the specification, and make sure that you have these in the data dictionary. Go through each procedure to make sure you have the necessary data to process the request as required by the UKAB; you might be amazed at what's easily forgotten. It's best to identify this during the analysis phase.

Consider, for example, that you need to generate statistics about the centres. Each centre will obviously need a 'name and address'! Therefore, some dummy names and address, centre names, candidate names and the like will need to be generated for setting up the system and for testing purposes. The data requirements for these extra features have not been done yet, so we need to consider them now!

Table 20.4 The data dictionary for the test-centre data

Name	Data type	No. of characters	Example	Description and notes
Centre number	Long integer	5 digits	20203	Limit to range 10000 to 80000 inclusive. This is unique
Centre name	Text	30 characters	Leigh College	Centre name – not necessarily unique. (Use centre number to identify centre, but put centre name on letters sent out to the centre.)
Title	Text	10 characters	Mr.	Mr, Mrs, Ms, Dr, Very Rev., etc. (These would be typical for the purpose of this exercise.)
Contact name	Text	30 characters	Wilson	Probably the examinations officer. Surname has been separated from initials so that it's easy to generate 'Dear Dr. ...' for letters to the centre.
Initials	Text	5 characters	A.N.	Capitals only, separated by dots with a dot at the end.
Address (1)	Text	30 characters	Porter's Lodge	
Address (2)	Text	30 characters	30 High Street	It is usual to put each line of the address as a separate entity so that you may search on entities like post code, town or county, for example.
Town/city	Text	30 characters	Middlington	
County/state	Text	30 characters	West Essex	
Post Code/zip	Text	30 characters	WE2 4BW	
Country	Text	30 characters	England	

Other information will include the Board's address, phone number and e-mail address (to be placed on the letter sent out to centres), and the Board's logo to go at the top of the page. There should also be the name of the examinations officer at UKAB, from whom the letter is sent. However, these data items do not change very often, and can be fixed within the system for the purpose of this exercise.

Inputting/editing data

It's important to ensure that an appropriate and easy-to-use user interface is designed *before* using the computer. From the data flow diagrams we see that there are several points at which data needs to be entered into the system, and these are as follows:

- A re-mark request has been made by the centre
- Re-mark information has arrived from the examiner
- Statistical information is requested by the Board.

The above assumes that much data has *already been entered* into the initial database. Therefore, the data must have already been set up to establish the re-mark database in the first place, and the user interfaces must be considered for these cases too. Typical of these would be the following:

- Entering information about each centre
- Entering information about each candidate
- Entering information about each examination.

The actual mechanism of data entry, including validation (if any) will be considered later, when the software chosen for the problem is analysed in detail. Here we concentrate only on the type of interface needed for the user to enter the data.

Outputting the data

It's important to ensure that an appropriate and easy-to-use user interface is designed for the production of the reports for the UKAB. Interfaces are needed to output the following:

- Re-marks for a particular subject
- Re-marks for a particular centre
- Daily lists of re-marks still outstanding
- Daily list of re-marks where the re-mark has altered the grade.

Bringing it all together

A variety of administrative tasks must be performed, and these can be broadly categorised as entering data about candidates, centres and examinations, then generating statistical information for the UKAB. A possible system is shown in Figure 20.3. Here, the hierar-

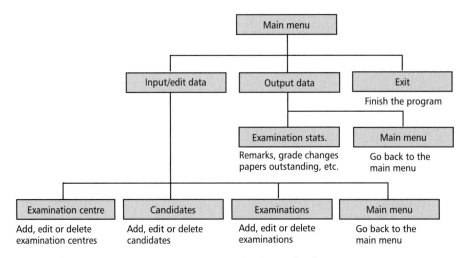

Figure 20.3 A possible heirachical structure showing the choices for the user

chical structure representing a menu system is presented to the user of the system. As can be seen, the user would have three initial choices: to 'input/edit data', to 'delete data' or to 'generate statistics for the UKAB', like 're-marks outstanding' or 're-marks to date', etc.

We have now made a reasonably comprehensive start to thinking about the **data requirements** of the UKAB system. You should note that *we have not yet made use of any computer software to implement the solution.* This much thought at least should be put into your analysis and design *before* starting work using your chosen software, be it a **high-level programming language** or a **relational database**.

Self-test questions

1 Which two types of software are acceptable for solving AQA module 3 projects?
2 Outline five good reasons for using a database to solve the UKAB problem.
3 Outline three good reasons for using a high-level language to solve the UKAB problem.
4 A data dictionary is useful for helping to define the data requirements of a system. What is a data dictionary?
5 The UKAB system needs to generate letters to the centres, informing them of the decision of the examiners. Outline, in principle, how this might be achieved automatically.
6 Considering the re-marking procedure, suggest three other items of data that could be stored in a real examination re-mark system.
7 For the three items of data you have chosen in question 6, construct a small part of a data dictionary, suggesting a suitable data type, the number of characters needed, an example and some helpful notes.
8 A data flow diagram must follow good design principles. What is wrong with the following small parts of these three data-flow diagrams?

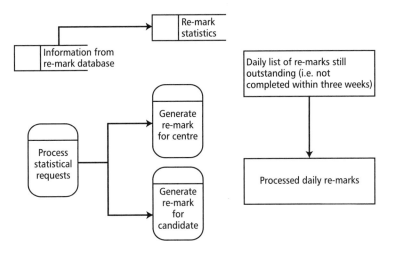

21 Database design for the module 3 project

Introduction

The work in this chapter follows on from the analysis of the UKAB module 3 problem outlined in Chapter 20.

Make sure you have read Chapter 20 before covering the material in this chapter.

The work shown here is not intended as a tutorial on Microsoft Access. Here we will concentrate only on the requirements for the AS examination.

Having defined the data requirements and a general method of solution using **data** flow **diagrams** and **hierarchical diagrams**, we now look at the design of the solution to the problem in more detail. You will recall that **high-level programming languages** or **databases** are the only acceptable methods of solution for the AQA module 3 AS project from 2004. We will therefore use a database because this is the method of solution that would be chosen by the majority of candidates. Microsoft's Access database will be used, as this is *the* most popular database available in schools and colleges. It is also a powerful **relational database** which has all the facilities to solve this particular problem. *If your school is a member of the appropriate scheme, students may purchase Microsoft Office Professional (Access is part of this) for a small annual charge.*

It is always advisable to check with your project supervisor that your chosen package or language is appropriate *before* getting to the implementation phase of your project (*see Chapter 22*). Make sure that the language or database you have chosen is supported by your centre, as it's unrealistic to do all your work at home.

Modelling the data using Access

We now put the work covered in Chapter 20 into practice, namely that of setting up a collection of **relational tables** that model the data for the UKAB re-mark system. We have already analysed the data requirements and now have the job of deciding which information needs to go into which tables.

A **table** within a database should model a particular **entity**. Obvious **entities** for the UKAB system are 'candidates', 'centres' and 'subjects', and this is a good way to model the tables. The first table is shown in Figure 21.1, where a *good description of the Field and Data Types is given. This prevents you losing a lot of marks (see later).*

Field Name	Data Type	Description
Centre Number	Number	An Integer within the range 10000 to 80000 inclusive. Not Null. Unique. Required.
Centre Name	Text	Up to 30 characters, the name by which the centre is known. Not Null. Required.
Contact Name	Text	Up to 30 characters, the name of the examinations officer. Not Null. Required.
Title	Text	Title for the person at contact at the centre - e.g. Dr, Mr etc. Not Null. Required.
Initials	Text	10 characters, capitals only, separated by dots with a dot at the end
Address 1	Text	Up to 30 characters, Not null. Required.
Address 2	Text	Up to 30 characters.
Town/City	Text	Up to 30 characters.
County/State	Text	Up to 20 characters.
Post Code/Zip	Text	Up to 10 characters.
Country	Text	Up to 20 characters. Not Null. Required.

Figure 21.1 A table set up in Access to store the information about the centres

When setting up tables like these, always refer back to the **data dictionaries** (shown in Chapter 20) to ensure that the **field names** used here reflect the **names** used in the dictionaries. It's not always sensible to make them exactly the same, but too many wasted hours could be spent wondering why a database does not work when the problem could be as simple as searching for 'Contact Name' when 'Name of Contact', for example, has actually been used. This simple act of checking could save you much frustration during the **implementation** and **testing phases**. Note that a centre number is unique, and can therefore be used as the **key field** (shown by the small key).

Some potential pitfalls

Examiners don't like vague **data types** like '**numeric**' or '**number**', even though this is what Access will display when you are designing the tables. Don't forget that Access qualifies the 'number' data type at the bottom of the screen, as shown for the centre number in Figure 21.2.

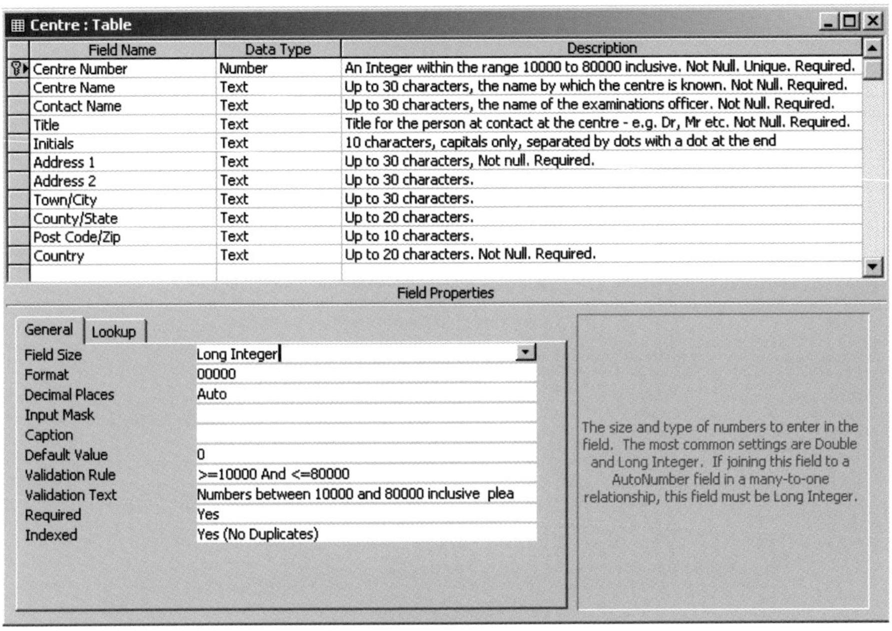

Figure 21.2 Qualifiying an Access 'number' data type as a 'Long Integer'

You will lose marks in the examination if you have not qualified your **numeric data types**, and this is why 'integer' is written in the data dictionary of Table 20.1. Microsoft Access has integer data types as displayed in Table 21.1.

Table 21.1 Some integer data types for Access

Name	Description
Byte	A single-byte **integer** for numbers between 0 and 255 inclusive
Integer	A 2-byte **integer** for numbers between −32 768 and +32 767 inclusive
Long integer	A 4-byte **integer** for numbers between −2 147 483 648 and +2 147 483 647 inclusive

Note that an *integer* used in Access has *not* got the range to store our centre numbers from 10 000 to 99 999 inclusive, and this is why a **Long Integer** has been chosen for this. However, it's perfectly proper to write **integer** in the data dictionary, because at that stage

Do write up the project as you are going along. It helps to clarify what you are doing and saves time when you might be struggling to get the final few things working.

As the report is written on a word processor, you can always alter it if you forget something important or change your mind.

you did not know which package you would be using, and therefore have little idea of the possible range for different numeric data types. Theoretically an **integer** is a whole number within the range $-\infty$ to $+\infty$!

On some occasions you might lose marks if you choose 'double' or 'long integer' instead of 'integer' when an integer is more appropriate. It really does depend on the software you are using. However, the small blue text in Figure 21.2 is reminding us that if we wish to join a numeric field to an auto number in a **many-to-one relationship**, then only a **double** or **long integer** will do. If you find yourself having to modify data types because of the way in which your package implements things, tell the examiners what you have done and why, or you may not get any marks for a part of your project which works perfectly, simply because they don't realise what you have done.

The other two tables

You should not forget the possibility that a single candidate may have more than one subject requiring a re-mark from the UKAB.

We could store multiple subject information per candidate, but most of these would be empty for the majority of candidates. Therefore, it's been decided to have a different request for each subject for each candidate. The same candidate may therefore have more than one entry in the candidate table, and this is catered for by the composite key field (three fields) in the candidate subject entry table.

The other entities to be modelled are 'Candidates' and 'Examinations', and some Microsoft Access tables to do this are shown in Figures 21.3 and 21.4. Note that 'Subject Reference Code' can't be null, or the candidate has no papers to be re-marked!

Field Name	Data Type	Description
Centre Number	Number	Long Integer, unique, range between 10000 and 80000, Not Null. Required.
Candidate Number	Number	Integer, not unique, range from 0001 to 9999, Not Null. Required.
Subject Reference Code	Number	Long Integer, 00001 to 99999 inclusive. Not Null. Required.
Surname	Text	30 characters, not unique. Not Null. Required.
Initials	Text	10 characters, capitals only, separated by dots with a dot at the end
Title	Text	Mr. Mrs. Ms, Dr etc. Not Null. Required.
Date Received	Date/Time	Date the request for a re-mark of subject received. Date field, Not Null. Required.
Date Processed	Date/Time	Date on which the request has been processed. Date field
Grade Before Remark	Text	'A', 'B', 'C', 'D', 'E' and 'U' only, Not Null. Required.
Original Mark	Number	Range from 0 to 100% inclusive, Not Null. Required.
Grade After Remark	Text	'A', 'B', 'C', 'D', 'E' and 'U' only
Re-mark Mark	Number	Range from 0 to 100% inclusive
Grade Changed?	Yes/No	Boolean - Yes or No only
Return Script?	Yes/No	Boolean - Yes or No only
Original Marker ID	Number	Integer - 4 digits, range from 1000 to 9999. Unique, Not Null. Required.
Re-mark Marker ID	Number	Integer - 4 digits, range from 1000 to 9999. Unique

Figure 21.3 A table set up in Access to store information about a candidate subject entry

Field Name	Data Type	Description
Subject Reference Code	Number	Range 00001 to 99999 Not Null. Required.
Subject Name	Text	50 characters. Not Null. Required.
Grade Boundary A	Number	Integer, 0 to 100 inclusive. Required.
Grade Boundary B	Number	Integer, 0 to 99 inclusive. Not Null. Required.
Grade Boundary C	Number	Integer, 0 to 99 inclusive. Not Null. Required.
Grade Boundary D	Number	Integer, 0 to 99 inclusive. Not Null. Required.
Grade Boundary E	Number	Integer, 0 to 99 inclusive. Not Null. Required.

Figure 21.4 A table set up in Access to store information about the subjects

Information to be stored concerning 'grade before re-marks', and other statistics like 'has the grade been changed' really belong to a particular candidate. Therefore, this information, stored in the data dictionary of Table 20.2, is also stored along with the candidate details in Table 21.3. The 'Overdue Date' (three weeks) can easily be generated from the 'Date Received' and therefore does not have to be stored.

It's important to remember that the candidate number is *not* unique and therefore can't be used as the primary key for the candidate table. It's easy to have a composite primary key (two or more fields) consisting of candidate number and centre number, for example, and this would make the composite primary key unique. This would be a good solution to finding a suitable primary key. However, in our system, this would not allow for an unfortunate candidate who might need more than one subject re-mark, because information on one subject only is stored in this table. If we include the subject code too, then the trio *now* produces a unique key field for each candidate-subject entry, as seen in Figure 21.3. Using this method, *a separate request would be needed by each candidate for each subject*, which is to be processed separately by our system.

The final 'subject' table is considered next, which contains information like 'Subject Code' and 'Grade Boundaries for that subject'.

Stop and take stock again

You will recall from Chapter 20, when defining the data dictionaries, we ticked off all the data items to ensure that the specification could be implemented in full. I suggest you do this again, to ensure that no item of data has been missed out. Tick all the entries in all the data dictionaries in Tables 20.1, 20.2, 20.3 and 20.4. Then tick all the corresponding entries in all the database tables of Figures 21.1, 21.3 and 21.4. Check that all items are ticked, and none are left out. *Time spent doing this now may save you a lot of hassle at a later stage when the database is up and running.* It is so easy to miss something out, especially if you are tired or doing your project late at night.

Relating the tables

The tables in Figures 21.1, 21.3 and 21.4 must now be linked. This means that some **relationships** need to be defined on fields that link these tables. This idea is shown in Figure 21.5.

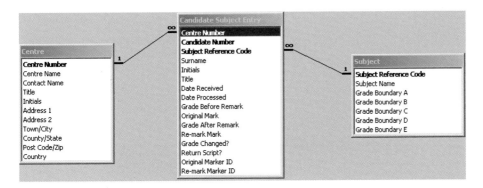

Figure 21.5 The relationships for the UKAB re-mark database

You can see from Figure 21.5 that a centre (left table) can have many candidate subject entries (middle table). Also, many candidate subject entries (middle table) can have the same subject reference code (right table). *Don't forget we decided that a candidate makes a separate subject entry for the purpose of this particular re-mark system. (See Figure 21.3 and accompanying text and the margin entry on the same page)*. If they need two subjects re-marked, they will submit two applications for the re-mark, one for each subject. The candidate can't be identified by 'candidate number' alone, because it's not unique to UKAB. So the trio of fields 'Centre Number' + 'Candidate Number' + 'Subject Reference Code' makes a unique field for each subject entry for each candidate.

The 'Centre' to 'Candidate Subject Entry' relationship is therefore one-to-many, and the 'Candidate Subject Entry' to 'Subject' relationship is many-to-one, to allow for those candidates who have more than one subject re-mark with the UKAB at any particular moment in time. The **entity relationship diagrams** (**E-R diagrams**) for these are shown in Figure 21.6.

Do check that each of your tables is related, and that the relationships are sensible in terms of the way that the data is being used.

A wrong relationship set up at this time could cost you a lot of extra time further down the line when you are struggling to find out why the queries or reports are not working.

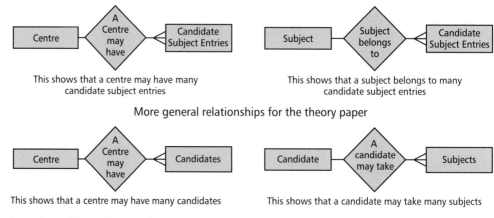

Figure 21.6 The E-R diagrams for our UKAB system relationships

You should note that the theory paper to accompany this project might *not* use the same tables and relationships that you have used in your project. For example, in the examination paper they might ask you to show the relationship between 'Centres' and 'Candidates' or the relationship between 'Candidates' and 'Subjects'. Think carefully when you answer this type of question, because the diagrams at the bottom of Figure 21.6 would be needed for the 'correct' answers to these questions, which are not necessarily a repeat of *your* relationships which you have used in *your* project.

Table 21.2 Data integrity for information about the Centre

Name	Data type	Comments and validation methods
Centre Number	Long Integer	Within the range 10000–80000 inclusive. Whole numbers only. Not Null. Required field.
Centre Name	Text	No validation, but verification could be used after initial data entry. Not Null. Required field.
Contact Name	Text	No validation, but verification could be used after initial data entry. Not Null. Required field. Could be selected from a drop-down list.
Title	Text	'Mr.', Mrs.', 'Ms.', 'Dr.', etc. Choose from a drop-down list, with the option to add specials like 'Most Rev.', for example, if needed. Not Null. Required field. Generate from a drop-down list.
Initials	Text	Capital letters only, separated by dots. Not Null. Required field.
Address 1	Text	No validation, but verification could be used after initial data entry. Not Null. Required field.
Address 2	Text	No validation, but verification could be used after initial data entry.
Town/City	Text	No validation, but verification could be used after initial data entry.
County/State	Text	No validation, but verification could be used after initial data entry.
Post Code	Text	No validation, but verification could be used after initial data entry.
Country	Text	No validation, but verification could be used after initial data entry. Not Null. Required field.

Data integrity

We now turn to ensuring the highest standard of **data integrity** that is sensibly possible. This means checking that data like 'invalid subject reference codes' or 'invalid centre numbers' don't get entered into the system. The validation process is also helped by making certain fields *'mandatory'* or *'required fields'*, and making sure they are *not null* (can't be blank). It would be unacceptable, for example to have no 'centre number' or 'centre name' for a centre which has an entry in our UKAB database.

Ensuring good **data integrity** means checking each and every item in Tables 20.1, 20.3 and 20.4, then deciding if it's possible to **validate** the entries. Tables are ideal for this, and appropriate data, together with possible **validation methods** and other comments are shown Tables 21.3, 21.4 and 21.5. We keep to the tabular arrangement, as this will be easier to manage for the project write up covered in Chapter 23.

It's important to have a sensible compromise on validation. It would be possible, for example, to get a database of post codes to ensure that all post codes conform to a set

Validation is not always possible. Verification (checking the data again) will have to be done manually in this project.

Table 21.3 Data integrity for information about candidate subject entries

Name	Data type	Comments and validation methods
Centre Number	Long Integer	Within the range 10000–80000 inclusive. Whole numbers only. Not Null. Required field. Candidate number is not unique, therefore centre number included here for correct ID of candidate.
Candidate Number	Integer	Within the range 0001–9999 inclusive. Not Null. Required field.
Subject Reference Code	Long Integer	Within the range 00001–99999 inclusive. Not Null. Required field. Needed here, together with the centre number and candidate number to create a three-field composite key to uniquely identify a subject entry.
Surname	Text	No validation, but verification could be used after initial data entry. Not Null. Required field.
Initials	Text	Capital letters only, separated by dots. Not Null. Required field.
Title	Text	'Mr.', Mrs.', 'Ms.', 'Dr.', etc. Choose from a drop-down list, with the option to add specials like 'Most Rev.', for example, if needed. Not Null. Required field. Choose from a drop-down list.
Date Received	Date	The 'Date field' ensures the correct date format and date validation. Not Null. Required field.
Date Processed	Date	The 'Date field' ensures the correct date format and date validation.
Grade Before Re-mark	Text	Choose from drop-down' list. Only values 'A', 'B', 'C', 'D', 'E' and 'U'. Not Null. Required field.
Original Mark	Byte	Number between 0 and 100% inclusive. Not Null. Required field.
Grade After Re-mark	Text	Choose from drop-down' list. Only values 'A', 'B', 'C', 'D', 'E' and 'U'.
Re-mark Mark	Byte	Number between 0 and 100% inclusive. Not Null.
Grade Changed?	Boolean	Yes or No only. Not Null.
Return Script?	Boolean	Yes or No only. Not Null.
Original Marker ID	Integer	4 digits: 1000–9999 inclusive, unique, Not Null, Required.
Re-mark Marker ID	Integer	4 digits: 1000–9999 inclusive, unique.

Do think carefully about what you are doing. If you make the 'Re-Mark Marker ID' or the 'Date Processed' a required field and this is not picked up later, it would be obvious that you have not tested your database in a sensible way!

Table 21.4 Data integrity for information about the subjects

Name	Data type	Comments and validation methods
Subject Reference Code	Long Integer	00001–99999 inclusive. Not Null. Required field. Number is unique.
Subject Name	Text	50 characters. Not Null. Required field.
Grade Boundary A	Byte	Integer, 0–100% inclusive. Not Null. Required field.
Grade Boundary B	Byte	Integer, 0–100% inclusive. Not Null. Required field.
Grade Boundary C	Byte	Integer, 0–100% inclusive. Not Null. Required field.
Grade Boundary D	Byte	Integer, 0–100% inclusive. Not Null. Required field.
Grade Boundary E	Byte	Integer, 0–100% inclusive. Not Null. Required field.

format. However, this would not work for foreign students, although databases of these too are available. If you observe some real foreign addresses, you will see that Town, County/State and 'Post Code' can't be required fields. A valid Hong Kong address, for example, is '85 North Bay Close, Repulse Bay, Hong Kong', which has no post code at all.

The original specification for UKAB is considerably simpler than real life, so we have to compromise on things that may be used in a real examination system. We need only validate the vitally necessary things like 'centre number' or 'candidate number' which, if entered incorrectly, would produce unacceptable errors, even in our simplified system. **Verification** of data means that either the computer or another person checks data that has already been entered 'correctly' by ensuring that it's identical to the data originally entered, usually by looking at the data written on a piece of paper (*something like the original application form for a new centre to become an approved UKAB centre*).

Drop-down lists can be used to help maintain a good level of data integrity. The grades, for example, can be chosen from a suitable drop-down list, thus negating the possibility of entering grades like 'G' or 'X', for example. With small lists like 'A', 'B', 'C', 'D' and 'E' this is very easy to do. Note that some fields, like 'Date Processed' and 'Re-mark Marker ID' are not required fields, *because information like this will not necessarily be known at the time of setting up the re-mark request*, and if set up, Access would not allow you to save the records, thus rendering the database useless!

Security of the system

We have not yet set up any **security** for the UKAB re-mark system. Examination results are sensitive and should only be accessed by the personnel who set up and maintain the database, and by the UKAB staff who run it.

If a professional operating system like Windows 2000 or Windows XP Professional is used, there may already be security set up by the use of file permissions and the process of logging on. However, it's easy to set up additional security on the database itself, because only those personnel involved with this database should see the actual data. Access enables us to set up a password before the database can be opened. You will have to decide on a suitable password a keep it safe. Make sure that it's hard to crack (by using a suitable combination of 'upper case', 'lower case', 'numbers' and 'punctuation') but easy to remember for the personnel involved. Something like the following should be OK, especially if you like curries!

```
Chicken_Tikka_Masala
```

The user interface – 'centre' information

We now come to the design of the **forms** for data input, and also the design of the **reports** for data output. You should technically consider these before using the database, but the AQA board require that you keep the project documentation very brief, so the actual screens used to design the real forms on Access will be used here instead, but do look at the margin entries. We need suitable forms to enter the 'centre', 'candidate' and 'subject'.

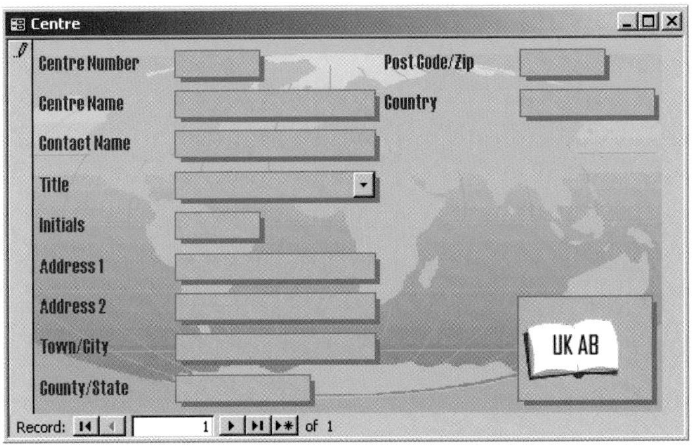

Figure 21.7 A typical user interface for the 'centre' information

Access will enable you to design a suitable interface very quickly indeed by using the Form Wizard. The interface is simple and effective, and reflects the international nature of the UKAB board (the Globe backdrop!). Don't spend too long making a fancy interface; you will get few extra marks for how good it looks over and above the utilitarian value of a minimalist approach which works well and suits the task in hand.

The user interface – 'candidate subject entry' information

Keep the design consistent across the range of database utilities. The candidate-information form is shown in Figure 21.8.

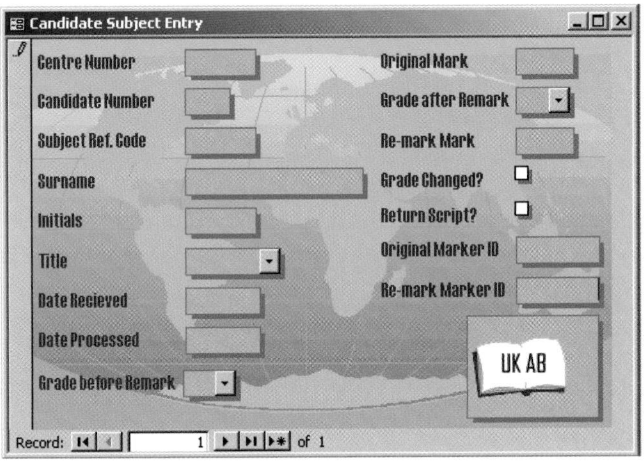

Figure 21.8 A typical user interface for 'candidate subject entry'

Finally, a typical form to enter the subject information is shown in Figure 21.9. Again we have kept a consistency across the range of user-input screens (*another good reason to make use of the Access facilities to help us achieve this*).

When using Access, the field names are the default values for the labels used on the forms. You may change these by editing the captions.

Make sure that your user interface looks professional, and no captions are obscured by the box used to display the data.

Think also about the length of the data-entry boxes. If you leave the default value of 50 on an Access text box you will end up with a box a mile long to enter a grade like 'B'. This looks silly, and shows that you have used the Wizards in Access without much thought!

Look at every detail to check that it is OK.

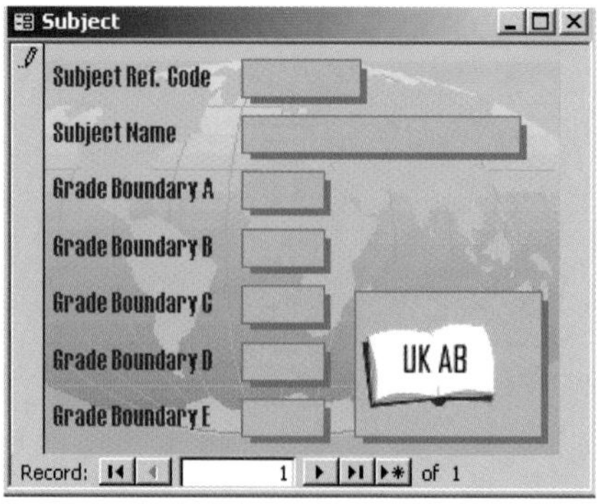

Figure 21.9 A typical user interface for 'subject information'

Note that drop-down lists (*shown by the down arrows at the end of the fields*) have been used to help maintain a high level of data integrity in Figures 21.7 and 21.8.

Output – reporting from the database

Having designed the database, you will recall that one of the major reasons for setting it up was to enable UKAB to produce **hard copy** of the following reports:

- A daily list of any re-marks completed where a mark change has affected the grade
- A daily list of any re-marks still outstanding, i.e. that have not been completed within a three-week period
- A list of re-marks that have been requested for a particular subject
- A list of re-marks that have been requested from a particular centre.

These are copied from the specification outlined in Chapter 20. Note that the design of the **user interface** for these **reports** does not have to deal with the mechanisms (i.e. the **queries**) for finding the information. You can use the report section from Access, and then assign appropriate queries during the **implementation phase** of your project (*see Chapter 22*). Here we concentrate on the printed outputs only.

Report for the list of re-marks resulting in a grade change

The UKAB is requesting this list, and it's up to the designer of the system (you!) to determine what should be on it. The grades before and after the re-mark are obvious, but how should the report be laid out, and what other information should be present? As the UKAB is requesting this, they will probably be interested in 'Centres', 'Subjects' and 'Exam Markers'. They will have the opportunity to list by any criteria like 'grade change by centre', and 'grade change by subject' in the next few reports. We now make some decisions about what information to include on this print out, making sure that important information like 'Date' is also included.

Much more information could be displayed, but this indicates which subjects have had the most re-marks, which is probably one of the most important statistics required by the board. Statistics like 'How many re-marks have resulted in a grade change for a particular subject' are also easily included.

In Table 21.6 we have already indicated the order in which the data will appear and how it will be sorted within each section. A calculation can also be done which displays the re-mark statistics (how many remarks) in a convenient form if thought necessary.

If the specification asks for 'hard copy', this means an actual printout produced by your system and included in your project report. Screen copies are not acceptable.

Any printouts will be on separate sheets, and are best included in an appendix to your report to save cluttering up your design, implementation and testing sections.

Table 21.5 Data to be included in the re-marks resulting in a grade change report

Name	Comments and additional formating
Heading	UKAB Daily list of re-marks that have resulted in a grade change
Logo	The UKAB logo.
Date Processed	This is to enable paper-based filing of these reports by day.
Subject Reference Code	Used as the primary index for presenting the data. Displayed in increasing numerical order.
Subject Name	Included as it's more convenient when reading a list. Subjects won't be in alphabetical order, as they are ordered by subject number from the above field.
Centre Number	Used as a secondary index. Centre numbers within a subject will be displayed in increasing numerical order.
Original Marker	Used as a secondary index. Displayed in increasing numerical order.
Grade Before Re-mark	Included to see the extent of the grade change when compared with the new grade.
Grade After Re-mark	Included to see the extent of the grade change when compared with the old grade.

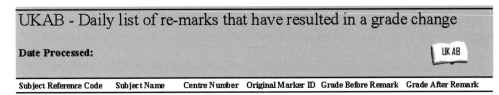

Figure 21.10 A typical report structure for the 're-marks' list

Report for the daily list of re-marks still outstanding

The actual query to filter the data on this report will be covered later. The format of the previous report should be fine, with the exception that it's the re-marker that's important here, because he or she is probably the person that needs chasing to get the job done as quickly as possible.

Table 21.6 Data to be included in the re-marks still outstanding report

Name	Comments and additional formating
Heading	UKAB – List of re-marks that are still outstanding after 3 weeks.
Logo	The UKAB logo.
Date Processed	This is to enable ease of filing of these reports by day.
Subject Reference Code	Used as the primary index for presenting the data. Displayed in increasing numerical order.
Subject Name	Included as it's more convenient when reading a list. Subjects won't be in alphabetical order, as they are ordered by subject number from the above field.
Centre Number	Used as a secondary index. Centre numbers within a subject will be displayed in increasing numerical order.
Re-mark Marker	Used as a secondary index. Displayed in increasing numerical order.

Access is a wonderful and powerful database program that's relatively easy to use. However, it will rarely give you exactly the right format when it comes to the production of reports.

It's essential that you manually intervene to produce the sort of hard copy reports that would be required for AQA module 3 projects.

As the re-mark marker is more important than the 'Centre number' in this report, this takes more prominence due to its position on the general report in Figure 21.11.

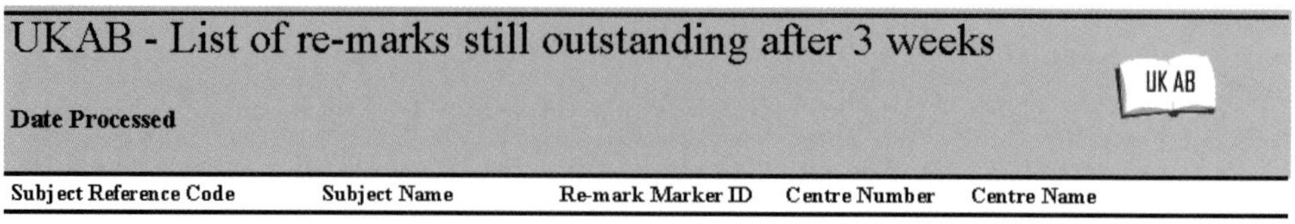

UKAB - List of re-marks still outstanding after 3 weeks				UK AB
Date Processed				
Subject Reference Code	Subject Name	Re-mark Marker ID	Centre Number	Centre Name

Figure 21.11 A typical report structure for the 're-marks still outstanding' list

Report for re-marks requested for a particular subject

This is for a particular subject only. It does not matter if a grade change has been effected or not, and the filter for this report will obviously be different (*see Chapter 22*). The 'Subject Reference Code' and 'Subject Name' need appear once only, because this is a request for a particular subject. This information is therefore included in the header information. The data for this report is shown in Table 21.8, and the layout of a typical report is as shown in Figure 21.12.

Table 21.7 Data to be included in the re-marks requested for a particular subject report

Name	Comments and additional formating
Heading	UKAB List of re-marks that have been requested for the following subject
Logo	The UKAB logo.
Date Processed	This is to enable ease of filing of these reports by day.
Subject Reference Code	Used as the primary index for presenting the data. Displayed in increasing numerical order.
Subject Name	Included as it's more convenient when reading a list. Subjects won't be in alphabetical order, as they are ordered by subject number from the above field.
Centre Number	Used as a secondary index. Centre numbers within a subject will be displayed in increasing numerical order.
Original Marker ID	To identify the marker whose script was requested for a re-mark.
Re-mark Marker ID	To identify the person who re-marked the script.
Grade Before Re-mark	To give an indication of the original grades.
Grade After Re-mark	To give an indication of the difference compared with the original grades.

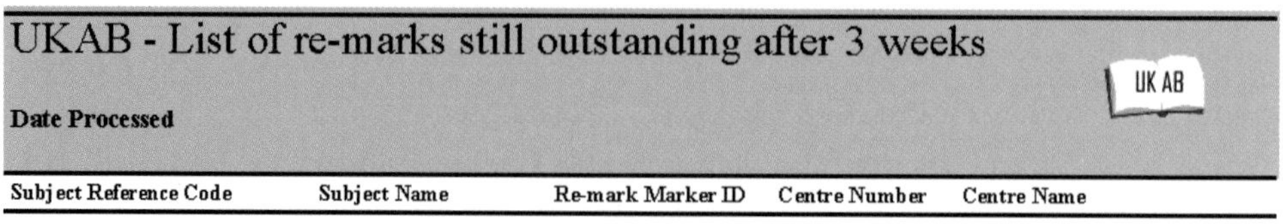

UKAB - List of re-marks still outstanding after 3 weeks				UK AB
Date Processed				
Subject Reference Code	Subject Name	Re-mark Marker ID	Centre Number	Centre Name

Figure 21.12 A typical report structure for a particular subject

You should note that there are no right or wrong answers regarding information that could appear on each report, but some information will be relevant, and other information won't be relevant. Don't include irrelevant information; you are likely to lose marks if you do. Note that the subject and subject reference code (*see Figure 21.12*) should now appear at the top of the report.

Reports for re-marks requested for a particular centre

The data shown in Table 21.8 will be suitable for this report. It is similar to the last report, but based on a centre, not a subject.

Table 21.8 Data to be included in the re-marks requested for a particular centre report

Name	Comments and additional formating
Heading	UKAB List of re-marks that have been requested for the following centre
Logo	The UKAB logo.
Date Processed	This is to enable ease of filing of these reports by day.
Centre Number	Used as a secondary index. Centre numbers within a subject will be displayed in increasing numerical order.
Centre Name	Included as it's more convenient when reading a list.
Subject Reference Code	Used as the primary index for presenting the data. Displayed in increasing numerical order.
Subject Name	Included as it's more convenient when reading a list. Subjects won't be in alphabetical order, as they are ordered by subject number from the above field.

A typical layout for this report is shown in Figure 21.13.

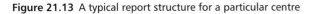

Figure 21.13 A typical report structure for a particular centre

A letter to the centre

You will recall that the centre needs to be informed of any decision made by the board. This is a standard letter, and can thus be generated by using an **Access report**, or the data exported to Word and used with the **mail merge** facility. A typical layout would be as shown in Figure 21.14.

Here you can see the letter headed paper containing a fictitious address, contact name and details like phone number and e-mail address. The letter is to an individual centre about an individual candidate. You will recall that our system works on a candidate subject entry, and therefore candidates with more than one re-mark will get more than one of these letters.

There is space for the contact name at the centre, the subject reference code and the candidate's name and number.

The scores and grades both before and after the re-mark are also included. As required by the specification (shown in green in Chapter 20), a sentence must be present to say if the grade has not changed. (*This is not shown in this example.*) You can make use of a **macro** to show or hide this sentence. A macro called 'Grade Change' could be created which operates on the 'Detail' section of the Access report. Specifically, it checks if the two fields 'Grade Before Remark' and 'Grade After Remark' are the same. If they are the same it displays the

UKAB
Excellence House
Successful Street
College Town
Brimberley
Surrey
GU 24 RC9
Contact: Dr. J. Dunn
Telephone: (0143) 222221
e-mail jdunn@UKAB.org

UK AB

Centre Number	**Candidate Number**
Centre Name	**Subject Reference Code**
Contact Name	**Candidate Name**
Address	

17 October 2003

Dear

RE: Re-mark for the above candidate.

Please be advised that the results of the re-mark for the above candidate is as follows:

Grade Before Remark	**Original Mark**
Grade After Remark	**Re-mark Mark**

Please don't hesitate to contact us if we can be of any further assistance.

Yours sincerely

Dr. J. Dunn.

Figure 21.14 A typical structure for the letter to a centre

label (*sentence*) but if they are different it hides it, as shown in Figure 21.15. In this particular example the sentence was typed into a label which has a name 'Label109'.

For the purpose of this simplified exercise it's not necessary to include more information than this. In a real letter for a real examination board there would be information about appeals that can be made if the centre still disagrees with the re-mark result.

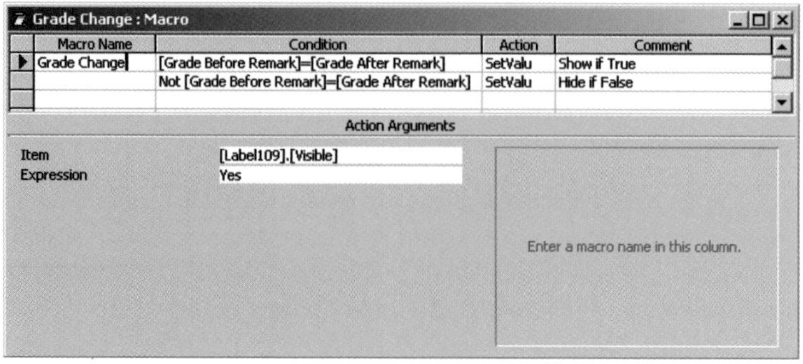

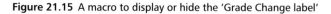

Figure 21.15 A macro to display or hide the 'Grade Change label'

Creation of an easier-to-use interface

You will recall from the **hierarchical diagram** of Figure 20.3 that we decided to provide the user of the system with an easy-to-use front end. This can be achieved in Microsoft Access by the use of Switchboards. This is a window on which buttons can be placed to launch things like 'Add a centre' or 'Add a re-mark request' or 'Print letters to the centres', etc. This makes the system more user friendly.

An effective switchboard should not have too many items on the main window, or it could be too confusing. A good start would be to separate the UKAB system into two or three parts, namely 'Adding and editing data', 'Creating reports' and 'Letters to the Centre' (this is also likely to be a report but the users don't need to know this). The 'Creating reports' section could then include 'List of re-marks for a centre' and 'Daily list of re-marks resulting in a grade change', etc. The ideas are shown in Figure 21.16.

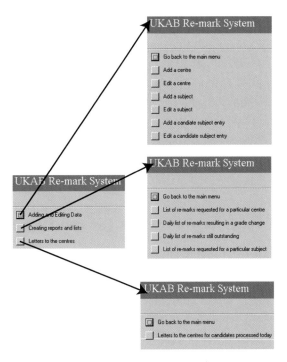

Figure 21.16 A typical menu-selection structure for ease of use

Self-test questions

1. A good systems analyst need not use anything other than a word processor to design the complete system outlined in this chapter. Why is it more acceptable for students to make use some of the Access database facilities, like those shown in this chapter, as they proceed with the project design?

2. If you do decide to make use of the Microsoft Access features like 'Form Design' and 'Switchboard Menu Systems' in the design of your project, you must be extremely careful. Why is this, and what should you do to ensure that you don't lose marks?

3. Draw an E-R diagram showing the relationship between candidates and centres. What type of relationship is this?

4. Why is the 'number' data type used by Microsoft Access not acceptable as a data type for AS Computing examinations?

5. 'Mail merge' is an alternative solution to the production of letters to the centre. Outline in principle what would have to be done to use mail merge with the **UKAB** system as set up in this chapter. Why might the use of mail merge give a better presentation than the Access reporting system being proposed here?

6. Why have we shown very little 'real' data on our output sheets when designing the forms and letters?

7. We could have used drop-down menus for entering information regarding subjects. What problems might this cause if a new subject had to be added later?

8. Outline five typical problems you might encounter if you were to attempt an implementation of the **UKAB** system using a high-level language.

22 UKAB test data and implementation

In this section you will learn about:

- Constructing suitable test data
- Constructing the detailed queries needed for the production of the reports
- Constructing parameter queries to produce the subject- and centre-specific reports
- Implementing the UKAB system using Microsoft Access

The work in this chapter follows on from the analysis and design of the UKAB module 3 problem outlined in Chapter 20.

Make sure you have read Chapters 20 and 21 before covering the material in this chapter.

Designing test data for the UKAB project – input of data

The last stage of the 'analysis and design' phase is to think up test data and the conditions under which the system will be tested. The project should work, where possible, for all valid and invalid data-entry scenarios. It's difficult to verify 'names', 'addresses' and other similar information, but make sure the data you use will test all important variations like 'candidates taking two or more subjects', 'exams where the grade has been changed' and 'exams where the grade has not been changed' to name but a few. This **test data** would be listed in an appendix as described at the end of Chapter 23.

To develop **test data** we need to recall what **inputs** to process and what **outputs** the system produces. The **data integrity** tables (Tables 21.2, 21.3, 21.4 and 21.5) are a good place to start; they contain a list of features you should be testing. The **black-box testing** methods outlined in Chapter 19 can also be used quite effectively. It would take a long time to be totally exhaustive, so a sensible selection of inputs and expected outputs will be chosen. They also refer back to the **data dictionaries** originally defined in Chapter 20. Table 22.1 shows the test data for Table 21.2.

Next we perform a similar operation for Table 21.4, and this is shown in Table 22.2. The table is not exhaustive.

Finally, we perform a similar operation for Table 21.5, and this is shown in Table 22.3. The table is not exhaustive.

Designing test data for the UKAB project – output of data

We also need to consider extra **test data**, specifically to test the operation of the database for valid data allowed by the input routines. We need to consider each output report in detail, and then decide on a suitable set of data. Don't forget that the data has already been validated; here we need check only that appropriate output reports are produced given a suitable set of input data. Some ideas about the choice of data are shown in Table 22.4 where grade changes on both today's and previous dates have been affected, and grades unchanged on both today and previous dates have been considered. *The actual data used (i.e. names and addresses, etc.) will be shown in detail later.*

Next we consider the data for the re-marks still outstanding after the required 3-week period. Table 22.5 shows that we consider >3 weeks, exactly 3 weeks and <3 weeks for candidates who have been processed already and other candidates who have not yet been processed.

Table 22.1 Some black-box test data for Table 21.3

Inputs		Outputs
Name	**Test data**	**Comments/expected results**
Centre Number	999	Too small – data should be rejected.
	80100	Too big – data should be rejected.
		A null value is not acceptable – should be brought to the user's attention and data should be rejected.
	ABC	Only numeric data should be accepted – data should be rejected.
	20003	This is a valid centre number – result should be accepted.
	20003 (again)	This is a valid centre number, but it has already been used – data should be rejected. (*Done by making sure there are no duplicates for this field.*)
Centre Name		A null value is not acceptable – should be brought to the user's attention and data should be rejected.
	Sandhurst	Data should be accepted. Can't easily be validated. Verification could be carried out by another person checking the entry at a later stage.
Contact Name		A null value is not acceptable – should be brought to the user's attention and data should be rejected.
	Hammer	Data should be accepted. Can't easily be validated. Verification could be carried out by another person checking the entry at a later stage.
Title	Mr.	Data should be accepted – drop-down list for ease of data entry
	Most Rev.	Data should be accepted – the user has the option of typing in data not contained in the drop-down list. Data should be accepted. Can't be validated. Verification could be carried out by another person checking the entry later.
Initials		A null value is not acceptable – should be brought to the user's attention and data should be rejected.
	F.	Data should be accepted. Can't be validated. Verification could be carried out by another person checking the entry later.
Address 1	Dunromin	Data should be accepted. Can't easily be validated. Verification could be carried out by another person checking the entry at a later stage.
Address 1		A null value is not acceptable for the first line of the address – should be brought to the user's attention and data should be rejected.
Address 2		Data should be accepted. Can't be validated. Verification could be carried out by another person checking the entry later.
Town/City	Bigmouth	Data should be accepted. Can't be validated. Verification could be carried out by another person checking the entry later.
County/State	Brighton	Data should be accepted. Can't be validated. Verification could be carried out by another person checking the entry later.
Post Code	BN 26 1EW	Data should be accepted. Can't be validated. Verification could be carried out by another person checking the entry later.
Country	England	Data should be accepted. Can't be validated. Verification could be carried out by another person checking the entry later.

Checking that a valid centre number is rejected if that centre number has already been entered into the centre's table shows that you have really been thinking about what could possibly go wrong.

Table 22.2 Some black-box test data for Table 21.3

Inputs		Outputs	
Name	**Test data**	**Comments/expected results**	
Centre Number	2003	Because we have enforced referential integrity when setting up the system, Access will not allow centres in this table which do not have an entry in the Centre table. Data should be accepted if there is an entry for this centre number in the 'Centre table'.	
Candidate Number	0023	Check that leading zeros are displayed in both 'form', 'data sheet' and 'printed output'. Data should be accepted.	
	35241	Too big. Data should be rejected.	
	0000	Too small. Data should be rejected.	
	ABC	Can't have text in a numeric field. Data should be rejected.	
Subject Reference Code	00000	Too small. Data should be rejected.	
	00001	Data should be accepted. Because we have enforced referential integrity when setting up the system, Access will not allow subject reference codes in this table which do not have an entry in the Candidate subject entry table. Data should be accepted if there is an entry for this centre number in the 'Centre table'.	
	99999	Data should be accepted (see above).	
	363533	Too big. Data should be rejected.	
Surname	Smith	Data should be accepted. No validation, but verification could be used after initial data entry.	
Initials	F.	Data should be accepted. Can't be validated. Verification could be carried out by another person checking the entry later.	
Title	Ms.	Data should be accepted. Can't be validated. Verification could be carried out by another person checking the entry later.	
Date Received	20/10/2003	Data should be accepted if it is not less than the current date. Data should be rejected otherwise.	
Date Processed	25/10/2003	Data should be accepted if it is not less than the current date. Data should be rejected otherwise.	
Grade Before Re-mark	A	Data should be accepted.	
	Y	Not 'A', B', 'C', 'D', 'E' or 'U'. Data should be rejected.	
Original Mark	108	Too big. Data should be rejected.	
	78	Data should be accepted.	
		Null value. Data should be rejected.	
Grade After Re-mark	B	Data should be accepted.	
		Null value. Data should be accepted. Won't be able to save initial re-mark request at this time if this is rejected!	
Re-mark Mark	B	Data not numeric. Data should be rejected.	
	58	Data should be accepted.	
Grade Changed?		Null value. Data should be accepted because a Null is a valid entry until the re-mark is completed.	
	Y	Data should be accepted.	
Return Script?	N	Data should be accepted.	
		Null value. Data should be rejected.	
Original Marker ID	0089	Too small. Data should be rejected.	
	7453	Data should be accepted.	
		Null value. Data should be rejected.	
Re-mark Marker ID		Null value. Data should be accepted because Null is a valid entry until the re-mark is completed.	

Table 22.3 Some black-box test data for Table 21.4

Inputs		Outputs
Name	**Test data**	**Comments/expected results**
Subject Reference Code	07352	Because we have enforced referential integrity when setting up the system, Access will not allow subject reference codes in this table which do not have and entry in the Centres table. Data should be accepted if there is an entry for this centre number in the 'Centre table'.
Subject Name	Computing	Data should be accepted. Can't be validated. Verification could be carried out by another person checking the entry later.
		Null value. Data should be **rejected**.
Grade Boundary A	89	Data should be accepted. Can't be validated. Verification could be carried out by another person checking the entry later.
	107	Too big. Data should be **rejected**.
Grade Boundary B	78	Data should be accepted.
Grade Boundary C		Null value. Data should be **rejected**.
Grade Boundary D	65	Data should be accepted.
Grade Boundary E	B	Not a number. Data should be **rejected**.

Table 22.4 Test criteria for the daily list of re-marks

Name	Test data	Name	Test data	Comments/expected results
Grade Changed?	**Yes**	**Date**	**Today's Date (*)**	Check this candidate is present in the list.
Grade Changed?	**Yes**	**Date**	**Other date**	Check this candidate is **not present** in the list.
Grade Changed?	**No**	**Date**	**Today's Date (*)**	Check this candidate is **not present** in the list.
Grade Changed?	**No**	**Date**	**Other date**	Check this candidate is **not present** in the list.
N.B. (*) This assumes that a daily list of re-marks is a list for the *current day* only				

Table 22.5 Test criteria for the daily list of re-marks still outstanding

Name	Test data	Name	Test data	Comments/expected results
Date Received	**>3 weeks ago**	**Date Processed**	**Null**	Check this candidate is present in the list.
Date Received	**Exactly 3 weeks ago**	**Date Processed**	**Null**	Check this candidate is present in the list.
Date Received	**<3 weeks ago**	**Date Processed**	**Null**	Check this candidate is **not present** in the list.
Date Received	**>3 weeks ago**	**Date Processed**	**Valid date**	Check this candidate is **not present** in the list.
Date Received	**Exactly 3 weeks ago**	**Date Processed**	**Valid date**	Check this candidate is **not present** in the list.
Date Received	**<3 weeks ago**	**Date Processed**	**Valid date**	Check this candidate is **not present** in the list.

Next we consider re-marks for a particular subject. Make sure that all the same subjects appear on the list, and other subjects do not appear on the list. As no data appears in our database that is not concerned with a re-mark we don't have to worry about these!

Table 22.6 Test criteria for the list of re-marks requested for a particular subject

Name	Test data	Comments/expected results
Subject Reference Code	Any valid code	Check this candidate is present in the list.
Subject Reference Code	Other code	Check this candidate is not present in the list.

Finally, we need to consider the list of re-marks from a particular centre. This is similar in principle to the above table, and is shown in Table 22.7.

Table 22.7 Test criteria for the list of re-marks requested for a particular centre

Name	Test data	Comments/expected results
Centre Number	Any valid code	Check this centre is present in the list.
Centre Number	Other code	Check this centre is not present in the list.

Entering the valid 'centre' data

Candidates sometimes spend so long checking that invalid data is not entered, they forget that a large amount of testing should be carried out on valid data too! How else can you tell if your project works!

Don't forget that you will also need some valid data! About ten centres, each with a few candidates should be suitable for demonstration of your reporting systems. Output from your reports will look very silly with only one or two entries on a sheet. However, don't spend too long thinking up names and addresses. The easiest way is to make use of the internet or a phone book. Don't use actual names and addresses, but mix them up to produce some fictitious ones. You could easily spend an hour or two of wasted time if you try to think up names from scratch. Look at some real addresses because this will check to see if you have a suitable address format, especially for foreign addresses like Hong Kong or Australia, for example, which the author has used in this database.

Entering the valid 'candidate' data

We will need some candidate data to test the reporting system. Look at the specification and you will see that a range of conditions must be met to test the following output.

- A daily list of any re-marks completed where a mark change has affected the grade
- A daily list of any re-marks still outstanding, i.e. that have not been completed within a three-week period
- A list of re-marks that have been requested for a particular subject
- A list of re-marks that have been requested from a particular centre.

The actual **test data** is reproduced in an appendix for the actual write up shown at the end of Chapter 23. To save duplicating the same material twice, it's not reproduced here.

The queries needed to produce the output reports

The only major thing left to do is to design the **queries** that will be necessary to **filter** the appropriate data for the above reports. In Chapter 21 we have already decided on appropriate data to display in each report (see Figures 21.10, 21.11, 21.12 and 21.13). These queries are now designed in the next few sections.

The 'list of daily re-marks resulting in a grade change' query

Here we require a list of the re-marks that have been completed today which have resulted in a grade change. Therefore, you will have to enter some grade-change re-marks with today's date or you will have no entries that satisfy this condition! If you work on this part of the project over a period of a few days you will need to alter the 'Date Processed' field so that you do have data to output in the final report. From Figure 21.10 you will recall that the required data for output from this report are 'Subject Reference Code', 'Subject Name', 'Centre Number', 'Original Marker ID', 'Grade Before Remark' and 'Grade After Remark'. These were not required from the subject specification shown in green in Chapter 20, but were thought to be sensible choices at design time.

The actual query needs to examine two things: firstly that the 'Date Processed' field from the 'Candidate Subject Entry' table is today's date, and secondly that a grade change has actually taken place. This can be achieved by examining the Boolean field 'Grade Changed?', also from the 'Candidate Subject Entry' table. All three tables will therefore need to be included in this query, and the methods for doing this using Microsoft Access are shown in principle in Figure 22.1. The logic behind this query is as follows:

```
IF the 'Date Processed' field = 'Today' AND the 'Grade Changed?'
field is 'True' THEN this is a re-mark which has been carried out
today.
```

Figure 22.1 shows how this query is set up in Access. You can see that the 'Date Processed' field is set to be 'Date( )', (Access's method of describing 'today') and the 'Grade Changed?' field is set to be 'True' (Access's method of checking the Boolean field to be true). If the criteria are on the same line, the 'AND' function is implied.

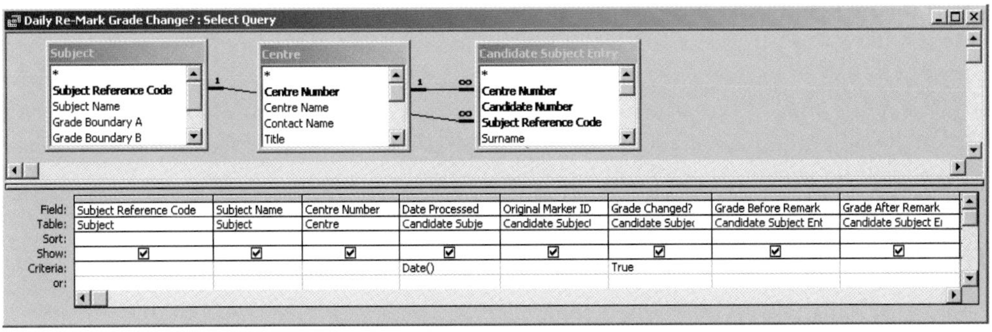

On some occasions it might be unclear to you what is meant by part of the specification.

In this specification, is a daily list of re-marks the list for today only, or all the re-marks that have been completed up until today?

If you have a problem like this, ask your teacher or lecturer. If they are unsure too, get them to phone the subject officer to clarify the point. Don't be unsure on important points like this.

Figure 22.1 Setting up a query in Access to be used by the daily re-mark report

Figure 22.1 shows what is called a **QBE** or **Query By Example** grid. Therefore, if both of these conditions are met, the eight fields outlined here will be reproduced when the query is run, shown in Figure 22.2. (*Only three test records match these particular criteria at the moment.*) The output from an Access query, although informative is not user friendly. You will recall from Chapter 21 that we wanted a nicely laid out headed **report** with the UKAB logo at the top laid out like the information shown in Figure 21.10. To do this we have to **bind** the **report** to the **query**. One way to do this is by inserting a report into the query in design mode, and laying out the report as suggested in Figure 21.10. The results displayed within the report will then be only those **records** and **fields** that satisfy the **filter** described above, *and* contain the **fields** from the **tables** specified in the **report** layout shown in Figure 21.10. This has been carried out and the result is shown in Figure 22.3. Don't forget

Figure 22.2 The result of running the query of Figure 22.1 on Sunday 26th October, when this particular part of the project was being tested.

Figure 22.3 The output from the report bound to the query set up in Figure 22.1

to select the fields from the 'Daily Re-mark Grade Change' **query** when you are setting up this **bound report**. If you use same fields from the original tables, you may think that the query is not working!

The data within the report has been grouped by subject reference code and subject. Therefore, different centres appear under the same subject reference headings if they have had a re-mark in that particular subject on that day. A grey background has been included to improve the display of the UKAB logo. Make sure that your report output looks functional and is attractive (*see margin entry*).

Don't forget that the specification (shown in green in Chapter 21) requires that you produce **hard copy** to show that your project works. *It would be soul destroying to work through the above, and receive few, if any marks for your efforts because you have put in a screen capture (like Figure 22.3) instead of an actual printout from Microsoft Access. We obviously can't produce hard copy here, or you would have a few loose-leaf pieces of paper in the book!* **Be warned – don't fall into this particular trap.**

The 'list of daily re-marks still outstanding' query

Next we require a list of the re-marks that have not been completed within the three-week period. To do this we need to examine the 'Date Received' and 'Date Processed' fields. We can do this using the following logic:

```
IF the 'Date Received' field is > 3 weeks ago, AND if the 'Date
Processed' field is Null (contains no entry) THEN this is a re-
mark which is still outstanding.
```

Figure 22.4 shows how this query has been set up in Access.

The Microsoft Access method to determine if a date is more than three weeks old is '<Date( ) – 21'. In the case of Figure 22.4, the 'Date Received' must be less than the current date (given by using Date( )) – 21 days. The 'Date Processed' field is set to 'Null' by using the entry 'Is Null', and because the two criteria are on the same line the AND function is used to join them together. You should make sure that there are some 'Date Received'

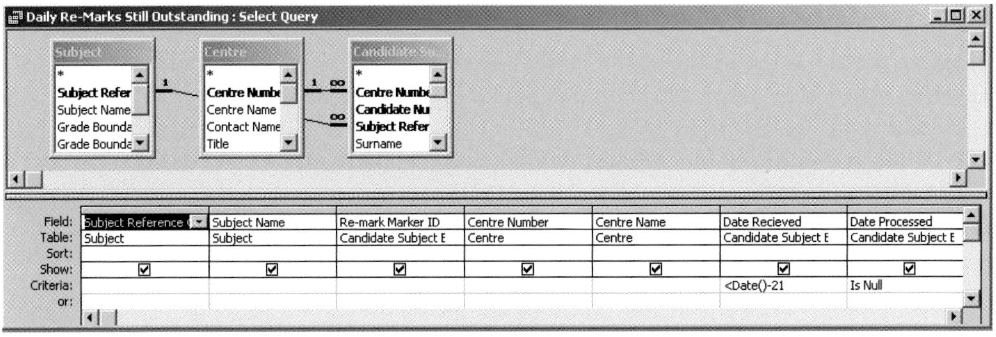

Figure 22.4 Setting up a query in Access to be used by the re-marks outstanding report

entries in the 'Candidate Subject Entry' table in which the received date is more than three weeks earlier than the current date on which you are testing, and the same entries have null values for the 'Date Processed' field. The result of running this query for a particular day is shown in Figure 22.5.

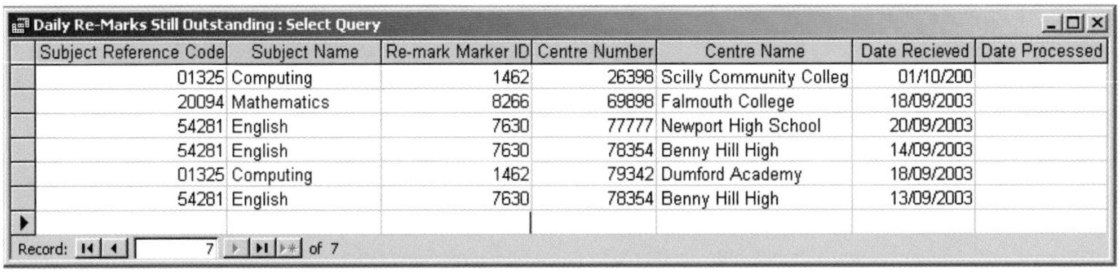
Daily Re-Marks Still Outstanding : Select Query

Subject Reference Code	Subject Name	Re-mark Marker ID	Centre Number	Centre Name	Date Recieved	Date Processed
01325	Computing	1462	26398	Scilly Community Colleg	01/10/200	
20094	Mathematics	8266	69898	Falmouth College	18/09/2003	
54281	English	7630	77777	Newport High School	20/09/2003	
54281	English	7630	78354	Benny Hill High	14/09/2003	
01325	Computing	1462	79342	Dumford Academy	18/09/2003	
54281	English	7630	78354	Benny Hill High	13/09/2003	

Record: 7 of 7

Figure 22.5 The result of running the query of Figure 22.4 on Sunday 26th October, when this particular part of the project was being tested

The report, which is bound to the query of Figure 22.4, is shown in Figure 22.6.

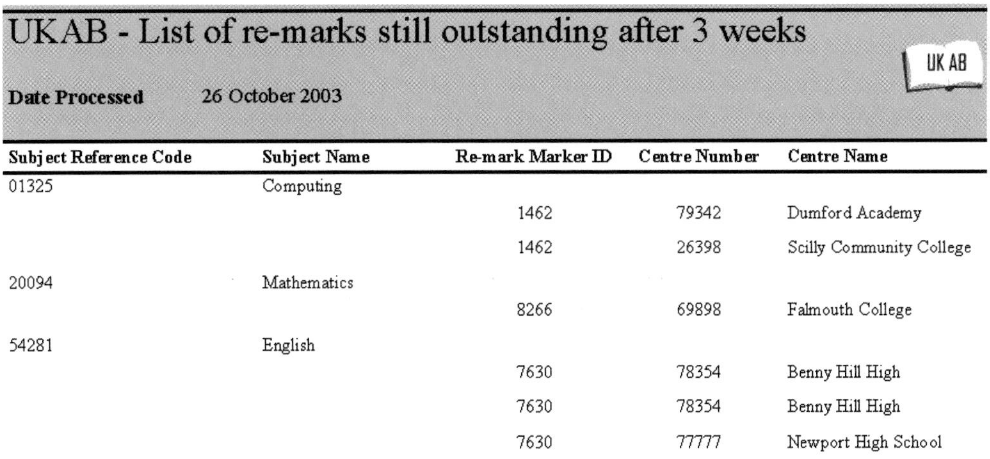
UKAB - List of re-marks still outstanding after 3 weeks

UK AB

Date Processed 26 October 2003

Subject Reference Code	Subject Name	Re-mark Marker ID	Centre Number	Centre Name
01325	Computing			
		1462	79342	Dumford Academy
		1462	26398	Scilly Community College
20094	Mathematics			
		8266	69898	Falmouth College
54281	English			
		7630	78354	Benny Hill High
		7630	78354	Benny Hill High
		7630	77777	Newport High School

Figure 22.6 The output from the report bound to the query set up in Figure 22.4

The 'Date Processed' title at the top of Figure 22.6 is actually a text entry, and the date is generated at the top of the form using the Access '=Now( )' function.

The 'list of re-marks for a particular subject' query

Next we require a list of the re-marks that are associated with a particular subject, irrespective of whether they have been completed or not. You might think that this is trivial compared with the previous two queries, but this time we need a method of letting the user of the system input the 'Subject Reference Code' that will be used when the query is run. This is called a **parameter query**, because the user can type a **parameter** (in this case the 'Subject Reference Code') into a box presented to them just before the query is run. The query will then use this code for the reference criteria.

Figure 22.7 shows the parameter query being set up. In the criteria box for the 'Subject Reference Code' field we have entered the following:

```
[Subject Reference Code:]
```

This instructs Access to display this message with a box to prompt the user to enter the information that has been typed in at design stage for the previous two queries.

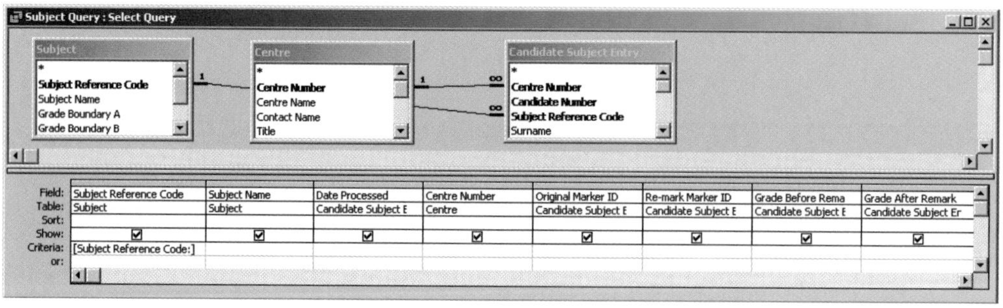

Figure 22.7 Setting up a parameter query for the subject re-marks report

The results of this query would depend on the parameter the user has entered into the box shown in Figure 22.8. Here the user has entered the Subject Reference Code 54281, and therefore the **bound report** for the **parameter** 54281 (English) is shown in Figure 22.9.

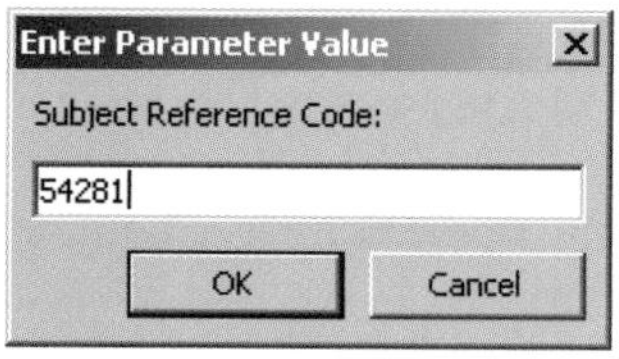

Figure 22.8 The box generated by Access for entering the parameter

List of re-marks requested for the following subject

54281 **English** UK AB

Date Processed 26 October 2003

Centre Number	Original Marker ID	Re-mark Marker ID	Grade Before Remark	Grade After Remark
78354	7551	7630	C	
63422	7551	7630	C	
78354	7551	7630	U	
77777	7551	7630	C	
63422	7551	7630	B	A

Figure 22.9 The output from a bound query using the parameter supplied in Figure 22.8

Note that the 'Subject Reference Code' (54281) and the 'Subject' (English) have been removed from the main body of the report and put in the page header information as shown at the top of Figure 22.9. If left within the main body of the report this information would be repeated many times, and thus look unprofessional. Note that the 'Grade After Re-mark' has been completed for one candidate only on 26 October 2003, when this particular report was produced.

The 'list of re-marks for a particular centre' query

For the last report we require a list of re-marks for a particular centre. This is another **parameter query**; very similar in principle to the parameter query just covered. The new expression for the parameter will be as follows:

```
[Centre Number:]
```

The parameter query for the centre is shown in Figure 22.10. The results of the query for centre number 24233 are shown in Figure 22.11. Here you can see that some unfortunate student with candidate number 0998 has had to have two subjects re-marked. He did badly in both 'Design Technology' and 'Computing'. Don't forget that we thought it important that our database catered for candidates having multiple re-marks with the UKAB, and this demonstrates that this particular part works too.

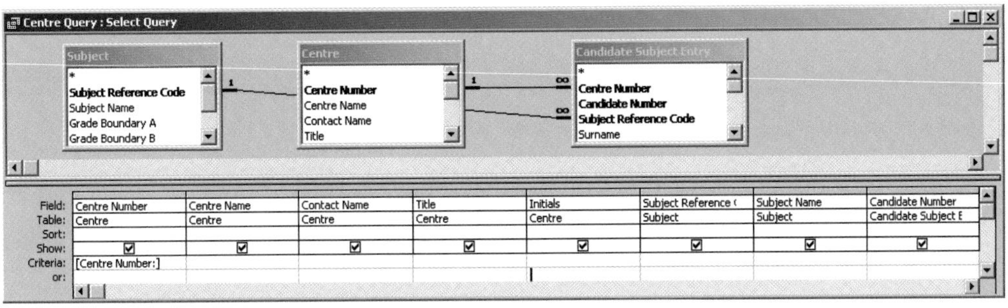

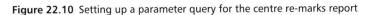

Figure 22.10 Setting up a parameter query for the centre re-marks report

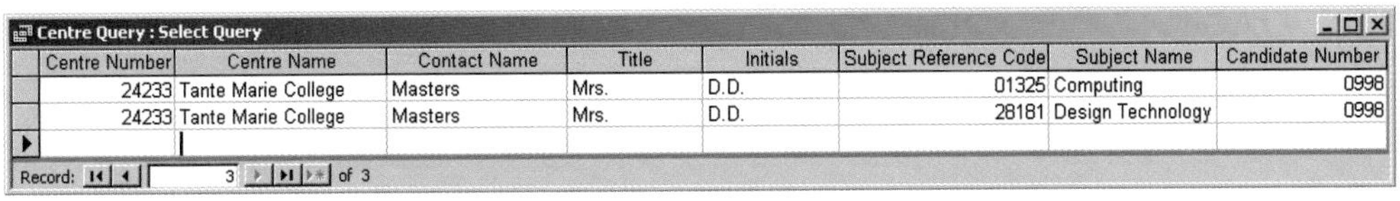

Centre Number	Centre Name	Contact Name	Title	Initials	Subject Reference Code	Subject Name	Candidate Number
24233	Tante Marie College	Masters	Mrs.	D.D.	01325	Computing	0998
24233	Tante Marie College	Masters	Mrs.	D.D.	28181	Design Technology	0998

Record: 3 of 3

Figure 22.11 The result of running the parameter query with centre number 24233

The bound report for the parameter query set up in Figure 22.10 is shown in Figure 22.12.

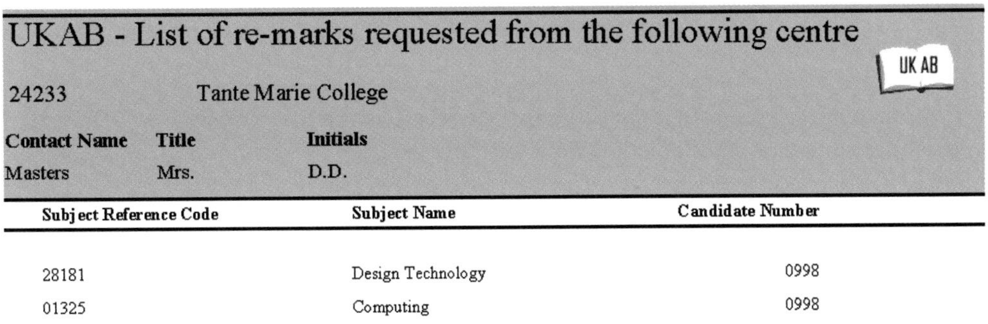

UKAB - List of re-marks requested from the following centre

UK AB

24233   Tante Marie College

Contact Name	Title	Initials
Masters	Mrs.	D.D.

Subject Reference Code	Subject Name	Candidate Number
28181	Design Technology	0998
01325	Computing	0998

Figure 22.12 The output from the bound query using the parameter supplied in Figure 22.10

Note that many of the fields described in Table 21.8 have been assigned to the page header in the parameter report of Figure 22.12. This information about the 'Centre Number',

'Centre Name', 'Contact Surname', 'Initials' and 'Title' don't need repeating over and over again. Make sure that your reports are well laid out like this too.

The letter to the centre

Finally, we require a letter to be addressed to the centre to inform them of any decisions made by the board. As with the subject entry, we will assume that a separate letter will be sent to the centre for each 'Candidate Subject Entry'. We can also do this by making use of a report.

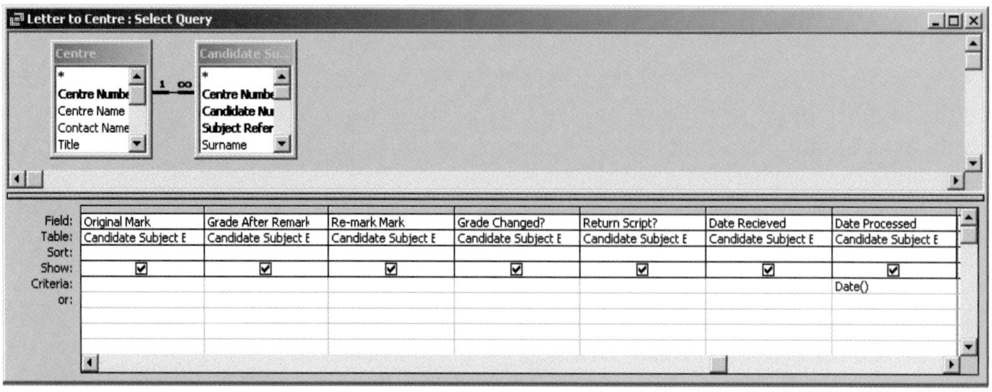

Figure 22.13 Setting up a query to help generate the letters to the centre

The only criteria needed for this is to make use of the 'Date Processed' field set to 'Today'. In other words, when a re-mark request is processed, the letter will be generated automatically by the system. Running this query for 26 October 2003 gives the results shown in Figure 22.14.

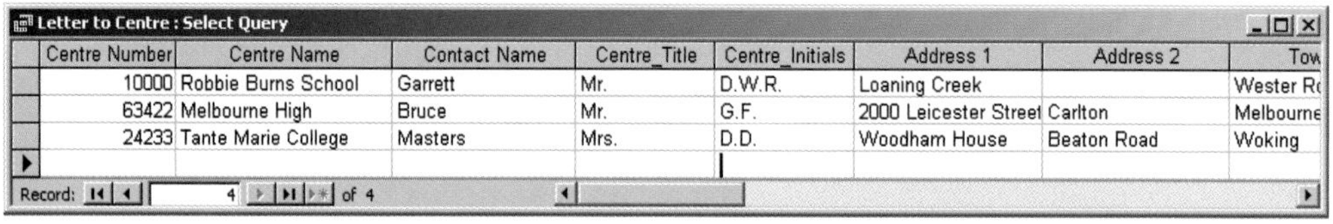

Figure 22.14 The result of running a query to see which re-marks have been processed today

There is far too much information to be displayed, but the important thing to note is that three letters need to be generated on that day. Also, we must make sure that each record goes on a separate piece of paper. This is done in Access by forcing a new page after the details section has been printed. The layout of the report is as shown in Figure 22.15.

Figure 22.15 shows the letter to Mr. Garrett (the contact at the Robbie Burns School), informing him of the results (D grade changed to C grade) for the candidate 0234 (Mr. R. B. English), who will no doubt be delighted with the result.

The other two candidate letters for 26 October have not been shown, but are formatted in identical ways, with the appropriate information for each centre. Because the letters are automatically generated on the due date, there is no need for a flag to be set to say that a letter has been sent to the centre. These letters should be passed to Dr. J. Dunn for his signature.

There are many ways to improve the above letter, but this should be sufficient to get very good marks. **Don't forget that a hard copy would actually be needed in your report**, probably included in the appendix.

UKAB
Excellence House
Successful Street
College Town
Brimberley
Surrey
GU 24 RC9
Contact: Dr. J. Dunn
Telephone: (0143) 222221
e-mail jdunn@UKAB.org

Centre Number	10000	Candidate Number	0234
Centre Name	Robbie Burns School	Subject Reference Code	01325
Contact Name	Mr. D.W.R. Garrett	Candidate Name	Mr. R.B. English
Address	Loaning Creek		
	Highland Hill		
	Wester Ross		
	Inverness		
	IV26 2K		
	Scotland		

26 October 2003

Dear Mr. Garrett

RE: Re-mark for the above candidate.

Please be advised that the results of the re-mark for the above candidate is as follows:

| **Grade Before Remark** | D | **Original Mark** | 53 |
| **Grade After Remark** | C | **Re-mark Mark** | 60 |

Please don't hesitate to contact us if we can be of any further assistance.

Yours sincerely

Dr. J. Dunn.

Figure 22.15 The first of the three letters sent to the centres on 26 October 2003

Implementing the detailed validation rules

You will recall that you need to convince the examiners that you have got a satisfactory level of **validation** to ensure **data integrity**. Here we consider just a couple of different examples to give you a flavour of what to do, then you need to produce a list of the 'Validation Rules', 'Validation Texts' and 'Required' fields for each field within the database. This table maps to the Access tables produced in Chapter 21. Figure 21.10 shows that the field 'Candidate Number' is highlighted and the attributes relating to this field in the 'Candidate Table' are displayed in the box.

Here you can see that the data is an integer, and the values are being forced to lie between 1000 and 9999 inclusive by use of the (>=1000 and <=9999) validation rule. Some suitable validation text (which explains to the user of the UKAB system why their data is being rejected) is added, and the user is forced not to leave this field blank by setting the required value to yes. This is how we implement the 'Not Null' properties in many of the tables shown earlier. Finally, we have created an index, because we might wish to make a quick search on 'Candidate Number' alone. It is not unique to this database because different centres can use the same candidate numbers.

Figure 22.18 shows that the field 'Centre' is highlighted and the attributes relating to this field in the 'Candidate Table' are displayed in the box. This time a 'long integer' has been used because '10000 to 99999' is outside of the range of an ordinary integer in Access, and the validation rule is changed (<=10000 and >=99999) to reflect the specification

*The data
dictionaries and
database tables
have already
shown that you
have considered
data integrity.
However, here you
prove that you
have actually set
them up in the
database.*

*You don't need to
show every single
rule, just a
selection of
different ones,
similar to those
shown here, thus
demonstrating that
you know how to
design the system
using your chosen
database.*

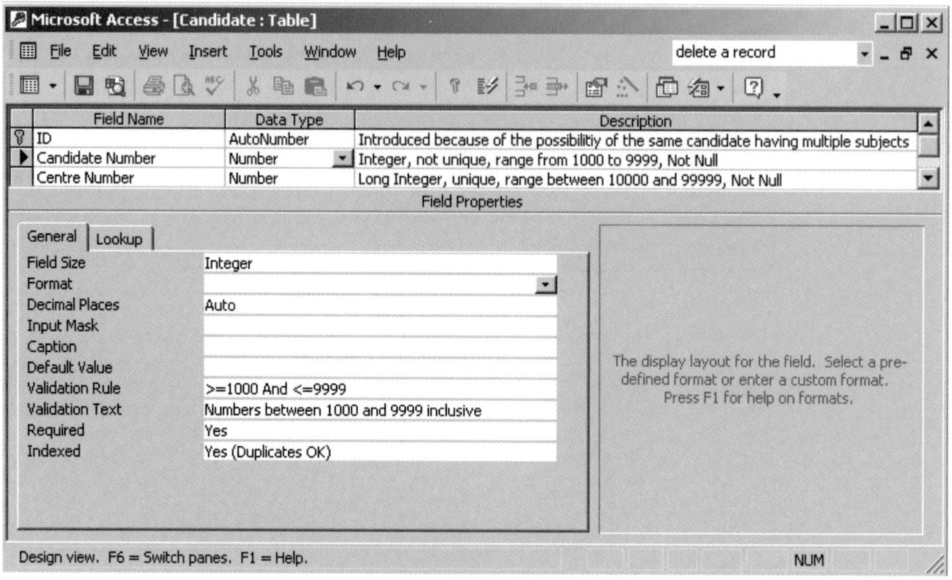

Figure 22.16 Showing the validation rules for 'Candidate Number'

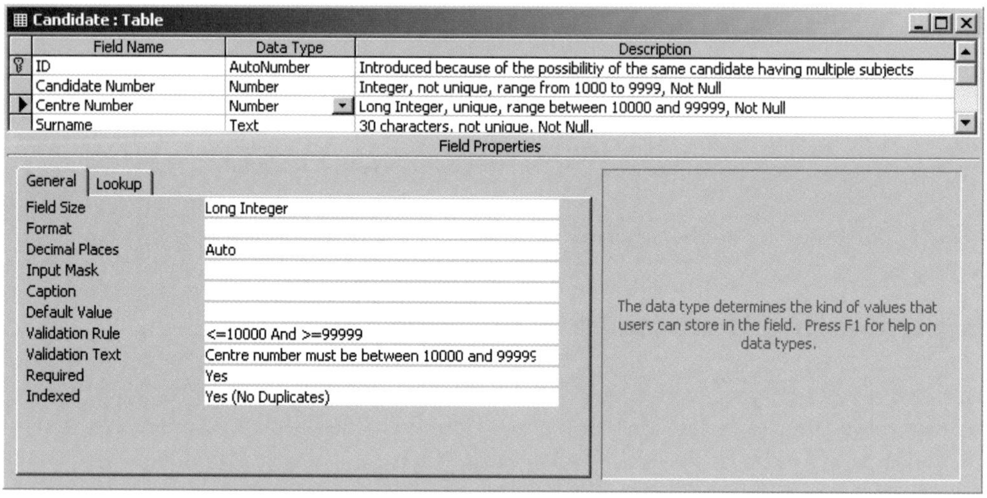

Figure 22.17 Showing the validation rules for 'Centre Number'

requirements regarding centre number. Again this is a required field, and an index is
created for a fast search on 'Centre Number'. This time the centre number is unique, and
thus no duplicates have been allowed.

It would take up too much space to 'prove' that you have done this for each and every field,
and a complete list of validation methods have already been shown in Tables 21.3, 21.4
and 21.5. In your write up you need not take too many screen shots like those described
above, because you can outline the code in small boxes within tables.

Taking suitable screen shots of the database in use

During the implementation phase of your project (i.e. setting up the database, entering the
data and testing the system) you need to collect evidence that your project is working. You
can do this by taking a number of screen shots to show important parts of the system in
operation. Don't take too many screenshots, especially not of the same sort of thing. The

examiners need only enough evidence to show that the system is working. The validation rules in the last section are good examples of screen shots, but you need some shots for the data entry in all three sections of the database. Try to demonstrate your genius by showing screen shots which appear to show that your project is working well. Figure 22.18, for example, 'demonstrates' that unusual postcodes can be entered, like the one shown here in Australia.

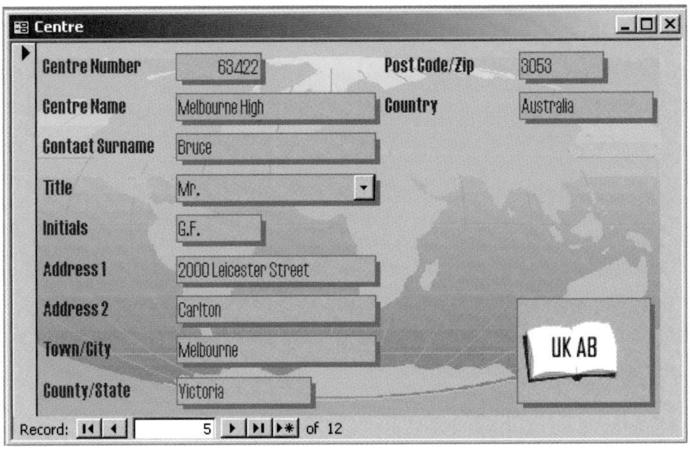

Figure 22.18 Data capture form for the 'centre information'

Figure 22.19 'demonstrate' that your project has been set up properly to accept subject reference codes with leading zeros. And Figure 22.20 shows that candidate numbers can have leading zeros too.

From these figures you can also tell that the UKAB logo has been used. It would take quite a lot of time and effort to fake screen shots in this detail, and examiners would probably notice if little details were missing or faked. You should note, for example, that similar screen shots *before* any data is entered are shown in Figures 21.7, 21.8 and 21.9 when the project

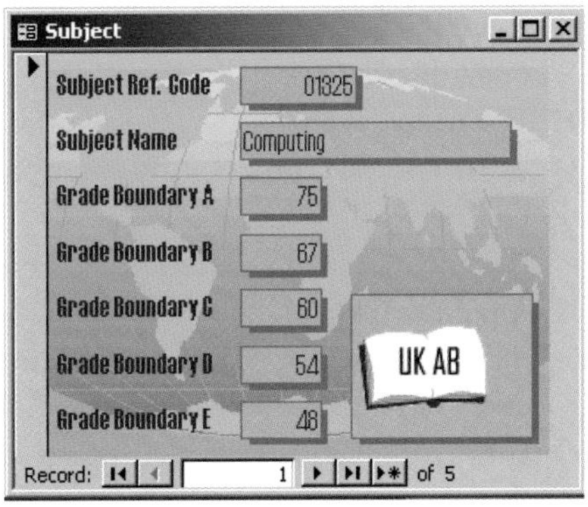

Figure 22.19 Data capture form for the 'centre information'

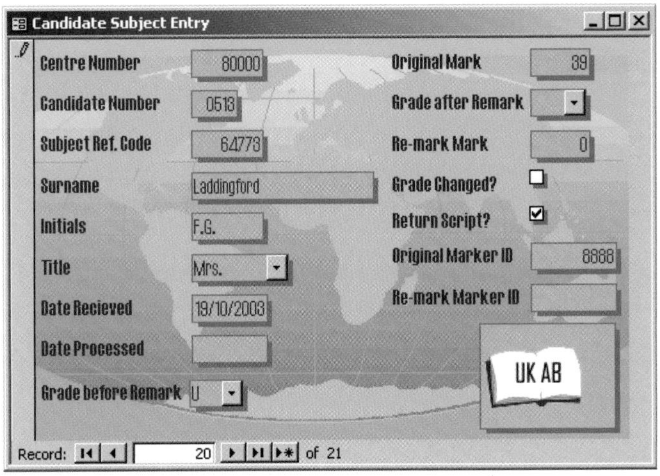

Figure 22.20 Data capture form for the 'centre information'

was being designed. However, in these earlier figures there are no extra records, and so the record data at the bottom of the screen showed 1 of 1 in all cases. Here Figure 22.18 shows 5 of 12 (indicating that 12 centres are now present in the database), Figure 22.19 shows 1 of 5 (indicating that 5 subjects have been entered), and Figure 22.20 shows 20 of 21 (indicating that 21 candidate-subject entries are present). Little details like these would easily give away the fact that you might be 'cheating' a little! Examiners will be watching out for this.

Remember that information shown in this chapter and in Chapters 20 and 21 do not constitute a project write up. Your project report should be very concise, and Chapter 23 concentrates entirely on this particular aspect of the module 3 project.

Self-test questions

1 A 'candidate number' of Genius123 would be rejected by the UKAB database as set up in this chapter. What causes this erroneous data to be rejected?

2 The first line of an address is entered as '13 Garfield Road' instead of '31 Garfield Road'. Would this be rejected by the UKAB system as set up in this chapter? What method of correction would you suggest for correcting this data?

3 A grade boundary for each subject should be an integer between 0 and 100 inclusive. If you are using Microsoft Access, what data type would be most suitable to store this data?

4 A drop-down list is used to enter the grades both before and after the re-mark. How does this list help with the process of data integrity?

5 The tables in the databases are related. What is meant by a relational database?

6 What are the names of the three tables used in the UKAB database as set up in this chapter?

7 List the field names used in the 'subject candidate entry' table.

8 A number like 'candidate number' might begin with leading zeros. What method has been used in this chapter to ensure that leading zeros in this field are displayed correctly?

9 How can a picture like the 'UKAB logo' used in this chapter be inserted onto an Access record?

10 What is a query? What queries have been used for the UKAB database as set up in this chapter?

11 A query may be described by code using terms like as 'IF', 'AND' and 'OR', etc. What code describes the query used to find the re-marks still outstanding for the UKAB database as set up in this chapter?

12 What is a report?

13 What advantage does an Access report have over an Access query? How might an Access query control what data is displayed inside an Access report?

14 Access enables you to perform a type of query known as a parameter query. What does this mean?

15 Access provides a system of Switchboards to enable novices to use a database more easily. Briefly describe how this benefits a novice user.

23 The module 3 project write up

In this section you will learn about:

- How to tackle a project write up in a very concise way
- The sections that should be included in your project
- The sections that should be included in an appendix

Where to start

Your solution needs to be *very concise* for the module 3 examination (*see Chapter 24*). The aims of an AS project are to demonstrate that you can **analyse, design, implement, test** and **evaluate** a solution to a set exercise. Here we make use of the UKAB project covered in Chapters 20, 21 and 22. The following sections show how major parts of a typical write-up may be undertaken, starting with a good cover page and a contents list, which refers to the pages in *this chapter* where the appropriate material can be found.

The material in this chapter will not make sense unless you have spent a considerable number of hours reading, understanding and preferably trying out the ideas and material covered in Chapters 20, 21 and 22.

The contents list shown here is typical of what to expect at the beginning of your project.

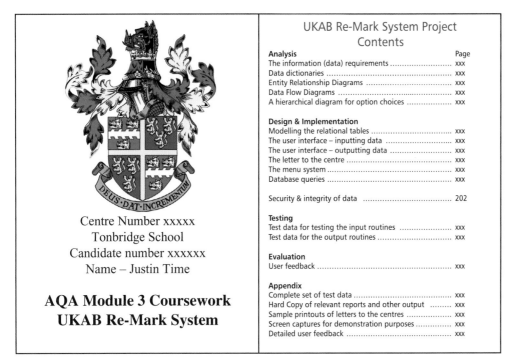

Centre Number xxxxx
Tonbridge School
Candidate number xxxxxx
Name – Justin Time

**AQA Module 3 Coursework
UKAB Re-Mark System**

UKAB Re-Mark System Project
Contents

Figure 23.1 Cover and contents page – Make an impressive start to any project documentation

Analysis – the information (data) requirements

The data requirements for each entity modelled for the UKAB project are as shown in the following data dictionaries. Assumptions regarding the detail are outlined in the comments. Data types are shown and typical validation rules are included where appropriate.

A candidate must submit a separate entry (*see Table 23.3*) for each re-marked subject. Therefore, if they have two subjects to be re-marked, they will have two entries in the 'Candidate Subject Entry' table.

Table 23.1 Data dictionary for a UKAB Centre

Name	Data type	Validation rules	Comments
Centre Number	Long integer	>=10000 And <=80000	An Integer within the range 10000–80000 inclusive.
	integer		Not Null. Unique. Required. No duplicates.
Centre Name	Text	None	Up to 30 characters, the name by which the centre is known. Not Null. Required.
Contact Name	Text	None	Up to 30 characters, the name of the examinations officer. Not Null. Required.
Title	Text	None	Title for the person at contact at the centre, e.g. 'Dr', 'Mr' etc. Not Null. Required.
Initials	Text	None	10 characters, capitals only, separated by dots with a dot at the end
Address 1	Text	None	Up to 30 characters. Not null. Required.
Address 2	Text	None	Up to 30 characters.
Town/City	Text	None	Up to 30 characters.
County/State	Text	None	Up to 20 characters.
Post Code/Zip	Text	None	Up to 10 characters.
Country	Text	None	Up to 20 characters. Not Null. Required.

Table 23.2 Data dictionary for a UKAB Subject

Name	Data type	Validation rules	Comments
Subject Reference Code	Long integer	>=1 And <=99999	Range 00001–99999. Not Null. Required. No duplicates.
Subject Name	Text	None	50 characters. Not Null. Required.
Grade Boundary A	Byte	>=0 And <=100	Integer, 0 to 100 inclusive. Required.
Grade Boundary B	Byte	>=0 And <=99	Integer, 0 to 99 inclusive. Not Null. Required.
Grade Boundary C	Byte	>=0 And <=99	Integer, 0 to 99 inclusive. Not Null. Required.
Grade Boundary D	Byte	>=0 And <=99	Integer, 0 to 99 inclusive. Not Null. Required.
Grade Boundary E	Byte	>=0 And <=99	Integer, 0 to 99 inclusive. Not Null. Required.

It's vital that you point out any assumptions that you may make regarding your implementation.

Separate subject entries in the 'candidate subject entry' table for the same candidate if they have more than one re-mark is of vital importance to understand how this solution works.

The Entity Relationship diagrams

The **Entity-Relationship diagrams** for the above entities (tables) are as shown in Figure 23.2. All three entities are linked because the 'Candidate Subject Entries' table is common to both systems, and these tables are therefore already in a form that can be modelled in a relational database system.

A main data flow diagram showing how the UKAB system is operated is shown in Figure 23.3, and the data flow diagram for the UKAB statistical requests is shown in Figure 23.4. All the main processes pertinent to the use of the UKAB system are shown in these diagrams.

Table 23.3 Data dictionary for a UKAB Candidate Subject Entry

Name	Data type	Validation rules	Comments
Centre Number	Long integer	>=10000 And <=80000	Range 00001–99999. Not Null. Required. No duplicates.
Candidate Number	Integer	>=1 And <=9999	Not unique. Range 0001–9999. Not Null. Required.
Subject Reference Code	Long integer	>=1 And <=99999	Range 00001–99999 inclusive. Not Null. Required.
Surname	Text	None	30 characters. Not unique. Not Null. Required.
Initials	Text	None	10 characters, capitals only, separated by dots with a dot at the end.
Title	Text	None	Mr., Mrs., Ms., Dr., etc. Not Null. Required.
Date Received	Date/time	None	Date the request for a re-mark of subject received. Date field. Not Null. Required.
Date Processed	Date/time	None	Date on which the request has been processed. Date field.
Grade Before Re-mark	Text	'A' Or 'B' Or 'C' Or 'D' Or 'E' Or 'U'	'A', 'B', 'C', 'D', 'E' and 'U' only. Not Null. Required.
Original Mark	Byte	>=0 And <=100	Range from 0 to 100% inclusive.
Grade After Re-mark	Text	'A' Or 'B' Or 'C' Or 'D' Or 'E' Or 'U'	'A', 'B', 'C', 'D', 'E' and 'U' only.
Re-mark Mark	Byte	>=0 And <=100	Range from 0 to 100% inclusive.
Grade Changed?	Yes/No	Yes/No only	Boolean – Yes or No only.
Return Script?	Yes/No	Yes/No only	Boolean – Yes or No only.
Original Marker ID	Long integer	>=1000 And <=9999	Integer – 4 digits range 1000–9999. Unique. Not Null. Required.
Re-mark Marker ID	Long integer	>=1000 And <=9999	Integer – 4 digits range 1000–9999. Unique. Not Null.

An easy-to-use menu system

It's important to keep the user interface simple, and the user of the system will therefore be presented with a series of menus from which appropriate options like 'add a centre' or 'edit a subject', etc. may be chosen. The hierarchical diagram showing these menu options is outlined in Figure 23.5.

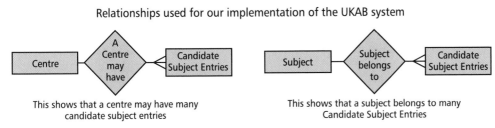

Relationships used for our implementation of the UKAB system

This shows that a centre may have many candidate subject entries

This shows that a subject belongs to many Candidate Subject Entries

Figure 23.2 The ER diagrams for the UKAB system

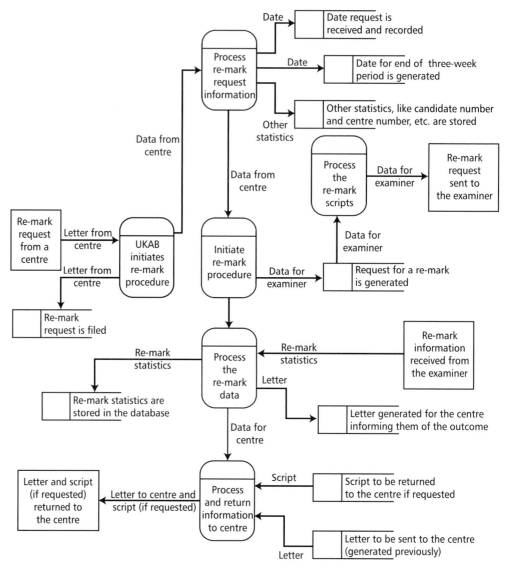

Figure 23.3 A possible data flow diagram for the main processing

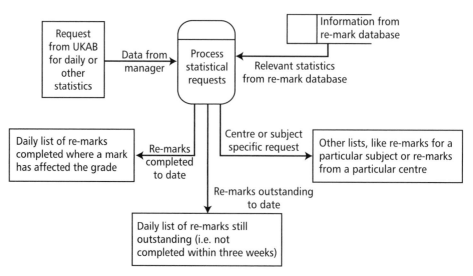

Figure 23.4 A possible data flow diagram for the UKAB statistical requests

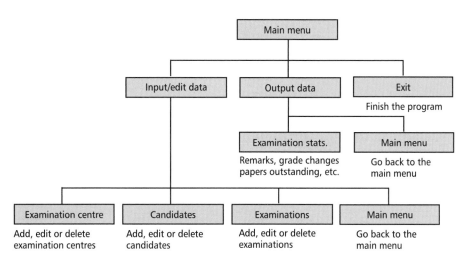

Figure 23.5 A possible hierarchical structure showing the choices for the user

Modelling the tables using a relational database

The system will be implemented using Microsoft's Access relational database, where a table will be set up to model each of the entities shown in Tables 23.1, 23.2 and 23.3. The table for a centre is described here using the conventional shorthand notation:

```
TABLE_NAME(Key field, field 1, field 2 etc.) as follows.
CENTRE(Centre Number, Centre Name, Contact Name, Title, Initials,
Address1, Address2, Town/City, County/State, Post Code/Zip,
Country)
```

The table for a subject is as follows:

```
SUBJECT(Subject Reference Code, Subject Name, Grade Boundary A,
Grade Boundary B, Grade Boundary C, Grade Boundary D, Grade
Boundary E)
```

Finally, the table for a candidate entry is as follows:

```
CANDIDATE SUBJECT ENTRY(Centre Number, Candidate Number, Subject
Reference Code, Surname, Initials, Title, Date Received, Date
Processed, Grade Before Re-mark, Original Mark, Grade After Re-
mark, Re-mark Mark, Grade Changed?, Return Script, Original
Marker ID, Re-mark Marker ID)
```

Note that a composite key field (consisting of three fields) is needed for the 'Candidate Subject Entry' table to create unique data which identifies a single candidate entered for a single subject. If a candidate takes more than one subject they will have more than one entry in this 'Candidate Subject Entry' table.

The relationships, described by the ER diagrams of Figure 23.2, are set up between the relational database tables as shown in Figure 23.6.

The shorthand notation shown here is a convenient way of describing the Access tables shown in Chapter 21.

If you find this confusing, look at Figure 21.1, which shows the 'Centre' table. Now compare it with the shorthand notation shown here. You will see that they contain identical information.

The key field(s) are underlined, and correspond to the field which displays the key in an access table.

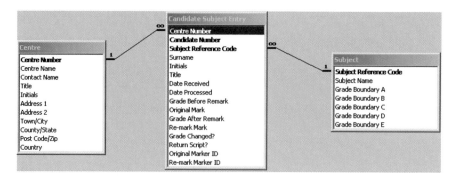

Figure 23.6 The relationships for the UKAB re-mark database

The user interface – inputting data

The data capture forms for the 'Centre information', 'Subject information' and 'Candidate Subject Entries' are shown in Figures 23.7, 23.8 and 23.9. Access is being used here simply to provide a convenient front end as an aide to the design of a professional form, which can be achieved more quickly than other methods like hand-written forms or a CAD package.

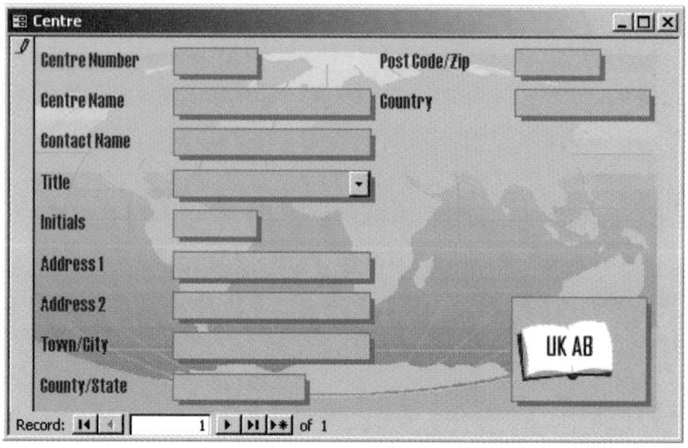

Figure 23.7 A typical user interface for the 'centre' information

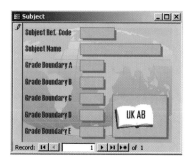

Figure 23.8 A typical user interface for the 'subject' information

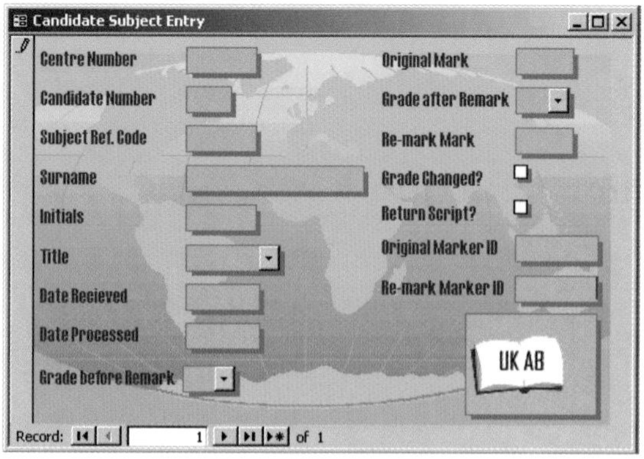

Figure 23.9 A typical user interface for 'candidate subject entry'

The user interface – outputting data

The designs for the four different reports and the letter to the centre informing them of any decisions made by the board are shown in Figures 23.10, 23.11, 23.12, and 23.13 respectively. The data to be displayed in each report is shown in the column headings under the grey area for each report.

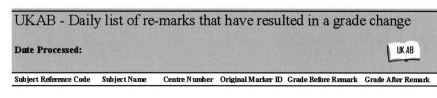

Figure 23.10 A typical report structure for the re-marks list

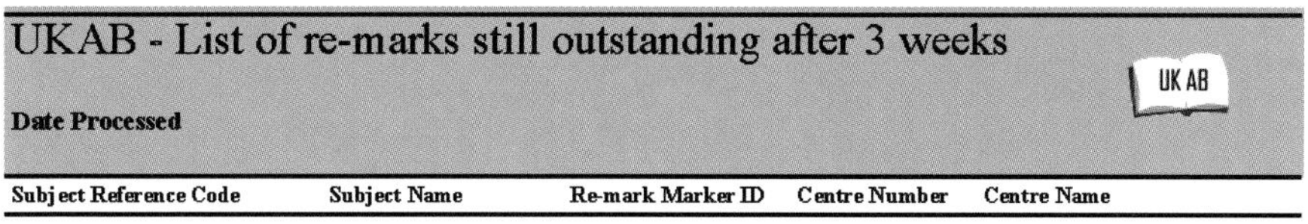

Figure 23.11 A typical report structure for the re-marks still outstanding list

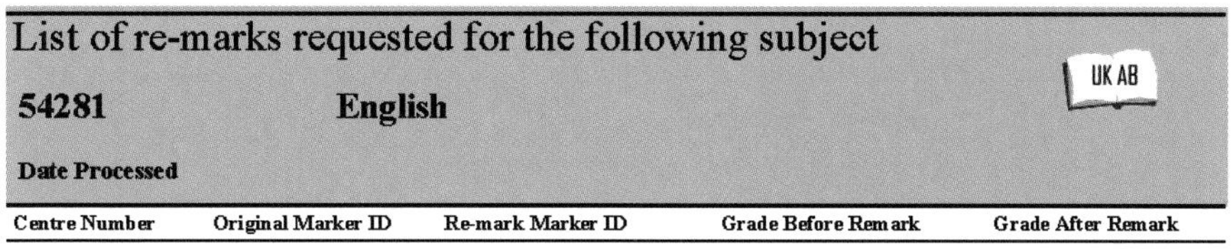

Figure 23.12 A typical report structure for a particular subject

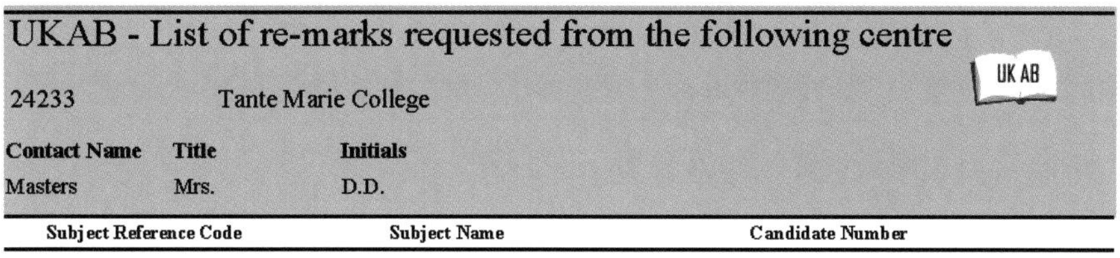

Figure 23.13 A typical report structure for a particular centre

The output reports shown here are designed making use of the Access reporting process, but they have been considerably altered to make the reports appropriate for the UKAB system.

Never accept the output from a report-generation Wizard 'as is', you will get far too many fields included, many which are not appropriate to your solution.

Finally, the letter to the centre may be formatted as shown in Figure 22.14. A hidden sentence (shown on this example letter) will carry the text information '*As you can see from above, a grade change has not been recommended*'. The method of including or excluding this is described more fully in Figure 23.16.

The menu-selection structure

The menu-selection structure, (modelling the hierarchical diagram shown in Figure 23.5) enabling the user to navigate through the system of options is shown in Figure 23.15. Again the Microsoft Access system has been used to generate an appropriate menu structure quickly and efficiently.

Displaying the hidden text

Figure 23.16 shows how a macro called 'Grade Change' is being used to display or hide the hidden text which controls whether the text 'As you can see from the above, a grade change has not been recommended.' is displayed or not. It does this by instructing the control (Label109 in this particular case) to make the text visible or invisible based on whether the 'Grade Before Remark' is the same as the 'Grade After Remark' or not. The visible property has been set to 'No' for other entries, and the second entry is needed to switch the visible property back on in case the next record does result in a grade change again.

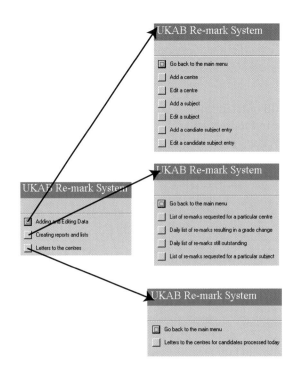

UKAB
Excellence House
Successful Street
College Town
Brimberley
Surrey
GU 24 RC9
Contact: Dr. J. Dunn
Telephone: (0143) 222221
e-mail jdunn@UKAB.org

Centre Number	24233	**Candidate Number**	0998	
Centre Name	Tante Marie College	**Subject Reference Code**	01325	
Contact Name	Mrs. D.D. Masters	**Candidate Name**	Mr. J.	Klander
Address	Woodham House			
	Beaton Road			
	Woking			
	Surrey			
	GU34 1N			
	England			

26 October 2003

Dear Mrs. Masters

RE: Re-mark for the above candidate.

Please be advised that the results of the re-mark for the above candidate is as follows:

Grade Before Remark	D	**Original Mark**	53
Grade After Remark	C	**Re-mark Mark**	60

Please don't hesitate to contact us if we can be of any further assistance.

Yours sincerely

Dr. J. Dunn.

Figure 23.14 A typical structure for the letter to a centre

Figure 23.15 A typical menu-selection structure for ease of use

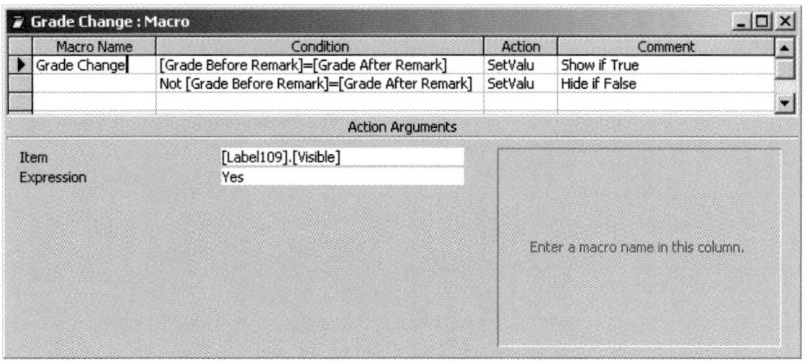

Figure 23.16 A macro to display or hide the 'Grade Change' label

Querying the database

Several queries need to be written to interrogate the database. These queries will be bound to reports to produce professional standard formatting for the output. The 'list of daily re-marks' query is constructed as follows:

```
IF the 'Date Processed' field = 'Today' AND the 'Grade Changed?'
field is 'True' THEN this is a re-mark which has been carried out
today.
```

The QBE design grid representation of this is shown in Figure 23.17.

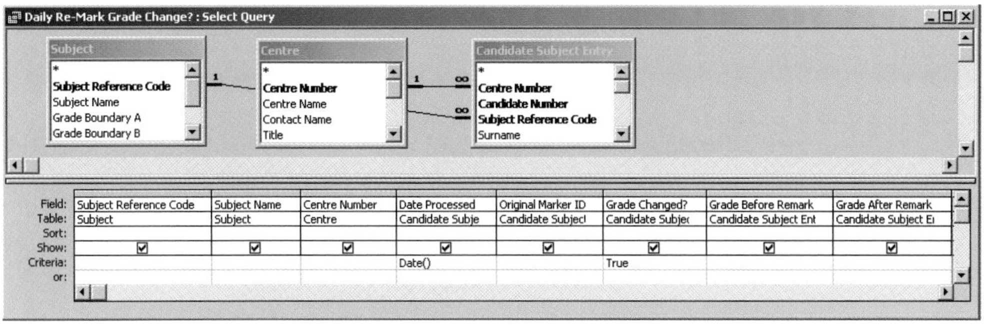

Figure 23.17 Setting up a query in Access to be used by the daily re-mark grade-change report

The 'list of re-marks still outstanding' query is as follows, with the QBE design grid representation being shown in Figure 23.18.

```
IF the 'Date Received' field is > 3 weeks ago, AND if the 'Date
Processed' field is Null (contains no entry) THEN this is a
re-mark which is still outstanding.
```

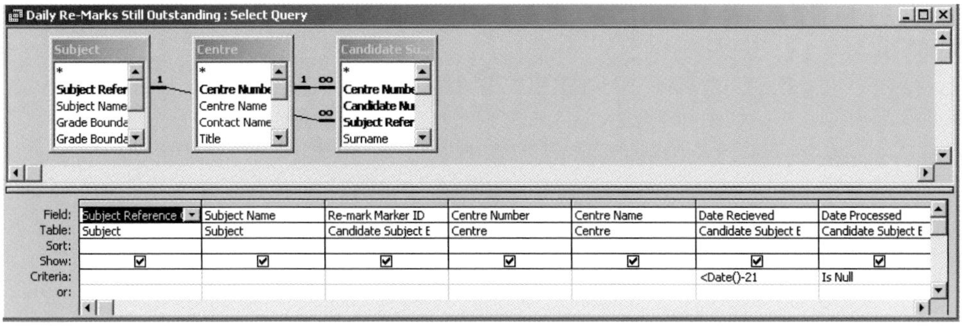

Figure 23.18 Setting up a query in Access to be used by the re-marks outstanding report

You must write down the logic behind your queries, like those shown here.

The QBE grid shows the same information, but the examiners like to know that you have thought about the query before designing the QBE grid!

Not all queries are covered here, but they have already been covered in detail in Chapter 22.

There is also much information contained in the appendices (see end of this chapter).

It would not easily
be possible to
provide an
exhaustive set of
test data for this
project.

The examiners are
looking for
representive and
reasonably
comprehensive
examples of
testing. You must
show them that
you have covered
most sensible
possibilities.

Table 23.4 Some black-box test data for Table 21.3

Inputs		Outputs
Name	**Test data**	**Comments/expected results**
Centre Number	999	Too small – data should be rejected.
	80100	Too big – data should be rejected.
		A null value is not acceptable – should be brought to the user's attention and data should be rejected.
	ABC	Only numeric data should be accepted – data should be rejected.
	20003	This is a valid centre number – result should be accepted.
	20003 *(again)*	This is a valid centre number, but it has already been used – data should be rejected. (*Done by making sure there are no duplicates for this field.*)
Centre Name		A null value is not acceptable – should be brought to the user's attention and data should be rejected.
	Sandhurst	Data should be accepted. Can't easily be validated. Verification could be carried out by another person checking the entry at a later stage.
Contact Name		A null value is not acceptable – should be brought to the user's attention and data should be rejected.
	Hammer	Data should be accepted. Can't easily be validated. Verification could be carried out by another person checking the entry at a later stage.
Title	Mr.	Data should be accepted – drop-down list for ease of data entry
	Most Rev.	Data should be accepted – the user has the option of typing in data not contained in the drop-down list. Data should be accepted. Can't be validated. Verification could be carried out by another person checking the entry later.
Initials		A null value is not acceptable – should be brought to the user's attention and data should be rejected.
	F.	Data should be accepted. Can't be validated. Verification could be carried out by another person checking the entry later.
Address 1	Dunromin	Data should be accepted. Can't easily be validated. Verification could be carried out by another person checking the entry at a later stage.
Address 1		A null value is not acceptable for the first line of the address – should be brought to the user's attention and data should be rejected.
Address 2		Data should be accepted. Can't be validated. Verification could be carried out by another person checking the entry later.
Town/City	Bigmouth	Data should be accepted. Can't be validated. Verification could be carried out by another person checking the entry later.
County/State	Brighton	Data should be accepted. Can't be validated. Verification could be carried out by another person checking the entry later.
Post Code	BN 26 1EW	Data should be accepted. Can't be validated. Verification could be carried out by another person checking the entry later.
Country	England	Data should be accepted. Can't be validated. Verification could be carried out by another person checking the entry later.

Test data for the UKAB system – inputting the data

Some black-box test data for each part of the project is shown in the following tables. Table 23.4 shows the test data for the 'Centre', Table 23.5 shows the test data for the 'Subject' and Table 23.6 shows the test data for the 'Candidate Subject Entry' system. The test data is not exhaustive, but extremes and erroneous data are input to be representative of different conditions that can be encountered when data is being entered into the UKAB system.

Table 23.5 Some black-box test data for Table 21.5

Inputs		Outputs
Name	**Test data**	**Comments/expected results**
Subject Reference Code	07352	Because we have enforced referential integrity when setting up the system, Access will not allow subject reference codes in this table which do not have and entry in the Centres table. Data should be accepted if there is an entry for this centre number in the 'Centre table'.
Subject Name	Computing	Data should be accepted. Can't be validated. Verification could be carried out by another person checking the entry later.
		Not null. Data should be rejected.
Grade Boundary A	89	Data should be accepted. Can't be validated. Verification could be carried out by another person checking the entry later.
	107	Too big. Data should be rejected.
Grade Boundary B	78	Data should be accepted.
Grade Boundary C		Null value. Data should be rejected.
Grade Boundary D	65	Data should be accepted.
Grade Boundary E	B	Not a number. Data should be rejected.

Test data for the UKAB system – outputting the data

The methodology for checking the output reports are shown in Tables 23.7, 23.8, 23.9 and 23.10, where suitable data is defined.

Test runs have been carried out using the test data shown in Appendix (1), and the results shown in Figures 23.19, 23.20, 23.21 and 23.22 were obtained. (*Don't forget these would be hard copy on your actual write up.*)

Security of data

Data security is controlled by placing a password on the Access database, as shown in Figure 23.23. This is in addition to the log-on password and file permissions provided by the operating system. The real database would obviously need backing up each day too, with several weeks of backups being the most likely scenario. Real backups are taken by the school each day, and tapes are kept in a fireproof safe in the main file server room serving the computer department. There are also backups of this project on Zip disks, which are password protected by using the WinZip compression utility with an encrypted password. Virus protection software is also used on the computers on which this database was constructed and used.

The measures outlined here should be sufficient.

Table 23.6 Some black-box test data for Table 21.3

Inputs		Outputs
Name	**Test data**	**Comments/expected results**
Centre Number	2003	Because we have enforced referential integrity when setting up the system, Access will not allow centres in this table which do not have an entry in the Centre table. Data should be accepted if there is an entry for this centre number in the 'Centre table'.
Candidate Number	0023	Check that leading zeros are displayed in both 'form', 'data sheet' and 'printed output'. Data should be accepted.
	35241	Too big. Data should be rejected.
	0000	Too small. Data should be rejected.
	ABC	Can't have text in a numeric field. Data should be rejected.
Subject Reference Code	00000	Too small. Data should be rejected.
	00001	Data should be accepted. Because we have enforced referential integrity when setting up the system, Access will not allow subject reference codes in this table which do not have an entry in the Candidate subject entry table. Data should be accepted if there is an entry for this centre number in the 'Centre table'.
	99999	Data should be accepted (see above).
	363533	Too big. Data should be rejected.
Surname	Smith	Data should be accepted. No validation, but verification could be used after initial data entry.
Initials	F.	Data should be accepted. Can't be validated. Verification could be carried out by another person checking the entry later.
Title	Ms.	Data should be accepted. Can't be validated. Verification could be carried out by another person checking the entry later.
Date Received	20/10/2003	Data should be accepted if it is not less than the current date. Data should be rejected otherwise.
Date Processed	25/10/2003	Data should be accepted if it is not less than the current date. Data should be rejected otherwise.
Grade Before Re-mark	A	Data should be accepted.
	Y	Not 'A', B', 'C', 'D', 'E' or 'U'. Data should be rejected.
Original Mark	108	Too big. Data should be rejected.
	78	Data should be accepted.
		Null value. Data should be rejected.
Grade After Re-mark	B	Data should be accepted.
		Null value. Data should be accepted. Won't be able to save initial re-mark request at this time if this is rejected!
Re-mark Mark	B	Data not numeric. Data should be rejected.
	58	Data should be accepted.
Grade Changed?		Null value. Data should be accepted because a Null is a valid entry until the re-mark is completed.
	Y	Data should be accepted.
Return Script?	N	Data should be accepted.
		Null value. Data should be rejected.
Original Marker ID	0089	Too small. Data should be rejected.
	7453	Data should be accepted.
		Null value. Data should be rejected.
Re-mark Marker ID		Null value. Data should be accepted because Null is a valid entry until the re-mark is completed.

Table 23.7 Test criteria for the daily list of re-marks

Name	Test data	Name	Test data	Comments/expected results
Grade Changed?	Yes	Date	Today's Date (*)	Check this candidate is present in the list.
Grade Changed?	Yes	Date	Other date	Check this candidate is not present in the list.
Grade Changed?	No	Date	Today's Date (*)	Check this candidate is not present in the list.
Grade Changed?	No	Date	Other date	Check this candidate is not present in the list.

N.B. (*) This assumes that a daily list or re-marks is a list for the *current day* only – see margin entry.

Table 23.8 Test criteria for the daily list of re-marks still outstanding

Name	Test data	Name	Test data	Comments/expected results
Date Received	>3 weeks ago	Date Processed	Null	Check this candidate is present in the list.
Date Received	Exactly 3 weeks ago	Date Processed	Null	Check this candidate is present in the list.
Date Received	<3 weeks ago	Date Processed	Null	Check this candidate is not present in the list.
Date Received	>3 weeks ago	Date Processed	Valid date	Check this candidate is not present in the list.
Date Received	Exactly 3 weeks ago	Date Processed	Valid date	Check this candidate is not present in the list.
Date Received	<3 weeks ago	Date Processed	Valid date	Check this candidate is not present in the list.

Table 23.9 Test criteria for the list of re-marks requested for a particular subject

Name	Test data	Comments/expected results
Subject Reference Code	Any valid code	Check this candidate is present in the list.
Subject Reference Code	Other code	Check this candidate is not present in the list.

Table 23.10 Test criteria for the list of re-marks requested for a particular centre

Name	Test data	Comments/expected results
Centre Number	Any valid code	Check this centre is present in the list.
Centre Number	Other code	Check this centre is not present in the list.

Evaluation

A questionnaire (see Appendix 3) has been given to sensible students who have evaluated this project by adding, editing and deleting different data items. They have also run some reports and checked a variety of different input mechanisms. The initial feedback from these students, as can be seen in Appendix 3 is very positive. The project has been tested to make sure that it complies with all the requirements outlined in the project specification (shown in green at the beginning of Chapter 20).

23

There is not sufficient space to include the appendices of the report here, but this database is available as one of the electronic resources that can be purchased in conjunction with other electronic resources for this course.

The module 3 project write up

UKAB - Daily list of re-marks that have resulted in a grade change

Date Processed: 26/10/2003

UK AB

Subject Reference Code	Subject Name	Centre Number	Original Marker ID	Grade Before Remark	Grade After Remark
01325	Computing				
		24233	1260	D	C
		10000	1260	D	C
54281	English				
		63422	7551	B	A

Figure 23.19 The output from the report bound to the query set up in Figure 22.1

UKAB - List of re-marks still outstanding after 3 weeks

Date Processed   26 October 2003

UK AB

Subject Reference Code	Subject Name	Re-mark Marker ID	Centre Number	Centre Name
01325	Computing			
		1462	79342	Dumford Academy
		1462	26398	Scilly Community College
20094	Mathematics			
		8266	69898	Falmouth College
54281	English			
		7630	78354	Benny Hill High
		7630	78354	Benny Hill High
		7630	77777	Newport High School

Figure 23.20 The output from the report bound to the query set up in Figure 22.4

List of re-marks requested for the following subject

54281   **English**

Date Processed   26 October 2003

UK AB

Centre Number	Original Marker ID	Re-mark Marker ID	Grade Before Remark	Grade After Remark
78354	7551	7630	C	
63422	7551	7630	C	
78354	7551	7630	U	
77777	7551	7630	C	
63422	7551	7630	B	A

Figure 22.21 The output from the bound query using the parameter supplied by the user

UKAB - List of re-marks requested from the following centre

24233   Tante Marie College

UK AB

Contact Name	Title	Initials
Masters	Mrs.	D.D.

Subject Reference Code	Subject Name	Candidate Number
28181	Design Technology	0998
01325	Computing	0998

Figure 23.22 The output from bound query using the parameter supplied in Figure 22.10

Some things to include in the appendices

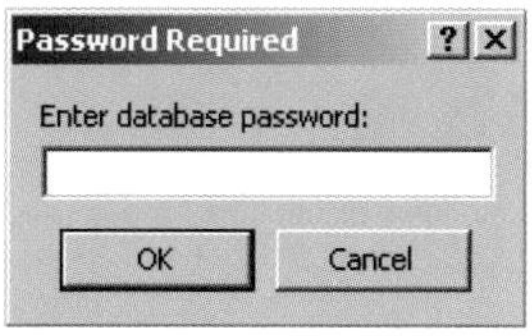

1 A *complete set* of test data (a small part of which is shown here).

The important parts of the test data should be annotated as shown here, so that you can convince the examiners you have entered data to test all important conditions. Many conditions like this need to be flagged in the test data.

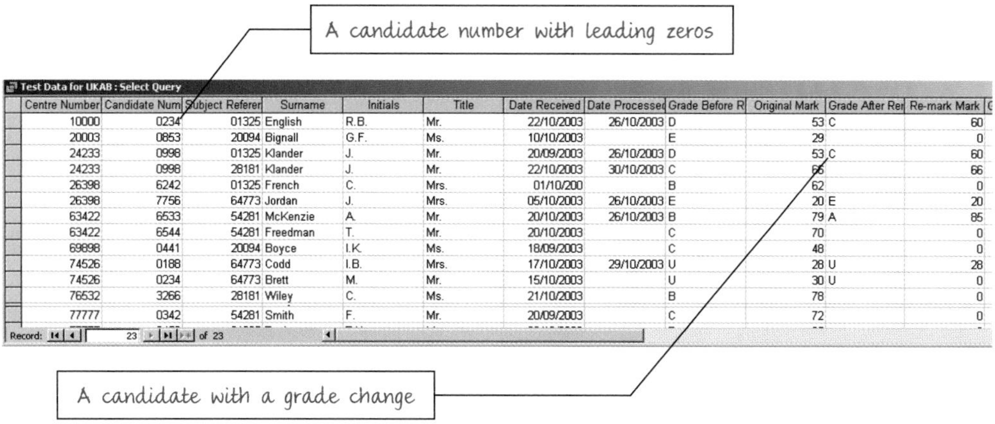

Password Required [?][X]

Enter database password:

[   ]

[OK] [Cancel]

Figure 23.23 A password has been set up on the Access database

A candidate number with leading zeros

A candidate with a grade change

Centre Number	Candidate Num	Subject Referer	Surname	Initials	Title	Date Received	Date Processed	Grade Before R	Original Mark	Grade After Ren	Re-mark Mark
10000	0234	01325	English	R.B.	Mr.	22/10/2003	26/10/2003	D	53	C	60
20003	0853	20094	Bignall	G.F.	Ms.	10/10/2003		E	29		0
24233	0998	01325	Klander	J.	Mr.	20/09/2003	26/10/2003	D	53	C	60
24233	0998	28181	Klander	J.	Mr.	22/10/2003	30/10/2003	C	66		66
26398	6242	01325	French	C.	Mrs.	01/10/200		B	62		0
26398	7756	64773	Jordan	J.	Mrs.	05/10/2003	26/10/2003	E	20	E	20
63422	6533	54281	McKenzie	A.	Mr.	20/10/2003	26/10/2003	B	79	A	85
63422	6544	54281	Freedman	T.	Mr.	20/10/2003		C	70		0
69698	0441	20094	Boyce	I.K.	Ms.	18/09/2003		C	48		0
74526	0188	64773	Codd	I.B.	Mrs.	17/10/2003	29/10/2003	U	28	U	28
74526	0234	64773	Brett	M.	Mr.	15/10/2003		U	30	U	0
76532	3266	28181	Wiley	C.	Ms.	21/10/2003		B	78		0
77777	0342	54281	Smith	F.	Mr.	20/09/2003		C	72		0

Record: 23 of 23

Figure 23.24 A small sample of the test data to be included in an appendix

2 Hard copy – the actual printouts representing the reports shown in Figures 23.19, 23.20, 23.21 and 23.22.

3 Sample printouts of the letters to the centres demonstrating grade changes and no grade changes.

4 A few sample screen captures to demonstrate the data validation in operation. (*Don't waste time doing lots of these.*)

5 Any code that you have produced when writing macros or VBA script for your database.

6 Any code that you have used to implement this project in a high-level language.

7 Any evidence that people have actually used the database (e.g. simple questionnaires, etc.)

8 A bibliography of any books or other material you have used to help with the project (also needed on the project cover sheet).

24 A module 3 examination

In this section you will learn about:

- The typical structure of a module 3 examination
- How the exam splits your project into natural sections like analysis, design and testing
- How to match a write up to the module 3 examination
- Typical questions that will appear in a module 3 examination
- The annotation methods that will be needed in the real examination (*see answers*)
- How the questions asked should influence your own project write up
- How the synoptic element of the course might get you to think in greater depth

Introduction

The examination paper used in this chapter contains 50% of material from the real AQA June 2003 examination for the module 3 UKAB project covered in Chapters 20, 21, 22 and 23. We are grateful to the AQA board for permission to use this material.

This chapter can be used as a mock examination paper. To use it as such you need to look at Chapter 20 to find out the background to this project, and Chapters 21 and 22 provide a complete solution in detail. Some of the answers in this examination paper will require additional thought and annotation on your part, and suggested answers can be found in the answers section at the back of this book, where the page references to the remaining answers can also be found. We obviously can't add the annotation here because it would mess up the book! If you wish to do this examination, it is suggested that you photocopy this chapter and Chapter 23, thus enabling you to add the annotation should you wish to get practice in this way for this vitally important part of your computing course.

Due to the large amount of explanation, Chapters 20, 21 and 22 *do not* constitute a suitably brief project write up. In practice, your documentation should be more concise, consisting of about 10 or 15 pages *plus* material in an appendix. Major sections of a write up are shown in Chapter 23, where the pages are arranged for a module 3 examination.

This examination constitutes the **synoptic element** for AS level computing. Virtually anything from any topic can be asked. During the examination you might, for example, be required to consider some of the **legal implications** of the exercise you have been undertaking. These types of question are included in the examination paper shown here.

A Module 3 practical systems development examination

Time allowed: 1 hour 30 minutes   Total marks: 65

Answer this paper using the documentation you have prepared for the UKAB Re-marks practical exercise as requested in the 2003 specification. A copy of the brief for this practical exercise has been included at the end of this paper if you need to refer to it.
(This brief (specification) is shown at the beginning of Chapter 20 in green.)

Many of these questions require you to give the page number in your documentation, where the evidence for the answer may be found. You should write the number of the question in the margin of that page in your documentation.

At the end of the examination you must hand in both your project and this answer booklet.

To do the examination in this chapter you need to use the project write up outlined in Chapter 23, which represents the material (except the appendices) that you would bring with you to the examination room.

Unless you have carefully read and understood the work covered in Chapters 20, 21, 22 and 23, you will not be able to satisfactorily undertake the questions in this chapter.

1 This question relates to the DESIGN process.

(a) List two extra data items that you have stored for the re-mark records (holding candidate name and number, centre number, subject code, etc.)

(i) First extra data item ....

(1 mark)

Where in your documentation have you defined or set up this data item?

Page number..

(1 mark)

(Write Q 1(a)(i) in the margin, in the correct place, on that page.)

How have you used this data item?

....

(2 marks)

(ii) Second extra data item ....

(Write Q 1(a)(ii) in the margin, in the correct place, on that page.)

How have you used this data item?

....

(2 marks)

(b) State what data type you have used for each of the following items, and explain your choice in each case. (Be as specific as possible when giving the data type.)

(i) Candidate Number...

Data Type ....

Why? ....

(ii) Whether scripts are to be returned to the Centre

Data Type ....

Why? ....

(iii) Original Mark
Data Type ....

Why? ....

(6 marks)

2 This question relates to the IMPLEMENTATION process.

(a) In order to produce the requested hard copy lists, your solution has to find certain records. Exactly how did your solution find:

(i) Records where re-marks have been requested for a particular subject;

....

....

(2 marks)

Where in your documentation is your coding to find this data?

Page number ....

(1 mark)

(Write Q 2(a)(i) in the margin, in the correct place, on that page.)

(ii)   Records where the candidate's mark has changed causing a change in grade;

....

....

(2 marks)

Where is a hard copy of such a list in your documentation?

Page number ....

(1 mark)

(Write Q 2(a)(ii) in the margin, in the correct place, on that page.)

(iii)   Records where re-marks have not been completed in the required three-week period?

....

....

....

(3 marks)

Where is a hard copy of such a list in your documentation?

Page number ....

(1 mark)

(Write Q 2(a)(iii) in the margin, in the correct place, on that page.)

(b)   You were asked to produce a daily list of those re-marks where the candidate's grade has been affected by a mark change. UKAB decides it also needs a daily list of those re-marks where the grade has not been changed, whether or not the mark has been changed.

(i)   Write an algorithm to produce this list.

(A larger space is available in the real paper)

(5 marks)

3   This question relates to the REPORT DESIGN process.

(a)   (i)   On which page of your documentation is a hard copy of the document to be returned to the centres, complete with the UKAB logo.

Page number ....

(1 mark)

(Write Q 3(a)(i) in the margin, in the correct place, on that page.)

(ii)   How did you input the logo and position it on this document?

....

....

....

....

....

(3 marks)

(b) Give two criteria that you have considered for the design of this document, other than using the logo, and say how you used each of them.

1. ....

....

2. ....

....

(*4 marks*)

(Write Q 3(b) in the margin of your document, in the correct place(s), on the page(s), where these two aspects of the design are demonstrated.

(*2 marks*)

4 This question relates to the TESTING and VALIDATION process.

(a) How did your solution ensure that 'subject reference codes' were stored and displayed with leading zeros if necessary?

....

....

(*2 marks*)

(b) What test data did you use to ensure that the following parts of your project were working properly?

(i) The centre number is a 5-digit number in the range 10000 to 80000;

....

....

(*2 marks*)

(ii) To ensure that the letters informing the centres of the results are sent at the appropriate time.

....

....

(*2 marks*)

(c) Show where you have considered these tests in your documentation.

Page number .... and ....

(*2 marks*)

(Write Q 4(c)(i) and 4 (c)(ii) in the margin, in the correct places, on those page.)

5 This question relates to the ANALYSIS process.

(a) (i) What type of relationship exists between the candidates and the centres in your project?

....

(*1 mark*)

(ii) Making use of an Entity Relationship Diagram, show the relationship you have described in part (i) above.

(*2 marks*)

(b) Draw an Entity relationship diagram showing the relationship between the subjects and the centres.

(2 marks)

(c) The UKAB is a simplified system. Imagine you are the systems analyst whose task it is to examine a real examination system. Describe three different techniques that could be used to gather information about the proposed system.

1. ....

2. ....

3. ....

(3 marks)

6 This question relates to the SECURITY and INTEGRITY of your project.

   (a) (i) What is meant by data integrity?

....

(1 mark)

      (ii) What is meant by data security?

....

(1 mark)

   (b) (i) Describe one place where you have implemented data integrity methods in your project and why

....

....

(2 marks)

      (ii) Describe one place where you have implemented data security methods in your project and why

....

....

(2 marks)

7 This question relates to the EVALUATION and MAINTENANCE of the new system.

   (a) Three criteria on which projects may be judged are (i) *effectiveness*, (ii) *usability* and (iii) *maintainability*. Briefly describe what is meant by each of these criteria.

(i) ....

....

(1 mark)

(ii) ....

....

(1 mark)

(iii) ....

....

(1 mark)

(b) Technical documentation and a user guide should accompany any real project. Briefly outline the two different types of user for whom these documents are intended, giving an example of a typical use for each.

1. ....

....

(2 marks)

2. ....

....

(2 marks)

Full answers to all end-of-chapter self-test questions

Complete answers are given to each self-test question. In many cases *extra material*, not covered in the main book is added to produce hundreds of comprehensive answers to the questions posed.

Chapter 1 – Data information and coding

1 ASCII is an **8-bit (1 byte) code** used for representing characters. ASCII is an acronym for the **American Standard Code for Information Interchange**. Because of the limited number of combinations, ASCII is *not suitable* for representing far-eastern languages like Chinese, for example, and so **Unicode**, a **16-bit (2 byte) code** is used for this purpose. Most languages, ancient and modern, can be represented using Unicode.

2 (a) A **byte** is **8 bits** (binary digits).
   (b) A **word** is a convenient number of bits, typically 8, 16, 32 or 64. It usually mirrors the number of bits that can be transferred into a 'single' memory location via the data bus.
   (c) A **bit** is a **binary digit**. This represents a '0' or '1'.

3 (a) **8 bits**.
   (b) Write down the column headings in binary

16	8	4	2	1

   Therefore 23_{10} is

1	0	1	1	1

   Therefore 5 bits are needed.
   (c) Write down the column headings in binary

8	4	2	1

   A_{16} is 10_{10} is

1	0	1	0

   Therefore 4 bits are needed.

4 (a) Write down the binary column headings

32	16	8	4	2	1

   39_{10} will be

1	0	0	1	1	1

   Therefore 39_{10} = 100111_2
   (b) Split up the number into two decimal digits

3	9

   Write down a 4-digit binary number for each decimal

0011	1001

   Therefore 39_{10} will be 0011 1001 in BCD.

(c) 39_{10} in binary (from part (a)) is   0010   0111
(Two leading zeros and group into fours)
Code each group of 4-digits into hex to get

2	7

Therefore 39_{10} is 27_{16}

5 Write down column headings

128	64	32	16	8	4	2	1
1	0	0	0	0	1	0	1

Write down the binary digits.
Add up the values $128 + 4 + 1 = 133$.
Therefore 10000101_2 = 133_{10}

6 Write down column headings

8	4	2	1	.	1/2	1/4	1/8
1	0	0	1	.	0	0	1

Write down the binary number
Note that $8 + 1$ is 9 (the integer part) and $1/8 = 0.125$ (the fractional part).
Therefore 9.125_{10} = 1001.001_2

7 (a) Write down the octal number   2   3   7
Replace each digit with the group-of-three binary equivalent   010   011   111
Therefore 237_8 = 10011111_2
   (b) Write down the octal column headings

64	8	1
2	3	7

Put the octal number underneath
Note that
$(2 \times 64) + (3 \times 8) + (1 \times 7) = 128 + 24 + 7 = 159$
Therefore 237_8 = 159_{10}

8 Write down the hex number   A   2   B
Replace each digit with the group-of-four binary equivalent   1010   0010   1011
Therefore $A2B_{16}$ = 101000101011_2

9 First write down the binary number, and then starting at the R.H.S., group the binary number into sets of 4-binary digits. Finally, for each group of 4 binary digits, write down the equivalent hex digit.
Here is an example. Convert 101111011_2 into hex.
Write down in groups of 4 (from right hand side)

1	0111	1011

Put hex number underneath   1   7   B
Therefore 101111011_2 = $17B_{16}$

10 **BCD** is *not a number base* in the true sense like pure binary, decimal or hexadecimal. All these bases generate numbers making use of column headings in the ways shown in previous questions. BCD does not use all the possible combinations of numbers – only the digits 0 to 9 are used. Binary codes, for example, can represent 0 to 15 as in hexadecimal. BCD is only a convenient way of representing decimal digits electronically, although it is possible to do mathematical operations with BCD.

11 Line up the binary digits to be added

```
      1  0  1  1
      1  1  1  1  +
   ─────────────
   1  1  0  1  0
   1  1  1
```

(Note: carry lots of two as we are working in binary.)
Therefore $1011_2 + 1111_2 = 11010_2$

12 Work out 11002 – 1102
Line up the digits to be subtracted

```
         2
   0  ̶0  2
   ̶1  ̶1  ̶0  0
      1  1  0  −
   ─────────────
      1  1  0
```

(Note: when we borrow one from the previous column we are really borrowing 2.)
Therefore $1100_2 - 110_2 = 110_2$

13 A **floating-point number** is one that consists of a **mantissa** and an **exponent**. A mantissa is a fractional number like 1.001, for example, and an exponent is an integer number that indicates how many places the binary point must be moved to the right or left, depending on whether it's positive or negative respectively. Consider the following representation.

     0.100   0011

Here, the exponent (2nd part) has a value of 3. Therefore, the binary point in the mantissa, (1st part) must be moved three places to the right, giving a final number of 0100. or 4.
Therefore 0.100 0011 is a floating-point number representing 4_{10}.

14 Line up the hex digits to be added

```
   2  B  C
      B  4  +
   ─────────
   3  7  0
   1  1
```

(Note: carry lots of sixteen as we are working in hex – i.e. C + 4 is 12 + 4 = 16 = 1 lot of sixteen with zero left over.)

15 To convert 111111111111111_2 into decimal you should realise that this number is one less than the number 1000000000000000_2. This is the same as 2^{16}; therefore the answer is $2^{16} - 1 = 65\,535$.
Therefore $111111111111111_2 = 65\,536_{10}$

16 Assuming the leading 1 is positive, the largest number is 111111111111111.
A quick way to work out its value is
$1000000000000000 - 1$ or $2^{16} - 1 = 65\,535_{10}$
The largest *positive* number that can be represented with 16 bits is 65 535.

17 To find the values of these negative numbers we must first find the values for the equivalent size positive numbers. This is done as follows:

	128	64	32	16	8	4	2	1
+29	0	0	0	1	1	1	0	1
+56	0	0	1	1	1	0	0	0

(Note: using 8-bit sign and magnitude notations, we have only to alter the most significant bit to a one to represent a negative number.)

	128	64	32	16	8	4	2	1
−29	1	0	0	1	1	1	0	1
−56	1	0	1	1	1	0	0	0

Note that each of the above numbers has a 1 for the most significant bit, thus confirming that they are negative. Therefore, the 8-bit sign and magnitude representation for the numbers is as follows.

$-29_{10} = 10011101_2$
and $-56_{10} = 10111000_2$

18 We start with the positive representations in pure binary.

+29	0	0	0	1	1	1	0	1
+56	0	0	1	1	1	0	0	0

Using the rules to convert to two's complement (page 6) we get

−29	1	1	1	0	0	0	1	1
−56	1	1	0	0	1	0	0	0

19 (a) The number 11110000 starts off with a leading one, therefore it's a negative number. The **two's complement** of 11110000 is 00010000 which has a value of 16.

 Therefore 11110000 represents –16.

 (b) The maximum positive number will be 01111111 which has a value of

 $2^8 - 1 = 128 - 1 = 127$

 Therefore the maximum positive number is +127.

 The maximum negative number will be 10000000. The **two's complement** of this number is 100000000, which has a value of 128.

 Therefore the maximum negative number is –128.

20 The number +30 has a binary value of 11110. With an 8-bit sign and magnitude representation this will be 10011110.

 Therefore +30 = 00011110 8-bit sign and magnitude.

Chapter 2 – Images, sound and analogue data

1 24 bits or 3 bytes are used to represent the number of different graphics colours or levels of grey. If 24-bits are used, then 2^{24} or 16 777 216 different combinations may be used for the colours. This is called true colour, as no more colours are needed to convince a human that he or she is looking at a real image.

2 (a) With just two bits we have the patterns 00, 01, 10 and 11 to represent 'colours'.
 Therefore, only 2^2 or 4 different colours are possible.

 (b) **With 8 bits we have 2^8 or 256 different colours.**

 (c) **With 16 bits we have 2^{16} or 65 536 different colours.**

3 **Bit-mapped graphics** is the system where an image is made up from pixels (or picture elements). If you zoom into the image it will start to appear pixelated (have jagged edges). If the resolution is very high, then at normal zoom levels the image will appear to be of high quality, rather like a photograph. Bit mapped images (bmp files) take up enormous amounts of memory to store the information.

Vector graphics is where a vector (a line) is used to make up an image. A **line**, or **vector** can be described by using a mathematical equation, and therefore intermediate points may be calculated rather than stored as pixels. A vector image therefore takes up far less memory than a bit-mapped image. Also, very high levels of zoom may be achieved with virtually no pixelation occurring, because the points are recalculated at the new zoom level.

You must understand that whatever system is used (bitmapped or vector), the final image you see on a monitor has to be made up of **pixels**, because that's how a monitor actually works.

4 2×3 inches gives us 6 in^2 and at 100 **dpi** (dots per inch) we need $6 \times 100 \times 100$ dots to represent the picture. 8-bit colour means one byte for each dot; therefore we need 60 000 bytes. Now there are 1024 bytes in a Kbyte, **therefore we need 60 000/1024 = 58.5 Kbytes.**

5 **MIDI** is an acronym for the **Musical Instrument Digital Interface**, a coding standard used by the music industry for digital keyboards and other MIDI-equipped musical instruments. It consists of data that describes musical notes, duration, attack (how hard a key on the musical instrument is pressed), etc. together with data about the type of sound that should be made (e.g. a violin or a piano, for example). It's possible to get a computer to control many different musical instruments at the same time by making use of this method.

6 As described in question (5), **MIDI** is data about the composition of the actual music. Sound encoding on a computer is a different system representing how a sound should be made (e.g. music, voice, sound effects, etc.) when played through a conventional sound card, amplifier and speaker system. There are numerous methods of encoding sounds, like Wav or MP3, for example. MIDI data can also be converted into a sound file that may be played through a conventional computer sound system.

7 **MP3** is an **audio compression method** for sending music files across the internet and for playing music on an MP3 player. It's important (and dangerous) for the music industry because it enables users to download music from the internet and to store files in a suitable form for portable players and mobile devices.

8 MP3 is a form of **digital compression** for **audio** (music) and **MPEG 3** is a compression algorithm for **graphics** and **video**. MPEG stands for the Moving Picture Experts Group.

9 An **analogue signal** is one that is continuously variable, and can take on any value between some minimum and some maximum. It should be contrasted with a digital signal, which can only take on discrete values. Many quantities in nature, such as sound, heat and light, for example, are analogue in nature.

10 An **A to D converter** is an **Analogue to Digital** converter (or **ADC**). This is an electronic circuit that converts signals from analogue (continuously variable form) into digital (discrete values) form that can be encoded using binary on a computer system.

11 Three other physical quantities which are analogue in nature are '**light**', '**voltage**' and '**pressure**'.

12 Sound may be encoded into binary by making use of an A to D converter circuit. An A to D converter circuit does this by taking samples of the analogue signals at frequent intervals, and changing the sample amplitude into an appropriate binary number. If the sampling rate is high enough (decided by Nyquist's criteria, which says that the sampling rate must be at least twice as high as the highest frequency component present in the signal being sampled) then high fidelity may be obtained. Because the limit of human hearing for a healthy young person is about 20 kHz, CD-quality sound is sampled at about 44 000 times per second (*about twice as high as the highest frequency a human can hear*).

13 A **Digital to Analogue** (or A to D) **converter**.

14 From using 8 bits we get 256 different levels. Now 5/256 = 0.0195. **Therefore a resolution of about 0.02 is available.**

15 **RGB** stands for Red, Green and Blue, which are the primary additive colours used to build up any other colours by adding light together. It is the system used inside a computer monitor where light from the Red, Green and Blue electron guns illuminate Red, Green and Blue phosphors on screen, enabling you to see the image on the monitor.

CMYK is the system used for colour printing. Cyan, magenta and yellow are the three primary subtractive colours used to produce other colours when the object being viewed reflects light. This is the system used when light reflected from the printer paper is being viewed by an observer. A large range of colours may be made up from a huge collection of dots printed on white paper using the Cyan, Magenta and Yellow inks in the colour cartridges or laser toners.

If cyan, magenta and yellow are used to produce black, in practice we get a dirty brown, which is unacceptable for typed written letters or the colour black in pictures. Therefore, an **extra black** cartridge is used if the colour black is actually needed, and this is called the **Key**. That is why it's called the **CYMK system**.

16 Remembering to use the **two's complement** system, (the 12-bit two's complement system here), we end up with the following patterns for the maximum positive and negative numbers: Maximum positive 011111111111   (Most significant bit must be zero for positive values) Maximum negative 100000000000   (Most significant bit must be one for negative values) From the above binary patterns,

$$011111111111 = 2^{11} - 1 = 2047$$
$$100000000000 = -2^{11} = -2048$$

Therefore, the range of the A to D converter is from −2048 to +2047 (giving a range of 4096) altogether. (Don't forget that 0 is also a value between these two extremes.)

Chapter 3 – Microprocessor fundamentals

1 (a) The **data bus** is a group of wires (usually 8, 16, 32, 64 or 128 bits wide) that carries signals representing the data going into or coming out of the microprocessor system. Typically this would be the route by which data travels from the main memory or peripheral devices connected to the computer system.

(b) The **address bus** is the group of wires that carries signals representing the addresses of memory locations or other devices connected to the computer system. The width of the address bus must be sufficient to address the amount of available RAM. A 32-bit address bus would be able to address 2^{32} or 4 294 967 296 (4 Gbytes) of RAM.

(c) The **control bus** is the group of wires that carries control signals like the read/write signal for the RAM, for example. Here the processor might place a 1 on the appropriate line of the control bus if a read operation is taking place, or might place a 0 on the appropriate line of the control bus if a write operation is taking place.

2 The **microprocessor** family (type of microprocessor) determines the **platform** for a particular computer. Therefore an Intel Pentium is one of several processors that define the PC platform, or the Motorola 68000 series chip and its derivatives define the Apple Mac platform. There are many others for specialist platforms like the high-end Sun workstations or supercomputers, for example.

3 **Primary storage** is the immediately available storage like RAM and ROM. It is usually fast (random) access, but RAM is volatile, which means that the contents of memory are lost when the power is removed from the system. Both ROM and RAM support random access methods. **Secondary storage** is the hard disks, floppy disks or tapes, etc. These are usually slower to access (with tapes being very slow), but data is maintained on these systems when the computer is shut down. Some secondary storage systems, like tape, are serial access only.
Primary storage is used for running the immediate programs, and secondary storage is used for keeping copies of the programs that are loaded into primary storage when they need to be run on the system.

4 **ALU** is an **acronym** for an **Arithmetic Logic Unit**. It consists of the registers and other circuits inside the microprocessor that works out the arithmetical (add, subtract, etc.) and logical (and, or, not, etc.) instructions.

5 **RAM** is needed for very fast access to run the operating system, utilities, applications and other user programs that need to be operated on 'immediately'. However, the computer needs to have a large amount of basic information

regarding the hardware connected to the system (like disks, for example), what processor is present and what speed is the processor to run at, etc. Information like this is needed before the computer can operate at all, and is therefore stored in non-volatile **ROM**. The **BIOS** (Basic Input Output System) is stored in **ROM**, and **settings** for the **BIOS** are stored in **CMOS RAM**. The contents of this RAM are saved from deletion by the CMOS battery on the motherboard. Modern computer systems may have the BIOS stored in a **Flash ROM**, which can be upgraded by the user under special conditions, thus saving the user the trouble of changing chips inside the computer to do a BIOS upgrade.

6 **Machine code** is the **pure binary** that operates inside the microprocessor. Manufacturers like Intel and Motorola, for example make up codes that represent instructions like 'ADD', 'LOAD' and 'ROTATE RIGHT', for example. Each manufacturer invents unique codes for operations like these, and that is why the machine code intended for one microprocessor will not work with any other type. Legacy code from earlier versions is often required to run on the later microprocessor systems.

7 There are several types of '**cache**' or very fast access memory. If very fast RAM (**static RAM**) is used to hold the part of the program being operated on at a particular moment in time, then it speeds up the **fetch-decode-execute cycle** compared to loading the same code from ordinary RAM (**Dynamic RAM**). RAM is very fast, but the memory used by the cache is even faster than this. It is usually much more expensive that 'ordinary RAM', and that's why the entire RAM is not made up from it. However, over the last few years RAM has undergone many transformations, making it even faster.
Many modern microprocessors have '**cache memory**' inside the processor itself. This is even faster than the external cache described in the first part of this question. This is known as on-board cache.

8 Put simply, it is the function of the **control unit** to act as a 'director of operations' under the guidance of the external electronic clock. The **control unit** sets up the paths to steer the data 'from and to' the appropriate places by obeying the program instructions supplied by the programmer of the microprocessor system. Instructions from the computer's memory must be fetched into the microprocessor, decoded and action taken (execution) depending on the nature of the instruction just fetched. This fetch-decode-execute cycle is all that goes on inside a microprocessor chip. It is able to do nothing else other than go through the **fetch-decode-execute cycle**. Even when a computer appears to be doing nothing, unless it is switched off, the microprocessor is still running programs by going through the fetch-decode-execute cycle.

9 The **fetch-decode-execute** cycle is the process of fetching instructions from memory, decoding them to determine what needs to be done and then carrying out the instruction (the execute phase).

10 Von Neumann developed the **stored program concept**. This is the idea that instructions stored in memory are fetched, decoded and then executed in a linear fashion (i.e. one after the other). No matter how fast a computer appears to be, or how many trillions of instructions it might be able to accomplish in a single second, it is still only executing instructions making use of the principles of the stored program concept developed so long ago.

11 Four different ways of connecting peripheral devices include **USB** (**universal serial bus**), **PS/2** (for some **mice** and **keyboards**), **serial interface** (for some **PDAs** and **modems**) and **parallel interface** (for some **printers**).

12 The function of the **motherboard** is to house and connect components like the microprocessor, memory, graphics and sound cards together. It also enables peripheral devices to be connected to the system.

13 Three different types of machine code instruction are **arithmetical** (ADD, SUB, etc.), **logical** (Shift Left, Shift Right, etc) and **Boolean** (AND, OR, etc.)

14 Research question.

Chapter 4 – Fundamental ideas about software

1 **Hardware** is the equipment that makes up the computer. It consists of the printers, screen, keyboards, base unit (system unit), etc. Indeed, a good description is 'anything you can physically touch is hardware'.
Software is a program like machine code, assembly language or a high-level language used to control the computer. It's the ideas that are important here, and software is an expression of these ideas. You can't touch software! If, for example, you hold a floppy disk in your hand, you are holding hardware, because you can touch it. If you print out a program (software) onto a piece of paper you are holding a piece of hardware (i.e. a piece of paper with ink placed onto it), but the ideas conveyed by what you are holding is the software.
In a nutshell, **software** is the set of program instructions, or the code that makes up the programs.

2 Ten different items of hardware are '**keyboard**', '**printer**', '**mouse**', '**motherboard**', '**graphics card**', '**sound card**', '**monitor**', '**graphics tablet**', '**USB hub**' and '**modem**'. Ten different items of software are '**word processors**', '**spreadsheets**', '**databases**', '**presentation packages**', '**CAD programs**', '**art programs**', '**operating systems**', '**e-mail packages**', '**desktop publishing systems**' and '**internet browsers**'.

3 **General-purpose software** is software like 'word processors', 'spreadsheets' and 'databases', for example.
Bespoke software is specially written software that satisfies a very specific need. An example might be software written to control the tills at a local supermarket, or a program written to help manage the interface enabling a severely disabled person to communicate with the outside world.
Systems software usually relates to the operations of the computer system. The operating system (like Windows XP or Millennium, for example) is an example of systems software. Third parties might also write special utilities (like disk defragmenters, etc.), which is also an example of systems software.

4 **Applications software** are programs that are designed to help with a specific tasks. These might be word processing, e-mail or running a presentation for a lecture.

Systems software is usually the vast collection of programs that make up the operating system or are related to it. Norton Utilities, from the Symantec Corporation, is a good example of third party system software, designed to repair disks, undelete files or create sophisticated recovery procedures in the event of a system emergency like a fault with Windows not loading, for example. It is to do with the management of the computer systems.

5 The **ROM BIOS** is the Read-Only-Memory Basic-Input-Output-System. This is usually a chip housed on the motherboard of the computer containing essential data that enables the hardware of the computer to interface with the operating system software. It uses user-configurable data (via the **CMOS RAM**) to manage all of the devices connected to the computer. Without this interface you would need a different operating system version for each motherboard! The **ROM BIOS** holds information needed by the computer to enable it to boot up properly at switch on. It also holds routines that test the hardware to make sure it's O.K. before the main operating system is loaded from disk. Without the BIOS the machine would not know that it had any disks connected to it!

6 Three things might include '**creating many new users on a network**', '**applying sets of unique file permissions (read/write/execute etc.) for individual users on a large file server**' or '**assigning users randomly generated passwords on a network system**'. All these operations could be carried out in a GUI environment, but it would be tedious in the extreme and very slow indeed to carry out these operations with Windows compared to using DOS, for example.

7 Three things might include '**double-clicking a mouse to run a program**', '**copying a large number of files from one directory to another**' or '**identifying different file types from a large number of others**'. All theses things could be done from the command line, but special syntax has to be learnt.

8 **High-level languages** are nearer to the way that humans think and **low-level languages** are nearer to the way in which machines operate. High-level languages are 'English like' and low-level languages are oriented towards assembly language mnemonics or pure binary.

9 Two examples are '**assembly language**' and '**machine code**'.

10 A **first-generation language** is the name given to machine code because it was the first type of language to be used to program computers.

11 A **third-generation language** is an imperative high-level language. An example is **BASIC**, or Beginner's All-purpose Symbolic Instruction Code.

12 An **imperative language** is one that typifies giving the computer a set of instructions called imperatives. When an **imperative language** is used it is up to the user to create the **algorithms** which tell the computer what to do.

13 FORTRAN – an acronym for **FORmula TRANslation**. It is used extensively for scientific and engineering applications. It has extensive mathematical processing and is often used to program applications like forecasting the weather on a supercomputer.
COBOL – An acronym for **COmmon Business Oriented Language**. It is used extensively in the data processing industry like commercial organisations and banking. It has extensive data processing and file handling capabilities.
PROLOG – An acronym for **PROgramming in LOGic**. It is a fifth-generation high-level language used extensively for **AI (Artificial Intelligence)** programming. It is often used to build inference engines in knowledge-based systems for use in Expert Systems.
VISUAL BASIC – Microsoft's version of **BASIC** in a visual (Windows) programming environment. It enables beginners and experts alike to develop general-purpose Windows programs that would be extremely difficult to do without the aid of the VB front end. Many sets of default values are set up so that users need not be too concerned at the beginning about how their multi-tasking programs will look on the desktop.

14 Three different utilities could include '**disk formatters**', '**disk defragmenters**' or '**tape backup systems**', for example.

15 A **compiler** compiles (turns the high-level language into machine code) the high-level language in one go, producing the object code (machine code) that will run on the target machine. This is ideal for maximum speed of execution and for distribution of the object code without your users being aware of the original

source code (*the original program written in the high-level language*). The resultant machine code may be run on the target machine without the need for a compiler.

An **interpreter** interprets (turns the high-level language in machine code) just one line at a time. If we go 10 000 times through a loop then the same code inside the loop is checked for errors and changed into machine code 10 000 times! This is ideal for debugging programs in a simple environment because errors may be corrected instantly without having to re-compile the entire program. To run the program on the target machine it must be reinterpreted, and this is slower than compilation. Also, the user will need to have access to an appropriate interpreter to change the high-level code into machine code.

16 An **interpreter** is easier to use than a **compiler** because you do not have to go through the complex compilation stages before getting feedback about what might be wrong with the syntax of your program. There is therefore a lot less to learn for the novice user.

17 A **library program** is a program within a suite of programs that may be called up by the operating system or by application or utility programs. Typically manufacturers will distribute libraries of routines (like the dynamic link libraries on the PC) or the C++ libraries, for example.

18 **Library programs** can typically do anything that programmers might care to dream up, but two typical things that might be accomplished by a library program are getting characters from the keyboard or printing information to the printer.

19 The **operating system** is the odd one out because it is software, the rest of the items in the list are hardware.

20 Delphi is a **high-level language**; therefore a **compiler** would be used. An assembler translates assembly language into machine code.

21 Three functions that are carried out by compilers include 'checking the syntax', 'producing a list of errors' and 'linking to any libraries'.

Chapter 5 – Programming fundamentals 1

1 An **identifier** is a **label** given to a string of characters that represents things like 'variables'

and 'constants' and 'procedure names', etc.

A **constant** is a value that can't vary during the execution of a program.

A **variable** is a value that can vary during the execution of a program. The range of values it can take on depends on the programming language.

2 **Pseudocode** is a set of statements that closely resembles the semantics of a high-level language. The syntax does not make any difference, but common key words like 'FOR TO NEXT' or 'DEFINE PROCEDURE', etc. are used to make the meaning of the algorithm clear.

3 **Syntax** is the rules governing the language. Examples would be how key words are spelt, or the structure used for a particular loop or procedure.

Semantics is the meaning given to a program, as opposed to the syntax rules which it must obey. Therefore, a set of program statements should convey a particular meaning (i.e. achieve a well defined set of unambiguous objectives) to the programmer.

A **statement** in a high-level language is a descriptive phrase that is compiled or interpreted into one or more machine code instructions.

4 This answer depends on the language. A typical answer for **Microsoft's Visual Basic 5.0** is as follows:

Data type	Range
Byte	0 to 255
Decimal	−79 228 162 514 264 337 543 950 335 to +79 228 162 514 264 337 543 950 335
Integer	−32 768 to +32 767
Long	−2 147 483 648 to +2 147 483 647
Single	-3.402823×10^{38} to $-1.401298 \times 10^{-45}$
Double	$-1.79769313486232 \times 10^{308}$ to $-4.9465645821247 \times 10^{-324}$ for negative: $+4.9465645821247 \times 10^{-324}$ to $+1.79769313486232 \times 10^{308}$ for positive.
Currency	−922 337 203 685 477.5808 to +922 337 203 685 477.5807

5 The following assumes a BASIC-like language.
```
r= 20 * x^2 + 10 * x - 1
a = (1/2) + (1/4) + (1/8)
b = (-6/(k + 1)) + t
y = (a^2 + b * c)^0.333
```

6 (a)
```
Total = 0
  For count = 1 TO 100
    Total = Total + count*count
  Next count
  Print Total
```
(b)
```
Total = 1000
  For count = 100 to 1 Step -1
    Total = Total - count*count
  Next count
  Print Total
```
(c)
```
For count = 100 to 1 Step -1
    Total = Total + SQR(count)
  Next count
  Print Total
```

7 A **dry run** means manually working through an algorithm or program to see if it functions as expected. The value of variables and any input and output should also be noted. A dry run is used to manually test the logic of a program.

Variables	a	b	counter	Printed
Initial conditions	1	3	10	–
1st loop	4	3	12	3
2nd loop	7	3	14	7
3rd loop	10	3	16	10
4th loop	13	3	16	13
5th loop	16	3	18	16
6th loop	19	3	20	19
7th loop	22	3	22	22

By observation, 22 is the final number to be printed.

8 A '**Repeat Until**' loop is always executed at least once, irrespective or whether the condition is true or false, because the condition to terminate the loop is not tested until the end of the loop. A '**Do While**' loop may never be executed because the condition to terminate the loop is tested before entry into the loop.

9 There is always a **one-to-one relationship** between a **high-level language** and the **machine code** into which it gets translated. This is how interpreters and compilers work.

Chapter 6 – Programming fundamentals 2

1 A **Boolean decision** is a decision based on '**true**' or '**false**' conditions, e.g. IF count = 6 THEN END.

2 A **function** may be called up by **name**, and **parameters** passed over to it. Only a **single parameter** may be returned from a function. A typical example of a function might be a **random number generator**. X = RND (10) might return a random number in the range 0 to 10 inclusive. The function is **called** by the name **RND**, the **parameter** passed over to it is **10**, in this case indicating the range. The parameter passed back from the function is the **value** of the **variable X**. A **procedure**, unlike a **function** may have many parameters passed back to the calling routine. Many parameters may also be passed over to the procedure.

3
```
If level >30 Then
   If level >80 Then
     Print "The water level is
dangerously high"
     If level >90 Then
       Print "The tank has exploded!"
     End if
   Else
     Print "Water level is
satisfactory"
   End if
Else
   Print "The water level is
dangerously low"
End if
```
The above may typically be carried out by using a CASE statement as follows:
```
Test = level div 10
case test of
0,1,2:Print "The water level is
dangerously low"
3,4,5,6,7:Print "Water level is
satisfactory"
8 : Print "The water level is
dangerously high"
9,10 : Print "The water level is
dangerously high"
        Print "The tank has exploded"
End case
```

4 Intrinsic functions are built-in functions, and user-defined functions are made up by the programmer.
An example of an intrinsic function is x = sqr(20). Here the parameter passed over to the function is 20, and the square root of 20 is returned as the value of x.
An example of a user defined function to work out the area of a circle given the radius is as

follows. It consists of two parts, the function definition and the function call.

```
Rem this is the function call
X = Area (5)
```

(*Here the parameter 5 is passed over to the function.*)

```
Rem this is the function definition
Function Area (r as real)
   Area = 3.142 x r*r
End function
```

5 If **data** is passed '**by value**' then this means that only the value of the data is passed over and the variable representing the data outside of the procedure does not get altered. If **data** is passed '**by reference**', then the original variable gets referenced and the original variable has its value changed by the procedure.

You typically use 'by value' if you don't want to mess up any other variable with the same name in the program, or use 'by reference' if you want the value of a variable to change.

6 **Procedures** help to **modularise programs** by splitting them up into definable modules. This makes the program easier to understand. **Procedures** also save us writing the same (or similar) code over and over again. The code can be called by name, having the same effect as executing the code without using a procedure.

7 **Comments**, good **program structure** and **meaningful variable names** are essential for program readability and therefore for good program maintenance. Without these things it would be more difficult for you or somebody else to understand what's going on. Without them it would be hard to modify the program at a later date.

8 The code in this question assumes a co-ordinate system of (1024 × 768). The code is written in Microsoft's Visual Basic 6.0.

(a) 50 Horizontal red lines

```
Private Sub Form_Load()
   ScaleMode = vbPixels
   Rem QBColor(12) is Red
   For y = 1 To 768 Step 768 / 50
      Line (0, y)-(1000, y),
QBColor(12)
   Next y
End Sub
```

(b) Screen covered with vertical and horizontal green lines (*similar to a piece of graph paper*).

```
Private Sub Form_Load()
   ScaleMode = vbPixels
   Rem QBColor(2) is Green
   For y = 0 To 768 Step 10
      Line (0, y)-(1024, y),
QBColor(2)
   Next y
   For x = 0 To 1024 Step 10
      Line (x, 0)-(x, 768),
QBColor(2)
   Next x
End Sub
```

(c) 45 degree diagonal lines

```
Private Sub Form_Load()
   ScaleMode = vbPixels
   Rem QBColor(2) is Red
   For y =-1024 To 1024 Step 10
      Line (0, y)-(1024, 1024 + y),
QBColor(2)
   Next y
End Sub
```

9 (a) This code is for the first quadrant

```
Private Sub Form_Load()
   ScaleMode = vbPixels
   For y = 0 To 350 Step 10
      Line (500, y)-(500 + y, 350)
   Next y
End Sub
```

(b) This is the code for the second quadrant

```
Private Sub Form_Load()
   ScaleMode = vbPixels
   For y = 0 To 350 Step 10
         Line (500, 350 + y)-(850-
y, 350)
   Next y
End Sub
```

(c) The full code for the entire shape

```
Private Sub Form_Load()
   ScaleMode = vbPixels
   For x = 0 To 350 Step 10
      Line (150 + x, 350)-(500, 350 - x)
   Next x
   For y = 0 To 350 Step 10
      Line (500, y)-(500 + y, 350)
   Next y
   For x = 0 To 350 Step 10
      Line (150 + x, 350)-(500, 350 + x)
   Next x
   For y = 0 To 350 Step 10
      Line (500, 350 + y)-(850 - y, 350)
   Next y
End Sub
```

(d) The following code draws the patterns shown here.

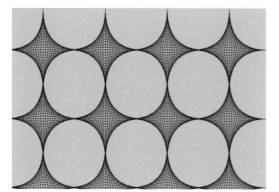

```
Private Sub Form_Load()
  ScaleMode = vbPixels
  For x_pos = 125 To 875 Step 250
    For y_pos = 150 To 900 Step 250
      Call DrawShape(150, x_pos,
y_pos)
    Next y_pos
  Next x_pos
End Sub

Sub DrawShape(Size, x_centre,
y_centre)
Rem - 2nd quadrant
For x = (x_centre - Size) To x_centre Step 10
  Line (x, y_centre)-(x_centre,
y_centre + (x_centre - Size) - x)
Next x

Rem - 3rd quadrant (Mirror of y
ordinates from 2nd quadrant)
For x = (x_centre - Size) To x_centre Step 10
  Line (x, y_centre)-(x_centre,
y_centre - (x_centre - Size) + x)
Next x

Rem - 1st quadrant
  For x = x_centre + Size To x_centre Step
-10
    Line (x, y_centre)-(x_centre,
y_centre - (x_centre + Size) + x)
Next x

Rem - 4th quadrant (Mirror of y
ordinates from the 1st quadrant
For x = x_centre + Size To x_centre Step -10
  Line (x, y_centre)-(x_centre,
y_centre + (x_centre + Size) - x)
Next x
End Sub
```

Chapter 7 – Programming fundamentals 3

1 A **data type** is a category of data like 'string', 'numeric' or 'Boolean'. A **string** is a data type that may take on any alphanumeric value. Strings may be split up or joined, but you can't do arithmetic with numbers held in a string data type.

2 The following code makes use of Microsoft's Visual Basic 6.0, but is similar in principle to many other high level languages.

(a) The code to extract the word 'mat' is
```
Private Sub Form_Load()
  Test$ = "The cat sat on the mat"
  a$ = Right$(Test$, 3)
  Print a$
End Sub
```

(b) The code to extract the word 'cat' is
```
Private Sub Form_Load()
  Test$ = "The cat sat on the mat"
  b$ = Mid$(Test$, 5, 3)
  Print b$
End Sub
```

(c) The code to replace the word 'cat' with 'dog' is
```
Private Sub Form_Load()
  Test$ = "The cat sat on the mat"
  beginning_of_string$ =
Left$(Test$, 4)
  end_of_String$ = Right$(Test$,
15)
  new_word$ = "dog"
  Final$ = beginning_of_string$ +
new_word$ + end_of_String$
    Print Final$
End Sub
```

(d) The code for the 'animal input' is
```
Private Sub Form_Load()
  Test$ = "The cat sat on the mat"
  beginning_of_string$ =
Left$(Test$, 4)
  end_of_String$ = Right$(Test$,
15)
  new_word$ = InputBox$("Please
type the name of an animal")
  Final$ = beginning_of_string$ +
new_word$ + end_of_String$
  Print Final$
End Sub
```

3 The code to reverse the words in a string is as follows.

```
Private Sub Form_Load()
  Target$ = InputBox$("Please type in
the text you wish to see reversed")
  End_of_word = Len(Target$)
  Beginning_of_word = Len(Target$)
  For x = Len(Target$) To 1 Step -1
    Test$ = Mid(Target$, x, 1)
    If Test$ = " "Then
      Beginning_of_word = x + 1
      Final$ = Final$ + Mid(Target$,
Beginning_of_word, End_of_word -
Beginning_of_word + 1) + " "
      End_of_word = Beginning_of_word
- 1
    End If
  Next x
  Print Final$ + Left(Target$, End_of_word)
End Sub
```

4 The code to translate the Umbonganeese language into English is as follows.

```
Private Sub Form_Load()
Dim English_word As String
Target$ = InputBox$("Please type your
Umbonganeese sentence")
Rem force a space at the end so that
the routine will work for the last
word also.
Target$ = Target$ + " "
  end_of_word = 1
  beginning_of_word = 1
  For x = 1 To Len(Target$)
    Test$ = Mid(Target$, x, 1)
    If Test$ = " "Then
      end_of_word = x
      Umbongan_word$ = Mid(Target$,
beginning_of_word, end_of_word -
beginning_of_word)
    If Umbongan_word$ = "toodle" Then
English_word$ = "have"
    If Umbongan_word$ = "mushi" Then
English_word$ = "I"
    If Umbongan_word$ = "umshi" Then
English_word$ = "mouth"
    If Umbongan_word$ = "targ" Then
English_word$ = "nose"
    If Umbongan_word$ = "urk" Then
English_word$ = "a"
    If Umbongan_word$ = "goop" Then
English_word$ = "big"
    If Umbongan_word$ = "jally" Then
English_word$ = "don"t"
```

```
    If Umbongan_word$ = "oojip" Then
English_word$ = "do"
      Phrase$ = Phrase$ + English_word$
+ " "
        beginning_of_word = x + 1
    End If
  Next x
Print Phrase$
End Sub
```

Answers to questions (5) to (7) *have not been given*. They are too large to be included here, and are more appropriate for mini projects lasting a number of hours. The graphical interface in question (7) could take many hours, depending on the level of sophistication you choose.

8 There are no right or wrong answers to this question. Here are some typical examples of suitable responses.

(a) The parts that make up a car

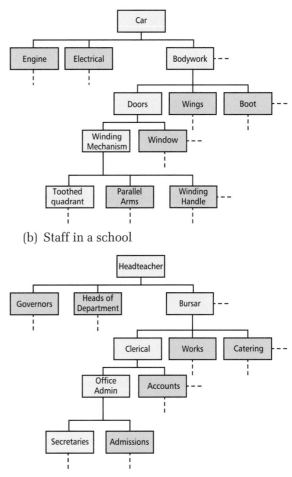

(b) Staff in a school

(c) Food and drink needed at a dinner party

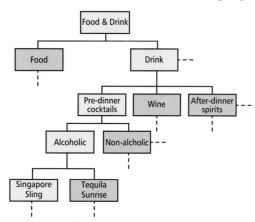

(d) Things to take on holiday

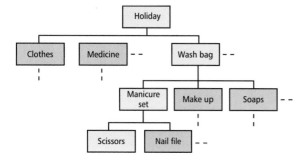

Chapter 8 – Communication basics

1 **Serial communications** make use of a single wire or communication channel such as a radio link. Information is sent one bit after another in a serial fashion. The data has to be sent at the appropriate rate, or it will be misinterpreted at the receiving end.

   Parallel communications make use of multiple wires or links, where several bits of information can be sent simultaneously. This usually happens under the control of a clock. It is not economic to have parallel communication over long distances, because of the number of wires or separate communication channels needed.

   Methods ideal for **serial communication** are **networks** and **modems**.

   Methods ideal for **parallel communication** are **bus systems** inside the **computers and local printers**.

2 **Synchronous communication** methods are under the control of a **clock**. The motherboard, which houses the processor and other interfaces to peripherals, is a good example of synchronous communication methods, as most of the devices on the motherboard are synchronised by the electronic clock.

Asynchronous communication methods depict those in which it is not possible to synchronise the transmitting and receiving end of the communications link. The only way to ensure that the data is interpreted correctly is to send it at an appropriate rate, together with start and stop signals that synchronise the receiving electronics. If you know where the signal starts, you can use a local clock to clock the data in at the appropriate rate.

3 **Modulation** means changing some aspect of the signal so that information may be detected or sent. Three typical methods used to modulate a signal are '**amplitude modulation**', '**frequency modulation**' or '**phase modulation**'.

4 The original telephone line was designed for transmission of **speech**, and used a **bandwidth** of just a few KHz. However, this assumes that signals (speech in this case) are sent in a raw form, which is not very efficient for modern communication methods. By using very clever modulation techniques, it's possible to send computer data in a variety of forms, which pack the data in ways that make very efficient use of the limited bandwidth. **Quadrature Amplitude Modulation** is a good example of one of the methods used on V90 modems.

5 Bit **rate** is the number of bits/sec that can be transmitted. **Baud rate** is the number of 'signal transitions/sec'. The actual information transmitted can be less than the number of bits/sec because of the **overheads** transmitted along with the signal like '**parity checking**' or '**CRC checks**', etc.

6 **Parity** is a method of sending extra bits along with the original data for the purpose of checking. Two methods, called **odd** and **even parity** exist, and are based on the assumption that an odd or even number of ones are always sent in each byte. Consider the following message, making use of the lower 7-bit ASCII codes.

	ASCII code (Using 7 bits of a possible 8 for each byte)						
	128	64	32	16	8	4	2	1
	7	6	5	4	3	2	1	0
B	0	1	0	0	0	0	1	0
A	0	1	0	0	0	0	0	1
S	0	1	0	1	0	0	1	1
I	0	1	0	0	1	0	0	1
C	0	1	0	0	0	0	1	1

Notice that bit 7 is not used, and thus this can be used for the parity bit. If we make use of even parity, this means that there should be an even number of 1s for each letter sent. Now 'B' has two 1s (an even number) and so has 'A' and 'S'. However, 'I' and 'C' have an odd number of ones, and therefore an extra 1 using bit 7 is added to make them both even. This is because 'even parity' is being used for this particular example. The new table now looks like the following.

	ASCII code (Using 7 bits of a possible 8 for each byte)							
	128	64	32	16	8	4	2	1
	7	6	5	4	3	2	1	0
B	0	1	0	0	0	0	1	0
A	0	1	0	0	0	0	0	1
S	0	1	0	1	0	0	1	1
I	1	1	0	0	1	0	0	1
C	1	1	0	0	0	0	1	1

When the data is received, the electronics can check to see if even numbers of 1s are present for each byte. If it is, then the data is assumed to be correct. If it's not, then an error has been detected.

Parity is useful for communication over short distances, or for checking the memory inside a computer, for example. However, it's found wanting when it comes to transmission of large amounts of data over long distances. Here the errors that occur usually corrupt many bits (or bytes) of data, rendering both odd and even parity methods (which is useful for single bit corruption) useless. More sophisticated checking mechanisms are used in modern communication systems.

7   In the early days of computing there were no **communication standards** at all, and people with data on one computer system could rarely share it with others who had a different computer system. As the need to share data between different systems developed, so did the development of standard method. The various types of **modems** and **Ethernet networks** are good examples of his. However, as technology advances, new methods of communications, making better use of bandwidth and pushing the speed of communications ever faster have been developed. Thus **new communications protocols**

are needed as the **new technologies** come on line. This obviously causes problems, but little progress could be made if we do not continue to develop these new methodologies.

8   A **modem** is used for **modulation** of a signal to be transmitted over and telephone line and for **demodulation** of the signal received from the telephone line. A standard telephone link was designed for low-bandwidth analogue speech. Computers use digital signals to communicate, and the digital information must be converted into analogue form for transmission over the link. The modem does this by encoding the signals into appropriate forms.

9   An **ADSL line** is a **digital communication** link and an **analogue modem** would therefore not work with these signals. Another reason is that the analogue modem would not be able to cope with the **speeds** necessary to link to an ADSL line. It is a completely different technology.

10   A typical analogue modem is 56 kbits/sec. However, in practice, little more than 33 Kbits/sec in achievable. A typical ADSL line is 500 Kbits/sec. On a good day the speed is therefore about 15 times that of an analogue modem.

Chapter 9 – Networking basics

1   A **network** is a means of connecting computers together so that they can share information and other resources. Typically, a network will consist of the connections, network interface cards, a network operating system, file servers and many other items.

2   (a)   At least **26 PCs** will be needed, consisting of 25 workstations and 1 server. One or two other PCs might be needed for connection to the internet or for other resources.
     (b)   A **tree network topology** making use of **Ethernet hubs** would be most suitable for this configuration.
     (c)   A suitable network bandwidth will be 100 Mbit/sec. This is perfectly adequate for such a small number of machines and is currently the most cost-effective option for a school.
     (d)   The **printers** may be attached to a couple of workstations and shared. These **shared printers** would be installed on all the other

workstations, thus giving the option of any student printing to them. A disadvantage of this system is that the computers to which the printers are attached would have to be switched on. A better solution would be to set up **network printers** on the **file server**. These are special printers with Ethernet connections. This would also relieve the two workstations of the added task of background printing.

(e) The pupils' work should be stored on the **file server** at the end of each day.

(f) A suitable structure would be **hierarchical**, based on the year in which the student joined. However, other systems like class or house might be suitable. The year is usually best because it will not change. A typical user name would be **surname** followed by **initials**. If two students have identical names and initials then a number can be added on the end. Another alternative user name would be a **unique** user ID.

3 **Network topology** covers the physical connections of the computers. Typical examples might be **ring**, **tree** or **star**. It's important to consider the topology for several reasons, including effective utilisation of network bandwidth and security.

4 A **LAN** is a **local area network**, usually set up within an organisation, and covering just a few kilometres. A **WAN** is a **wide area network** and usually stretches over a much larger distance, and makes use of the public communications systems. A LAN would be useful in setting up a computer network for a school or office. A WAN is typical of offices in different cities connecting together, perhaps making use of the internet, which is the largest example of a WAN.

5 A **proxy server** is a **file server** set up with an **internet** connection. Typically the proxy server will deal with all the requests from the users on the LAN and pass them over to the internet connection. When information is received via the internet, the proxy server will route the information to the appropriate client on the LAN. Only one internet connection is being used, but hundreds of people may surf the net via this means.

A typical connection speed for 25 users in a classroom would be a standard **500 Mbit/sec**

ADSL link with a low **contention ratio**. (Preferably no other people should be sharing the line.)

6 The **internet** is the worldwide network of networks, i.e. the physical connections and the computers, etc. connected to it. The **World Wide Web** is the name given to the resources on the internet, which typically refer to the information available via http and other systems.

7 Five different protocols used on the internet are as follows:

(i) **http** – **hypertext transfer protocol** – used to access file servers on the internet.

(ii) **https** – The **secure version** of the **http** protocol – this means that the information is encrypted.

(iii) **ftp** – **file transfer protocol** – used to transfer large files of any type over the internet.

(iv) **smtp** – **simple mail transfer protocol** – the main protocol used for e-mail on the internet.

(v) **pptp** – **point to point tunnelling protocol** – used for virtual private networks.

8 The **domain name system** is used for organising information on the **World Wide Web**. **Domain name** servers contain databases consisting of the domain names and **IP addresses** which are needed to route information to and from the right places. Top level domains like '.com', '.co.uk' and '.org' define the start, and are prefixed by the names of companies or individuals to build up a **URL** or uniform resource locator, which details the exact computer (web server) from which a resource may be found.

9 A **URL** is a **uniform resource locator**. It defines exactly what resource is to be loaded from the file server on the internet. A typical example is

http://www.revisecomputing.com/project_work/ project_johnson/post_quick_intro.pdf

Here the **protocol** being used is **http**. The **top level domain** is '.com' and the **web site** is **revisecomputing.com**. The directory path is **project_work/project_johnson/** and this indicates that the resource is in the 'project_work' directory, and a subdirectory called 'project_johnson'.

Finally, the resource to be loaded is a pdf file called '**post_quick_intro.pdf**'.

This is the URL needed to load Ben Johnson's AS project from the author's revisecomputing website.

10 When a **domain name** like 'revisecomputing.com' is resolved into an **IP address** (a number made up from 4 sets of digits like **217.44.141.94**), a search is made on a database, which hopefully resolves the name into the numbers which enable the routing to be accomplished. Special **domain name servers** hold this information, but ISPs may also hold their own databases to speed up the process. If a name can't be resolved, a request is made from one of the **definitive** **domain name servers** which hold the main database, (e.g. the main database for '.com'). If the name still can't be resolved it does not exist, or a brand new name has not been registered yet.

11 **Internal mail** can be accessed by using a **file server** set up as a **mail server**. If the mail server has a connection to the internet, then external mail can be dealt with in this way.

12 The term **internet** refers to the **network of networks** which hosts the information on the World Wide Web. An **intranet** refers to an **internal system**, with facilities similar to the internet, but set up on a LAN environment. An **extranet** is the name given to accessing private material from an intranet via the internet, possibly by using a VPN.

13 The security set up on a VPN is usually achieved by using **user names**, **passwords** and **encryption**.

14 The extra hardware needed would be a computer or **file server** set up as a **web server**.

15 Four different file servers set up on a LAN could be as follows:
    (i)   A **file server** set up to store peoples' work
    (ii) A **proxy server** set up to enable internet access
    (iii) A **web server** set up to enable an intranet to be set up
    (iv) A **mail server** set up to deal with internal and external mail.

Chapter 10 – Applications and effects

1 The **information requirements** of a system are basically what the system has to do in terms of the inputs required and the outputs needed. From the information requirements of the system it's possible to design a system specifications cost for processing the information.

The **communication requirements** of a system deal specifically with how information between the users and the computer is communicated. Typically this would concentrate on which types of computer interface would be ideal for a particular application.

2 (a) Five different information requirements of the attendance module might be 'date of attendance', 'student name', 'flags set for lateness, 'student address' and 'parent's name'. These would be useful for correlation of statistics and sending letters home.

   (b) Five possible different communication requirements of the attendance module could be 'an interface for the office secretary', 'an interface for students or parents to view statistics via the net', 'an interface to produce an attendance report', 'an interface to generate lateness statistics for the head teacher' or 'an interface to analyse statistics such that letters may be automatically sent home'.

   (c) The flags set up in the attendance module could be used to automatically trigger the conditions to produce reports (e.g. absent for more than three times without a suitable excuse). The database could automatically print out reports (individual letters to the parents) which could then be presented to the headteacher or head of year to sign and send home.

   (d) A teacher's view of the attendance module might require that they can only view statistics for pupils they teach; a head of house might only be able to view pupils within their house but more senior staff may be able to view all pupils. A governors' view might not include the names of the individual pupils, but present the entire statistics regarding absence and lateness.

3 (a) A computerised timetable could help to achieve a 'balanced curriculum' by monitoring unacceptable combinations of subjects and bringing this to the attention of the teacher or pupil trying to enter the data into the system.

   (b) A student is unlikely to be allowed to drop maths and English, and may not be allowed to do too many foreign languages if this means dropping history or geography, for example. The information requirements (particular restrictions imposed) would need to be programmed by the person in charge of the curriculum at the school.

(c) If a student is filling in a form via the internet, then the system used (active server pages, for example) would need to monitor information being entered before being saved to the database. Validation would thus be taking place before information is saved. Help messages would need to pop up so that the user is aware of the reasons why the system is not accepting the data.

4 (a) The style and information contained in the end-of-term reporting system will need to vary for a particular target audience. Reports to parents, for example, would need to be more formal than reports to pupils. A private communication between teachers might contain information that it would be best if the pupil did not see. Also, communication between teachers might contain information that should not be viewed by the parents.

   (b) The 'senior management' and 'governors' have different views of the system because they are observing it from a macroscopic view. In this case statistics about certain groups of pupils or teachers are more appropriate than detailed information about any one pupil. Don't forget that the senior management team can also have access to the detail if the system has been programmed for them to do so.

5 (a) Five possible information requirements for the medical practice could be 'the patient's name and address', 'the patient's doctor', 'important medical history', 'appointments history' and 'previous medication'.

   (b) (i) It will be necessary to ensure that the prescriptions are printed in a form suitable for acceptance by local and other pharmacies. The doctor's signature could be a problem, and a computer-based signature might not be acceptable.

       (ii) A drug database could be consulted to check the prescriptions (type of drugs and dosage, etc.) against known and sensible limits. This could help any mistakes made by a doctor to be rectified before the prescription is printed out.

   (c) Two **social considerations** are 'Can the reception staff use the technology?' and 'Will the system cause problems due to the perceived lack of the human touch?'
   Two **moral considerations** are 'Is the security tight enough to prevent unauthorised people breaking into the system?' and 'Is the cost of the system justified in relation to what could have been spent elsewhere on patient care?'
   Two **ethical considerations** are 'Do the requirements of the system comply with the current data protection act?' and 'Are any of the systems open to misuse by the doctors or the reception staff?' (e.g. could the reception staff produce prescriptions for drugs without the knowledge of a doctor, for example).

6 (a) Five different modules for the police system could be as follows:
   (i)   A **link to a national crime database**. (This module could enable searches to be made for known criminals working in other areas.)
   (ii) A **fingerprint and/or dna module**. (This could enable identifying information to be entered into the database and correlated with other information.)
   (iii) A **statistics module**. (This could be used to provide statistics for the chief constable or the government.)
   (iv) A **current information module**. (This could be set up to act like a notice board providing topical information in a variety of categories.)
   (v)   A **criminal profile database**. (This could be used to enable police to enter information in an appropriate form to build up a profile of a criminal.)

   (b) Two typical **information requirements** (inputs and outputs, etc.) for each of the modules listed above could be as follows:
   (i)   Appropriate **passwords** to be entered with a sensible degree of complexity (e.g. 10 character minimum including numeric and punctuation). **User names** and **user** IDs need to be entered into the system.
   (ii) Possible fingerprint sources include **actual fingers** or existing prints on a **card**. It should be possible to get print information from a **computer** too.

(iii) Local crime **statistics** to be entered by **categories**. Print out of statistics in a variety of forms including **graphical**.

(iv) Local **social events**, **conferences**, etc. It's possible to include **training information**.

(v) Criminal **types** (e.g. serial killer!). **Similar crimes** to others that have been committed either locally or nationally.

(c) Two typical **communication requirements** (interface needs) for each of the modules listed above could be as follows:

(i) **Password protection** and authentication based on rank and other privileges. A huge variety of **pre-prepared and customised search criteria** needs to be available.

(ii) A system enabling **finger prints** to be **automatically entered** into the system. A system which will enable old **fingerprints** contained on **conventional cards** to be scanned into the new system.

(iii) An **automatic print out** of local crime statistics based on many different criteria like burglaries or traffic offences, etc. A system could be set up to **correlate local crime statistics** with national figures to determine the effectiveness of a local force.

(iv) A system can be set up to enable police to **post information** in a form that can be viewed easily by the local and other forces. A system of **filtering** needs to be set up so that police are not swamped with a mass of irrelevant detail.

(v) A system of **entering profile information** in the appropriate form needs to be established. A system of **extracting information** based on **known profiles** and filtering the results on various criteria could be established.

(d) Two **legal considerations** are as follows: The data protection act much be adhered to, and this has implications for the use of the database. The database must also be secure, and the system needs to be set up so that hackers can't access sensitive data. There will be a variety of European legislation with which the database must comply.

Two **social considerations** will be the training of the staff needed to operate the system and the possible consequences for less administrative staff being needed in the force.

Two **ethical problems** might be police misusing the system by passing on sensitive information about crimes to unauthorised personnel (e.g. leaking of crime statistics to the press) and police or administrative staff leaving a workstation logged on, unlocked and unattended so that unauthorised personnel could observe or alter the data in the database.

Chapter 11 – General purpose packages

1 (a) Typical things that a **database** can do are 'create record cards', 'validate data entry', 'manually sequence through a series of records', 'create related tables', 'produce reports based on queries', 'select a subset of records based on a query', 'provide different users with different views of the data', 'provide security access to the data via password protection', 'allow access to the data via different programming languages', 'sort data into order on using many subsets', 'export data to other databases and the web' and 'import data from other packages'.

(b) Typical things that a **word processor** can do are 'formatting text', 'check the spelling in a variety of languages', 'layout a document using multiple columns', 'insert mathematical equations', 'create mail merge lists', 'cut and paste large sections of text, complete with formatting', 'view a document in a variety of sizes and formats', 'find text, or find and replace text in a document', 'perform a word count', 'insert tables', 'insert pictures into the document', 'paste the formatting of one part of the document onto another', 'provide templates for styles and layouts'.

(c) Typical things that a **spreadsheet** can do are 'add up columns of numbers', 'relate cells either by absolute or relative references', 'carry out complex "what if" scenarios', 'produce graphs from the data', 'sort data into alphabetical or numeric order', 'perform goal seeking analysis', 'link multiple worksheets for working in different dimensions', 'hot link data with other applications like word processors', 'set up complex simulations', 'generate pseudo random numbers' and 'perform a huge variety of mathematical, financial and business functions'.

(d) Typical things that a **presentation package** can do are 'customise a demonstration with an appropriate style', 'provide templates for lectures and other talks', 'enable a lecturer to navigate easily through a talk', 'provide the lecturer with notes', 'provide a large degree of animation and slide transition functions', 'record minutes of meetings as the slide demo progresses', 'hide or reveal parts of the slide', 'import pictures and text from other applications to include in the show', 'link to other applications like a spreadsheet or database, and other links to the web', and 'presentations may be run in continuous loop for unattended demonstrations'.

(e) Typical things that an **e-mail package** can do are 'display e-mails that have been read or are yet to be read', 'send attachments along with the e-mail', 'verify the authenticity of the user via a digital signature', 'notify the sender when a message has been opened by the recipient', 'allow aliases to be used for contacts', 'allow the creation of groups and contacts enabling a single e-mail to be sent to multiple people', 'message management by assigning priorities', 'synchronise contacts and settings with PDAs and portables', 'add a standard signature to each message sent', 'block unwanted spam e-mails', 'provide blind carbon copies to a number of people' and 'messages are held on the server until they are downloaded'.

2 A **mail merge** means using a standard letter or document into which parameters may be inserted which represent data imported from an outside source. Typical of these are 'names', 'addresses', 'telephone numbers' and 'order items'. As an example, many letters could be sent out to customers confirming items which they have just ordered. A typical word processor can link to a database using CSV or other suitable formats.

3 A **template** is a **pre-designed document** in which the layout, types of text and any pre-written parts of the document are provided as a base from which you can add your own material. A typical use for a template might be the creation of an invoice, containing the company name and logo at the top, company registration numbers, vat numbers and membership of institutions at the bottom, and tables set up so that the invoice total at the bottom is automatically calculated.

4 A **what if scenario** might typically model a business strategy. If a company were to reduce the price of the goods it sells, then it is usually the case that more goods are sold. However, the profit that the company makes on each item will be less. Nevertheless, if they sell more, then the overall profit might be higher than if they had sold fewer items making more profit on each. This scenario can be programmed into a spreadsheet, and typical assumptions may be made. The company can play around with the prices they charge, saying things like 'If I reduce the price to £145, what would be the likely effect on the overall profit?' You must always be aware that 'what if scenarios' are only as good as the spreadsheet model, and may not necessarily mirror what actually happens in practice.

5 A 'typical' one-arm bandit programmed in Microsoft's Excel can be seen in the diagram. The system is extremely trivial to program, and the author carries out this exercise with 13-year olds at his school. A macro is assigned to the object, (an option in Excel) which simply causes the spreadsheet to recalculate. In fact, only the word '**calculate**' is needed between the 'Sub Spin()', the name of the macro, and End Sub. This causes the spreadsheet to recalculate when the macro is executed. The only other things to set up are three random numbers, placed in the cells as shown, and the cell that determines what happens when you win. You could, for example, flash a picture when three identical numbers are encountered in the cells. The sophistication of what happens is up to the user. It can be very simple, as shown here, or a complex simulation if you have time to program it.

```
Sub Spin()
'
' Spin Macro
' Macro recorded 23—04—2003 by Ray
Bradley
'
' Keyboard Shortcut: Ctrl + Shift + S
'
    Calculate
End Sub
```

The rest of the sheet is simply disguised to look like a one-arm bandit.

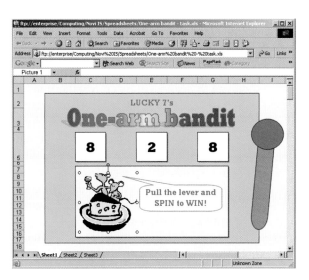

6 A **query** is the interrogation of a database to find out if any particular information matches the criteria set up in the query. Let's suppose that a 'Boolean field' is set to 'true' if a customer's bill has been outstanding for more than 30 days. Running the query would result in the selection of a subset of records that contain customers with this particular field flagged.

A **report** is the information displayed, usually using a detailed output template with headings, page numbers and other information. A report is usually associated with a query. If a suitable report is set up and associated with the query outlined above, then individual customers might be listed by name and account number, sorted into a list with 'who owes most' at the top. It is possible to automatically generate the letters to be sent to the customers by this method.

7 Different uses may be given **different views** of a database by designing **different front ends** to the database. Although the same data is being accessed, each user will see only what the database designer has intended that they can see. For example, data entry clerks may see customer details and accounting statistics, but only the management may see the total profit which is calculated from the records able to be viewed by the data entry clerks.

Only the **database administrator** would be able to design a new front end, and other users would be prevented from viewing unauthorised data by a system of **user names** and **password**.

8 A **database** could be set up on a **web server**. This means that the data contained within it could be viewed by a browser using Active Server Pages or some similar system. A means of transferring the word processed reports into the database should be set up, and this could be achieved by getting the staff to **export** the data from their **word processors** in the appropriate form. A **template** should be set up to make sure that the data is in the appropriate form.

When the reports have been placed into the appropriate fields within the database, they would be assigned **security** by **user name** and **password protection**. This means that when a parent logs on via the internet, they may see only the records belonging to their pupils.

9 A **broadband** **internet** **connection** would be needed if the lecture is to be interactive with any degree of success. It depends largely on whether the lecture is to be delivered to large groups in lecture theatres around the world, or to individuals sitting at PCs. If we assume the lecture theatre scenario then you would need projection TV facilities in addition to other hardware which would consist of computers with fast internet connections, and presentation packages like PowerPoint. Software capable of receiving broadband streaming video would be ideal for this purpose.

A video camera may be needed to present the lecturer to the audience in real time, and individual video cameras may be needed at each lecture venue if real-time student feedback, including vision, is needed.

A means of controlling who speaks to whom and when will need to be set up, and therefore some sort of video conferencing software would be useful. It may also be possible for people to chat in real time via the internet if video links would prove too expensive.

A web server would be needed on which the lecture could be controlled and distributed to the masses via the internet.

10 Three possible reasons why e-mail has revolutionised communications are as follows:
   (i)   **Instant communication** of **textual** and **pictorial** material is now possible.
   (ii) **Copies** may be sent to **numerous people** simultaneously.
   (iii) **Records** are **automatically generated** regarding the date and time at which information has been sent. This saves the user the bother of having to set up a filing system.

E-mail will replace much of mail sent by letter, but it can never replace the post entirely because physical things can't be sent. People don't usually want to print out a large catalogue, even though many of these can be delivered to your home via the internet. People still prefer reading things on paper, and parcels containing physical objects cannot be sent via e-mail.

11 It is usual to send confirmation details of a transaction to a particular e-mail address. This often includes the crucial code that will unlock the software. Some codes to activate software are now so long and convoluted that the only sensible way to send these codes is by e-mail. This means that the user can 'cut and paste' the code into the appropriate box.

12 It's important to be able to determine that an e-mail is from a particular person, not someone masquerading as them, and that the information contained in it has not be read by any unauthorised people. It's possible to use what's called a digital signature to do this. Your digital signature and your public key combine to produce authentication called a digital certificate. This will encrypt your e-mail, verify the sender and make sure that only you can read the message, because only you have a copy of your private key.

13 (a) It is likely that the statistics are held in a **database** or on a spreadsheet. The data would probably be exported to a **spreadsheet** for the analysis and the production of appropriate statistics like 'class sets' and 'year groups', etc. Finally, a **word processor** could be used with mail merge to produce the appropriate documentation to be printed out or sent to the staff, possibly as an **e-mail** attachment.

(b) This system depends largely on the numbers of cards involved. If it's more than a few thousand, then it's likely that a **word processor** would be used in conjunction with the **customer database mail merge mode**, and the resulting file sent off to a printing company to distribute the cards.
A less sophisticated system could print out **labels** into which information can be stuck into pre-printed stationery. The biggest problem here is the card. It's a problem for a standard printer to print really thick card, but

card of sufficient quality can be fed through a laser printer. However, this process would usually be quite slow for a standard office printer, especially if lots of customers were involved. It also depends on whether the cards need to be personally signed by the staff at the restaurant.

(c) It is assumed that all the employees will have **internet** access. The software update would need to be packaged into an appropriate form so that it can be installed quite easily. The update itself can either be sent by an **e-mail attachment**, or an e-mail could be sent indicating that a critical update is available from the company's **web site** or accessed via the **intranet** and delivered via a **VPN**.

Chapter 12 – Social, economic and ethical consequences

The answers to this question will depend largely on the type of high-tech system introduced. Here we assume it's a computer-based solution to a particular problem.

1 Arguments **for** a high-tech solution to a problem in a third-world county might be:
(i) No legacy systems in operation to complicate installation of a new system.
(ii) After initial training, the system might enable the people to compete with their higher-tech competitors.
(iii) Labour is usually cheap, and assuming the people can be trained, it will create employment.

Arguments **against** a high-tech solution to a problem in a third-world county might be:
(i) Local people might not be able to operate the system.
(ii) Is the infrastructure available to support the system (i.e. electricity, internet access, etc.)?
(iii) Are there any ideological reasons for not having the system introduced (e.g. internet access might cause cultural problems)?

2 The first problem would be to define what is meant by the term '**intelligence**'. Most dictionaries would regard intelligence as the ability to '**think**' and '**learn**'. There is no doubt that computers can learn, so the problem would be one of deciding if a computer can think. So we need to decide what is meant by '**thought**'.

Various definitions might say something like 'to use the mind to make certain types of judgement'. We are therefore into the argument about whether a computer needs a mind to be able to think.

Strong AI (**Artificial Intelligence**) scientists believe that computers will be able to think at some time in the future, but others feel that they will never be able to do so. This will bring up arguments about whether a machine can be regarded as a sentient being, and if it were, whether it would have any rights. There are no right or wrong answers here, just opinions based on known facts and current research. It's an interesting topic for debate about moral, social ethical and legal issues.

3   Computers are no doubt **addictive** for certain people. This usually includes 'children or adults and **games**', but could also include 'the **internet**'. It's unlikely that people would be addicted to word processing or databases! Your arguments should therefore centre on what is meant by 'addiction'. Addiction is really a total dependence on something, usually to the detriment of other things. Therefore, if someone is addicted to the computer, they will spend a disproportionate amount of time playing games or using the internet and other parts of their life, like social interaction, doing a job of work or getting other things done may suffer.

Addiction would not normally apply to those individuals who spend a couple of hours a night playing games, or to those who will temporarily spend a long time playing a new game because they are engrossed in it. If other parts of a person's life, like holding a full time job, having a social life and being interactive with the family at home are not affected, then they are not addicted to computers.

4   **Computer aided learning** (or **CAL**) enables pupils to receive individual attention for 100% of the time, and can tailor the learning to a particular individual. It is excellent to use the computer for learning, but it does become very tedious and boring if no other form of learning takes place. At the author's school we have an interactive learning package which teaches the pupils the ECDL course (ECDL is the European Computer Driving Licence). Pupils love using it, but if it is used day after day after day with no variation, then it does become boring. Pupils

appreciate the teacher interaction, and we intersperse the CAL with lectures and videos. Human interaction will be needed, and computers fail to provide this. Teachers will probably be needed for some considerable time yet! Not least with making sure that the pupils are actually doing the work they should be!

5   Six different areas of misuse in the workplace could be as follows:
    (i)   Downloading inappropriate material from the internet.
    (ii)   Using the internet when other work should be in progress.
    (iii) Using someone else's account without authority.
    (iv)   Divulging sensitive company information to others.
    (v)   Sending inappropriate e-mails.
    (vi)   An employee trying to hack into the system to get around security set up by the company.

6   The Data Protection Act.

7   Tax can be automatically deducted at source (i.e. the price you pay for the goods may be included in the purchase price). VAT is an example of this. The companies operating on the internet would have to agree to pay taxes to the appropriate government, and international legislation would be needed to do this effectively.

8   Just a few of the many areas in which European legislation affects computers are as follows:
    (i)   Anonymous access and use of computers.
    (ii)   Harmful and illegal content on the internet.
    (iii)   Offences related to hacking and denial of service.
    (iv)   Network and information security.
    (v)   Data protection and the telecom framework.
    (vi)   Identity theft.
    (vii)   Setting up computer emergency response teams.
    (viii) Raising public awareness.
    (ix)   Security in government use.
    (x)   International co-operation.

9   Three areas of ethical concern are 'identity theft', 'child pornography' and 'privacy of information'.

10 Complete privacy can never be maintained without compromising security. If complete

privacy is adopted then people would be allowed to break the law with impunity. An acceptable degree of privacy (easily enough for most sensible people) can be maintained with good security. See the 'Policy Central' software outlined in Chapter 12.

Chapter 13 – File organisation and structure

1 A **record** is a set of related information. In the context of a file, this might be a record about a particular student in a college, or a record giving details about a particular item in stock in a shop. A record is made up from one or more **fields**. The student example just quoted might have 'surname', 'middle name' and 'first name' fields, together with a variety of others like 'address' fields, etc. A **field** is split up into **characters**. For example, the surname field might contain the characters 'Bloggs'.

2 (a) **Name** would be a **text field**. Let's assume that a 50-character description is sufficient.
   (b) **Product description** number would be an **integer**, depending on the system used, let's assume that 2 bytes are needed to store an integer.
   (c) **Price** is **currency**, so let's assume 8 bytes to store this variable.
   (d) **Description of item** will be a text field, and could be quite a lot longer than a name. Let's assume 256 characters or 256 bytes for this one.
   (e) **Page number** in the catalogue would be an **integer**, and we will assume 2 bytes. Therefore, each record would need 50 + 2 + 8 + 256 + 2 = **318 bytes**. Therefore, for data only, 10 000 records would need 3 180 000 bytes or about **3 Mbytes**. In practice, a little more than this would be needed for overheads. **5 Mbytes would be easily enough to hold all the data**, account for any overheads and leave a little room for expansion.
   (Note: different assumptions can easily be made – without knowing the actual programming language or database used to implement the system, much of the above would be guesswork. In an examination you would be given marks for how you arrived at the answer, not marks for an absolute value.)

3 A **serial file** is one in which the data has been saved without any regard to order. Such a file could be the result of transactions in a shop during the day. A **sequential file** is one in which the data is placed in some pre-determined order, like 'alphabetical listing of items' or 'ascending order of item number', for example.

4 **Disks** and **tapes** support serial access.

5 An **indexed** sequential file is a sequential file (a file in a specific order), which has pointers pointing to salient parts of the file made up from an index. The following diagram shows part of a **large** sequential file in which alphabetical pointers point to the start of the names as shown in the list.

Index (Pointers)		Sequential file (Names)
Alpha pointer to 'A's	⟶	Abbey
Alpha pointer to 'B's		Able
Alpha pointer to 'C's etc.		...
Etc.		Arnold
		Barnhold
		Baterby
		...
		Etc.

The **index** on the left consists of **pointers** that can be sequentially followed until the desired part of the sequential file is found. The list of names belonging to a particular index can then be followed **sequentially** until a particular name is found.

6 **Hashing** is a convenient way to generate addresses within a given range from numbers like customer ID or bank account. It provides for **very quick access** to the information stored within the file because the address at which the information is found is calculated from the hash address, and the file is accessed randomly. If two or more numbers generate the same address, then an **overflow table** is generated, but the search is still very fast indeed.

7 A **surname** is usually no good for the key field because the primary key field must be unique. It is very likely that a large business will have many customers all sharing the same surname. A far better system would be to use a **unique customer account number**.

8 (a) A typical bank account number might be something like 31759628. A hash function to generate addresses in the range 0 to 1499 would be to use modulo 1500. A suitable hashing function would therefore be as follows.

Address = Account number (Mod 1500) + 1

(b) Consider the account numbers 31720000 and 31730000. The hash addresses for each would be:

31720000(Mod 1500) + 1 = 500 (i.e. the remainder after division of the account number by 1500)

31710500(Mod 1500 + 1 = 500 (i.e. the remainder after division of the account number by 1500).

Two different account numbers (many actually) generate the same address, and under this system, both would need to be stored at location 500.

(c) To get over the problem outlined in part (b), an overflow table is set up. All the account numbers which generate the same address are stored in a sequential overflow table. When an account number is used to generate a hash address, if an overflow table exists, then the accounts within the overflow table are followed until the required account is found. Although this might sound slow, just a few comparisons will normally be needed.

Chapter 14 – Security, integrity and management of data

1 **Data integrity** refers to making sure that the data is correct. It may get corrupted due to human error, or due to a malfunction in the computer system. A file, for example, may have been corrupted due to a fault on a disk, rendering the data unreadable.

Data security means keeping data secure from attacks by hackers. Data security attempts to make sure that unauthorised users can't gain access to private data, and uses systems such as encryption, for example.

2 A **batch total** is a number used to check the integrity of data in a batch. Typically invoices might each have a total, and a batch total could be calculated by adding together all the individual totals to create a batch total. If any of the data is missing or has been changed in some way, then the batch total received is unlikely to be the same as the original batch total that was generated when the data was sent.

3 It's possible that the first letter of the first word in each report could be changed into its ASCII value and this could be used as a number for each report. These numbers could then be added together to form a '**hash total**' or '**control total**' for the **batch** of school reports.

4 A **check digit** is a single digit, which is calculated by using some algorithm on the data being transmitted. The idea is that the received data can have the same algorithm applied to it, and a new check digit calculated. If the check digit is the same as the one that has been received, then the data is assumed to have been received without error.

5 The calculation of the check digit for 795436 is as follows:

Number	7	9	5	4	3	6	CD
Weighting	7	6	5	4	3	2	1
Product	49	54	25	16	9	12	—
Sum	49 + 54 + 25 + 16 + 9 + 12 = 165						
Mod 7 division	165/7 = 23 remainder **4**						
New number	7	9	5	4	3	6	4

The **check digit**, put on the end of the number is **4**.

6 A cyclic redundancy check is one of the best methods because it's ideal for transmission over networks and small numbers of digits are generated for large number of digits that are checked.

7 There are two aspects to security – **data security** and **physical security**. To keep the data secure you make sure that the files are password protected, including any backups that might be made of the file. The operating system security and protection via fire walls, etc. also play a part in this. The physical security means making sure unauthorised personnel can't enter the rooms in which the computers are stored that hold the information on the file. The security of the building is important here (i.e. code locks, etc.) and ID cards for clocking in any visitors is also a help.

8   A **computer virus** is a threat to **data integrity** because malicious viruses will often destroy or alter the data. However, a computer virus can also be a threat to **data security** because some viruses are designed to sniff out passwords and other sensitive information, which could then be passed back to the hacker, leaving the system open to abuse.

9   Four different methods for **physical security** could include 'combination locks on the computer room doors', 'a system of ID cards needed to enter the building', 'a finger print log on system' and 'video surveillance cameras in the room'.

10 A **master file** is no different to an 'ordinary file'; it is just the use to which it is put. It contains definitive information, usually about a business like a shop. Such information could be 'customer names and addresses', 'amount owing' or 'bank account details'.

    A **transaction file** is more transitory. It is a file which represents the transactions of a business, often on a daily basis. Using the shop example again, the transaction file could be the 'business transactions' that have taken place that day. At the end of the day the transactions in the **transaction file** are used to update the information in the **master file** so that a new, more up to date master file is produced.

11 Once all the **transaction files** are received from each branch they will probably be merged into one large transaction file ready to update the **master file** at head office. After the merge has taken place, the large transaction file, containing all the branch transaction files will need to be sorted into order before being used to update the master file.

    Once the large transaction file is ready, the transaction processing will sequentially go through the large transaction file and the master file to produce a new master file containing the updated transactions and any new customers for that day.

    The new master file is called the '**son file**' because the file from which it was made (the old master file) is called the '**father file**'.

    The next day a new transaction file will be produced, and the new master file will be called the 'son file' the previous day's master file will be called the 'father file' but the master file used

before that will be called the '**grandfather file**'. In this way three generations of files are kept, called the **grandfather, father** and **son files**.

12 The two serially-based files must first be in some suitable order, like customer ID number, for example. The serial transaction file and the serial master file must both be opened such that you are looking at the first record of each file. The main points of the algorithm are as follows.

    (i)   The key fields (customer ID in this example) in the transaction file and master file are compared and if the **key field** in the **master file** < key field in the **transaction file**, this means that *no transaction has taken place* for this master file record, and it's simply copied to the new master file (son file).

    (ii) If the **key field** in the **master file** = key field in the **transaction file** *a transaction has taken place*, and the record in the master file (son file) is updated.

    (iii) If the **key field** in the **master file** > key field in the **transaction file** then the record in the master file does not exist and a *new customer record is created* in the new master file (son file).

    Some suitable pseudocode for the above algorithm would go along the following lines:

```
OPEN MASTER-FILE for INPUT
  OPEN NEW-TRANSACTION-FILE for
INPUT
  OPEN NEW-MASTER-FILE for OUTPUT
  READ MASTER-FILE-RECORD INTO
MASTER-RECORD
  READ TRANSACTION-FILE-RECORD
INTO TRANSACTION-RECORD
  * Need to get first records
from each file
  * Working records are called
MASTER-RECORD and TRANSACTION-
RECORD
  WHILE NOT END-OF-MASTER-FILE
AND NOT END-OF-TRANSACTION-FILE
  IF KEYFIELD-MASTER-RECORD <
KEYFIELD-TRANSACTION-RECORD
    *No update necessary for this
record
  WRITE MASTER-RECORD TO NEW-
MASTER-FILE
    READ MASTER-RECORD INTO
```

```
MASTER-RECORD
  ELSE
    IF KEYFIELD-MASTER-RECORD =
KEYFIELD-TRANSACTION-RECORD
      *Update the record before
writing
      PERFORM UPDATE procedure
      WRITE MASTER-RECORD TO NEW-
MASTER-FILE
      READ MASTER-FILE-RECORD
INTO MASTER-RECORD
      READ TRANSACTION-FILE-
RECORD INTO TRANSACTION-RECORD
    ELSE
      KEYFIELD-MASTER-RECORD >
KEYFIELD-TRANSACTION-RECORD
      *New record to be added
      PERFORM NEW-RECORD
procedure
      WRITE NEW-RECORD TO NEW-
MASTER-FILE
      READ TRANSACTION-FILE-
RECORD INTO TRANSACTION-RECORD
    END IF
  END IF
ENDWHILE
WHILE NOT END-OF-MASTER-FILE
  * Transfer any remaining
master-file records to new master
file
  WRITE MASTER-RECORD TO NEW-
MASTER-FILE
ENDWHILE
WHILE NOT END-OF-TRANSACTION-FILE
  * Transfer any remaining
transaction records to new master
file
  * New record/s to be added and
transferred to new master file
  PERFORM NEW-RECORD procedure
  WRITE NEW-RECORD TO NEW-
MASTER-FILE
    READ TRANSACTION-FILE-RECORD
INTO TRANSACTION-RECORD
ENDWHILE
CLOSE MASTER-FILE TRANSACTION-
FILE NEW-MASTER-FILE
```

13 Data **files** are usually backed up onto tape or copied onto a second disk. The frequency with which this is done depends on the volatility of the data (*how often it changes*). Typically an incremental backup will be made at the end of each day. An incremental backup will backup only those files that have changed since the last backup was made. If the data file is a transaction file in a business, then it might be processed as described in question (12).

The **system** and **application files** are usually backed up by using a disk imaging system. This backup system takes a snapshot of the disk (probably arranged in a partition to prevent it getting mixed up with the data files) and keeps this as a single file, or two or three files if the system is large. If applications or any operating system files get corrupted, then the system image may be restored. This will restore the system and applications back to the state that they were in when the image was taken. This will also save you having to reinstall the operating system.

14 A **backup** is a copy of a file for use in the event of an emergency. This enables you to recover your system to a point when the backup was made. An **archive** refers to taking 'little used data' off line, so that it may be recovered and used if you ever need it in the future. A typical example of an archive might be a building plan for houses that were built ten years ago. It would be silly to waste space storing this information 'on line' if it might never be needed again. However, if an extension to one of the houses is planned, the original builders might be asked to produce a copy of the plans, and this could be done by loading the appropriate archive.

15 A **physical drive** is the actual drive present in a computer. Typically this would be the 'C drive', but you could have the letters 'C' and 'D' if you had two drives in the computer.

It is often convenient to partition large hard drives into logical units called '**logical drives**'. As far as the computer is concerned you might have only one physical drive, but you might have three partitions, and from a user's perspective this would look like they had three different drives labels 'C', 'D' and 'E', for example. Partitions are useful for backup and organisational purposes, and the storage of data is accomplished more efficiently.

16 (a) The **fat clients** (i.e. workstation with local hard disk and conventional PCs) will need a disk image taken for each partition on the

drive. This would be needed in the event of an emergency, when the disk image, probably stored on a file server, could be used to get the workstation back up and working. It would need careful consideration if any important data files were stored on the local hard disks, but if this has been done then these data files will need a suitable backup mechanism carried out with suitable frequency. The data files for the users would probably be stored on a file server, and this would need suitable backups taken with suitable frequency too.

(b) A **thin client** has no local hard disk, therefore any data or applications or operating systems used by the thin client are server based. This means that no local backup is needed. However, the files servers and data stored on the file servers will need backing up, and this can be done using the same methods outlined for fat clients in part (a).

Chapter 15 – Databases

1   A **flat-file database** is one in which the entire database consists of a single table or file. A **relational database** is one in which the data has been split up into two or more smaller tables, which are related to each other in some way by using one or more fields. A relational database is the most efficient way to store data in the majority of databases, unless the database is trivial.

2   A **table** within the database corresponds exactly to a **file** on disk.

3   A **row** in a relational database represents a **record**, and a **column** represents a **field**.

4   (a) The term 'data inconsistency' as applied to a database means that data stored in one part of the database is different from the same data stored in another part.

(b) An example of **data inconsistency** could be a misspelled name. For example, the publisher 'Nelson Thornes' might be stored correctly in one part but as 'Nelson Thorns' in another. The database would interpret these as different publishers, and data inconsistency is to blame for this.

(c) A badly designed database might have the publisher name stored 1000 times. It would

be more efficient to have some sort of publisher ID, and the name stored just once. This not only saves on storage space, but minimises the problems outlined in part (b). If the name is stored once only it can't be spelt differently in different parts of the database.

5   A **primary key** is a **unique field** (or group of fields) by which a particular **record** is **identified**.

6   **Surname** – **text** – Consists of letters and some other characters (e.g. '-', for example)
Age – **integer** – (Probably limited in range)
Male or **Female** – **Boolean** – True/false field
A **picture** – Depends on format, but possibly a **bitmap** or **jpeg**
A **telephone number** – **text** (*not numeric*) if spaces or '-' signs, etc. are used to separate code. Also, international codes might have '+' in them too.

7   A **primary key** is a **unique field** (or group of fields) that defines a record in a file. Mapping a field from one table to another table sets up a relation, and the key to which the first field is mapped is called a **foreign key**.

8   A **relationship** in a **relational database** is a mapping (a common association) between two different attributes. Relationships may be one-to-one, one-to-many or many-to-one.

9   A **primary index** is an index set up on the primary key. This enables quick searching of information in this particular filed. A **secondary index** is an index based on a key other than the primary key. This too can speed up certain operations. However, you should not put an index on every key, as this will create too many overheads and slow down the system.

10   **Data validation** is using a set of rules to ensure that data is entered without error. Assuming that the pensionable age for a male is 65, and assuming that no one lives to more than 130, then a suitable validation rule could be $65 \leqslant age \leqslant 130$.

11   The best way to choose data from a pre-defined list would be by the use of a **drop-down menu** system. A default value could be displayed, and if this is not suitable, moving the mouse over an arrow would produce a list of possibilities. This is one way of achieving data validation.

12 Data may be **validated** to see if it conforms to a particular rule like a 'numerical range' or 'belonging to a particular set', for example. Data can also be chosen from a **drop-down list**, and this saves typing (or mistyping) data that would be rejected on validation.

13 A **query** is a request for information from the database that obeys certain criteria. It is usual to search all records or a subset of records using the query as a guide to information that is either presented on screen or passed over to a report.

14 A **Boolean operation** is one that may be carried out on Boolean data (**true/false**). Examples of Boolean operators are '**AND**', '**OR**' and '**NOT**'. The Boolean operator 'AND' could be used in a database query to search for women who are over the age of sixty-five. A typical query for this might contain the syntax

```
WHERE (Sex = Female) is true AND age
> 65.
```

15 Keeping **referential integrity** of a database means maintaining the validity of relationships between tables in a database. There are a large set of rules with many possible examples, but trying to enter a value in a foreign key when the primary key or other key does not exist is one particular example.

16 Let's assume that the report on the pupils is to list their surnames and first names, house, year and form. Now house is the first item to be used for the grouping. Therefore, when the report is created, you instruct the database to do an alphabetical listing of house. The following assumes we have four house colours in the school, namely 'red', green', 'blue' and 'yellow'. Instead of getting a listing of the complete school sorted alphabetically by house, we need to sort by year. Let's assume that there are five years, namely '1st', '2nd', '3rd', '4th' and '5th'. Therefore, we instruct the database to sort each house by year, and we therefore get a listing of pupils, in alphabetical order, first sorted by 'house' then by year' and finally by alphabetical name.

Lastly, we require the forms within each house year. Let's assume that we have form 'a', 'b', 'c' and 'd'.

The report layout will be arranged something like the following. (Only a small extract is shown.)

Pupils listed by house, year and form			
House	Year	Form	Pupils' names
Blue	1st year	Form a	
			Billy Bloggs
			Betty Mumps
		Form b	
			Bertie Bassett
			Dolly Dimples
		Form c	
			Etc.
		Form d	
			Etc.
	2nd year		
		Etc.	Etc.
	3rd year		
		Etc.	Etc.
	4th year		
		Etc.	Etc.
	5th year		
Green	Etc.	Etc.	Etc.
Red	Etc.	Etc.	Etc.
Yellow	Etc.	Etc.	Etc.

17 Data may be **exported** from a database in a variety of formats, like **CSV** (Comma Separated Value) for example. Spreadsheets like Excel can easily import CSV data, and therefore the statistics can be analysed in the conventional way. If necessary, data could be imported back into the database, filling fields with the new statistics. The process could be automated by the use of scripts and macros if necessary.

18 VBA is **Visual Basic for Applications**, which brings much of the power and functionality of Visual Basic to any application that supports it. It would, therefore, be possible to write any mathematical functions using VBA, which could act on the contents of one field, work out some statistics, and then place the results into the same or another field.

Chapter 16 – Operating systems

1 A **command-line operating system** is one in which strings of commands are given at a prompt

to undertake tasks similar to those that would be carried out using a mouse in a **GUI** operating system. The best known command line operating system is DOS.

2 A **batch operating system** is one in which commands can be issued to run a batch of jobs. Typical examples of batch operating systems are to be found in the banking and utility billing sectors. Here large quantities of batch processing such as 'clearing of cheques' or the 'production of electricity and gas bills' need to be carried out each day, and the computers are set up especially to do this.

A **real-time operating system** is one that has been designed specifically to respond to external events in an appropriate amount of time. Typical examples of this are to be found in the **process-control industry** where chemical plants or nuclear power stations are controlled by specially adapted computers. The **response time** of a real-time operating system is **usually very fast**, such as those found in the control of cruise missiles, for example.

3 Allocation of **RAM** to applications and other tasks running on a computer is a good example of a resource managed by the operating system. Others could include checking to see if there is sufficient disk space before saving a file, or allocation of processor time to each task in a multi-tasking operating system.

4 A **file server** usually has **public** and **private** areas. In a school, for example, hundreds of pupils should have access to their own work, but not to that of others. Similarly, applications might be served to work stations, but users should not be able to delete these applications. This is usually achieved by applying **file permissions** to the users' files and applications, which are a combination of options like 'full control', 'modify', 'read and execute', 'read' or 'write', etc.

In addition, you can **audit** actions taken on files, such as who is reading them and when. Users would usually have to log onto a file server using **passwords**, so that they can be identified to the system. Logs may also be kept about who has logged on, when they log off, and the resources that they have used.

5 A **multi-user system** is one in which more than one user can use the system at any particular moment in time. In a single-processor system this would have to happen on a time-sharing basis, but each user would have the illusion of having 'his or her' own resources, assuming that the system is fast enough. Thin clients connected to a server farm, or many users using a mini or mainframe computer are typical examples of multi-user systems.

6 A **fat client** is usually able to deliver higher performance on graphics and audio-intensive applications. The response from a **thin client** could be very slow for these particular applications. A fat client is often able to function if the network is down, although there would obviously be no access to network resources on the fileservers if this did actually happen.

7 **Thin clients** are very easy to maintain compared to a **fat client**. They usually have no hard disks or floppy disks, and little hardware to go wrong at the client end. Any applications that needs updating can be done very easily using the server farm. Nothing has to be stored locally on the thin client machines, and they are therefore usually more reliable than a fat client.

8 Things appear to be happening on the screen at the same moment in time to the user because they are happening very quickly, thus deceiving the eye (and therefore the brain) into thinking that things are happening simultaneously. However, without a second processor, it is physically impossible to do more than one thing at the same instant in time.

9 A **batch** of **commands** is often essential for network administration because it would be far too time consuming to carry out the same processes manually in a Window's environment. Typical operations would be 'applying file permissions to hundreds of thousands of files' or 'creating hundreds or new users', for example.

10 Without **network security**, people would be able to inadvertently or deliberately interfere with work belonging to other people, be able to view material that should be private, or be able to alter the intended way that applications should be run. They would also be able to install applications, some of which might contravene the network licensing arrangements for the

institution, or fill up the hard disks with 'rubbish', thus rendering the computer system inoperable because it has run out of disk space.

11 (i) You should be able to put a file to read only. This would ensure that unauthorised personnel do not delete or alter the contents of the file.

(ii) You can alter the **security settings** on a file such that only administrators of the system are able to change the security settings. This can prevent an ordinary user, even if they have other permissions set, from being able to take full ownership of the file.

(iii) You change the **system settings** such that users can't run executables. This ensures that users could not add illegal or unlicensed programs from CD-ROMs or other possible sources like the Internet, for example.

12 It is possible to run a **batch file** at certain times that warns the users that they should log off of the computers now. Several minutes later another batch file could automatically log them off and shut down the computer in a controlled way. This can usually be done remotely from the file server by running a batch command at certain times. The scheduler would normally manage this task.

13 If groups of individuals within a company need similar or identical settings, then it's possible to form what's called a **group**. You can set attributes (identical to those described in earlier questions) for members of the group. Very sophisticated permissions may be granted by making individuals members of several groups. At the author's school, for example, only A level Computer Science students are allowed to compile and run programs using Microsoft's Development Studio. As another example, all students are members of the internet group, which allows them to make use of the proxy server to gain internet access. If they misuse this privilege, we simply remove them from the internet users group, and they can no longer gain access to the net.

14 It is possible to set **auditing** on this particular file. This would create a **log** of what happens to this file, including the people who have accessed it, and the times at which it has been accessed. Assuming that nobody can use the system with

an anonymous log on, then it should be possible to track down the account being used. Note that this will not necessarily identify the person involved, as several people might use the same account, or the password might have been compromised, for example.

15 If **file auditing** has been set up correctly, then the administrators are also under the same restrictions as others. Therefore, the **log files** on a file server might be acceptable in a court of law as evidence of what has actually taken place. It might be possible for a corrupt administrator to alter the files, but this would have to be argued in court.

16 An operating system that controls **navigation systems on an aircraft** would need added reliability. Often two or three different computer systems must agree with each other before the plane is allowed to take off.
Control of a **nuclear power station** would also need added reliability with fail-safe systems being the norm. It would not be acceptable for the computer to fail under these circumstances.

17 Systems like **theatre-ticket booking**, **airline ticketing** or **container ship loading** have to respond in real time. It would be unacceptable, for example, to have to wait too long for confirmation of a seat in a theatre or for the container to be delayed while the computer works out where it should be placed for efficient loading or unloading. Even though these system don't need a lightning-fast response, they are still good examples of a **real-time operating system**.

Chapter 17 – Input and output devices

1 It is easily possible to imagine that the **keyboard** will be replaced by voice input for certain applications. At some time in the future this is inevitable, but in the short-term voice recognition systems need to be improved, and context-sensitive language analysis is in its infancy. Nevertheless, most people producing word-processed documentation still find voice input an unnatural form of getting data into the computer, unless they are trained in the art of dictating letters to a secretary. Most people are not precise enough when using voice input, and are often annoyed with having to speak the

formatting commands too. For users who are disabled and not able to use a conventional keyboard, or for people who have abysmal typing skills, voice input is a real bonus.

2 **Personal Digital Assistants** now have a variety of peripherals, and pen-based handwriting is now a common method of data input. However, extra (larger) **keyboards** can sometimes be plugged into PDAs. There is usually a method of backing up data to a computer, for example via a cradle connected to the serial or USB port. Infrared ports are also common, which enables the PDA user to print directly to a printer that has an infrared link. There are numerous other special peripherals, such as bar code readers, modems, radio and network links to name but a few.

3 A **QWERTY keyboard** would enable data to be entered much more efficiently than using the conventional mobile phone keypad. Without a QWERTY keyboard, buttons have to be pressed many times to send a message. While this is O.K. for small text messages, and the current generation of youngsters seem to manage this at tremendous speed, especially with predictive text, it is not convenient for larger e-mails.

4 (i) OCR can be used to scan in a page of typewritten text. After processing, the text is then in editable form, as though it had been typed in using a word processor.

(ii) A second use of **OCR** would be to read **turnaround documentation**. An example of this is the bills produced by the utility companies. The customer invoices, produced and printed out by a computer system in the first place, are fed into a machine that automatically reads the information written at the bottom of the form (hence the name turnaround document). This enables people to pay bills quickly without the need for the operator to re-key information that is already written on the utility bill.

5 **OMR** is often used for getting the computer to automatically analyse the results of questionnaires that have been manually filled in by the user. This is ideal for multiple-choice questionnaires where a written response is not required. OMR is also used in some hospitals when patients order meals. A selection of starters, main courses and vegetables, etc. can easily be marked with a pen and analysed by computer so that the cooks know which meals to prepare.

6 The typed page must be input into the computer as a bitmap, making use of a scanner. The resultant image is then scanned by pattern recognition software, which attempts to match the text to a particular font. After the pattern-recognition process, the text, complete with flagged errors, is then in computer editable form.

7 **Pedals** could be placed under the computer that simulates the **rudder controls** on the **aircraft**. The cockpit instrumentation can be simulated in hardware that interacts with the pilot in ways similar to the real aircraft. Examples of this could be switches and levers that simulate throttles, and other control devices. A microphone could be used to simulate (and eventually record) conversations with air traffic control personnel. This could be useful when doing a post flight debriefing.

8 A **key-to-disk terminal** is used to key data onto disk ready for later processing. This has been superseded by the humble PC, which enables data to be prepared in virtually any form ready for analysis at a later date. If large amounts of data need to be input to a mainframe, then PCs acting as workstations or thin clients might be used instead.

9 **Video conferencing** is an obvious candidate – without video input this would not be able to operate. Computer security systems often have video cameras in which footage gets saved straight onto the computer system. Finally, biometric input of data such as facial recognition would also rely on video input of data.

10 (i) In some jobs data must be input when the operator needs to use both hands at the same time. For example, in the meat processing industry, animal carcasses are lifted onto a scale for weighing. At the same time, information has to be entered about the animal, and the human operator's voice is used to do this.

(ii) **Speech input** might be used when some disability prevents the user from using a conventional keyboard. It is ideal for people who have little or no control over their hands, or have lost arms in accidents.

11 MIDI is an acronym for the **Musical Instrument Digital Interface**. It is ideal for musicians to input music, which can either be entered from a conventional keyboard, played in via a MIDI keyboard (a musical one) or via any suitably equipped MIDI instrument such as a guitar or violin with the appropriate attachments.

12 **Sound input** may be used to get the pet to respond to a spoken command like 'fetch' or 'chase the ball'. A device to simulate stroking the pet may use touch sensors. A cat, for example, could be made to purr if stroked in this way. Finally, light sensors could tell the pet if it were night or day, and could thus make the pet go to sleep after a suitable period of time in the dark.

13 A **data capture form** is useful to gather information off line. For example, the results of a questionnaire taken in the street, or the capture of data that is currently in manual format (e.g. you might be building a database for science laboratory equipment). A data capture form enables users to enter data at remote locations without the need for a computer. It is also useful to focus the minds of systems analysts when deciding what data should be captured for a particular project.

14 One of the most useful ways to gather information from the internet is by the use of a **form** within a browser. This can be displayed on conventional **web browsers**, and requires the user to fill in boxes identical to those that would be present when filling in a record card for a database. Indeed, the information from these forms (in the form of individual fields) get sent back to the server for processing (using **CGI**, **ASP** or **JSP**), which in turn may be put into a **database** that resides on the server or another machine. In the same way the data captured from internet users is placed into a conventional database for further processing and analysis.

15 The following is only a particular example. The detail obviously depends on the school. For example, it might be a boarding school, a girls' school or a religious school, in which case extra information might need to be entered.

Provisional entry form to St Trinian's School			
Surname		First name	
Other names		Known as	
Desired date of entry			
Address 1		Telephone	
Address 2		Fax	
Town		e-mail address	
County/State Other			
Country			
Post Code/Zip			
Date of birth		Present Age	
Place of birth		Religious denomination	
Full name of father		Maiden name of mother	
Nationality		Nationality	
Profession or occupation		Profession or occupation	
Full name of guardian		Boarder or Day girl	
Nationality			
Profession or occupation		Any other relevant information	
Name of present school			
Telephone number			
Fax number			
Name of head teacher			

The above would be typical for a boarding school. It is the minimal amount of information. Other possibilities include any qualifications already achieved, medical history or other more confidential information such as criminal records!

16 A similar amount of information would be needed to the above. However, parents' or guardians' names and addresses might not be required. Next of kin probably would, as they need a contact in the event of any accident that might happen. The following extra information would probably be needed *in addition to the information* described in question (15).

Extra information for a university candidate			
Proposed course			
Course code			
GCSE or other equivalent qualifications		GCE Advanced Level (or equivalent qualifications) if known	
Subject	Grade	Subject	Grade

Other information, such as proposed address (if known), while staying at the university may also be needed.

17 This is a vast area, and some pointers here are shown. The questionnaire could be broken down by category, starting with the four main categories, namely CDs, cassettes, videos and DVDs. Let's take the DVD section as typical. If the user has ticked a box indicating that they are interested in purchasing DVDs, then we could respond by asking the user to designate the categories in which they would be interested. Typical categories for DVDs might be as follows: 'Action and Adventure', 'International', 'Children's DVDs', 'Classic films', 'Comedy', 'Drama', 'Horror and suspense', 'Music', 'Performing arts', 'Science fiction', 'Fantasy', 'Sport and fitness' and 'Television', etc. Each category might have a sub-category consisting of the type of material. For example, if you selected that you are interested in the Sport and fitness category, then you might divide this up into different sports like Football, Rugby, Golf, Tennis, American Football, Formula One Racing, Gymnastics, etc. Being such large categories, we would need a form which starts of something like the following.

Please help us by completing this questionnaire, and you will get a chance to win £100 worth of free DVDs, Videos, Cassette or CDs.				
Please tick the media in which you are most interested	DVD	Videos	Cassettes	CDs
	☐	☐	☐	☐

Notice the incentive at the top. Most people would not want to fill in a questionnaire unless there was a possibility of some sort of reward.

The next part of the form to be displayed depends on the boxes that are ticked. If a user ticks all the boxes, then all four forms would be displayed in sequence, after the previous form had been completed.

The DVD sub-form is typical of what might come next.

Please tick the category of DVD in which you are most interested			
Action and adventure	International	Children's DVD	Classic films
☐	☐	☐	☐
Comedy	Drama	Horror and suspense	Music
☐	☐	☐	☐
Performing arts	Science fiction	Fantasy	Sport and fitness
☐	☐	☐	☐
Television			
☐			

Other information might be as follows:

Please tick the following boxes relating to your DVD buying habits				
How many DVDs have you purchased in the last month?	☐ None	☐ One	☐ Between one and five	☐ More than five
Of these DVDs, how many were purchased from us?	☐ None	☐ One	☐ Between one and five	☐ More than five
Did you find the DVD you wanted on our site?	Yes ☐		No ☐	
Please fill in the following information:				
Name				
Address				
E-mail				
Telephone				
Do you wish us to send you marketing information?	Yes ☐		No ☐	

There can be many other types of question, but the above are typical of that which would help the marketing department of the company gather data about the users' surfing habits and requirements.

18 This is an ideal machine on which to print out large architects' drawings for building plans. These are usually A2 or larger, and an ordinary laser printer would therefore not do.

19 **LCDs** are **Liquid Crystal Displays**. They typify the technology used in modern flat-screen monitors, and are also used in PDAs and calculators, etc. **LEP** are **Light** Emitting Polymers and are set to challenge the LCD market. One of the advantages of an LEP display is that it can be very large indeed (the size of the wall of a normal house) and can be moulded into a variety of shapes. They can also fold up inside your pocket.

20 Some modern computer programs (like games and CAD packages) make intense demands on the computer system to compute the mathematics needed to display high-resolution pictures in colour. A graphics card will relieve the main processor of much of this work. Good graphics cards have copious amounts of RAM which is usually faster than the RAM used on the main motherboard inside the computer.

21 There is little difference now between the quality of output, and both printers will produce first class output if the appropriate paper is used (e.g. photographic quality on glossy paper). The main difference in the two systems lies in the **running costs**, **reliability** and **speed of operation**.
Ink jet printers are usually very cheap to buy, and are intended for the home market and low volume office work. They tend to be built with lower quality components, and are subsidised to some extent by the very high costs of the cartridges they need to operate. They are, however, ideal for use at home, and cost effective if you don't print too much work.
Although cheap laser printers (£100) are available, laser printers tend to be built like a battleship, and easily capable of taking the pounding of continuous use, as could be found in a busy office or a school environment. The expensive **laser printers** are much faster than ink jet printers, and the amount of paper they can handle at any one time is usually much greater (e.g. 500 or 1000 + sheets). They are quite

expensive to buy, and the cartridges (especially the colour ones) can cost a few hundred pounds to replace. (Don't forget you need a C,Y,M and K cartridge.) However, the cost (per sheet) of running a laser printer is much less than for the equivalent ink jet printer.

22 A **COM reader** is a machine that can read **Computer Output** on **Microform**. This means microfiche and microfilm, and is typical of some machines found in libraries and garages for cataloguing spare parts. A film is put into the machine and a light projects the image onto a screen to be read by the operator.

23 An **offset litho machine** is a high-quality machine used by the printing industry in the production of newspapers and magazines. The larger machines, once set in operation can produce thousands of copies per hour.

24 **Dot matrix printers** are still the only type of printers to be able to produce carbon copies on continuous stationery (the paper with the sprocket holes down the side). This is still used extensively in the retail industry, especially for stock lists where different copies need to be given to different people.

25 A modern **laser printer** can typically do about 30 pages/minute. However, specialist and expensive printers can go much faster than this.

26 As a coating on a **manikin**, to give the optical illusion that it is real by creating facial expressions. (This is used is some theme parks and museum exhibits.)

27 Computer monitors.

Chapter 18 – Primary and secondary storage devices

1 **RAM** is needed to store users' programs, applications and the operating system. **ROM** is needed to store the BIOS, but **CMOS RAM** would hold the **BIOS settings**.

2 **Volatile** means that the contents of memory are lost if the power is removed from the system. A **UPS** or **Uninterruptible Power Supply** may be used. This will not enable long periods of work to be undertaken, but ensure that the computer can be powered down safely so that no work is lost in the event of a power cut.

3 When a program demands more **RAM** than is physically available, it's possible to make use of disk space that is pretending to be an extension of the actual RAM in the computer. The act of storing some of the contents of RAM on a disk is called **virtual memory**. The process will obviously slow down the operation considerably compared to execution of the entire program in RAM. The secret is to use the disk to store parts of the program that are not needed immediately.

4 **Primary storage** is electronic memory such as RAM. It is used to store programs that are currently being executed by the computer. **Secondary storage** is storage used for programs that are not needed immediately. These programs, usually stored on **disk**, can be loaded into RAM as and when needed.

5 Hard drives are contained inside a **dust-free housing**, and **spin very fast** (currently 15 000 rpm for a fast disk) compared to a floppy, which spins at only a few hundred rpm. The floppy disk has its magnetic surface open to the elements. This means that particles of dust and smoke may easily damage the surface. It is also easily possible to inadvertently place a floppy disk near to an audio speaker, which being magnetic might corrupt the disk. Floppies are therefore notoriously unreliable compared with a fixed hard disk.

6 A brand new disk will store files very efficiently, putting one after the other with little space in between. However, when files are deleted, the space is returned to the system and used to store parts of other files. Under normal use, files are continuously placed on and deleted from the disk, and the efficiency of storage becomes poor, because parts of the same file might be distributed all over the surface of the disk. This will mean that the response time for disk access gets worse and worse. When this happens the disk will need to be defragmented. This means that spare spaces are gathered together to form a contiguous space, similar in nature to when the disk was new. Also, parts of files that are placed in positions all over the disk are gathered together in a more efficient way. After **defragmentation** has taken place, the response of the system should be faster.

7 (i) One way of using a **RAID array** is to ensure continuity of service in the event of a disk crash. This is called mirroring. The content of one disk is mirrored on another identical disk. If a disk crash occurs, because the same data is available on the other disk, service may continue uninterrupted. A new disk may then be placed into the machine (hot swappable ones are available) and the data rebuilt on the new disk to mirror the one still in operation. With luck, the service to the end users will not be interrupted at all.

(ii) The second major way of using a **RAID system** is to have two disks operating in parallel, such that different parts of the data are simultaneously stored on two different disks. This will obviously double the speed of access (slightly less in practice) and thus give a significant speed advantage.

(iii) If four disks are used, then mirroring and high speed can be used simultaneously, and other combinations of RAID are used in different computer systems.

8 As programs get more sophisticated and computers become faster, the size of the programs become enormous. Not long ago programs were distributed on several **floppy disks**. The advent of the **CD-ROM** meant that the pile of floppies could be replaced with a single CD-ROM disk. However, recent large suites now take several CD-ROMs, and the Microsoft Tech Net actually takes about **20 DVDs**! As you can see, 60 Gbytes will not last the new user for as long as might be indicated by obtaining a disk many times larger than his or her old one.

9 **Serial access** means that data must be read one item after another until the item of interest is found. This is typical of finding data on a tape backup system, for example. If you can go directly to the item of interest without having to read all items that are stored before it, then this is called direct or random access. Both types of access supported by floppy and hard disk drives.

10 Assuming that each pupil is given 100 Mbytes of disk space, then 2000 pupils would need 2000 × 100 or 200 Gbytes of data. This is a generous allowance from the school's point of view, but individual pupils can regularly use in excess of this, even for genuine schoolwork. At the author's school we have **120 Gbytes** of data storage for about **700 pupils**.

11 Many programs are not designed to take advantage of a drive having this speed capacity. Also, the time taken to get up to speed is

considerably longer, and the errors produced by reading the drive at this speed are considerably higher than for slower speeds. Hence the speed of response will not be 100 times better than a single-speed drive.

12 The **internet** is becoming a common method for downloading software. With a high-speed connection relatively large applications can be downloaded within a few tens of minutes. With a slow (28 K or 56 K) connection, this is not yet viable, as large applications may take many hours to download. However, even this is not a deterrent if you do not have to pay anything for the phone calls. The internet is an essential medium for downloading the latest patches and drivers, which used to be distributed on floppy or CD-ROM.

13 **CD-R (Compact Disk Recordable)** is now an inexpensive mechanism whereby users can record data (once only in this case) onto a special CD making use of a special drive and software. Legitimate uses of this technology would be 'backing up files from your hard disk', recording your own music (not ripping off audio CDs!) onto CD and archiving some of your little-used data to CD.

14 **CD-R** is a **write once technology**, whereas a MO **drive** can be written many times. MO drives vary from the small 3.5 in. floppies capable of holding a few hundred megabytes, to larger non-portable versions. MO drives are not as fast as conventional disks, and are not as popular as CD-R or CD-RW technologies.

15 An **archive** is removing little-used data to a medium where it can be retrieved at some later date. A **backup** is making copies of important files for recovery in the event of an emergency. A CD can hold about 650 Mbytes of data. It depends on how the data is distributed across this range. Many CDs could be a good idea if it were possible to retrieve data on a single CD only. However, if the files are integrated so that the CDs had to be swapped many times during the course of searching, some other medium, more suitable to storing many Gbytes on a single medium might be more suitable. A tape could be a possibility here.

16 It depends where the data is stored. If, for example, it is on several file servers, then a tape for each file server would be the ideal method. If all the data were on a single file server, assuming a large enough tape backup is available, then this would be a better idea. It is possible to get a tape unit where many tapes appear to the system to be one continuous tape, and this would probably be the best idea for such a large volume of data backed up each day.

17 If continuity of service is required in the event of a hard disk crash, then a **RAID array** with **mirroring** would be the best possibility. Here a second disk would store identical data to the first, and would be able to maintain the system in the event of one of the disks crashing. A new disk can be inserted without switching the system off, and the data is rebuilt on the new disk to maintain the original level of reliability.

Chapter 19 – Systems development and testing

1 This is a detailed study of a problem that has the potential to be computerised. The analyst must look at the problem in detail to see if it is suitable for computerisation, and produce a feasibility report, coming to the conclusion that it is either suitable or not. Realising early on that a problem is not amenable to computerisation can save much money. Sometimes millions of pounds are spent on computerisation only to find that the final solution does not work as was intended.

2 (a) A **questionnaire** may be constructed to gather a variety of information from the users of the system. This is ideal if you want to get the views of hundreds of people and correlate the results. The questionnaires may be anonymous, in which case you can't easily follow up good ideas, or the personnel filling them in may be identified, in which case they might not be so open with criticism. Constructive criticism is essential at this stage of the development.

(b) **Interviews** may be conducted to find out the views of key personnel. This can often reveal the most useful information, but remember that the people being interviewed might feel threatened by the introduction of a new computer system. The potential end users of the system usually know considerably more about the day-to-day running of the office or factory than the analyst who is undertaking the study.

(c) **Observation** by the analyst is another possibility. It sometimes comes to light that people actually carry out activities that are not in the manual, or skip some functions that should be carried out in their jobs. It is only by careful observation over a period of time that the real methodologies are seen.

3 A **data flow diagram** shows the movement of data through a system. It is particularly useful because any data, manual or computerised can be processed. The symbols used are general enough represent people, machines, processes and manual operations.

4 **One-to-one** and **many-to-one** relationships are shown in the following diagram.

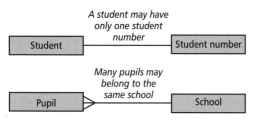

5 The **program flowchart** to determine and output the **largest** and **smallest numbers** from a list of ten numbers is as follows.

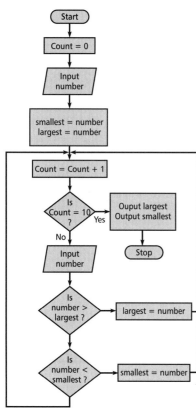

6 The **flowchart** to work out the **average mark** for the examination results is as follows.

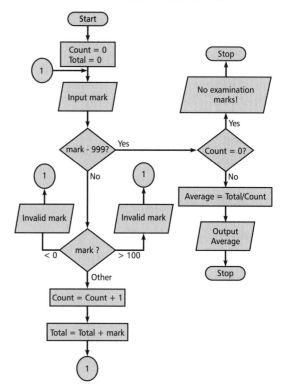

7 The flowchart to create a **four function calculator** is as follows.

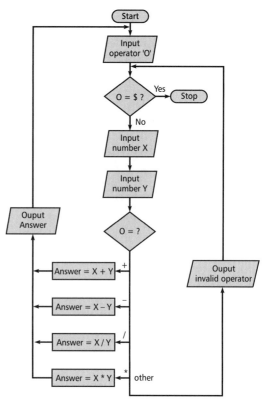

Note the **alternative method** of coping with 4 outputs from a **decision box**. This is an acceptable alternative to using many different decision boxes when 4 or more outputs are needed.

8 There are no 'right' or 'wrong' answers to the **newsagent shop**. One possibility is shown as follows.

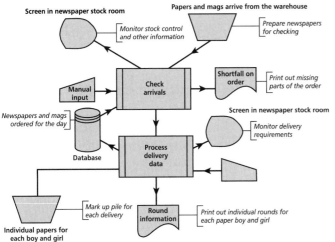

9 There are no 'right' or 'wrong' answers for the **registration of pupils**. One possible system is as follows.

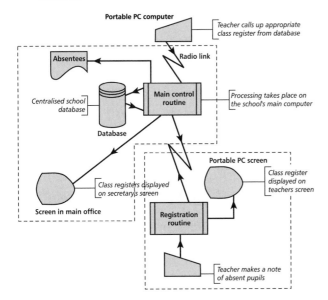

10 It's possible to provide a variety of aids to help users entering data. **Drop-down menus** are a good example when pre-set items (such as houses in a school, for example) have to be entered. **Validation** should also be used whenever possible, as it minimises the risk of error when entering data. This can take on a

variety of forms such as using an appropriate data type (date or Boolean, for example), using input masks (ideal for dates or phone numbers) and restricting numerical ranges to sensible values to name but a few.

11 Factors that could influence the **HCI** might be the environment in which the interface is used. A conventional keyboard, for example, is inappropriate for data entry on a muddy building site. The age of the people could drastically affect the interface. Small children, for example, like bright colours and large buttons, whereas professional adults usually prefer conventional interfaces with subdued colour schemes. The disability or otherwise of the person using the system will also have great effect on the way in which the interface is to function. Blind people might require voice input or a Braille keyboard. Finally, the system might be used under conditions of stress, such as might be encountered in a medical emergency. Quick conformation that all is as it should be might be important here.

12 A **dry run** is manually working through some computer code carefully checking to see that it performs exactly as it should. Consider, for example, checking the code to print out the first 5 Fibonnacci numbers. The pattern should be as follows:

1, 1, 2, 3, 5, ... (Up to the 5th term only here – it will take too long to dry run otherwise!)

As you can see, the next number in the sequence is obtained by adding up the previous two numbers. One example of some Visual Basic Code to do this is as follows.

```
Private Sub Form_Load()

x = 1            'Set up the value of
the first number
Nextnumber = 1   'Set up the value of
the next number
Print x          'Print first two
numbers in the sequence
Print Nextnumber

    For Counter = 3 To 5       'Work
out next

        Newnumber = Nextnumber + x
```

```
'Work out next number in sequence and
print out
        Print Newnumber
'Set pointers for next pair in the
sequence
        temp = Nextnumber
        Nextnumber = Newnumber
        x = temp

    Next Counter

End Sub
```

To dry run the above code we need to make a list of the variables, and check to see that the code produces the following list.

1, 1, 2, 3, 5.

It's best to set up some sort of tabular arrangement, showing what happens to the variables as we go round the loop. We essentially have four variables, called x, NextNumber, NewNumber and temp. We also have a loop variable called Counter. Therefore, we need a table having 5 columns with an extra couple of columns. The table, including a column for actual printed output and comments is as follows.

Counter	X	Next number	New number	Temp	Output	Comments
—	1	1	—	—		Set up first two numbers
—	1	1	—	—	1	Print out x (first number)
—	1	1	—	—	1	Print out next number
3	1	1	2	—	2	Work out and print out new number
3	1	2	2	1	—	Set up pointers for next loop
4	1	2	3	1	3	Work out and print out new number
4	2	3	3	2	—	Set up pointers for next loop
5	2	3	5	1	5	Work out and print out new number
5	3	5	5	3	—	Set up pointers for next loop
6	3	5	5	3	—	Loop terminated by for-to-next counter

13 A **prototype** is useful to formulate possible ideas to see if they work in practice. Once a possible prototype is developed, users can use it under simulation conditions, so that vital feedback is developed. A typical example where a prototype might be useful is in the development of a new mobile-phone interface. This may be simulated on the computer screen, making sure that you don't use any of the functionality of the computer that would not be present in the actual mobile phone. (E.g. if you are entering names into the phone book, then you can't use the computer keyboard as this will not be available when the actual phone is used!!) You will have to simulate letters like the real phone – e.g. pushing buttons several times to cycle through the appropriate sequence. This, of course, assumes that the mobile phone does not have a QWERTY keyboard.

It is often the case that the prototype brings up problems that are not brought to light at the design stage. Nothing beats a good prototype for ironing out possible problems. However, one must be careful not to overdo any functionality that can't be delivered in practice. A simple interface on a prototype might be very difficult to get going in the real system due to interactions with other parts of the system not covered by the prototype interface.

14 **Extensive testing** may not find all the bugs because there are so many different possible paths through the system. On complex projects it would take longer than the Universe has been in existence to go through every single combination of code. All we can do in practice is to modularise the system, and apply black and white box testing techniques to each module. We then add modules together and test the system again, to see if any undesirable action results. Object-oriented programming methodologies help with this in practice, but it's impossible to say with 100% certainty that a complex project will always work under all conditions of use.

15 Three tasks that the interface might have to perform could be as follows:

- Building up the phone book for pre-dial numbers
- Editing a number already entered
- Providing suitable messages when the Internet connection is being used.

When editing a number that has already been entered, we would need to test that the number can be edited properly, and the edited version is saved automatically when the editing has been carried out. As we are editing numbers, we must ensure that letters or other characters can't be entered in error. It might be possible to bring up help messages at salient points too.

16 **Module testing** means performing tests, like black-box and white-box testing, for example, on individual modules in a system. This means that the module should work under all possible conditions. If the module is small enough then the designers can be reasonably confident that this will be so.
When modules are joined together to see if they integrate properly, then this is called **integration testing**. In this way modules can be added gradually, and the overall system tested. If an error suddenly occurs, then it's usually a case that the last module added to the integration testing is at fault, and this is the first thing that should be investigated.

17 (a) Braille is a possible way to enter the numbers. Voice could also be a possibility.
(b) Very large displays or voice output would be suitable here.
(c) The **visually impaired** might be able to see certain colour combinations better than others, and this could be investigated further. It might also be possible to have part of the interface set up for different colours and sizes to optimise it for a particular individual.

18 If **integer arithmetic** is being used then the number range must be stated. For example, what is the maximum value negative number or the maximum value positive number that the calculator can cope with? Are suitable error messages displayed if the results of any arithmetic exceed these limits? The unit should be tested for the numbers at the extremes of this range to see if it works properly. Zero addition could be tested too to see that no errors occur here. A range of valid numbers should also be tested to see that the answers are actually correct.

19 First, a detailed look at the **design** or **system specification** must be undertaken. All important points must have been achieved for a successful project. You should evaluate the degree of success by comparing the actual outcomes with the suggested outcomes when the project was designed.

20 **System maintenance** is checking to see that the system is working after it has been commissioned. It is often the case that errors, not detected during the testing and commissioning phases come to light. These errors must be corrected, and suitable documentation produced to say what's been altered to overcome the errors.

System maintenance also deals with modifying the system in the light of changing user requirements. These modifications can also be built into the system so that anybody maintaining the system in future can keep up with events. It would not usually be feasible to modify the system too much, or it gets very unwieldy. If great change is needed then a new system should be designed.

21 Two different **system maintenance scenarios** are 'errors coming to light after the system has been in use for some time', or 'the user requirements have changed slightly'.

The engineers would need the user and technical documentation that accompanied the original design of the system, or they would not be able to make detailed changes to the code or other parts of the system. Without this documentation they would not understand the system.

Chapter 20 – A module 3 project – the analysis phase

1 The only two types of software acceptable for AQA module 3 projects are relational databases and high-level programming languages.

2 Five good reasons could include the following.
(i) A database mirrors the entities used to model the data.
(ii) A database provides many routines for maintaining data integrity like validation.
(iii) A database provides a comprehensive system of queries to filter the data.
(iv) A database provides comprehensive reporting mechanisms.
(v) A database provides export routines to export data to other packages like a word processor.

3 Three good reasons could include the following. 'A high-level programming language could provide compiled code which would need no proprietary software to enable it to run.'

'A high-level programming language would enable complete customisation of the system.'
'The compiled code from a high-level programming language would mean that even technical users could not alter anything fundamental about the database.'

4 A data dictionary is data about the data used in a system. Information about the data could include the 'data type', 'names', 'a description of the data', 'typical examples' and 'the number of characters needed to store the data'.

5 There are two ways of doing this. A query could be built up to filter the data, and a report (mirroring the format of the output for the letter) could be set up and bound to the query. Thus a standard letter would contain personalised information about a centre, candidates and results etc. An alternative way is to export the data to a word processor where the fields from the database could be used as the source of data for the fields used in a mail merge document. This would give a greater degree of control for the final formatting.

6 Three other items of information that could be stored for the re-mark procedure are 'name of the re-marker', 'a counter to keep a tally on how many re-marks have been requested for a particular original marker' and 'the percentage difference between the original mark and the re-mark marks'.

7 The data dictionary for the three items chosen in question (6) is as follows.

Name	Data type	No. of characters	Typical example	Description
Surname	Text	30 characters	Smith	The name of the re-marker. Not unique
Counter1023	Integer	5 digits	78	Counter for re-marker who has the ID 1023
PercentDiff	Integer	5 digits	34	Number between 0 and 100%

8 (i)   Storage of data can't feed into another storage of data device without any processing in-between.
   (ii) The same output from the process symbol can't go to two different places.

(iii) A source or data destination can't feed into another source or destination symbol with no processing in-between.

Chapter 21 – Database design for the module 3 project

1 An analyst would be completely familiar with all the facilities offered by a relational database like Microsoft Access. He or she would therefore be able to design the data requirements, validation rules, data entry forms, queries and reports, etc. without reference to any software. However, a student may not know how a query or report works, and will need to experiment with the system. As they are experimenting they can develop a good deal of the queries and reports needed for their projects. As long as you do not do the design after the database has been implemented, you should not go far wrong.

2 You must make it perfectly clear to the examiners that you are not using screen shots of your final project implementation. This can be done by making sure that there is no data present in the database. If you make use of the wizards it's highly unlikely that the reports or other output will be in an appropriate form without manual intervention. With appropriate 'tweaking' this can be a good method to produce acceptable designs.

3 There is a 'Centres' table in the solution to our database but no 'Candidates' table. This is because we decided to use a 'Candidate Subject Entry' table. Therefore, the relationship between candidates and subjects is not explicit from the work covered in this chapter. However, it's obvious that that a centre can have many candidates, and therefore the relationship between candidates and centres is many-to-one. The ER diagram for this is as follows.

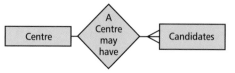

4 A number type is regarded as being too vague. There are several different 'number' data types and the examiners like to know that you have thought about the type of number you need to process. Therefore, 'byte', 'integer', 'long integer', 'single' or 'double' would be better descriptions.

5 Using a mail merge involves exporting the data from a query in a form that can be understood by Microsoft Word', the word processor. A mail merge document is then constructed in Word, which uses the exported data as a data source for the fields within the document to be sent to the board. A Word processor has more extensive formatting facilities than the reports section from an Access database. Therefore, virtually any request for layout and style could be accommodated if a mail merge system is used.

6 When you are designing a database the real database does not yet exist, or it exists only in skeletal form. Therefore, there is little, if any, data to show at this stage of the project cycle.

7 If drop down menus are used for the subject entry, then the user of the system would need to add a further menu entry if a new subject is added. This is a more complex operation than is usually carried out by the database operatives (the personnel who will use the database), and would thus be classed as maintenance, because an 'expert' would probably need to oversee this operation.

8 It would be a lot harder to implement the UKAB system using a high level language. Five typical reasons are as follows.
   (i) You would have to set up a complex system of interrelated files to manage the database (accomplished by using tables in a relational database).
   (ii) Complex validation routines would have to be written for all data types (variables) entered into the system (easily accomplished by using a database).
   (iii) Queries needed by the users would have to be constructed from scratch (easily accomplished by using a database).
   (iv) All the reporting would need to be programmed from scratch (easily accomplished with a database).
   (v) Any export routines to mail merge documents would have to be programmed from scratch (easily accomplished with a database).

Chapter 22 – UKAB test data and implementation

1 'ABC123' would be rejected by the database because it is *not* a number, and a numeric data type (integer) is required.

2 The database would not detect this transposition error. Verification could be used to detect this error. This means that the same data is checked again after it has been input to the system.

3 A byte would be the best data type because this deals with numbers between 0 and 255. Only one byte is needed to store this information.

4 It minimises the risk of entering erroneous data like 'X' or 'J', for example. However, it does not eliminate the possibility of entering 'B' instead of 'A'. It thus increases data integrity standards.

5 A relational database is a database in which tables contain related information, joined together by means of relationships of the type 'one to one', 'one to many' and 'many to one'. Each of the related tables contains at least one field that is identical, and this is used to set up the relationships.

6 The tables are called 'Centre', 'Candidate Subject Entry' and 'Subject'.

7 The field names used in the 'Subject Candidate Entry' table are as follows.

   Centre Number, Candidate Number, Subject Reference Code, Surname, Initials, Title, Date Received, Date Processed, Grade Before Remark, Original Mark, Grade After Remark, Re-mark Mark, Grade Changed?, Return Script?, Original Marker ID and Re-mark Marker ID

8 Access has been instructed to display leading zeros in these fields by making use of '0000' in the number format when it is being displayed. This ensures that leading zeros are included.

9 The picture must first be turned into computer-readable format, and then saved with a suitable file type (a bitmap image has been used in this project). The size of the picture may need to be resized to suit the output format being used. Access has the facility to include graphics of this type in any part of the reporting system. It has been included on the headers of all the reports in this project.

10 A query is a filter set up to choose a subset of data from the database. The queries used in this project are as follows.
   (i) To filter out the daily list of re-marks

(ii) To filter out the daily list or re-marks still outstanding

(iii) To filter out the list of re-marks for a particular centre.

(iv) To filter out the list of re-marks for a particular subject.

(v) To filter out the re-marks that have been processed 'today' to produce the letters to the centre.

11 The general code (not the Access SQL) for the re-marks still outstanding is as follows.

```
IF the 'Date Received' field is > 3
weeks ago, AND if the 'Date
Processed' field is Null (contains no
entry) THEN this is a re-mark which
is still outstanding.
```

12 A report is a mechanism for helping to display information chosen from the database, usually by means of a query. A reporting system will give the user a large number of options to group various items of data and to provide features like headers, footers and formatting information for all the data being output. The list of reporting facilities for Access is extremely comprehensive.

13 A report has the advantage of giving the user a great deal of choice when formatting the output from the query. A report can be bound to a query in Access by inserting the report into the query.

14 A parameter query is a query which accepts one or more parameters from the user when the query is run. This enables the user to modify the output of the query based on the parameters they have just typed in. (e.g. the list of re-marks for a particular centre where the user is able to type in the parameter 'centre name'.)

15 A switchboard is a menu-driven system which enables users to load forms in 'edit or add' mode, to run queries, run reports and exit the system etc. without having to have a detailed knowledge or Microsoft Access.

Chapter 23 – The module 3 project write up

There are no self-test questions for this unit.

Chapter 24 – A module 3 examination

1 (a) (i) First data item is 'Date Received' (see Table 23.3).

(ii) Second data item is "Date Processed' (see Table 23.3).

(Other data items are Original Marker ID and Re-Mark Marker ID).

(b) Candidate Number – **Integer** – This numeric data type is the most efficient to store whole numbers in the range 0 to 9999.

(ii) Return Script? – **Boolean** – This data type will limit the data to Yes/No True/False responses only.

(iii) Original Mark – **Byte** – This numeric data type is the most efficient to store whole numbers in the range 0 to 100.

2 (i) See the **QBE design grid** in Figure 22.7, where a 'parameter query' has been set up, inviting the user to enter a 'Subject Reference Code' for the subject in question. The report (showing output details) which is bound to this parameter query can be seen in Figure 22.9.

(ii) See **QBE design grid** in Figure 23.15, where the date processed has been put equal to Date(), Microsoft Access' method of setting a date to 'Today' and the Boolean field 'Grade Changed?' is equal to 'True'. The report bound to this query is shown in Figure 23.9. Hard copy would be a printout of Figure 23.17, would be shown in an appendix which would accompany your script taken into the exam room.

(iii) See **QBE design grid** in Figure 23.16, where the 'Date Received' field must be more than 21 days ago, (set up by using <Date()-21) and the 'Date Processed' field is Null (i.e. the mark has not yet been processed). The report which is bound to this query is shown in Figure 23.18, and a hard copy would be a printout of Figure 23.18, shown in an appendix which would accompany your script taken into the exam room.

(b) Note that an *algorithm* is needed; therefore a suitable flowchart or pseudocode solution will be sufficient.

We basically need to cycle through all of the records, examining only those which have a 'date processed' field equal to today's date, and then look only for those whose grades have *not* been changed. This is accomplished, (*making use of the field names used for this project in Chapter 23*), as follows.

```
Open Re-mark Database file
Start at record number one
While not End Of File Do
  Read Record
  If 'Date Processed' = Today THEN
    If 'Grade Changed?' = False THEN
      Print 'Subject Reference Code'
      Print 'Subject Name'
      Print 'Centre Number'
      Print 'Original Marker ID'
      Print 'Grade Before Remark'
      Print 'Grade After Remark''
    End If
  End If
  Next record
Endwhile
Close Re-mark Database file
```

3 (a) A screen dump of the letter to the centres is shown in Figure 23.13. A Hard copy would be a printout of Figure 23.13, shown in an appendix which would accompany your script taken into the exam room.

    (ii) The logo was obtained from the 2003 subject specification. The part of the page containing the logo was scanned into an art package, and then cropped to an appropriate size, tidied up and then saved as a bitmap image. Microsoft Access allows you to insert a picture on a report, and the bitmap image of the logo was imported into the database using this method.

(b) (i) A letter head containing the Board's name and address, a person to contact and further contact information is present at the top of each letter.

    (ii) The letter is formatted using a very clear layout; so required fields may be inserted without affecting other fields on the letter, and a space for a hidden sentence gives the ability to print out information about no grade changes.

4 (a) Subject reference codes were stored as a long integer' but formatted using '00000', which is Microsoft Access' way of ensuring that leading zeros are inserted and displayed (see Figure 21.2).

(b) (i) The test data, to ensure that the centre number is a 5-digit number in the range 10000 to 80000 is stored correctly in the 'centre' table is '999', '80100', 'Null', 'ABC' and '2003'. '20003' was entered a second time to make sure that it is rejected if a centre with that number already exists (see Table 23.5).

    (ii) To ensure that the letters to the centre are sent at the appropriate time, they are only generated once at the end of each day, by making sure that 'Date Processed' = 'Today'. This query should be run once only.

(c) The evidence is given by observing the letters printed out for a particular day, which should be shown in the appendix which accompanies your script.

5 (a) (i) There is no 'candidate' table explicitly used in this way, because we have a 'Candidate Subject Entry' table, where candidates would have two entries for two remarks. However, the relationship that exists between candidates and centres would be many-to-one, because one centre may have many candidates.

    (ii) The ER diagram is as follows. Note that these diagrams do not necessarily mirror the ER diagrams in your project. It depends how you have provided the solution to the UKAB problem.

    (iii) The ER diagram showing the relationship between subjects and centres is as follows.

(c) Three different methods to gather information about the proposed system could include:

    (i) Interviewing the prospective users
    (ii) Producing a questionnaire for the prospective users
    (iii) Looking at similar systems set up already.

6 (a) (i) Data integrity means ensuring that data is 'Correct'.

(ii) Data security means protecting data from hackers and other similar hazards like 'fire and theft'.

(b) (i) When setting up the 'Candidate Subject Entry' table, it's impossible to enter a centre number that does not exist in the 'Centre' table. This has been set up to ensure that no candidate is present from a centre which does not exist.

(ii) A password has been set up using the password security feature provided by Microsoft Access.

7 (a) (i) A project is effective if it carries out the tasks outlined in the specification in an effective way.

(ii) Usability means making sure that the system is easy to use by the people for whom it has been designed.

(iii) Maintainability means making sure that the project is designed such that it can be easily altered to accommodate the changing needs of the UKAB.

(b) (i) The user guide is intended for the people who will use the system on a day-to-day basis. It contains non-technical information about the operation of the UKAB system. An example in the guide might show how to produce the report for 'List of re-marks' still outstanding.

(ii) Technical documentation is intended to be used by competent personnel who might find they have to maintain the system at a later date. Typical of this might be altering the 'candidate number' to be a five digit code.

Index